*F*oundations of Music Education

Foundations
of Music
Education *Second Edition*

Harold F. Abeles
Teachers College, Columbia University

Charles R. Hoffer
University of Florida

Robert H. Klotman
Indiana University

Schirmer Books
An Imprint of Simon & Schuster Macmillan
New York

Prentice Hall International
London · Mexico City · New Delhi · Singapore · Sydney · Toronto

Schirmer Books
An Imprint of Simon & Schuster Macmillan
1633 Broadway, New York, NY 10019-6785

Library of Congress Catalog Card Number: 93-1877

Printed in the United States of America

printing number
       6 7 8 9 10

Library of Congress Cataloging-in-Publication Data

Abeles, Harold F.
Foundations of music education/Harold F. Abeles, Charles R. Hoffer, Robert H. Klotman. — 2nd ed.
p. cm.
 Includes bibliographical references and index.
 ISBN 0-02-870011-2
 1. Music—Instruction and study. I. Hoffer, Charles R.
II. Klotman, Robert H. III. Title.
MT1.A25 1994
780'.7—dc20   93-1877
                                                                               CIP
                                                                               MN

The paper used in this publication meets the minimum requirements of American National Standard for Information Sciences—Permanence of Paper for Printed Library Materials. ANSI Z39.48-1984. ∞ ™

Contents

Preface

MANY UNIVERSITIES, realizing the importance of an understanding of the "larger picture" of music education, offer graduate courses in the foundations of music education. Usually these courses seek to provide students with insight into the many significant matters that affect music instruction in the schools and colleges. As the brief introductory section of *Foundations of Music Education* points out, historical, philosophical, sociological, and psychological issues greatly affect what music teachers do when they teach.

Because a course dealing with fundamental matters in music education has a small clientele, very few textbooks have been written for it. Although information related to fundamental topics may not change as much or as quickly as it does in other areas of music education, it does change, and the material discussed and the point of view from which it is examined need to be revised periodically. In fact, most of the current material consists of books or articles dealing with only a limited portion of the content of the course. In the early 1980s, after several years of using lists of assigned readings in the teaching of the foundations course, the authors concluded that a new comprehensive textbook was badly needed. The result was the first edition of *Foundations of Music Education*, a textbook that not only dealt with the more frequently covered areas of philosophy and psychology, but also included chapters on sociology and social psychology, which had seldom been written about for music educators. Other chapters concerned curriculum, teacher education, research for the "consumer," and many other topics not usually discussed in the literature.

The gratifying response to *Foundations of Music Education*, together with the emergence of many new events and trends that affect music education and education in general, prompted the authors to undertake the present revision. Featuring approximately 40 percent new material and expanded by 10 percent, the second edition of *Foundations of Music Education* expands the scope of the original volume to include such issues as the perception of an educational crisis in the last decade, exemplified in the report *A Nation at Risk* (National Commission on Excellence in Education. *A Nation at Risk: The Full Account.* Westford, MA: Murray Printing Co., 1984); the ever-growing impact of new technologies; the increasing urgency of calls for cultural pluralism; and the implications of new theoretical positions in the psychology of education.

This book does not attempt to include every subject that merits attention in a foundations-type course. Rather, it provides a core of material upon which each instructor can build. Since no book can hope to be completely up to the moment in its content, instructors may wish to supplement this text with readings on current topics.

This book is addressed to women and men alike. Initially, we wrote *he/she* and *himself/herself* before we reluctantly accepted the criticism that this procedure was both cumbersome and unreadable. Until a nongenderized pronoun comes into common usage we are using the generic *he* and *him* to include *all* people.

We would like to thank the many scholars and researchers in music education and its related fields whose work can be used by instructors today to develop courses and books in the foundations of music education. Without the previous efforts of Edward Bailey Birge, James Mursell, Charles Leonhard, Thurber Madison, Bennett Reimer, Edwin Gordon, and other music educators, as well as MENC projects such as the Tanglewood Symposium, Ann Arbor Symposium, and Commission on Teacher Education, the study of fundamental matters in music education would not be as rewarding. Also due thanks are the scholars who reviewed the manuscript: Keith P. Thompson of the Pennsylvania State University, John Grashel of the University of Illinois, and J. David Boyle of the University of Miami.

Foundations of Music Education

Introduction:
Why Study Foundations
of Music Education?

AT FIRST GLANCE, teaching a group of children to sing a song may appear to be an obvious activity. Pitches are given, a tempo indicated, and the children start singing; mistakes are then corrected and the interpretation refined until the song is learned. However, teaching a song is just the tip of the proverbial iceberg; it is only the portion that is immediately visible. Below the surface and out of sight are forces and factors of enormous importance. In fact, without the huge body of what is not seen, there might be no tip, or if it were visible its appearance would be very different.

What are some of the important but unseen influences? Some are matters of philosophy and belief. For example, are songs something that people discover or something that they create? Are they eternal or transitory? What constitutes a good song? How do we perceive and understand a song—or anything else, for that matter? Do people sing songs for emotional release, physical well-being, or artistic expression? What makes something a work of art? Do art works communicate? If they do, how do they communicate?

Some of these unseen influences are sociological in nature. Are the songs of our culture better than those of other cultures? Is music valued enough in our society so that it is included in school curricula? Do different age or economic groups in American society consider music and songs in different ways? What role or roles do the playing and singing of music occupy in our society? How have television sets and record players affected the way children learn songs and what they think about them?

Some of the factors are psychological. Do people learn songs through the accumulation of small bits of information or in larger chunks? Do they learn through singing or intellectual thought? What is music talent? How

1

does it affect what a teacher does when teaching a song? Are there differences in how children learn to sing at different age levels? What determines how well students remember what they have learned? How does a teacher motivate the children to learn a song?

Then there is the influence of history and tradition. Is the singing of songs included in music instruction as a carryover of what has transpired? What ways of learning music used in the past have been revived in contemporary music education? Are there trends that give indications of where music education is headed in the future?

From the basic academic disciplines of history, philosophy, psychology, and sociology, music teachers utilize and synthesize information and beliefs to come up with what they think is the best way to teach a song or an instrumental work. Is it best learned by rote or by trying to read the notation? Is it better learned in one long session or in several shorter lessons? What aspects of music will the students learn? Will they learn many facts about it? Will they learn only to sing or play it? How thoroughly will they learn it? How will the performance be evaluated?

Although the preceding paragraphs may appear to have identified most of the factors affecting the teaching of a piece of music, they have in fact only begun to explore the elements of learning. They have, however, made the point that there is much more to music teaching than appears at first glance.

It is easy to assume that what is not obvious is also impractical or not worth knowing. It may seem like a long way from Socrates and his dialogues in ancient Greece, or Pavlov and his drooling dogs, or the concept of social stratification to teaching music to students in the schools today. However, remote as such considerations may appear to be, the connection is very much there. When all is said and done, an understanding of such topics is as practical and useful as knowing the procedures for teaching songs or learning to play an instrument.

As undergraduates, future music teachers are taught specific methods for teaching songs and other aspects of music. This training enables them to begin as teachers. As graduate students, however, music educators should consider the "larger picture" of music education, and realize some of the significant conditions and factors that greatly affect their work, as well as consider ways in which to better their teaching.

History of Music Education

In 1838 the Boston School Committee, or Board of Education as we know it today, formally adopted music as a branch of instruction in the schools of that city. To many this was the beginning of music education in America, but actually it was just another milestone for what was inevitable in a society based on Western civilization and Western culture. Much music education had preceded this date, not only in America but in early and ancient societies that were precursors of our culture. In virtually every society—ancient, tribal, or preliterate—some form of music education existed. In order to understand some of the importance attached to the official date of the first formal action introducing music instruction into the education of the young of this nation, a brief review of how music was valued and taught in earlier civilizations would be appropriate.

Early Greek and Roman Music Instruction

The chief function of education in the early Greek era was building individuals of character, grace, and stamina. Inherent in these goals were the incipient concepts of developing the mind, the body, and the soul. To accomplish these goals, the early organization of Greek education was structured with rhetoric or oratory for the mind, gymnastics for the body, and art and music for the soul. With the expansion of writing, astronomy, and the science of mathematics in the Greek educational curriculum, con-

3

troversy and debate regarding music became an issue even among the Greeks. Aristotle in his *Politics* not only was dubious of the need for music, but doubted its educational potential as well. He questioned whether or not music served education or entertainment. (It is interesting that the attitudes and issues that existed in the fourth century B.C. regarding music education were articulated with much of the same rhetoric that one hears in the twentieth century.)

The Greek and Roman philosophers and poets wrote and spoke paeans of praise in the name of music. Plato in his *Republic* (Book III) wrote:

> Literature, music, art ("musical" education) have a great influence on character. The aim of "musical" education is to inculcate rhythm, harmony and temperance of the soul, and thus develop good moral character. Proper "musical" education and proper gymnastics constitute the first stage to knowledge of Ideas, for the harmonious soul and beautiful body in the concrete individual are copies of the Ideas. Censorship of all arts is therefore necessary to prevent the inculcation of harmful qualities which will corrupt the soul. Rhythm and harmony produce grace of body and mind, and recognition of and sensitivity to beauty in the concrete. This is the first step to the recognition of Ideas. The individual who possesses a harmonious soul in a beautiful body stimulates a noble love in others like himself. Thus through love of beauty, harmony is increased. (Bryan, 1898, pp. 138–139)

To the Greeks the doctrine of *ethos*, or moral qualities and effects of music, emanated from the Pythagorean view of music "as a microcosm, a system of sound and rhythm ruled by the same mathematical laws that operate in the whole of the visible and invisible creation" (Grout, 1973, p. 7). According to this concept, music was not something that one passively enjoyed, but rather was governed by mathematical laws that operated both in the visible and invisible organization of the universe. Music was considered a force that affected everything that existed, and as a result one can find in Greek mythology many feats and miracles attributed to legendary musicians. This concept of an *ethos* was followed by a later position, one that emphasized the effect music might have on the individual's will and thus his or her character and behavior. Aristotle in his *Politics* pointed out how music influenced the will of human beings through the principle of imitation. He said that music

> directly imitates the passions or states of the soul—gentleness, anger, courage, temperance, and their opposites and other qualities; hence, when one listens to music that imitates a certain passion, he becomes imbued with the same passion; and if over a long time he habitually listens to the kind of music that arouses ignoble passions his whole character will be shaped to an ignoble form. (Grout, 1973, p. 7)

In other words, Aristotle was saying that if one listened to the wrong type of music he or she would become the wrong kind of person. On the other hand, if one listened to the right kind of music he or she would become the right kind of person. Thus there was considerable agreement between Plato and Aristotle regarding what is necessary to produce the appropriate individual. The two principal elements in their philosophy were gymnastics and music. Gymnastics was for the discipline and development of the body and music for that of the mind.

It was in the fifth century B.C. that music reached the apogee of its function as a part of the life and culture of the Greek people. It was during this period that Pythagoras, the mathematician, developed the musical theories that influenced scale and interval practices still utilized today. It was a period when the professional musician emerged as a virtuoso, new musical forms were developed, chromaticism was introduced, and scholars of the day even found evidence of quarter tones.

Little is known of these developments other than what was written by Phrynis of Mytilene (c. 450 B.C.), Euripides (c. 480–406 B.C.), and Timotheus of Miletus (c. 450 B.C.), who were some of the leading proponents of chromaticism during that period. Scholarly evidence shows, however, that music festivals, singing societies, and music contests, along with rhetorical societies, existed virtually everywhere. It was a period of great involvement in the arts, especially music, which was, along with poetry, the chief art form of the time. Anacreon of Teos (c. 563–478 B.C.), a court poet, traveled throughout the land writing songs on love and wine. In addition, the plays of Aristophanes (c. 446–385 B.C.) and Euripides contained essential choruses who sang and chanted dramatic sections that were integral to the action.

The Middle Ages

It was at the beginning of the Middle Ages that music assumed its place in the quadrivium that constituted the higher division of the seven liberal arts (arithmetic, astronomy, geometry, music). During this period the Christian church assumed control of education and became the chief disseminator of knowledge. After the Edict of Milan in A.D. 313 Christianity became a legal religion that people were permitted to practice openly, and since music was an integral part of the service it became a necessary part of the formal instruction offered by and to priests. Schools were organized to educate the Christians. These schools were the *scholae cantorum*, and they were expanded under Pope Gregory near the end of the sixth century. The curriculum was broadened to include instruction in singing, playing instruments, and basic elements of harmony and composition.

Boethius, who died about A.D. 525 wrote a treatise, *De Musica*, on musical theory in the fifth century. It was regarded as a source of erudition and was copied many times; even as late as the period of Columbus's discovery of America it was printed in numerous editions. Much of Boethius's work dealt with the Greek modes, and his musical nomenclature and musical system remained, at least in theory, fairly stable until the eleventh century and the appearance of Guido of Arezzo's famous treatise, *Micrologus* (c. 1025).

Henry Cady (1974) further illuminated the position of music in the medieval university by pointing out that the liberal arts that were formed in the seventh century A.D. were actually composed of two parts, "verbal" and "numerical" in character. Music was essentially the study of the numerical ratios that Pythagoras, Aristophanes, and other ancient Greeks had found in their acoustical studies. It was not related to learning the art of performance. However, this was primarily true only of music as an academic study; when formal music instruction was given for purposes of performance, considerable emphasis was placed on the prevailing practice and style.

During the early development of music instruction, no formal system for writing music existed, and the instruction consisted of oral transfer from one church group to another. Without a systematic form of notation, the major churches and monasteries of Europe utilized different music in their various services. As a result, in the ninth century, about the time of Charlemagne, in an effort to standardize the chant, a method was devised for writing music so that the same music would be sung in similar services throughout the churches of Europe. This development brought about a more urgent need for formal instruction in music and a period of expanded instruction. It is interesting to note, as one traces the development of music and music education, that when the function of music changes, a change occurs not only in the music but in the training of musicians.

The Founding of Conservatories and Schools of Music

The precedent for using schools of music to improve singing in the church actually began in the 1500s, with the church organizing these schools for the express purpose of having plainsong performed properly in the service. First organized in Italy, these institutions were actually the precursors of modern schools of music in that they offered many subjects that led to professional training.

The Italian "conservatories" (from *conservatorio*, a home for foundlings) were indeed orphanages. In fact, some modern Italian-English dictionaries still include "poorhouse" in their definition of the word. It may be that orphans were selected to be trained as performers because they had no families; a life "on the road," which was typical for musicians of that period, caused them little concern.

Venice was the great center for girls' conservatories, while Naples was recognized for its boys' "music orphanages," the first being established in 1537. A letter sent in 1739 to the Président de Brosses, in describing the music of the Venetian orphans, said: "They are educated and maintained at the expense of the State, and their sole training is to excel in music. Thus they sing like angels."

As a result of having observed these schools in Italy, Charles Burney in 1774 distributed a *Plan for a Music School* in England. His idea was to establish a school in connection with the Foundling Hospital in London, but the idea was most unpopular. It wasn't until 1822 that the Royal Academy of Music was established in England, and it was not organized as an orphanage but rather as a boarding school for young students. The Royal College of Music came half a century later in 1873 and operated under a royal charter.

The earliest school of music in Europe (apart from the orphanage schools in Italy) that still exists is the school now known as the Paris Conservatory. It was founded in 1784 and started the proliferation of many small conservatories throughout France.

Probably the oldest conservatory in central and northern Europe is the Prague Conservatory, which was established around 1811. This was followed by the school in Vienna, the Musikakademie Hochschule für Musik, which originated in 1817 but did not become a state school until 1909. Mendelssohn originated the Leipzig Conservatory in 1843, and the Berlin Conservatory was founded in 1850. There were many others, but these examples are cited to point out that the conservatory, as we know it, was a European product of the first half of the nineteenth century. Such institutions did not begin to appear in the United States until the latter part of the 1800s, with the Peabody Conservatory in Baltimore, which was established in 1857, being one of the first.

Music Education in the United States

When the first colonists set foot on this land, the only indigenous music that existed here was that of the American Indians. It was completely alien to English ears, and little effort was made to assimilate it into the British-American music culture. Furthermore, most of the early colonists came to the new land seeking either religious freedom or escape from indebtedness. The former brought their own church music and musical ideas, whereas the latter were either a part of one religious sect or another or were too preoccupied with the rigors of making a place for themselves in the New World to be concerned about an indigenous music. As a result, little of the Native American music found its way into the formal music of the early colonials. In fact, many of the early missionaries were far more interested in teaching their own religious rites and accompanying music than integrating the musical culture of those they were trying to convert.

The earliest significant development in the musical culture of this country occurred in 1619, when the first slaves of the American settlers made their appearance in Virginia. These people brought with them a musical heritage from their native Africa that was unique and creative, and it fused itself into the musical idioms of this country. As a form of expression, this amalgamation of western European and African music became the unique product of the New World.

Just as it had done in the Middle Ages, the church in the early days of the United States became the chief dispenser of music education. Since singing was a part of the religious ritual, it became the basis for early instruction in the church schools. It is true that the Franciscan friars who settled in the area around St. Augustine, Florida, as early as 1603 did offer some instrumental instruction to the Native Americans, whom they wished to convert and educate, but basically, instruction in music centered around the Catholic ceremony, which involved considerable chanting a cappella.

With the advent of the Pilgrims' landing in Plymouth, the Protestant element of the church made its appearance.

> Where the Franciscans and Catholic education embraced music as an indispensable part of their liturgical service, the English did not permit music in any form during their church service. Music, being overtly joyous and emotional, was tabooed as worldly and secular. The early colonizers were not interested in accepting Old World practices, musical or other. (Sunderman, 1971, p. 10)

The Puritans brought with them from England the Ainsworth version of the psalms. Although this was essentially a manual of psalmody, it served as a basis for teaching music to the members of the choir and the congregation. Out of this manual evolved what some refer to as the first published songbook in America, *The Bay Psalm Book* (c. 1640). It was actually the product of a revision of the Ainsworth edition of the psalms that was done by about thirty ministers who came to the colonies in 1636. The music in *The Bay Psalm Book* was purely vocal or choral, and singing was dependent on a "call and response" or "lining out" method, as it was referred to in colonial times. This consisted of the preacher or pastor singing a phrase or line and the congregation imitating it by rote. Although *The Bay Psalm Book* went through several revisions between 1640 and 1773, little concern was given toward improving the singing of the congregation. In fact, little singing occurred in early colonial workshop services, and usually the congregation's repertoire was limited to a few songs.

Incidentally, this is not to be construed as implying that no musical culture existed in colonial times. There were English artists who visited Boston and many shops involved with music. Private schools offered a wide variety of music study on instruments such as the violin, flute, spinet, harpsichord, violoncello, and bassviol. However, one can begin to sense that the terrible condition of singing in the churches led to the establishment of singing schools by several ministers and lay persons around 1720. These schools flourished on the hope that they would improve the singing quality of their students for church purposes. Furthermore, it was inevitable that as people began to seek ways to enhance or enrich their daily existence, some would want to learn to read music notation.

The first singing school was established in Boston in 1717. It probably was the initial step toward stimulating the later movement to include music instruction in the public schools. The rationale was that it would improve the quality of singing in the churches. Schools such as this concerned themselves very little with the teaching of music fundamentals, concentrating more heavily on correct vocal production. They were mainly concerned that the melody be sung correctly, melodically as well as rhythmically. "The first music instruction books were the product of John Tufts, a minister, who in the early eighteenth century wanted to teach the churchgoing colonists to sing psalms and hymns. He devised a tetrachord system of notation in which the octave is broken into two identical halves. Tufts chose the tetrachords E F G A and B C D E, which he identified by the syllables *mi, fa, sol,* and *la*" (Lowens, 1964, ch. 3). His system was later adapted into "shape notes" in which each of the four shapes of the noteheads indicate a syllable. Shape notes are still seen occasionally in the notation of some hymnals, especially in the music of southern states and in Appalachia.

Prominent people in this period included Samuel Holyoke of Salem, Massachusetts, who in 1806 expanded his singing school to include a second school devoted to instrumental music. William Billings, one of America's first native composers and composer of *The New England Psalm Singer of the American Chorister*, was another. Holyoke's classes were so successful that in 1808 his school performed the "Hallelujah" chorus from Handel's *Messiah* in its public concert. Billings created and popularized an interest in American music that was composed for purposes other than the church. His tune "Chester" became the battle song of the American Revolution, since it was the only song that the Continental pipers would use on the march.

Shortly after the singing schools made their appearance, singing societies began to spring up. The oldest singing society still in existence was formed in Stoughton, Massachusetts, in 1786. Actually, the major difference between the singing societies and the singing schools was that the former were devoted to performance that sought a higher musical level, while the latter were concerned with teaching people to read music so that the societies could attain the performance level they sought. In a sense, they were interdependent.

Sunderman (1971) points out that the importance of these early singing societies lay in their ability to (1) provide an outlet for the development of American singing talent; (2) set standards of attainment for other musically minded individuals and groups; (3) bring outstanding choral works before the public; (4) increase commercial and professional opportunities for concert singers and conductors; and (5) give impetus to the singing school movement. The singing society, in promoting opportunities for lay and professional musicians, also became the major agent in encouraging the creation of secular songs.

The Pestalozzian Schools

Probably the most influential system of education in the United States prior to the Civil War was that based on the theories of the Swiss educator Johann Heinrich Pestalozzi. He was born in Zurich in 1746, the son of a local doctor. Following the French destruction of the canton of Unterwalden, Pestalozzi provided shelter to the orphans of the area and became interested in education. As one of the proponents of the concept that the best education is acquired through participation or the senses, Pestalozzi urged educators to include music instruction, which was then basically vocal music instruction, in their schools. His early-nineteenth-century treatise, *How Gertrude Teaches Her Children; An Attempt to Give Directions to Mothers on How to Instruct Their Own Children*, which was written in a dialogue format, stated that the only true foundation of human instruction was that acquired through direct participation—a forerunner of the Dewey concept of education! He was one of the first educators to distinguish between "real knowledge" and "book knowledge," the ivory tower versus the clinical experience.

In reality one cannot give Pestalozzi credit for initiating vocal music instruction in schools other than his own. However, his principles did provide other proponents with a philosophical basis for introducing such instruction. In 1810 Hans George Nageli produced a work entitled *The Theory of Instruction in Singing*, which was based on *Die Gesangbildumstehre nach Pestalozzischen Grundsatzen*. It combined the educational objectives of Pestalozzi with basic musical knowledge. It was this treatise that opened a new era in music instruction to children and had a great deal of influence on William C. Woodbridge, one of the early American leaders in music education. The same publication was later utilized as the foundation for vocal music instruction offered by Lowell Mason at the Boston Academy of Music later in the nineteenth century.

One of the earliest proponents of Pestalozzian ideas in this country, Joseph H. Naef, had been a member of Pestalozzi's staff in Europe before he emigrated around 1806. In 1809 he founded an elementary school here that was based on the Pestalozzian methods. Music in this school was considered a basic subject and all children were given appropriate music instruction.

In 1830, at the American Institute of Instruction meeting in Boston, Naef presented the following outline of "Principles of the Pestalozzian System of Music":

1. To teach sounds before signs and to make the child learn to sing before he learns the written notes or their names;

2. To lead him to observe by hearing and imitating sounds, their resemblances and differences, their agreeable and disagreeable effect, instead of explaining these things to him—in a word, to make active instead of passive in learning;

3. To teach but one thing at a time—rhythm, melody, and expression, which are to be taught and practiced separately, before the child is called to the difficult task of attending to all at once;

4. To make him practice each step of these divisions, until he is master of it, before passing to the next;

5. To give the principles and theory after the practice, and as induction from it;

6. To analyze and practice the elements of articulate sound in order to apply them to music, and

7. To have the names of the notes correspond to those used in instrumental music.

Many of these principles are still topics for discussion in current music education meetings.

Naef did not remain long in the East and moved to the Midwest, where he settled in New Harmony, Indiana, and established a settlement based upon Pestalozzi's ideas. Remnants and historical preservations of this colony still remain in New Harmony, and one can visit many of the first sites established there.

Lowell Mason, often referred to as the father of music education, was actually the first recognized official supervisor of elementary *vocal* music in the Boston public schools. He spearheaded the idea that music could be taught to children in the public schools and became the first teacher of music in the schools of Boston.

As a youth Mason had learned to play many instruments, including the organ, piano, violoncello, and clarinet. This versatility equipped him to assume the leadership of his hometown band in Medfield, Massachusetts. By the time he was sixteen he was already teaching singing in a singing school, and by the time he was twenty he had already been conducting a parish choir. Mason then moved to Savannah, Georgia, where he proceeded to perform as a solo violoncellist and singer. In addition to his musical involvement he worked as a clerk in a local bank. In spite of these demands, he still found time to organize a band and a church choir, to conduct many community groups, and to assume the responsibilities of a large Sunday school of the Independent Presbyterian Church in Savannah.

Mason continued to write music and was urged by his friends in Savannah to present his manuscripts to the Handel & Haydn Society of Boston. His friend Jubal Howe persuaded Mason to go to Boston, where they presented Mason's work to the society. It was favorably received and was published by the society under the formidable title *The Boston Handel & Haydn Society Collection of Church Music, Harmonized for Three and Four Voices, with Figured Bass, for Organ and Pianoforte.*

Mason's later publications met with considerable success, and the society convinced him to return to Boston so that they could have a closer working relationship. In 1827 Mason was elected president of the society, a position that he retained for four years. As president he established a studio in the society's building that enabled him to give vocal instruction to the members in an effort to improve the quality of the society's performances. It was during this period that he became acquainted with William Woodbridge and learned about Pestalozzi's work in Europe. In 1836 Mason petitioned the Boston school board to include vocal music in its elementary school. A special committee appointed to consider the proposal submitted its positive recommendation in 1837 and to justify its favorable decision presented the following position:

Let music be examined by the following standards:

1. Intellectually. Music had its place among the seven liberal arts, which scholastic ages regarded as pertaining to humanity. Arithmetic, Geometry, Astronomy, and Music—these formed the quadrivium. Memory, comparison, attention, intellectual faculties—all of them are quickened by a study of its principles. It may be made to some extent a mental discipline.

2. Morally. It is unphilosophical to say that exercises in vocal music may not be so directed and arranged as to produce those habits of feeling of which these sounds are the type. Happiness, contentment, cheerfulness, tranquillity—these are the natural effects of music.

3. Physically. It appears self evident that exercise in vocal music, when not carried to an unreasonable excess, must expand the chest and thereby strengthen the lungs and vital organs. Judging then by this triple standard, intellectually, morally, and physically, vocal music seems to have a natural place in

every system of instruction which aspires, as should every system, to develop man's whole nature. (Birge, 1966, pp. 41–42)

The report further stated:

> What is the great object of our system of popular instruction? Are our schools mere houses of correction, in which animal nature is to be kept in subjection by the law of brute force and the stated drudgery of distasteful tasks? Not so. They have a nobler office. They are valuable mainly as a preparation and a training of the young spirit for usefulness and happiness in coming life. Now, the defect of our present system, admirable as that system is, is this, that it aims to develop the intellectual part of man's nature solely when, for all the true purposes of life, it is of more importance, a hundred-fold, to feel rightly than to think profoundly. Besides, human life must and ought to have its amusements. Through vocal music you set in motion a mighty power which silently, but surely, in the end, will humanize, refine and elevate a whole community.

From this place first went out the great principle, that the property of all should be taxed for the education of all. From this place, also, may the example, in this country, first go forth of that education rendered more complete by the introduction by public authority, of vocal music into our system of popular instruction (Birge, 1966, pp. 47–48).

In 1837 Mason visited Europe to observe the schools and see how music, as advocated by Pestalozzi, was taught. He became completely convinced of the efficacy of this approach and began preparing his own texts based on the method. Mason was convinced that any child who could read could sing. He felt that it was an educational responsibility to make a musical heritage available to all children. The emergence of this concept, which was a deviation from the elite concept of the European culture of that period, was most opportune. This was the period when Horace Mann was advocating wide dissemination of free public education and the American educational system was growing. As a matter of fact, Mason and Mann became close friends and Mann invited him on many occasions to appear as lecturer and demonstrator at meetings, conventions, and workshops.

Mason believed that music contributed to the well-being of the individual; it united him with his God. To him and his followers, music brought comfort and solace. It created better homes, better citizens, and happier human beings. In Mason's estimation, everyone could enjoy music. All that was needed, according to both Mason and Horace Mann, was proper education and proper training.

In the early months of 1838, in order to sell his plan of teaching music to the Boston public schools, Mason worked without pay. He was so effective that a sufficient demand was created to warrant the school system employing him in August as the nation's first public school music teacher.

Normal Schools in the United States

The normal school became the chief source for trained teachers during the next sixty years. Its development can be traced to July 3, 1839, when the first state-supported school was opened in Lexington, Massachusetts, for the express purpose of preparing teachers. American society had been committed to education as an instrument of upward socioeconomic mobility; the opening of these schools was the initial move toward establishing a better means to achieve progress toward democracy, prosperity, and culture.

The first normal-school building, which was financed by the state of Massachusetts, was constructed in 1846 at Bridgewater. (Actually, a law was passed on March 6, 1818, that gave Philadelphia the right to train teachers, but the Normal School of Philadelphia was not established until February 1, 1848.) The Honorable William G. Bates of Westfield, Massachusetts, speaking at the dedication of the Bridgewater Normal School, said that "the common [public] schools could have an adequate teaching force only if the education of their teachers were provided for by the state" (Harper, 1939, p. 12).

Prior to the 1839 event that marked the first state-supported school, many private teaching institutions were springing up in communities because of a concern and dissatisfaction with the manner in which the young of this nation were being educated. As early as 1823 a private academy for the preparation of teachers was organized in Concord, Vermont. In 1825 Governor DeWitt Clinton, speaking to the New York legislature, recommended that it be concerned with the need to supply competent teachers. Others in that year were making similar appeals, as well as sponsoring and contributing numerous articles for publication in newspapers and journals.

From these early beginnings the normal schools began to proliferate throughout the East. These schools began to establish a separate and distinct profession of teaching. They were preparing young people to go out into the community with a knowledge and understanding of the art of teaching that enabled them to provide instruction far superior to what was offered by teachers who had not attended such schools.

By the latter part of the nineteenth century the normal-school movement had gained a secure place in the public's confidence, and such schools were being established throughout the nation. At the turn of the century (1900–1920) normal schools developed into teachers colleges. This educational evolution can be attributed to the increasing complexity of life in a maturing, developing society. Another issue in the struggle to change to teachers colleges was the growing power of colleges and universities in general, both private and state-supported. By expanding, normal schools were able to extend their programs to four years and enrich the curriculum. In addition, they secured better financial support—public and private—and were given the legal authority to grant degrees. Most importantly, the move preserved the distinct nature of the institution as a place to train teachers.

Expansion Following the Civil War

Public school music, as it was first known, or music education, as it is currently identified, had its real beginnings in the large cities following the Civil War. Much of the delay since Lowell Mason had first introduced music into the Boston public schools was attributable to the American system of financing schools. Boards of education in each local district totally managed their own affairs, which included levying taxes, adjusting curricula as recommended by guidelines from the state, and hiring teachers. To insert music into the curricula these boards had to be convinced of the importance of music in affecting the daily lives of the children and then in turn convince the local voting population of the need to provide the funds.

Even in pre–Civil War times most board members were of the opinion that music was for the talented and that these talented students could secure instruction through private studios or singing schools; they felt that it was not the taxpayer's responsibility to provide such instruction for every child.

However, the momentum for adding music into the curricula as a part of each child's daily life continued to grow. Some of this support came from (1) the increasing number of private teachers who were being trained in the singing schools, (2) increased choral activities resulting from the growth of choral societies, and (3) the impetus provided by the incipient stage of the formation of symphony orchestras. Concerts by international artists were being presented throughout the United States, and American composers such as George Chadwick and Edward MacDowell were having their music performed both here and abroad. In the fall of 1869 the first tour of the Theodore Thomas orchestra covered the Middle Atlantic states and New England. All these developments not only began to affect large numbers of people who became supportive of music instruction in the schools, but also produced a more musically sophisticated public. All this led to a rapid development of music in institutions of higher education such as conservatories and schools of music. In addition, liberal arts colleges began to include music courses in their offerings.

At the same time, an "even more immediate influence upon the generality of people was the large number of excellent regimental and concert bands which appeared after the Civil War under such leaders as [Patrick] Gilmore, [David] Reeves, and [Thomas] Brooks [Brooke], to which may be added the fact that the highly versatile bands maintained by such huge traveling shows as P. T. Barnum's were heard annually by millions" (Birge, 1928, p. 84).

Benjamin Jepson of New Haven, Connecticut, had been most successful in training children's choruses even prior to the Civil War. Upon returning from military service in 1865, he persuaded the New Haven Board of Education to employ him to introduce music into its schools as part of an experiment. He developed his own materials and later published them as a textbook called *Music Reader*. The experiment was eminently successful.

Similar developments were occurring throughout the United States. In 1866 George B. Loomis developed and published his own method for the Indianapolis public schools. *Loomis Progressive Music Lessons*. Other prominent figures included Nathan L. Glover, the first supervisor of music in Akron, Ohio, who served in that capacity for 49 years (1872–1920); Milton Z. Tinker, who taught for years in the Evansville, Indiana, schools; Henry M. Butler of St. Louis; Orlando Blackman of Chicago; and N. Coe Stuart of Cleveland, who was credited with initiating the concept of having classroom teachers teach music. The Cleveland Board of Education had established music as a part of the basic required courses for the education of its children as early as 1846; this set the stage for similar experiments in Tennessee and Virginia from 1870 to 1880.

In addition to the appearance and founding of orchestras in the schools at the turn of the century, the study of music appreciation became a specific course objective. Frances E. Clark initiated music history courses in the Ottumwa, Iowa, schools as a part of the appreciation movement. Will Earhart started similar courses in Richmond, Indiana, while at the same time Peter Dykema was introducing pupils in the Fletcher School in Indianapolis to the operas of Wagner. In the East, Mary Regal of Springfield, Massachusetts, was organizing high school appreciation courses, and Frederick Chapman added the study of harmony, melody, and counterpoint to the music offerings in the high schools of Cambridge, Massachusetts.

It should be noted that the high school was much different than from what we know it as today. In the early 1900s it was almost entirely a preparatory step toward college and, as a result, a much smaller percentage of students attended high school. These programs were therefore unique and innovative at the time. With the success of these programs, however, it became implicit in the emerging school music teaching profession that it was the school's responsibility to make music available to all children. As a result the post–Civil War period saw the development of new techniques, materials, and methods devoted to the instruction of larger groups, as opposed to the available materials and methods that were used in the singing schools and conservatories, where a one-to-one type of instruction prevailed.

Early in the twentieth century the pragmatic philosophy of John Dewey initiated an emphasis on and concern for educating the whole child. To attain this goal, it was essential that the arts be considered a part of the total school experience. Furthermore, this was a period of prosperity in which society began to concern itself with the quality of living. This concern included an awareness of the need for developing a cultured America. It helped bring about the establishment of symphony orchestras in major cities such as Detroit and Cleveland. However, even before this period, as early as 1889, Will Earhart had started a school orchestra in Richmond, Indiana, that later became an example for instituting and developing a quality instrumental program in a school setting.

In 1910 Albert F. Mitchell, a supervisor of music in the Boston schools, was given a year's leave of absence to study violin class instruction in England. He was so impressed by the class teaching approach he observed that he was inspired to write the *Mitchell Class Method* for the violin. In Boston, Mitchell's violin classes met only after school hours, but they were very successful. Classes spread across the country as the violin class movement was imitated by others. The concept of class instrumental teaching spread to all of the instruments and a new technique to meet the class-ensemble challenge was developed. Some of the early and significant texts were Joseph Maddy and Thaddeus Giddings's *Instrumental Techniques for Orchestra and Band* and Raymond N. Carr's *Building the School Orchestra*.

About 1913 piano class instruction began to appear in the schools of Cincinnati and other places. These piano classes were initiated in high schools but soon moved to the elementary schools, where class techniques for early piano instruction evolved.

After World War I

World War I helped project bands into the limelight. The groundwork for school bands had been laid prior to the war by leading instrumental educators such as A. R. McAllister in Joliet, Illinois, and many others. However, with the end of the war, and the interest in band music stimulated by it, returning army bandsmen were employed by school boards to initiate band programs in the schools. This was also the period of famous touring bands headed by the "March King," John Philip Sousa. The entire atmosphere made it easier for instrumental music to become a staple in school instruction. Instrumental music began to flourish.

In 1918 George Eastman, the founder of Eastman Kodak, purchased 300 instruments for the Rochester public schools. Joseph Maddy, who later founded the National Music Camp at Interlochen, was employed as the school's instrumental teacher. In 1919 J. W. Wainwright organized the band program in Fostoria, Ohio, which in 1923 won first place in the first National Band Contest held in Chicago. Also in 1919, Detroit's Cass Technical High School was opened. Because music was treated in its curriculum as a technical subject, graduates were so well prepared that they were equipped to seek employment as professional musicians. Instruction in music, including instrumental music, was becoming an accepted part of the total school curriculum.

Actually, the major expansion in secondary school music occurred with the growth of the secondary school itself during the thirty years between 1910 and 1940. During this period the chances that a child would attend high school increased from one in ten to three out of four. As a result of this expansion in the secondary school population, curriculum changes had to be made to accommodate many students who were not planning to attend college and who regarded high school as a terminal program.

Other shifts occurring in population centers at the turn of the twentieth century were not only affecting these curricular changes, but were also bringing into the classroom a more enlightened student. Around 1900 the United States was essentially a rural nation. By 1970 it was 85 percent urban. Because school music expanded at such a rapid rate, there was not a sufficient number of trained school music teachers to meet the growing demand.

To offset the shortage of trained personnel, secondary schools often turned to professional performers to teach in the schools. This brought people into the classroom who were not only skilled musicians but were also oriented toward the ultimate goal of performance. These musicians held "rehearsals" much as one would in a professional group, and their whole orientation was directed toward performance. The trend to use performing musicians as teachers was accelerated by two events: "talking pictures," which began in 1927, and the Depression, which followed in 1929.

Unfortunately, the nation's financial collapse in 1929 had traumatic, devastating effects on the population's attitude toward culture. It became a question of whether or not the economy "could afford it." Community orchestras began to fold because of lack of financial support. In addition, there were technical developments that affected employment for live performing musicians. The "talking pictures" began their slow attrition and gradual elimination of pit orchestras and theater bands. Organists were gradually replaced by "sound tracks."[*] This threat to live performances has reached such magnitude that in 1990 an independent group, Coalition for the Advancement of Live Music (CALM), was founded in New York

---

[*]Threats to live music did not end with the "talkies." In fact, they are a concern that will probably be with us at all times. In an article in the July 24, 1981, *Wall Street Journal*, "Magic Flutes: Instruments Powered by Computers Invade the World of Music," it was reported that what people heard during a CBS movie, *Word of Honor*, may have sounded like an orchestra but was actually a digital synthesizer that was a computer. The article suggested that the computer and one player might be able to perform the work of many musicians thanks to the microprocessor revolution. In this particular movie, the article pointed out, "those sitting in the theater thought that they were hearing violins and flutes, as well as oboes, trombones, clarinets, and French horns on the sound track; yet, all of these sounds

for the express purpose of developing "a marketing campaign whose chief function would be to attract more business for live music and musicians in the commercial announcements field" (*International Musician*, 1992, p. 1). The need for such supportive organizations was seen as early as 1935, when the government created an agency called the Works Progress Administration (WPA). Its purpose was to stimulate and support creativity and artistry through federal support, and thereby assist in overcoming the national economic disaster. One can only conjecture what would have happened to American culture if it had not been for this agency. It was through the WPA that the creative efforts of American artists actually flourished beyond any previous point in our national history (Sunderman, 1971, 262–65). It not only provided employment to vast numbers of performing artists, but supplied educational funds to employ teachers to prepare the multitudes that would benefit by low-cost or free performances that were being presented under the WPA's auspices. It was the largest single force in advancing American culture during the 1930s.

World War II and the Postwar Period

With the advent of World War II and America's entry into the conflict in 1941, cultural pursuits had to be held in abeyance for the duration. In the all-out effort that was involved in the war, manpower became a crucial concern, and the schools were confronted with a shortage of trained male personnel. To meet this threat to music instruction, new techniques and skills were developed to enable individual classroom teachers to conduct their own music programs. So successful was this approach in terms of meeting minimum programs that long after the war ended and male teachers returned, the prevailing philosophy—based on the classroom teacher in the elementary school conducting the music program on a daily basis, with the music specialist acting as a consultant or appearing once or twice weekly to introduce certain skills—continued. This philosophy dominated the school literature and was pretty much the accepted practice, although many school systems, such as Detroit's, still maintained the attitude that music as a special subject should be taught by specialists, even in the elementary schools. In 1972 the Music Educators National Conference's (MENC) *Teacher Education in Music: Final Report* sought to reestablish

---

were coming from this mechanical instrument." True, as one musician pointed out, mechanized instrumentation cannot provide the aesthetic pleasure that one gets from a live performance, but as a New York trumpet player indicated, "a lot of people can't tell the difference." Today one can see this as a serious threat to live movie studio musicians. Music educators are now confronted with the challenge of developing perceptive audiences with sensitive ears that can distinguish between music produced by live musicians and music that is re-created "plastically" through electronic devices. Much of the beauty of music stems from the subtle nuances of live performances, which cannot be satisfactory duplicated with electronics.

the position of the music specialist in the elementary school by taking a position that "music in the elementary be taught by music specialists" (Klotman, 1972, p. 20). It did, however, acknowledge that there should be times when the classroom teacher will assume some responsibility for musical experiences in the classroom.

In the meantime, instrumental music continued to flourish. Following World War II there was a decline in strings and orchestras in the schools because of the increased popularity of bands, created by use of the latter in the war and by the proliferation of professional sports events that utilized bands for "show-business" types of entertainment. To counteract this decline, a concerned group of string educators met in Cleveland in 1948 and formed the American String Teachers Association. Through publications, workshops, public relations programs, and financial support from key industry figures such as Heinrich Roth of Scherl & Roth, this group was able in the ensuing years to restore the orchestra movement to some of its previous status in the school music program.

In 1957 the Soviet Union launched the first satellite into space, and the space race was underway. Concern was expressed by scientific leaders and educators in the United States that the Soviets had succeeded in this task ahead of us because of alleged shortcomings in our educational system.

As a result, the support given to education during this period was focused on the sciences and related subjects. However, the rallying cry was "the pursuit of excellence," and this pervaded every subject area, including the arts. It was during this period that the aesthetic education movement emerged as an effort to form a firm philosophical framework that would meet fundamental concerns in the pursuit of excellence. The aesthetic education proponents emphasized that they were proposing a more fundamental approach to education in music. They were far more concerned with the artistic values of music than with the traditional "performance for performance's sake." The 1970 biennial convention in Chicago of the Music Educators National Conference featured several panels and served as a catalyst for generating interest in the movement. Aesthetic foundations in music education will be discussed in chapter 3.

In the period following the 1970 convention, music in most school systems was affected by compacted schedules that allowed more time for so-called required academic subjects and fewer periods in the school day for electives. This restricted the time available for subjects not in the basic group required for graduation and college. In music, "excellence" was interpreted to mean excellence in performance and greater emphasis on cognitive knowledge in the general music areas. In those affected schools, classes and performing groups were generally smaller, but the quality of performance improved. Unfortunately, it was at the expense of one of music education's basic tenets, which was "music for every child." This goal was a commitment to reach out and offer opportunities for as many children as were interested.

Jazz in the Schools

During World War II virtually all units in the armed services had a dance/jazz band along with their military bands. The U.S. Navy School of Music even included jazz and swing band training in the preparation of its musicians and directors. After the war these musicians who were trained in the armed forces were discharged and returned to civilian life, where many went to universities under the G.I. Bill and earned degrees in music education. They began directing school bands and included jazz ensembles in their schools where they didn't already exist. "As early as 1944, a Rye, N.Y. music department chairman was editing a weekly mimeographed jazz publication distributed to 180 high schools" (Baker, 1979, p. iv).

By the 1960s jazz-type ensembles were appearing not only in high schools but also in middle and junior high schools, although the impediments to incorporating jazz in the school curriculum were, at times, discouraging. However, leaders in the professional field such as Stan Kenton, Art Dedrick, Sammy Nestico (arranger for the official U.S. Air Force Stage Band) and others began writing charts and arrangements for school groups as early as 1954. It was largely through their efforts and support that jazz began to assume its role as a viable musical form to be expressed and studied in the school music curriculum.

When the Tanglewood Symposium met in 1967 at Tanglewood, the summer home of the Boston Symphony, a complete session, "Music In Our Time," was an integral part of the program. It featured jazz artists and jazz pedagogues. David P. McAllester, one of the presenters, highlighted the efficacy of teaching jazz in school programs when he stated:

> The popular music of our own youth embodies high art and a content both cultural and aesthetic, that must inevitably receive serious attention from the entire musical community. (Music Educators National Conference, 1968, p. 97)

The Elementary–Secondary Education Act

It was in 1965 under President Lyndon Johnson, who envisioned a "Great Society," that the Elementary-Secondary Education Act was passed. This provided renewed support for the arts in the schools through cultural enrichment programs. Musicians were brought into the schools to perform and to offer workshops to supplement and improve instruction. Financially depressed school areas were provided with funds to purchase equipment to help compensate for their economic disability. Innovative programs and experiments in music teaching were encouraged. It was a period of growth and expansion for music education in areas that had been disadvantaged by economic limitations. Once again, music education was reaching out to provide experiences and training for "every child."

Other events occurred in the 1960s such as the Yale Seminar and the Tanglewood Symposium. These significant meetings are discussed later in this chapter. Unfortunately, a mild economic recession in 1969 stunted the growth and development that had occurred as a result of the 1965 Elementary-Secondary Education Act, and educators in the arts and other areas fell into a pattern during the period from 1969 to 1974 of being content to retain their previous advances. They could not, however, withstand the impact of the major recession that occurred in 1974. Declining school enrollments and limited funding initiated the slow attrition that ate into and practically eliminated the gains achieved in staffing and providing time allotments for the arts that had occurred in the previous decade. With the impact of reduced funding, taxpayers began to ask whether or not the arts were essential subjects, and the sound of "back to basics" began its beat. In spite of the popular acceptance of the back-to-basics movement, which was economically motivated, school music for every child remained a part of the curriculum. It is true that in many areas programs suffered, and some were eliminated altogether. These measures, however, were primarily efforts to alert the public to the educational implications of failing to provide funds for school programs in question, and the programs were restored once the tax funds were provided. This indicated that music and the other arts had substantially proven their value and importance in the American educational scheme.

The Yale Seminar and Tanglewood Symposium

Two conferences held in the 1960s merit special mention: the Yale Seminar and the Tanglewood Symposium. (Both of these projects are discussed further in chapter 10 since they were designed to have an impact on the school curriculum.) The Yale Seminar, which met in 1963, was one of the first federally supported developmental conferences in arts education. At the time it created quite a furor among music educators, since it appeared to be an imposition of views upon music education by those involved with musicology. The chief criticism leveled at the seminar at that time was that among the thirty-one participants, there were only a few music educators.

In its final report the seminar advocated that the young people of the nation be exposed to what the seminar participants considered "good" music. In its criticism of school music programs the seminar focused on the literature used in the school music programs but ignored the competencies expected of students as a result of music instruction.

In the summer of 1967 the MENC, in cooperation with the Berkshire Music Center, the Theodore Presser Foundation, and the School of Fine and Applied Arts of Boston University, convened a symposium to consider major issues related to the theme "Music in American Society." This symposium met in Tanglewood, the summer home of the Boston Symphony Orchestra. Participants included not only music educators but also performing musicians, sociologists, labor leaders, scientists, educators, and representatives from corporations, foundations, and government. The symposium was assembled not only because of the urgent issues confronting the arts and music but also as a result of some of the many criticisms and attacks that were being made on music education. The project was organized by Robert Choate, a former president of the conference, and Louis Wersen, the current president of MENC.

The symposium focused on the problems and potentials for music activities and musical development in American society. Music education as an integral part of life and living, not only within the individual but as it extended to society, was the prime focus. The symposium, a milestone for the profession, culminated in the *Documentary Report of the Tanglewood Symposium* (Choate, 1968), which contains all the papers presented and positions adopted.

In its final declaration, the symposium stated: "Educators must accept the responsibility for developing opportunities which meet man's individual needs and the needs of a society plagued by the consequences of changing values, alienation, hostility between generations, racial and international tensions, and the challenges of the new leisure."

The symposium seemed to unify and provide some philosophical guidance badly needed by the profession. It gave direction on such topics as youth music, music in urban education, electronic music, music in the related arts, and music for the child in "special education." It was the profession's attempt to make its programs more current and more relative to the issues of the day.

Manhattanville Music Curriculum Project

Another project in the '60s designed to promote creativity was the Manhattanville Music Curriculum Project (MMCP). The program was funded by grants from the U.S. Office of Education and was named for Manhattanville College in Purchase, New York, where it was initiated in 1965. Initially it was designed to identify innovative and experimental music programs in the United States. Ninety-two programs were examined, and fifteen were selected for in-depth study. The project, which began in 1966, consisted of three phases:

1. Phase one studied how students learn, as well as curriculum and classroom procedures.
2. Phase two refined and organized the information obtained in phase one into a course of study.

3. Phase three was intended to field test and refine the course as well as develop a plan for teacher training and assessment. However, the project expired and was not renewed before an assessment could be conducted.

The primary objective of the MMCP program was to have children learn to hear and perceive music much as a composer does. Students were asked to compose, perform, conduct, listen, and not to stand back and consider music reverently (Thomas, 1968, p. 64).

Field tests of the program in its third phase revealed that some modifications were necessary and that a teacher in-service training program was essential to implement the program.

In 1975 Congress enacted "The Education for All Handicapped Children Act." This legislation mandated that all handicapped children were entitled to special education in the schools. Its impact was that school systems were now required to provide some music teachers who had special training in working with these children. Its curricular implications are discussed in chapter 9, p. 291.

A Nation at Risk

With the growing national concern for the so-called "declining quality" of education given the young people of this nation in the '70s and early '80s, President Ronald Reagan appointed a National Commission on Excellence in Education. This commission issued a report in 1983 entitled *A Nation at Risk: The Imperative for Educational Reform*. The report indicated that American education experienced a serious decline over approximately the past twenty-five years (LeBlanc, 1983, p. 29).

In reviewing this educational decline, the report attributed it to a "weakness of purpose, confusion of vision, underuse of talent, and lack of leadership." The specific educational shortcomings were attributed to deficiencies in four areas that exist in the current educational process: content, expectations, time and teaching.

The criticism leveled at content was that over the past twenty-five years courses of substance were replaced by less demanding or less rigorous offerings. Expectations were cited as deficient because, in the commission's opinion, teachers were less demanding in their subject areas. The examples they cited to verify this criticism were grade inflation, simplified texts, lowering of requirements for high school graduation, and relaxed requirements for college admission. When the commission compared the requirements for time devoted to education in other industrialized nations, it found U.S. standards considerably below those of the other countries. The quality of teaching was described as inadequate because of low teacher salaries, poor working conditions, and shortage of qualified teachers in specific areas that were more remunerative outside the classroom. Furthermore, because of these limitations the teaching profession seemed to be attracting academically weak students. The preparation of those teachers was faulted, in the commission's opinion, because of the emphasis on methods at the expense of content in the teacher education curricula.

The commission attacked these concerns with the following remedies. Concerning content, the commission recommended "five new basics": English, mathematics, science, social studies, and computer science. For those wishing to attend college, the commission recommended two years study of a foreign language, along with study in the fine and performing arts (LeBlanc, 1983, p. 30). This recommendation will be discussed in further detail later.

To improve standards and eliminate grade erosion, the commission urged that stricter grading be enforced and higher standards be required for graduation from high school and admission to colleges. In its concern for the substandard time allocation attributed to the education of students, the commission recommended that more homework be assigned, that there be fewer intrusions in class teaching time, and that the school day be lengthened. In addition, the commission expressed a need for better support for teachers in maintaining discipline and enforcing stringent attendance policies.

To improve teaching, the commission recommended that higher standards for admission to teacher education programs be established. In addition, it suggested that higher salaries be given teachers, along with an eleven-month contract. It noted that programs recognizing the work of outstanding teachers needed to be initiated and outstanding students who wanted to become teachers should be encouraged and given financial assistance.

It its final suggestion, the commission stated that elected officials and educators should be held responsible for implementing these needed reforms. Furthermore, these responsible individuals needed to provide fiscal support necessary to finance and implement these recommendations.

In its statement regarding the fine and performing arts, the report stated: "A high level of shared education in these Basics, together with work in the fine and performing arts and foreign languages, constitutes the mind and spirit of our culture" (National Commission on Excellence in Education, 1984, p. 70). Interestingly, it specifically endorsed arts education at the elementary level.

The most disappointing aspect of the exposure given this report by the media and public discussion was the lack of emphasis or even concern over the the comments on the arts. Historically, "every individual or group that has made a major contribution to educational thought since Plato has spoken of the importance of the arts in education" (Music Educators National Conference, 1984, p. 27).

In order to be assured that the concern for education in the arts be given its proper perspective in the discussion and recommendations that would emanate from the commission's report, MENC took the following positions:

1. MENC supports efforts to improve the quality of American education at every level and in every phase of the curriculum. Further, we support efforts to develop more rigorous and measurable standards for education in all fields.

   Each elementary and secondary school should undertake to implement, in stages if necessary, the specific recommendations of MENC with respect to curriculum, staff, scheduling, physical facilities, materials, and equipment as presented in *The School Music Program: Description and Standards*.

   Teachers should be fully qualified, not merely legally certified, in the specific subjects they are assigned to teach.

2. MENC supports efforts to raise the standards for admission to higher education and to ensure that each college or university student possesses knowledge and skill in the arts.

   Each high school student in a college-preparatory program should receive a comprehensive program of instruction in the arts as specified in *Academic Preparation for College* by the College Board. Each student should demonstrate the knowledge and skills specified by the board in at least one field of the arts.

3. Offerings in the arts should not be reduced or jeopardized in efforts to increase graduation requirements or improve the quality of other offerings at the secondary level. Specifically, there should be sufficient flexibility in the curriculum and a sufficient number of periods in the school day to provide a balance program in music and the arts.

   The school day should be extended, when necessary, to ensure that all students have the opportunity to elect courses in the arts. (Music Educators National Conference 1984, p. 12)

The *A Nation at Risk* report stimulated the most vigorous interest and discussion at a public level in years. It is interesting to note, however, that although there were forty commissioned papers in this study, none dealt with the arts. Hearings were held on science, math, computer technology, language, and literacy, but other than a visit to a high school for Performing and Visual Arts in Houston, little else was done reflecting concern for the arts. Arts educators and arts-interested citizens were disturbed by the glaring omission of the arts in this reform effort to remedy a situation that the commission described as a "rising tide of mediocrity," especially since its critical assessment will have impact on American education well into the twenty-first century.

College Entrance Board Report

In contrast to the disregard for the arts in the *A Nation at Risk* report, the College Entrance Examination Board published a report titled *Academic Preparation for College: What Students Need to Know and Be Able to Do* (College Entrance Board, 1983) that strongly supported arts education. This report named the arts, along with English, mathematics, science, social science, and foreign languages, as one of the six major areas of study. The reasoning and significance of this recommendation is contained in the following excerpt from the report:

> Why?
> The arts—visual arts, theater, music, and dance—challenge and extend human experience. They provide means of expression that go beyond ordinary speaking and writing. They can express intimate thoughts and feelings. They are a unique record of diverse cultures and how these cultures have developed over time. They provide distinctive ways of understanding human beings and nature. The arts are creative modes by which all people can enrich their lives both by self-expression and response to the expressions of others. . . .
> Preparation in the arts will be valuable to college entrants whatever their intended field of study. The actual practice of the arts can engage the imagination, foster flexible ways of thinking, develop disciplined effort, and build self-confidence. Appreciation of the arts is integral to the understanding of other cultures sought in the study of history, foreign language, and social sciences. Preparation in the arts will also enable college students to engage in and profit from advanced study, performance, and studio work in the arts. For some, such college-level work will lead to careers in the arts. For many others, it will permanently enhance the quality of their lives, whether they continue artistic activity as an avocation or appreciation of the arts as observers and members of audiences. . . . (Hodsoll, 1983)

If music preparation is given to college entrants, they will need the following knowledge and skills.

- The ability to identify and describe—using appropriate vocabulary—various musical forms from different historical periods.
- The ability to listen perceptively to music, distinguishing such elements as pitch, rhythm, timbre, and dynamics.
- The ability to read music.
- The ability to evaluate a musical work or performance.
- To know how to express themselves by playing an instrument, singing in a

group or individually, or composing music. (College Entrance Examination Board, 1983)

Toward Civilization

In 1988 The National Endowment for the Arts presented President Bush and Congress with a report on arts education titled *Toward Civilization: A Report on Arts Education*. The report attempts "to identify the arts that should be taught in school, to present the reasons for studying them, to show why the present state of arts education is unsatisfactory, and to suggest avenues for its improvement." (p. v) The research undertaken and the writing of the report was supervised by Frank Hodsoll, chair of the National Endowment for the Arts during this period.

The problem identified in the report is that basic arts education does not universally exist in our educational system. The report emphasizes that a balanced education is essential to an enlightened citizenry and a productive work force and that such a comprehensive education should include study in three branches of learning—the arts, humanities, and sciences. It points out that arts education is important to understand civilization, to develop creativity, to learn the tools of communication, and to develop the capability of making wise choices among the arts.

The report identifies a gap a between commitment and resources for arts education and the actual practice of arts education in the classroom. "Resources are being provided, but they are not being used to give opportunities for all, or for even most students, to become culturally literate. In general the arts are not being taught sequentially. Arts students are not being evaluated. Many arts teachers are not prepared to teach history and critical analysis of the arts." (p. v) Following this theme, the report does not advocate new resources but a redistribution of resources. Resources that are now allocated to support performances and exhibitions should be employed to help students "move toward civilization."

To accomplish this recommendation the report proposes that:

1. State education agencies and school districts should develop a consensus on what all students should know in the arts before graduating from high school, and provide required and optional courses to achieve this.

2. State education agencies, with federal assistance, should develop evaluation procedures to determine how successful school districts are in meeting the identified arts goals.

3. Certifying agencies should strengthen and broaden arts teachers' certification requirements, and special procedures designed to permit artists and arts professionals to teach the arts where there are shortages of arts education specialists should be developed.

4. More support for arts education research that focuses on improving classroom instruction is needed.

5. The U.S. Department of Education and the National Endowment for the Arts should strengthen research to help educators improve arts education in schools.

6. Supporters of the arts as a basic part of education should work together to develop a consensus on the purpose and content of arts education.

7. The National Endowment for the Arts should continue and strengthen its arts education efforts. (p. vi)

Soon after the report was delivered, funds for arts agencies were decreased. While many of the themes promoted by the report continue to guide arts bureaucrats, there is little money to implement them. During the early part of the 1990s, attention turned instead to preserving arts programs as economic pressures diminished the funds available for supporting them at the local levels.

The Early Days of the Music Educators National Conference

Although some instruction in music, particularly singing, was generally given in classrooms throughout the world, it was in the United States that the term "music education" and the reference to its instructor, "music educator," were first conceived. According to Allen Britton, it was not merely the love for music, which in itself is sufficient, but also "the necessity historically felt by school music teachers to justify the expenditures of public monies on their behalf, [that caused] such a term (music educator) . . . to be invented" (Britton, 1966, p. 15). The scope of the American program far exceeded any instruction carried on by educators anywhere else in the world. It was organized in a sequence that carried from elementary school through high school and even extended into adult life and higher education. It was broader than ever conceived elsewhere in the world in that it included almost every facet of vocal, choral, general, and instrumental music in virtually every school.

Much of music education's success in becoming an integral part of the school curriculum can be directly attributed to the efforts of its chief proponent and professional arm, the Music Educators National Conference (MENC). This conference evolved out of what was originally a group of supervisors who met in April 1907 in Keokuk, Iowa, and formed the Music Supervisors National Conference.

Philip C. Hayden, who was teaching in Keokuk, was so enthusiastic about his rhythmic approach to learning to read music that in November 1906 he invited a group of supervisors not only to observe his techniques and materials but to help evaluate the success of this program. In addition, if there was sufficient interest it was planned to have a program discussing problems of general interest and including papers and discussion groups to review new concepts. Twenty-six individuals accepted the initial invitation. This led Hayden and the others to believe that there was considerable interest in a conference just for music teachers. Armed with this support and the possibility of National Education Association (NEA) meetings being held on the country's East and West coasts, the group requested that the NEA appoint a committee to help them arrange for a Midwest conference. The initial meeting was held in the Westminster Presbyterian church in Keokuk on April 10–12, 1907, with three sessions on each day. The program included demonstrations by Hayden and his students from the Keokuk schools.

According to Edward Bailey Birge (1928), those in attendance had no idea of making this ad hoc meeting a basis for forming a permanent organization. Up to this point the music section of the National Education Association was considered the official national organization for school music teachers. However, as the meeting progressed it became evident that there were special concerns that needed to be reviewed and discussed apart from a central organization such as the NEA. Many of those in attendance in Keokuk began to express a desire to form a permanent, separate organization. Committees were formed and the incipient stages of what was commonly referred to as the "Music Supervisors Conference" were underway. It was not until 1910 that the formal name was adopted at a meeting in Cincinnati. The total membership by then had reached about 150.

In 1919 at the St. Louis meeting, Osbourne McConathy formulated one of the basic tenets of music education when he stated: "Every child should be educated in music according to his natural capacities, at public expense, and his studies should function in the musical life of the community" (Birge, 1928, p. 251). By 1923, at the meeting in Cleveland, the membership had reached 2,200. It was there that Karl Gehrkens phrased his famous "Music for every child, every child for music," which has remained a guiding objective for music educators to this day.

Most significant in the growth and efficacy of the supervisors national conference was its official publication, the *Music Supervisors Bulletin*. It began in 1914 as a regularly issued bulletin. In 1916 it formally changed its name to the *Music Supervisors Journal*, and thus began a journal publication that presented issues and disseminated information to its members regarding the activities of the conference.

The name Music Supervisors National Conference remained as such until 1934, when the organization broadened its perspective by changing its name to Music Educators National Conference. The *Music Supervisors Journal* was renamed the *Music Educators Journal*, and what had once been a gathering of individuals identified primarily as supervisors became a profession embracing every aspect of music as it was taught in the schools.

In 1952 the National Executive Board of MENC decided to consolidate its Chicago office with the NEA office in Washington. This period was a significant one. During the same year the board established the Commission on Accreditation and Certification, whose responsibility was to develop standards for evaluation of curricula in colleges that were responsible for training school music teachers. During the following year, 1953, the first issue of the *Journal of Research in Music Education* was published.

With support from members of the music industry and direct contributions from individual MENC members, state organizations, and student chapters, MENC finally realized one of its long-sought ambitions in 1975: a home of its own. A permanent residence that members of the profession could identify as their own base of operation was completed and occupied in Reston, Virginia.

Music education as we know it is a unique product of the American system. Until it was first developed in the United States it was merely traditional instruction given on a one-to-one basis in a studio, or possibly a class that had little to do with what was going on within the school system.

The distinctive feature of music education in this country is that its programs are conceived and carried out in such a way that they are designed to benefit all the children of each community. This is not to be confused with a position of offering each child an identical musical experience. It emphasizes instead the need for a variety of opportunities in the school to provide sufficient differentiation for all levels of musical ability and interest. It is the basic tenet of music education that each student may advance at a rate of speed consistent with his or her interest and ability.

Under the aegis of the American educational system music education was permitted to prosper and flourish in this country in a manner that has now become an exemplar for music training in schools throughout the world. This accomplishment has been the result of the combined forces of dedicated teachers, appropriate funding to permit installation of programs in schools, and the establishment of realistic goals and objectives that enable the profession to make students informed and literate about music and the world around them. It is the ultimate goal of the profession that such individuals may participate in a musical society that is both vital and enlightened.

Music Educators National Conference Professional Certification Program

In the late 1980s, in order to improve the quality of music education in the United States and encourage professional growth in the music teaching profession, MENC departed from its long-established position of being primarily an advocacy organization, rather than a certifying or evaluating agency, and established the "MENC Professional Certification Program." This program is designed not only to improve the quality of instruction in music in the schools but also to recognize outstanding music teachers who meet the criteria set by the organization for elementary and secondary music education. The first "registered" awardees were named in 1990.

The program is divided into two levels: level one, "Nationally Registered Music Educator," and level two, "Nationally Certified Master Music Educator." The first level documents the individual's professional achievements, professional growth, and contributions to music education through participation on committees, attendance at professional meetings, and involvement in other music education activities. Candidates are required to have eight years of teaching experience before being eligible for consideration. Attainment of the second level indicates that the applying music educator has met the criteria of level one, and that a panel of qualified music educators have determined that the applying teacher's competencies have also complied with MENC's established national standard for teaching after twelve years of classroom experience.

To receive professional certification, teachers need to submit an "Application and Certification" booklet along with letters of recommendation and a videotape demonstrating their music teaching skills to the MENC office. The assessment is then done by a peer review committee. The entire program is voluntary.

The impetus for MENC's assuming this new role of being a certifying agency for music educators resulted from the many reports and publications that focused on the concern for education in the United States as it prepared to enter the twenty-first century.

Summary

Education in music and debates regarding its value can be traced as far back as the fourth century B.C. Musical education has not developed in isolation but rather in the social, religious, and economic context of the times. Understanding the sequence and the nature of the historical development of this movement helps us understand better how the music profession arrived at its present position and may assist music educators in predicting future directions for music in the American schools. The major events in music education history are summarized in table 1.1.

TABLE 1.1
Chronological Table: The History of Music Education

DATE	MUSIC EDUCATION EVENTS
5th century B.C.	Pythagoras, the mathematician, developed his musical theories, which influenced scale and interval practices still utilized today. The professional musician emerged as a virtuoso.
4th century B.C.	Early Greek education was structured with rhetoric for the mind, gymnastics for the body, and art and music for the soul. Aristotle, in *Politics*, questioned the need for music and doubted its educational potential as well. However, he did philosophize that music influenced the will of human beings [concept of *ethos*]. Plato, in his *Republic* (Book V), wrote that "literature, music, art ("Musical" education) have a great influence on character." He and his student Aristotle were in agreement.
A.D. 313	The Edict of Milan permitted Christians to practice their religion openly. Soon Rome organized the *scholae cantorum*.
5th century A.D.	Music assumed its position in the quadrivium.
6th century A.D.	Boethius (d. A.D. 525) wrote his treatise on musical theory (*De Musica*). Pope Gregory expanded the *scholae cantorum* to include instruction in singing, playing instruments, and harmony and composition.
9th century A.D.	In an effort to standardize the chant, a method for notating music was devised.
16th century A.D.	Churches organized schools in a type of orphanage called a *conservatorio*.
A.D. 1784	The Paris Conservatory, the earliest school of music in Europe, was founded.
19th century A.D.	The Royal Academy of Music was established in England in 1822. The Prague Conservatory was established c. 1811. The Musikakademie Hochschule für Musik originated in 1817 in Vienna. Mendelssohn organized the Leipzig Conservatory in 1843. The Berlin Conservatory was founded in 1850. The Peabody Conservatory was established in the U.S. in 1857.

Music Education in the United States

c. 1640	The first published songbook in America, *The Bay Psalm Book*, appeared.
1717	The first singing school was established in Boston.

TABLE 1.1 (*continued*)

DATE	MUSIC EDUCATION EVENTS
Early 19th century (1800–1850)	Samuel Holyoke of Salem, Massachusetts, expanded his singing school to include a second school devoted to instrumental music. William Billings, a native American composer, wrote *The New England Psalm Singer of the American Chrositer*. Joseph Naef founded an elementary school based on Pestalozzian methods in 1809. Lowell Mason introduced music as a subject in the Boston public schools in 1838. The first state supported normal school devoted to teacher training was opened in Lexington, Massachusetts, in 1839.
Late 19th century (post–Civil War)	Following the Civil War, increased activity in music in the nation led to an upsurge of music in the schools. Benjamin Jepson persuaded the New Haven Board to employ him to introduce music into the elementary schools as an experiment. He developed his own textbook, *Music Reader*. Will Earhart started music appreciation courses and a school orchestra in Richmond, Indiana. Frances E. Clark started similar courses in Ottumwa, Iowa, as did others throughout the nation.
Early 20th century	In Boston, Albert F. Mitchell started violin class instruction in the schools. Following World War I, George Eastman of Eastman Kodak purchased 300 instruments for the Rochester, N.Y., schools and Joseph Maddy was employed as the school's instrumental teacher. The "talkies" in 1927 and the Depression of 1929 forced many professional musicians to seek employment elsewhere. Some were aided by the WPA. Others found jobs teaching music in the schools.
Mid–20th century	In 1963 the Yale Seminar, a federally supported conference on arts education, met in New Haven. An outgrowth of this seminar was the Juilliard Project.

The MENC

1907	The music supervisors who were members of the National Education Association held their first meeting on April 10–12 in Keokuk, Iowa.
1910	This group formally adopted the name "Music Supervisors National Conference" at its meeting in Cincinnati.
1918	The Supervisors Council initiated the National Education Research Council.

Date	Music Education Events
1919	In St. Louis, Osbourne McConathy formulated one of the significant tenets of music education: "Every child should be educated in music according to his natural capacities, at public expense, and his studies should function in the musical life of the community."
1923	Karl Gehrkens, at the conference's Cleveland meeting, set the goal of "Music for every child, every child for music." The Music Education Research Council became a formal body.
1926	The national meeting was changed from an annual event to a biennial meeting, and the Music Educators Exhibitors Association was formed.
1934	The Music Supervisors National Conference changed its name to the Music Educators National Conference, and the *Music Supervisors Journal* was renamed the *Music Educators Journal*.
World War II and the postwar period (1942–)	Because of the manpower shortage during the war, the self contained elementary classroom became popular. It made it easier to supply special teachers. In 1957 the Soviet Union's successful launch into space caused a shift in American education toward preoccupation with the sciences. In 1965 Congress passed the Elementary Secondary Education Act, which had cultural enrichment as one of its goals. The declining economy in 1962 and 1974 revived the "back to basics" movement, causing a reduction in school enrichment programs.
1952	The national office of MENC was moved from Chicago to Washington, D.C.
1967	The Tanglewood Symposium met.
1975	Congress enacted "The Education for All Handicapped Children" Act.
Late 20th Century	In 1983, President Reagan's National Commission on Excellence published a report entitled *A Nation at Risk: The Imperative for Education Reform*. The disappointing aspect of the commission's report was its lack of emphasis or even concern over the comments on the arts. At the same time (1983), the College Board's published report, *Academic Preparation for College: What Students Need to Know and Be Able to Do,* strongly supported arts education.
1985	The Holmes Group submitted its report for improving teacher education in America. (See chapter 12.)

TABLE 1.1 (*continued*)

Date	Music Education Events
1986	The Carnegie Forum on Teaching as a Profession published its report, *A Nation Prepared: Teachers for the Twenty-first Century*. (See chapter 12.)
1987	MENC introduced its "Professional Certification Program." It named the first registered music educators in 1990.
1988	The National Endowment for the Arts presented President Bush and Congress with a report on arts education, *Toward Civilization*, which expressed a concern for the lack of arts instruction in the educational system.
1989	President George Bush met with the nation's governors in Charlottesville, Virginia, to initiate a decade long campaign to raise educational standards and qualities of performance at all levels of instruction. (See chapter 12.)

STUDY AND DISCUSSION QUESTIONS

1. How did the ancient Greek doctrine of *ethos* affect instruction in music?

2. What was the main reason for including music in the quadrivium of studies in the medieval universities?

3. What were the circumstances that led to early efforts to create a form of music notation?

4. Describe how conservatories were formed.

5. How does the original idea for a music conservatory differ from that of a music department in American colleges and universities today?

6. For each significant historical period (e.g., the Middle Ages) answer the following questions.

   a. What was the political/social climate like?

   b. What was the general education system like? Who was educated? How?

   c. What was the music "cultural life" like?

   d. What was music education like?

      1. Who taught?

      2. Who was taught?

3. What methods were used?

4. What were the underlying rationales?

7. For what reasons was music instruction first offered in the early days of the United States?

8. What guidelines for music teaching were adopted by the American followers of Pestalozzi? Which of the guidelines are still useful today?

9. Why were Lowell Mason's efforts at establishing music in the schools limited to vocal music at the elementary level? On what basis did he justify the inclusion of music in the school curriculum?

10. What concept of the teaching profession did the normal-school education of teachers represent? In what ways has that concept changed over the years?

11. What conditions in the first half of the twentieth century contributed to the expansion of music in the schools, especially the secondary schools? What forms did this expansion take?

12. What events occurring in the following years influenced the course of education and music education?

(a) 1927   (e) 1985

(b) 1929   (f) 1986

(c) 1957   (g) 1989

(d) 1965

13. What were the circumstances of the founding of the MENC in the early years of the twentieth century? How has the organization changed over the years from its original purpose?

14. What were the significant points made in the Tanglewood report?

15. What conditions are dictated by federal legislation that requires handicapped students to be placed in regular classrooms?

INDIVIDUAL OR CLASS ACTIVITIES

1. Select a significant period in music education and explore in detail what was occurring in world events at that time. Who was being educated and what was occurring socially during that period? How did these events and attitudes affect music education?

2. Out of past events, discuss what still remains in music education and why it has or has not changed.

3. In response to the threats against the arts in the early '90s, MENC initiated several actions. Discuss the impact these actions had and are currently having on music education.

4. Secure MENC's "Application and Certification" booklet and assess your skills at this stage of your career.

SUPPLEMENTARY READINGS

GOODMAN, H. A. (1982). *Music education: Perspectives and perceptions.* Dubuque, IA: Kendall/Hunt.

HART, P. (1973). *Orpheus in the New World.* New York: W. W. Norton.

International musician. (1992). New York: American Federation of Musicians.

KEENE, J. A. (1982). *A history of music education in the United States.* Hanover, NH: University Press of New England.

LEONHARD, C., & HOUSE, R. (1972). *Foundations and principles of music education* (2d ed.). New York: McGraw-Hill.

MARK, M. L. (1982). *Source readings in music education history.* New York: Schirmer Books.

MARK, M. L., & GARY, C. L. (1992). *A history of American music education.* New York: Schirmer Books.

SEYFFERT, O. (1963). *Dictionaries of classical antiquities.* Cleveland, OH: World Publishing.

REFERENCES

BAKER, D. N. (1979). *Jazz pedagogy.* Chicago: Maher.

BIRGE, E. B. (1928. Reprints 1966). *History of public school music in the United States.* Washington, DC: Music Educators National Conference.

BRITTON, A. (1966). Music education: an American specialty, source book III. In B. Kowalt (Ed.), *Perspectives in Music Education.* Washington, DC: Music Educators National Conference.

BRYAN, W. and BRYAN, C. (1898). *The republic of Plato with studies for teachers.* New York: Charles Scribner's Sons.

CADY, H. (Fall, 1974). The department of music in contemporary society. *College Music Symposium,* 14, 43. Boulder, CO: College Music Society.

CHOATE, R. A. (Ed.). (1968). *Documentary report of the Tanglewood Symposium.* Washington, DC: Music Educators National Conference.

COLLEGE ENTRANCE EXAMINATION BOARD. (1983).

FISHER, RENEE B. (1968). Learning music unconventionally—Manhattanville Music Curriculum Program. *Music Educators Journal,* 54(9), 61–64.

GROUT, D. J. (1973). *A history of Western music.* New York: W. W. Norton.

HARPER, C. (1939). *A century of public teacher education*. Washington, DC: American Association of Teachers Colleges, National Education Association.

HODSOLL, F. (1983). Music education for the eighties. *American-Education, 19*(8), 2–4.

INTERNATIONAL MUSICIAN. (1992). New York: American Federation of Musicians.

KLOTMAN, R. H. (Chair). (1972). *Teacher education in music: Final report*. Washington, DC: Music Educators National Conference.

LEBLANC, A. (1983). A nation at risk: Opportunities within the essentials report. *Music Educators Journal*.

LOWENS, I. (1964). *Music and musicians in early America*. New York: W. W. Norton.

MUSIC EDUCATORS NATIONAL CONFERENCE. (1984). Excellence in education. *Indiana Musicator*. Muncie: Indiana Music Education Association.

NATIONAL COMMISSION ON EXCELLENCE IN EDUCATION. (1984). *A nation at risk: The full account*. Westford, MA: Murray Printing.

NATIONAL ENDOWMENT FOR THE ARTS. (1988). *Toward civilization: A report on arts education*. Washington, DC: Author.

SUNDERMAN, L. (1971). *Historical foundations of music education in the United States*. Metuchen, NJ: Scarecrow.

CHAPTER 2 _____

Philosophical Foundations of Music Education

WHAT DOES THE TOPIC of philosophy have to do with music teaching? Philosophical inquiry is fine for philosophers, but why do teachers of beginning instrumental classes and high school choral directors need to think about philosophy? Such questions are logical ones to raise, and therefore a discussion of the important role of philosophical thinking opens this chapter.

Reasons for Considering Philosophical Matters

There are at least three practical reasons for teachers to probe some fundamental issues about the nature of the world in which they live.

1. Music teachers (and almost everyone else) must make decisions and take actions. They cannot avoid doing so, even if they can avoid thinking or talking about the reasons for doing something. In a very real sense, each person defines a philosophy when he or she makes a decision. Therefore, it is not a question of whether decisions are made and actions taken, but of whether the person making a decision is aware of its larger implications and how one action relates to another. The difference between teachers and most other people is that the decisions teachers make affect not only

41

themselves but also a number of students. Furthermore, these decisions and their associated actions are made under a broad authorization from society in the form of tax funds for education and compulsory attendance laws.

2. A comprehensive, systematic understanding of what one is trying to do serves as a guide for action. It is somewhat like a rudder on a ship. The ocean may move the boat back and forth and try to push it off course, but the rudder guides the ship toward the desired destination. Also, an understanding of what one is doing will help a teacher through the tough places of teaching. Every teacher encounters days and situations that are discouraging and frustrating. A solid philosophy gives one a sense of direction and perspective, which in turn aids in overcoming problems and disappointments.

3. Teachers need to be consistent in what they do. Inconsistency at best leads to a lack of follow-through and completion; at worst it can lead to undoing the work of previous classes. The need for consistency does not mean that one should never change one's mind, but it does mean that the reasons for changing one's goals or viewpoint should be known.

Why should music teachers delve into the esoteric world of Plato, Descartes, Dewey, and the other giants of philosophy? Granted, teachers need a sense of direction in their work, but can't they find it on their own without getting into the subject so deeply? The answer is that they can, but they can do a much better job of understanding fundamental issues and applying them in their teaching if they have the benefit of the thinking of some of the great philosophical minds. Like trying to design and construct, for example, an alarm clock, it is a great deal easier if you don't have to invent it but instead can build on the experience and knowledge of others. Therefore Plato, Descartes, and Dewey are included in this book because they have devoted their considerable abilities to dealing systematically and deeply with the fundamental intellectual issues of life and education.

Three Basic Philosophical Viewpoints

Philosophical approaches have been grouped in a variety of ways under a variety of titles. Three have been selected for discussion in this book: rationalism, empiricism, and pragmatism. These three philosophical viewpoints are not, of course, all-inclusive. However, they are the most systematic and comprehensive ones, while philosophical views such as existentialism and others are narrower in scope. Categorizing philosophies into schools has the same benefits and drawbacks as does the division of music history into style periods such as Baroque, Classical, Romantic, and so on. The classifications allow for generalizations about characteristics that exist in common among works of music or philosophical ideas. Unfortunately, the terms used for the categories in philosophy seem less standardized than the names of historical periods in music.

Caution should be exercised in the application of philosophical categories, however. There is some overlap among music styles and among philosophical schools; they do not differ on every point. Some of the differences among philosophical viewpoints are a matter of emphasis; some points are more important to some philosophies than to others. Nor are the viewpoints uniform among proponents of a particular position; each one possesses many interpretations and shades of opinion. Finally, none is without its strengths and weaknesses; each contains some valid ideas, and each has its problem areas.

Differences among philosophical viewpoints include differing explanations about *why* something is so. For example, one philosophical viewpoint favors teaching masterpieces of music because it sees them as the best musical manifestations of the eternal and therefore "real" world; another favors them because people knowledgeable about music generally agree on who some (but not all) of the master composers are.

The three philosophical viewpoints differ on two fundamental questions. One is *metaphysics*, the question of what is real and true. The other fundamental matter is *epistemology*, the study of knowledge, including how we find out what is real. Although the questions of what is real and how people find out what is real may appear to have obvious answers, that is not the case, as will soon become apparent.

Rationalism

Rationalism is often referred to as *idealism*, and it has several variants, including *phenomenonology*, which maintains that a person's consciousness of what is perceived is an integral part of reality (Reese, 1980, p. 428). The central thesis of rationalism is that knowledge is a fixed body of truth that applies in all times and places. It began with Socrates (470?–399 B.C.) and Plato (427–347 B.C.) in ancient Greece, and proponents include René Descartes (1596–1650), Immanuel Kant (1724–1804), Georg Hegel (1770–1831), and a number of English and American philosophers. According to Plato (who wrote down many of his and Socrates's thoughts), some ideas are so real and lasting that, in comparison, things that we know about through the senses are only fleeting and transitory. The basic reality is thought, not external objects, as represented in the phrase of Descartes *Cogito, ergo sum* ("I think, therefore I exist"). Physical objects are just imperfect embodiments of the ideas they represent, which are universal and eternal. For example, the chair that you are sitting on as you read this page is merely an imperfect rendition of the "ideal" chair, which can only be realized through thought and is perfect throughout the world—for all time. Some ideas, of course, cannot be represented in physical form—beauty, goodness, truth, and so on.

How are these ideas to be known? They can be found by rigorous intellectual examination for logic and consistency. When Socrates taught as he sat on the steps of the Academy (in ancient Greece there were few formal classes), he usually answered a question from a student by asking the student another question. His purpose in doing this was not to develop a better teaching method (although in fact that may have been what happened), but to probe with the student for truth, much as one might peel away the layers of an onion. Over the centuries these philosophers developed intricate logical structures to help determine truth. One such technique was the *syllogism*, which consists of two true statements and their logical conclusion.

> *All men are mortal,*
> *Socrates is a man,*
> *Therefore, Socrates is mortal.*

Many rationalists concern themselves a great deal with questions of ethics and values. In a sense, the utopian ideas of Sir Thomas More (1478–1535) are one result of rationalistic thinking. Rationalistic aesthetic values are also expressed by the German philosopher Arthur Schopenhauer (1788–1860). He viewed the arts as the "flower of life," because through them the individual can rise above everyday struggles and tedium (Schopenhauer, 1896, p. 345). He believed that it is through the arts that one can sense, even if for only a short period of time, the eternal and lasting Platonic ideas—the realities behind the physical objects we see and touch. When this happens, the observer or listener loses his or her preoccupation with personal feelings and mundane matters and becomes a part of something far greater, more lasting, and more satisfying.

Empiricism

The roots of *empiricism* (often called *realism*) reach back to Aristotle (384–322 B.C.), who was a pupil of Plato but differed with him on a number of matters. Aristotle did not agree with the notion of the ultimate reality being ideas; instead he wrote such phrases as "It is clear to everyone that there are many kinds of things . . ." and indicated the need to "distinguish what is and what is not evident" (Aristotle/Ross, 1930, Book II, Section I, p. 193a). The heart of realism is the acceptance of "what is clear to everyone." Things are what they appear to be, not representations of some greater but invisible reality.

Over the centuries this rather simple idea has been subjected to a wide variety of interpretations, so the empirical viewpoint is by no means a homogeneous one. Some of the important names associated with it include Baruch Spinoza (1632–1677), John Locke (1632–1704), and the American philosopher-psychologist William James (1842–1910). Despite differences in emphasis and explanation, these philosophers agreed on the reality of the physical world "out there" beyond the mind, and the mirror-like character of the mind in receiving images, which it then organizes and tries to interpret. The mind is grounded in the existence of the body, and cannot probe into worlds beyond what the senses perceive, as the rationalists claim. The road to truth is through observation and scientific evidence.

An important variant of the empirical philosophic viewpoint is often called *naturalism*—the belief in the reality and rightness of the natural world. Its roots also reach back to ancient Greece, but its beliefs were refined and expanded by Thomas Hobbes (1588–1679), Jean-Jacques Rousseau (1712–1778), and Herbert Spencer (1820–1903).

The belief in the ultimate reality of the natural world led logically to the belief that the most acceptable life is achieved by staying close to the ways of nature. The chief spokes-person for this position was Rousseau. Partly in reaction to the excesses of the court of Versailles, he spoke out for the simple, "natural" life. He believed in the natural goodness of the human race and the corruption of humans by society. Mankind in society was bad; individuals were naturally good, unless spoiled by society. Nature yielded many good things, but society and especially governments perverted and misused them. Rousseau was influential in bringing about the revolution in France, and his thinking affected Thomas Jefferson and other founders of the United States. Some naturalist language even found its way into the American Declaration of Independence: "the separate and equal station to which the laws of Nature and of Nature's God entitle them. . . ."

Naturalist empiricists believe that the arts should be natural in character and not carry any great meanings or truths. They reject complexity in art: thematic development, complex counterpoint, and similar features found in some music. Rousseau himself composed quite a bit of music, including a folk opera.

Empiricists generally have an interesting position on aesthetic matters. They see a close relationship between a person's ability to perceive what is really there and the enjoyment of aesthetic objects. For example, if someone does not find Beethoven's Fifth Symphony interesting, the problem lies in the inability of that person to hear all that is present in the music: the manipulation of themes, the subtle changes of harmony, the changes of timbre, and so on. Because it is "known" that Beethoven's Fifth Symphony is great music, the problem is, therefore, with the listener, who is not perceiving adequately (Sellars, 1932, pp. 451–52).

Pragmatism

Although the roots of *pragmatism* go back to Heraclitus (sixth to fifth centuries B.C.) and the Sophists in ancient Greece, this philosophic viewpoint did not flower until it reached nineteenth- and twentieth-century America.

Heraclitus emphasized the idea that all things change; nothing is permanent (Heraclitus/Bakewell, 1939, p. 33):[*]

> *All things flow; nothing abides.*
> *One cannot step twice into the same river.*
> *Into the same river we step and do not step;*
> *We are and are not.*

The early predecessors of pragmatism were often subjected to criticism for this view, and with some justification. If nothing can be known in a lasting way, that is just a short step from saying that nothing can really be known—a type of nihilism.

Although Francis Bacon (1561–1626) and Auguste Comte (1798–1857) anticipated some of the features of pragmatism, it was the American Charles Sanders Peirce (1839–1914) who began its systematic formulation. His main contribution was this idea: "To determine the meaning of any idea, put it into practice in the objective world of actualities and whatever its consequences prove to be, these constitute the meaning of the idea" (Butler, 1968, p. 367). To Pierce, it was pointless to accept the conclusions of logic or the opinions of authorities. What made sense to him were the results of an idea when tested.

Peirce's notion was adopted and promoted by two other famous American philosophers: William James, who in many respects was an empiricist, and John Dewey (1859–1952), who is the figure most often associated with pragmatism today. Both James and Dewey followed Heraclitus in believing that nothing is lasting, and that it is impossible to gain knowledge of ultimate reality. Dewey believed that the testing of hypotheses was the best approach to finding truth that human beings could have. Therefore, not science, which had fascinated intellectuals since Aristotle, but rather the scientific method was to be applied in all possible situations. Although it may seem like hairsplitting to emphasize the difference between the results of a scientific observation and the process of scientific experimentation, the distinction is very crucial to Dewey and the followers of pragmatism. According to their beliefs, truth is not permanent, so what is most useful is the process of arriving at information. For this reason, Dewey emphasized means as being equal to ends; that is, the way in which one gains information is as important as the information itself. Clearly, pragmatism's long suit is its epistemology.

The logic of pragmatism is the scientific method, which is quite a change from the reasoning that had been traditionally associated with philosophy. Dewey proposed five steps of thinking: activity, awareness of the

---

[*]Charles M. Bakewell, from *Source Book in Ancient Philosophy*, revised edition. Copyright 1907, 1939 by Charles Scribner's Sons; copyrights renewed 1935, 1967. Reprinted with the permission of Charles Scribner's Sons.

problem, observation of data, formulation of a hypothesis, and testing of a hypothesis (Dewey, 1933, p. 107).

Dewey also argued that values are derived from the experiences of society and life, not from a supernatural mandate. He wrote specifically about aesthetic values. Most experiences have an aesthetic side, he believed, as well as a practical side. That is, they possess and yield meanings that people may want to preserve. Aesthetic values are often retained and communicated (in the broad sense of that word) by means other than words, because words are used for communicating everyday experiences. Ultimately, Dewey wrote, the enjoyment of beauty is related to the cycles of life, the "ups and downs," the "rhythms." At times, life is stable and we feel content, while at other times it is disturbing and difficult. It is in such a world that aesthetic values can exist. If everything were finished, perfect, and complete, there would not be unknowns or struggles. Without difficulties to reflect back on, there would be no present moments of satisfaction to enjoy. It is the artist and musician who through their media allow us to contemplate the experiences of overcoming difficulties and tensions and to enjoy the times of satisfaction. In that sense, the arts express human experience, and they make life richer because they make us more conscious of its qualities (Dewey, 1934, p. 56). That is why humanity finds the arts valuable. Therefore, pragmatism puts the arts in the middle of life, not "up in the clouds" of some ultimate or cosmic scheme of things.

Pragmatists place much emphasis on education, which is consistent with their interest in the process of determining truth. Dewey established the Laboratory School in Chicago in 1896 and took an active part in the education of the children. His writings were very influential in American education for the first half of the twentieth century. What Dewey said (or was purported to have said—some of his followers misinterpreted him) was a part of virtually every curriculum in teacher education during those years. Some of his views on education will be discussed shortly.

Strengths and Weaknesses of the Three Viewpoints

The following discussion of the strengths and weaknesses of each of the three basic philosophical viewpoints is from the point of view of their effect on what happens in classrooms. It is not a technical discussion such as is found in writings on philosophy. Those matters are important to philosophers, but of only limited value to music educators.

Rationalism

Probably the greatest strength of rationalism is its conscious intellectual approach to reality, the way in which reality is known, and the values that should be held. It is more systematic and thorough in seeking answers to the difficult questions of philosophy than the other philosophic viewpoints. Few scholars question the intellectual qualities of rationalistic philosophers, although their conclusions have been vigorously disputed.

Another strength of rationalism is its stability. It provides conclusions that are not going to be buffeted about by each novel breeze or whim. What is true is true, always was true, and always will be. It will not go out of fashion like a suit of clothes.

However, that notion of lasting truth also presents some major problems. If there are certain eternal verities, why in over 2,000 years has it been so difficult to arrive at some agreement about what those truths are? Granted, seeking what is eternal and true is no easy task, but 2,000 years would seem to be an adequate amount of time.

Furthermore, how do rationalists account for the diversity of views and beliefs found throughout the world? If truth be truth, why is it so different in so many times and places? Different societies display too much diversity for one to be impressed with the universal nature of ideas.

Also, rationalists have a difficult time accounting for new developments and change. There is little disagreement that Bach and Mozart composed great music, music that has met the "test of time" and therefore has demonstrated outstanding qualities. But has all the great music now been written? Should no new music be accepted? If so, on what basis? Are there universal criteria that can be used to evaluate music from all places and ages? If there are, musicologists, theorists, and aestheticians have had a difficult time agreeing on what those criteria are.

Finally, logic—the main means of rationalist philosophers to determine truth—has proved to be a less precise tool than they would like to admit. Not only is the process itself subject to error, but people generally make judgments according to their personal values rather than on the basis of rational deductions. For example, it can be demonstrated economically and logically that it would be an efficient practice to terminate everyone's life once he or she reaches the age of 65 or 70. The idea is, of course, abhorrent. Why? Because in our system of values, human life is far more important than economic gains. (That has not always been true at all times in all places—not by any means!) Logic is a good and useful way of examining issues, but it is not a solution for philosophical and moral problems.

Empiricism

The main strength of empiricism lies in its practical quality. Empiricists take whatever information they have and work with it as best they can, even though they realize their knowledge is not perfect or complete. Because no one can know what lies beyond what the senses are able to perceive, there is no use worrying about it. Empiricists do not wonder if the wall in front of them is the ultimate, "real" wall; they simply realize that if they bump into it, that experience will be one of reality. In short, this philosophic position deals with reality as it can best be known.

The practical, direct nature of empiricism is also its weakness. Our knowledge of reality as perceived through the senses is subject to error. A stick in the water appears to bend at the surface; the pitch of the horn on the diesel railroad engine appears to change as it goes by; when our hands have been in hot water, warm water seems cool by comparison, while the same water seems warm if our hands have been in cold water. The portion of the physical and psychological world that can truly be known, even with sophisticated scientific equipment, is probably only a small part of what is actually there—if one wants to think about it as a empiricist.

Empiricists place more reliance than any other philosophic positions on the opinions of experts and authorities. If, for example, you want to know what should be included in the content of a chemistry course, you should listen to recognized chemists, not to people who have little knowledge of the discipline of chemistry. As Harry Broudy states: "We rely upon the expert or the *consensus of the learned* and hopefully, the wise. . . . A roster of the learned societies furnishes our culture with definitions of norms within each of the intellectual disciplines" (Broudy, 1967, pp. 10–11). The importance attached to authorities is one of the strengths of empiricism.

However, the reliance on experts also has some negative aspects. Who decides who is an expert? In some cases there are specific standards, such as those maintained by state board examinations in medicine and law and certification procedures for teachers. In other cases there are no guidelines established by the state; the ministry is one example. What happens when the experts disagree? No science or profession has a fund of knowledge so complete and final that there are no instances of disagreement. One doctor may recommend surgery, while another doctor may not; psychiatrists often appear on different sides of a court trial or hearing to determine a person's mental condition; on the same day one economist predicts that things will improve while another economist says they will grow worse. The music profession's experts disagree on everything from the correct embouchure for playing the trumpet to the content of freshman theory courses. Another problem is the possibility that one group of experts may become restrictive and reject valid ideas that do not agree with theirs. Such a practice may keep a profession or academic discipline "pure," but it also shuts out other legitimate viewpoints. The troubles encountered thirty and forty years ago in including jazz in the curricula of university departments of music is one example of this phenomenon.

The naturalistic branch of empiricism presents different strengths and weaknesses. Its main appeal is its simplicity. It seeks to ignore or reduce the complexities and artificialities of life. Such views are fueled in this century by the fact that there is much about contemporary civilization that is not very heartening. Pollution, wars, hatred, and other vices of society tend to cause people to become disillusioned and to believe that somehow humanity has gotten from its true destiny.

But the strength of these views is also its weakness. At first glance it may seem easy to decide what is natural, but it is not. Is it natural for people to cooperate or compete with each other? Is it natural to try to save lives through medication or surgery? Furthermore, nature is by no means simple and good. Although it produces beautiful mountains, birds, gentle rain, and flowers, it also produces earthquakes, animals that kill and eat each other, and diseases. Finally, if children are allowed to develop "naturally," will they become good and unselfish people who are competent to operate in society? Or will their knowledge and skills be a mosaic of personal desires and experiences?

Pragmatism

The strength of pragmatism lies in its attention to the process of uncovering the truth. It does not depend on what one thinks is natural, or on mental cogitation, or on the perception of the world. Instead, it proposes the scientific method as the best means for determining reality. The results of science—ranging from atomic energy to kidney transplants—are truly impressive. The notion of testing hypotheses does seem to have succeeded, if one considers it from a pragmatic point of view. Nor is pragmatism burdened with the problem of who is an expert. The process itself determines truth; truth is not determined by persons.

The weakness of pragmatism lies in its devotion to a single means for determining truth. That process works well in small, tightly controlled situations. One can apply the scientific method and find out about the effect of a certain fertilizer on fields of corn or the behavior of atoms in a critical mass. Unfortunately, many questions, especially the important ones in life, are too large or too unwieldy to be subjected to experimental examination. No one can set up the conditions to test experimentally the causes for World War I or World War II, or the 1992 riots in Los Angeles, or the dominance of the Austro-German style of music during the eighteenth and nineteenth centuries.

Nor can the scientific method answer questions of value any better than logical thinking. It provides information to aid in making decisions, which can be very useful, but it cannot tell which decision is the right one. Pragmatism can also be faulted for its lack of concern for values. In many respects the notion of lasting values is inconsistent with the pragmatic view of continual change. Without values and goals, teachers have little guidance as to what should be taught. It may be somewhat helpful to say that the schools should prepare young people to be able to function in the society, but that guideline is not very useful if the nature and goals of society are themselves unstable.

Eclecticism

As can be seen, no philosophical position is without its strengths and weaknesses. This fact may tempt one to consider the idea of taking the best points of each philosophical view and then combining them into a virtually faultless system. The idea of synthesizing the best of several different styles or systems is called *eclecticism*. Unfortunately, it works little better with regard to philosophy than it would in the world of music. The combination of the best features of the music of Bach, Mozart, Brahms, Bartók, and Dave Brubeck would probably be more comical than impressive; it would end up being a goulash of styles. While one may consider points from various philosophical schools, in the end people must make decisions that reveal a tendency to subscribe principally to one of these schools.

If pressed for their opinion *as music educators*, the authors admit to finding the empiricist viewpoint without naturalistic inclinations the most useful of the three. The idea of accepting what can be known and working with it as best one can seems defensible, practical, and reasonable. This is not to deny the possible existence of the great and eternal truths of rationalism. There is considerable evidence for believing that there is more to life and the world "than what meets the eye," as du Noüy and others have established through scientific dialectics (du Noüy, 1947, p. 36). The problem is that not enough is known about things beyond human perception on which to operate in a systematic way. The nature of an eternal verity (God) or verities is as much a matter of faith and intuition as of reason and observation, and therefore is more a matter of religion than philosophy. Pragmatism and its reliance on scientific method is very attractive in restricted situations, but seems inadequate for the larger questions.

Philosophical Viewpoints and Education

What practical effects do these three philosophic viewpoints have on what happens in music classes and rehearsals? To answer this question, each viewpoint is examined here in relation to four aspects of teaching: curriculum and content, methods of instruction, evaluation, and the roles of teachers and students.

Rationalism

Rationalists are eager for those aspects of music that are great and lasting to be learned. What good does it do the students to learn something that is only transitory and ephemeral? It is only by learning things of lasting value that the students are properly served. Therefore, much attention is given to the organization and planning of what the students are to learn. The curriculum should include general knowledge (definitely including the arts), moral and scientific truth, and the development of critical and logical thinking.

Rationalists have a rather great interest in evaluating students' learning. They see evaluation as an important part of education. Although they assess the learning of specific information, they are especially concerned about comprehensive understandings. They want the students to be able to synthesize and apply knowledge and to have the "big picture" of the material covered.

Traditionally the rationalists, especially Socrates, followed the dialogue procedure in which teacher and student probed and searched together to uncover truth. Over the ages the emphasis changed more to the students learning what was believed to be valuable and lasting. Methods that are effective in achieving the learning of the material are the ones favored. Often this means listening to lectures or reading books. Student originality and exploration are acceptable under certain conditions, one of which is that the student be well grounded in the subject.

Many rationalists see the students as part of a larger scheme of things. Herman Harrell Horne writes: "Our philosophy dares to suggest that the learner is a finite person, growing, when properly educated, into the image of an infinite person, that his real origin is deity, that his nature is freedom, and that his destiny is immortality" (Horne, 1942, p. 155). If Horne's words sound like quite an assignment for a teacher, they are intended to be, for the rationalistic viewpoint places much emphasis on the teacher. Not only do teachers have the obligation to impart knowledge, they are also to be models for the students. Teachers personify the reality of the adult world, are capable of commanding respect, learn along with the students, are specialists in their field of study, and awaken in the pupils the desire to learn. Rationalists realize the limitations of teachers. Horne also has written:

> The development of mind is from within out, not from without in. . . . The teacher may lead the pupil to the fonts of learning, but he cannot make him drink. Teaching is not so much the cause of learning . . . as it is the occasion or condition of learning. The cause of learning is the pupil himself and his effort. . . . The ultimate responsibility for winning at education rests with the will of the pupil. (Horne, 1930, pp. 273–74)

Rationalists see discipline as a part of teaching. However, discipline is not an end in itself, but rather a means of securing patterns of behavior that will eventually benefit the students.

RATIONALISTS AND TEACHING MUSIC. Music teachers who operate from the rationalistic viewpoint tend to pay much attention to choosing music. They favor the established "classics," especially the recognized works that have stood the "test of time." They have little use for marching bands and swing choirs.

Rationalistic music educators also place emphasis on the intellectual understanding the students gain in music classes. While these teachers do not reject or ignore the performing of music, they do not attach as much importance to playing and singing as do their empiricist colleagues. And the type of information rationalists favor is not so much factual as it is the acquisition of concepts and broad understandings. Such music teachers are more interested in having students understand sonata form, for example, than they are in students learning how many piano sonatas Beethoven composed. Grades are not looked upon as being very important.

Rationalists see teachers as role models for students, and therefore avoid improper or slovenly behavior or what is sometimes called the "artistic temperament." In addition, they are more interested in the subject of music than they are in satisfying their egos.

Rationalists strongly favor good discipline in classes because more effective learning can take place in an organized situation. Good student behavior, they believe, results from healthy student involvement in the search for understanding. The selection of students, if any, is based on the student's desire to learn and willingness to put forth the appropriate effort.

Rationalist music teachers are more inclined to engage in question-and-answer sessions with their students. They are also more likely to encourage individual student projects. Student learning is evaluated not just on factual knowledge or skill development, but rather from more subjective, more probing, and comprehensive evaluations of the students' work by both students and teachers. The motivation for learning is seen as coming largely from the student.

Empiricism

Because empiricists see the mind as functioning in relation to objects outside the mind, they also emphasize the learning of subject matter. As F. S. Breed writes, "There is no perception without the perception of *something*; no memory without remembering *something*. This condition prevails in every mental function" (1939, p. 135). A. N. Whitehead makes the point even more bluntly: "The ordered acquirement of knowledge is the natural food for a developing intelligence" (1929, p. 47).

In totalitarian countries empiricists see the learning of what is prescribed by the state as of primary importance, because that is what is essential in those societies. Empiricists in democratic societies believe in teaching what authorities in an academic discipline say is worth knowing, as was mentioned earlier. For example, the "America 2000" federal educational effort of the early 1990s had as its goal the achievement of "world class" standards by American students in the various areas of the curriculum. Sizable grants were awarded by appropriate governmental agencies to professional associations, including MENC, to develop curriculum and assessment standards for their academic disciplines ("MENC leads effort," 1992, pp. 17–18). These standards documents, when completed, will emphasize the acquisition of information and the development of concepts and skills.

Like rationalists, empiricists are interested in evaluating the results of instruction. However, they are more interested in the acquisition of specific information and skills—the ones deemed necessary to function in society and in an area of work. The empiricist piano professor, for instance, would have his or her student learn the Beethoven piano concertos because that is what is perceived as essential repertoire for successful concert pianists.

Whatever works in getting the material over to the students is favored. Often this consists of lecturing or reading, or in more contemporary settings working with a computer on a learning program.

Although empiricists emphasize imparting knowledge, in their view the teacher has the responsibility for molding the pupils like an artisan forming an object.

A logical outcome of the realists' view of instruction and molding the young is an impatience with distracting behavior. Time is too short to allow for fooling around. Empiricists, with the exception of those with naturalist leanings, are strong believes in orderly classrooms.

Empiricists see teachers as central in the educational process. Teachers (or the state in totalitarian societies) largely decide what will be taught and how it will be taught. If they are not the only source of information, teachers tell the students where to locate it.

Empiricists who take a naturalistic view of reality come to some quite different conclusions regarding education. They, too, believe that reality is "out there," but it is a very different reality that they perceive. Instead of to society and authorities they think that reality is best determined by looking to nature, especially to how children are believed to evolve "naturally."

To begin with, they feel that children learn best when they are interested in a topic, and if they are not, it does little good to impose the topic on them. For this reason, teacher-prepared curricula and courses find little favor.

Followers of this outlook are not very interested in the evaluation of learning, either. They tend to see the goals and objectives being evaluated as society's goals, which often are not valid in their eyes. Evaluation—and this includes grading—is also seen as a force encouraging conformity and reducing individuality. Since learning is an individual matter, anything that detracts from individual interest is undesirable.

Persons with naturalistic inclinations favor letting pupils learn on their own with a minimum of teacher intervention. The way of learning is largely the responsibility of the student, not the teacher. The learning process should proceed according to these guidelines:

1. Education should conform to the natural growth and mental development of the child.

2. Education should be pleasurable.

3. Education should utilize a great deal of spontaneous self-activity.

4. The acquisition of knowledge is an important part of education.

5. Education is for the body as well as the mind.

6. Learning should generally follow the inductive approach; that is, children should generalize from particular bits of information.

7. Punishments should be the result of natural consequences of doing the wrong thing, but the teacher should be sympathetic when this happens. (Butler, 1968, pp. 92–95)

It is easy to see the similarity of several of these statements with some present-day thinking on education. Most advocates of "open education" would support the previous list with enthusiasm. The admirers of Jean Piaget (discussed in chapter 7) would also point out the first statement about the natural order of maturation and its importance in education.

The teacher's role, therefore, is more that of a benevolent helper than a dispenser of information. Discipline is viewed as the result of the natural consequences of actions (e.g., letting the plants in the classroom die if the students forget to water them). It definitely does not consist of teacher-imposed rules.

EMPIRICISTS AND TEACHING MUSIC. The division between those empiricists who think that students should learn what they ought to and those who believe in the natural development of children leads to quite different practices in music lessons, classes, and rehearsals. Most empiricists teach what it takes to have a good band or choir, to be a fine pianist, or to fulfill the curricular demands of the state or school district. Their subject matter is determined by what they think the reality "out there" requires, whether that reality is a contest list or the opinions of experts. They are not so concerned about broad understanding as the rationalists are. For example, if the student can play Beethoven's "Waldstein" Sonata, whether or not he or she understands the forms of its movements is not all that vital.

The empiricists who believe that a child's natural development is the meaningful reality reject such structured learning in favor of the individual development and motivation of each child. In addition, they are far more tolerant of individual differences and favor pursuing individual interests over group demands. If a child wants to play the bells instead of sing, that is fine with teachers who hold this view.

The empiricist views of teaching music seem to differ more among various grade levels than expressed philosophical differences, probably because the nature of music instruction differs somewhat according to age level. Teachers of children of preschool or primary age are more inclined to favor natural development. On the other hand, directors of performing organizations at the secondary school level are much more inclined to use teaching methods that meet the realities as determined by experts and other demands, like performances for school events, that are expected of the group.

These differences, in turn, affect the type of discipline the teacher favors. The naturalist empiricist favors self-discipline and self-direction. Most empiricists believe in having students adhere to the rules so that learning can take place.

Different views are also held about motivation. Most empiricists believe in extrinsic motivation, ranging from pep talks to rewards such as favorable ratings at contests, medals, and certificates. The group favoring the naturalist view sees motivation as coming from within each student according to his or her interests. The child who is interested in playing the bells doesn't need additional motivation.

The teaching methods of empiricists also differ depending on what they believe to be the primary reality "out there." Most favor whatever is most effective in getting the students to learn the particular material—lectures, authoritarian commands, computer-assisted instructional programs, questions to reinforce the correct answers, and so on. If the clarinet players are suppose to play certain notes, then they should learn to do so as quickly as possible. If a teacher has to be a bit of an autocrat to get them to learn the clarinet parts, then so be it. What matters most is that the students learn to play those parts.

Those who believe in following the natural development and interests of children rely a great deal on student discovery. In fact, some of them believe that such learning is virtually the only truly effective type of learning, especially with younger students. They believe that trying to teach students things they are not interested in is about as useful as asking them to memorize the license plate numbers of the next five cars they see.

Most empiricists favor admitting only qualified students to music groups. No one is helped, they believe, by accepting students with substandard preparation, ability, or interest. Such students detract from the level of performance or study of the group, and the substandard student is frustrated because he or she is not able to keep up with the other students.

Pragmatism

Pragmatists place much emphasis on learning how to acquire skills and gather information, and they see experiences as the basis of learning. Because things are always changing, in their view, all knowledge lacks permanence and will need to be replaced—hence the emphasis on process rather than product. Pragmatists are also interested in the nonmusical outcomes of music study. If music contributes to nonmusical goals such as citizenship or health, that is fine, even if these are not a part of the subject matter.

Logically, pragmatists are more interested in evaluation than are the holders of other philosophical positions, since consideration of the results is a part of the scientific process. The evaluation, however, is not concerned solely with what content has been learned, but concentrates on the methods of learning employed by the students.

Pragmatists place much importance on the means of learning, because that is at the heart of their philosophy. Their process of education is similar to Dewey's steps of thinking, which were described earlier in this chapter. A problem is encountered, information gathered, solutions considered, hypotheses tested, and data analyzed. (The basic procedure will be examined again in chapter 11 in conjunction with research.) Such thinking has led to the institution of "general methods" courses in many departments of education. The rationale is that essentially the same process is employed whether the subject be a foreign language, music, or science.

Dewey stressed the need for the consistency of means and ends; e.g., one cannot hope to teach students to conduct themselves in a democratic manner by using autocratic teaching methods. Even if one does not agree with the pragmatic philosophy, there is much to commend in the idea of consistency. To music teachers, it says that consistency is needed between the subject of music and the manner in which that subject is taught. If the nature of music is organized sound and silence—an often-used definition of music—then it seems that music classes should deal with and relate to organized sounds as much as possible. For example, the learning of rhythmic values in notation, which is something that is experienced in terms of time and sound, is not effectively achieved when the note values are treated as mathematical fractions. One may add $1/4 + 1/4 = 1/2$ and know little about quarter and half notes in music (or about sixteenths and eighths, depending on the association attempted).

Pragmatists see pupils as biological, psychological, and sociological beings caught up in the flow of history and life. Growth is considered as beginning with biological birth, followed by physiological growth and development. The development of language is believed to be the great socializing force in personality, which is followed by the gradual acquisition of a concept of self. Pragmatists also see youngsters as individuals. To a greater degree than holders of other philosophical viewpoints, they consider the influences both within and without the individual. As a result, each person, young and old, is to be treated as someone worthy of dignity and esteem.

Pragmatists see teachers as agents who impart to the young the techniques for living and acquiring knowledge. Teachers also instruct students how to meet the new situations that will inevitably arise; in a sense, the students are educated for change. In the course of their education they are expected to pursue information and to be occupied in constructive activity. The conventional ideas of discipline (e.g., no talking without permission, no throwing spitballs) are not as important as the results of the learning activity. Pointless and/or disruptive fooling around is not tolerated, however, although pragmatists have often been accused of being too lenient.

PRAGMATISM AND MUSIC TEACHING. The thing that makes pragmatist music teachers different from rationalists and empiricists is their interest in helping the students to learn how to learn. They know that they will not always be around to tell the students what to do, and they also realize that their students will encounter new music in new situations. Therefore, teaching the "right" answers, whether those answers are products of the mind or outside of it, is a false goal, because the right answers of today may not be the right answers of tomorrow. The ease of transposing to any key on the better electronic keyboards and organs today, for example, was unknown fifty years ago, and many new works of music have been composed in the past fifty years.

Pragmatist music teachers do not even have a set method for teaching their students how to learn, because situations change. Methods are different for each student because of individual backgrounds, interests, and abilities. What works with one student sometimes does not work with other students. However, the basic principle prevails for pragmatists of giving students as much responsibility for learning as they can handle, given their experience and ability.

According to pragmatists, the role of the teacher is not one of collaborator in the search for truth (as it is with rationalists) or dispenser of knowledge (as it is with most empiricists), but rather one of being a combination organizer-cheerleader in helping students to learn. For example, the students might be taught an approach for learning unfamiliar music such as: (1) look at the meter and key signatures; (2) scan the work for special problems, features, and patterns; and (3) run through a portion of it mentally before attempting to play or sing it. Such a procedure could have been developed by the students after much trial and error, but the pragmatist teacher provides such an approach to save time and avoid student (and teacher?) frustration and resulting loss of interest.

Other aspects of teaching are secondary to the main goal of teaching students to become musically more independent. Aspect such as subject matter, selection of students, and grading practices are not major concerns. Student motivation is seen as arising from successful and meaningful experiences. When a student learns the correct use of the pedals on the piano, for example, his or her playing is improved, which is motivating to the student.

Classroom behavior is also a minor matter, as long as student activity is purposeful and "on task." It's all right for the students to talk in class, for example, if their talking pertains to the task at hand and is not social chatter.

Coda

Your decisions about a philosophical viewpoint are not likely to be a process of saying to yourself "Now I have decided that I will be a rationalist" or a believer in some other philosophical viewpoint. Instead, it is more often a matter of realizing, after analyzing a pattern of decisions you have made, that you are more of an rationalist than anything else. Furthermore, it is not so much a matter of rejecting other philosophies as it is of agreeing with a particular philosophy's priorities. For example, if you are an empiricist with naturalistic tendencies, you will give priority to the interests of the students as they unfold naturally; if you are inclined toward pragmatism, you will be more concerned about how students learn. That does not mean that you must reject the process of inquiry and the scientific method.

The topics that have been discussed in this chapter are certainly fundamental in life—and in teaching. In a real sense, a teacher's decisions about what to do begin with what he or she thinks is real and true, and how that reality is known and learned. Although the connection between Plato, Aristotle, and other philosophers and music instruction in the classrooms of American schools today may not be easily and immediately visible, it is there. Fundamental beliefs and understandings make a significant difference in what teachers do.

Summary

The chapter opened by listing some of the reasons why all music educators should think about philosophical matters as they relate to teaching music. One reason for doing this is that all teachers make decisions as a part of their work, and most of these decisions have philosophical implications. A second reason for considering such matters is the fact that basic understandings and beliefs provide, or at least should provide, a sense of direction and perspective. A third reason for thinking about philosophical topics is that teachers should be consistent in the different actions they take.

Three basic philosophical approaches were presented in terms of what each considers real and true ("metaphysics") and how that truth is determined ("epistemology").

Rationalism is based on a belief in the reality of thought, not objects. The eternal and universal world of ideas is known through rigorous intellectual examination and logic, including formal propositions such as syllogisms. The arts are thought to be of value because they reveal a bit of ultimate reality in their expression of the quality of human experience.

Empiricism is based on the idea that things are what they appear to be, and that the human mind is incapable of knowing anything beyond what the senses perceive or science reveals. Truth is what those who are most knowledgeable in a particular academic area say it is. The enjoyment of the arts depends on the viewer or listener perceiving what is actually present in the art object.

Pragmatism is based on the proposition that the truth of an idea is determined by the process of testing the idea in the real world. Whatever the results of that testing, these constitute the truth of the idea, at least for the situation in which the testing occurs. The arts are valued because they are manifestations of the feelings associated with experiencing life.

Each of these philosophical schools has its strengths and weaknesses, as are indicated in table 2.1.

Eclecticism—the idea of taking features from different philosophies and combining them into a new philosophy—has also been found wanting. The results of such efforts are often an incongruous mixture.

Each of the three philosophical viewpoints contains implications for education. These implications—for curriculum and content, evaluation, methods, and teachers and students—are presented in table 2.2.

STUDY AND DISCUSSION QUESTIONS

1. Why is it important for music teachers to have clearly thought out goals for what they want to accomplish and why are those goals significant?

2. Why is it useful for music educators to be familiar with the fundamental ideas of Plato, Dewey, and other recognized philosophers?

3. Which philosophical position is represented by the following statements? Be prepared to offer reasons for your choice of position.

   (a) "The basic reality is thought, not external objects."

   (b) "The need is to distinguish what is and what is not evident."

TABLE 2.1
Comparison of Strengths and Weaknesses of the Four Philosophies

	STRENGTHS	WEAKNESSES
Rationalism	Conscious intellectual approach	Unable to determine reality in 2,000 years.
	Stability of ideas	Cannot explain different forms of truth found around the world.
		Has trouble accepting new truths.
		Logic is not infallible.
Empiricism	Practical	Perception is sometimes inaccurate.
	Realistic	Matter of who is expert is debatable.
Pragmatism	Method of determining reality	Devotion to only one means of determining truth.
		Method is not adequate for "big" questions.
		Lack of interest in values.

(c) "To determine the meaning of any idea, put it into practice in the objective world of actualities, and whatever its consequences prove to be, these constitute the meaning of the idea."

4. What is the main weakness of eclecticism?

5. Dewey strongly emphasized the need for consistency between ends and means. What examples (other than the one cited on page 57) of inconsistent ends and means have you observed in the teaching of music (by others, of course)?

6. What are the strengths and weaknesses of relying, as Broudy suggests, on the "consensus of the learned"?

7. How does each of the three basic philosophical positions determine aesthetic values?

8. What are the epistemological (concerned with the way of knowing the truth) strengths and weaknesses of each of the three philosophies?

TABLE 2.2

Four Philosophical Viewpoints on Various Aspects of Education

PHILOSOPHY	CURRICULUM AND CONTENT	EVALUATION	METHODS	TEACHERS AND STUDENTS
Rationalism	Very important. Learn what is lasting and eternal. Interested in general knowledge.	Important. Looks for comprehensive understandings.	Logical inquiry to uncover ultimate truth, often resulting from dialogue between student and teacher. Lectures and readings often used.	Teacher and prescribed sources provide knowledge. Teacher is model for students. Students have ultimate responsibility for learning. Discipline exists so that students may learn.
Empiricism	Very important. Learn prescribed subject matter determined by experts.	Important. Wants to be sure specified content has been learned.	Lectures and readings usually used.	Teacher and prescribed sources provide knowledge. Schools and teachers mold students. Discipline exists so that students may learn.
Naturalistic Empiricism	Not much interest in content.	Does not like it. Should be only in terms of student.	Minimum of teacher intervention. Follows child's natural development.	Students and teachers work together as equals. Teacher is enabler or helper.
Pragmatism	Interested in process of learning, not particular subject matter.	In terms of student's ability to learn. Seen as part of scientific process.	Learning how to learn through methods of inquiry and testing ideas. Methods and goals should be consistent. Learning is lifelong process.	Views students as individuals. Teachers help students to acquire skills in gathering information. Results are more important than orderliness.

INDIVIDUAL OR CLASS ACTIVITIES

Have the class members consider the music teachers with whom they have worked. Discuss which of the three philosophical positions most music teachers appear to follow. Reasons should be offered to support any claimed philosophical "winner" among music teachers.

REFERENCES

ARISTOTLE. (1930). *Physica* (W. D. Ross, Trans.). Oxford: Clarendon.

BREED, F. S. (1939). *Education and the new realism*. New York: Macmillan.

BROUDY, H. S. (1967). The case for aesthetic education. In R.A. Choate (Ed.). *Documentary report of the Tanglewood Symposium*. Reston, VA: Music Educators National Conference.

BUTLER, J. D. (1968). *Four philosophies* (3rd ed.). New York: Harper & Brothers.

DEWEY, J. (1933). *How we think*. Boston: D.C. Heath.

DEWEY, J. (1934). *Art as experience*. New York: Minton, Balch.

DU NOÜY L. (1947). *Human destiny*. New York: New American Library.

HERACLITUS. (1939). *Source book in ancient philosophy* (rev. ed.). (C. M. Bakewell, Comp.). New York: Scribner's.

HORNE, H. H. (1930). *The philosophy of education* (rev. ed.). New York: Macmillan.

HORNE, H. H. (1942). An idealistic philosophy of education. In *Forty-first Yearbook of the National Society for the Study of Education* (Vol. 1, p. 155). Bloomington, IN: Public School Publishing.

MENC leads effort in developing standards. (1992). *Music Educators Journal, 79*(1), 17–18.

REESE, W. L. (1980). *Dictionary of philosophy and religion: Eastern and Western thought*. Atlantic Highlands, NJ: Humanities Press.

SELLARS, R. W. (1932). *The philosophy of physical realism*. New York: Macmillan.

WHITEHEAD, A. N. (1929). *The aims of education and other essays*. New York: Macmillan.

3

The Musical and Aesthetic Foundations of Music Education

WHY SHOULD MUSIC and the other fine arts be included in school curicula? That fundamental question occupies the first portion of this chapter.

Reasons for Music and the Arts in Schools

The place of the arts in the lives of human beings rests on a fundamental proposition: *Living is not the same* as *existing*. Living is more than just getting through life, more than having something to eat and shelter from the rain and cold. Living is making life interesting, satisfying, and meaningful. Human beings live; animals exist. Perhaps the most important distinction between people and animals is the human desire and ability to make of life something more than biological existence.

When you think about it, it is amazing that the human race survived to dominate the earth, because in virtually every sensory capacity and physical ability humans are outclassed by animals. Birds have far superior distance vision and cats can see in the dark; dogs and many other animals have a vastly superior sense of smell; horses, lions, and hundreds of other animals can outrun humans; birds can fly and fish can swim and remain underwater; many animals are larger and stronger; even human hearing is much inferior to that of dogs and birds. Why weren't early humans squashed or swallowed up by some more able species?

There are two basic reasons. First, humans have the capability of abstract thought; they can do more than respond by instinct to stimuli. Anyone who has trained a dog knows that the reinforcement for an action must be made within ten seconds, otherwise the association is lost in the dog's brain. Humans can figure out that they can trap an animal by digging a hole for the animal to fall into, even though it may be days before the event might occur. Not only can they plan over a period of time, but they can perceive the relationships between digging the hole to trap an animal and the eventual satisfaction of their need for food and clothing. The ability to think led to the ability to use symbols, which in turn made possible one of humankind's most important accomplishments: language. Language permits the communication of ideas, facilitates thinking, and, through writing, enables humans to preserve thoughts.

The ability to think and plan would have kept the prehistoric humans alive, but they would not have become human as we think of human beings today without the second basic reason: an aspiration for something more than existence. Humans were not, and are not now, content to grub their way through life in a cave with a fire at its mouth for warmth and safety. They are never quite satisfied; constantly, it seems, people are trying to find better ways and new ideas. It was this quality of restless aspiration that kept humans trying until they were able to fly, to develop the electric lightbulb, to preserve food first through using spices and then canning and now freezing, to design clothes and furniture that are attractive as well as functional, to create different types of music, and to grow different types of flowers.

Where do music and the arts enter into all this? Music and the arts are one of the most significant manifestations of the ability of human beings to think and to aspire restlessly for something more than survival. Music has much to do with what makes us different from the animals and marks us as human. In *Human Destiny*, which analyzed the evolution of the human race, the scientist du Noüy writes about the cave drawings and other manifestations of artistic interest in the Cro-Magnon people:

> These *useless* manifestations—the word is taken in the sense of "not absolutely necessary to maintain or defend life"—mark the most important date of all the history of mankind. They are the proof of the progress of the human spirit in the direction of evolution, that is, in the direction leading away from the animal. (1947, pp. 125–26)

Granted, it can be argued that for a few people in miserable circumstances it may be better to be insensitive, to be "dead," psychologically speaking. Unfortunately, this could be true in a few cases. The basic point of the difference between living and existing is still valid, however. What needs to be changed for such people are the conditions under which they exist.

It is not difficult to demonstrate that people have found the arts and music to be important to the quality of their lives. All over the world, people spend countless hours listening to music and performing it, and they spend vast amounts of money for instruments, recordings, and sound reproducing equipment. People dance, sing lullabies, and create new tunes in just about every part of the globe. Many millions of Americans attend concerts of popular and "classical" music, and they spend huge amounts of money for recordings and related equipment, as well musical instruments and instruction.

Music has also been present in every age. The walls of ancient Egyptian buildings show people playing instruments and singing, and the Bible tells how David soothed King Saul with his music. In the Middle Ages courtly gentlemen serenaded the lady of their choice, and competitive guilds were organized to reward excellence in music performance. The breadth and depth of humankind's interest in music is indeed impressive.

Why Listen to Art Music?

As the preceding paragraphs have demonstrated, it is not difficult to provide evidence that music and aesthetic experiences are important to people. Attempting to find out *why* they are important is a much more tricky and complex matter. The trouble is that no one really knows why, or at least knows a single overriding reason. There are a number of theories and educated speculations, but such endeavors are not solid information, even though they may represent great intellectual insight. Human feelings and motivations are very complex; they are at least as complex as the wordy writings of some scholars about aesthetics and philosophy.

It is unlikely that any one theory or reason can ever explain why people create and listen to music; the matter is too multifaceted for that to happen. A person listens to the same work on different occasions in different ways for different reasons, and certainly different people listen for dissimilar reasons.

It should also be pointed out that not all music is used in an artistic, aesthetic way. In fact, most music (about 96 percent by one count) is not intended primarily for objective, passive listening (Malm, 1982). The idea of listening to music in a contemplative way is largely a product of Western civilization, with its objective manner of thinking. Even in the Western world only a minority of people listen to music in the sense that a musician uses the word "listen." Both within and outside of Western civilization music is used to accompany other activities, a topic that is discussed in chapter 5. In other words, the aesthetic use of music is only one of several uses of music, and it is one with which most people have had only a limited experience.

As is true of the philosophies outlined in the preceding chapter, the reasons given for wanting to listen to music can be organized into groupings. There are three categories in considering why people listen to music: referentialism, expressionism, and formalism. However, it should be remembered that each writer on the subject expresses an individual view, so there are as many variations and syntheses of viewpoints as there are people who have written on the topic.

Referentialism

This theory holds that the value of music lies in its "references" to things beyond the music itself. A song or a painting can, of course, denote for the observer or listener a specific nonmusical idea, but the referentialists believe that even instrumental works have this capability. For example, in the former Soviet Union the arts were seen as contributing to the "new socialist man" and the ideological education of the people in the spirit of socialism (Beardsley, 1977, p. 360). The "message" for referentialists, however, is not always that specific. It can also be moods or affective states. Deryck Cooke (1959, pp. 90–133) has devised what he believes are the proper referents to intervals and scales. For example, he considers the major third as referring to "joy," the major seventh as indicating "violent longing, aspiration in a contest of finality," and an ascending minor pattern of the first five pitches in the scale as "an outgoing feeling of pain—an assertion of sorrow, a complaint, a protest against misfortune."

It is true that programmatic works of instrumental music have nonmusical associations designated by the composer, and that almost all vocal music has words whose specific meanings combine with the music. However, the associations can only be as specific as the words make them. Therefore, Vivaldi's *The Four Seasons*, with its references to the lines of a sonnet interspersed among the lines of the score, is much more referential than Richard Strauss's *Death and Transfiguration*, for which there is only the title to indicate the association.[*]

The referentialist view presents a music teacher with a number of problems. For one thing, the search for a nonmusical message in absolute music distracts from the music by drawing attention away from its intrinsic qualities. Instead of centering attention on what is happening in terms of sound,

---

[*]Actually, the "program" was written by Alexander Ritter *after* Strauss had completed the music (Finck, 1917, p. 169).

the listener tries to fit the right nonmusical referent to the work. Looking for the correct referent is also largely guesswork, and it is prone to error.[*]

As a theory for music listening, referentialism appears to be flawed. Not only does it focus attention on things other than music itself, it also doesn't work. If a composer truly wanted to "tell a story" in instrumental music, he or she would find it necessary to make the sounds so similar to the real thing that the work would no longer be of interest as a piece of music. In fact, the effect would be more comic than artistic. On the other hand, if music is subtle and interesting, the specific message cannot be perceived by the listener; only a generalized feeling or mood is sensed. If composers wish to present a nonmusical idea, it seems more logical for them to write vocal music with words and their designated meanings.

Vocal music with its words presents an interesting aesthetic situation. The text of a song or choral work presents definite referents for the listener. When in *Messiah* Handel uses the words "Wonderful, Counselor, The mighty God, The everlasting Father, The Prince of Peace," listeners are provided a specific religious message. As is true of virtually all texts, the words in the chorus "For unto us a child is born" contain some poetic properties, although that is not their primary purpose. What makes the arias, recitatives, and choruses that make up *Messiah* aesthetically interesting are the qualities added by the music Handel composed to enhance those texts. In the case of the words "Wonderful, Counselor . . ." Handel set them to vibrant, rapidly moving sixteenth notes. What Handel achieved so well in *Messiah* has also been accomplished by Schubert, Debussy, Brahms, Ives, and hundreds of other composers of artistic vocal music: the aesthetically satisfying setting of texts enhanced and enriched by music.

Not only is there the actual setting of the words, there is also the larger work in which the words are set. The particular sections fit into a larger mosaic. "For unto us . . ." includes "And the government shall be upon his shoulders" as well as "Wonderful, Counselor. . . ." In addition, that chorus is preceded by the aria "The people that walked in darkness" and is followed by the "Pastoral Symphony." These works are but three parts of the total of fifty-three that make up *Messiah*.

Clearly there are also songs in which the artistic setting of a text is not the objective. Many songs and church hymns consist of tunes to which several different sets of words have been set. "America" and "God Save the King" are well-known examples. One can think of such songs and hymns

---

[*]One music teacher used Shostakovich's Symphony No. 5 to teach his students about "war." There was one problem: The symphony was composed in 1937. four years *before* Russia's involvement in World War II. Apparently, this teacher had confused the Fifth Symphony with the Seventh (*Leningrad*) Symphony (Moses, 1971, p. 25).

aesthetically, of course, but they lack the deeper expressive and musical properties of vocal music created for artistic purposes. For example, their harmonies are generally merely functional. Although they may have much entertainment or religious usefulness, such music usually lacks sufficient qualities for a listener to gain much satisfaction from just listening to it.

Expressionism

A more sophisticated theory of music's expression of meaning beyond itself is contained in the writings of Susanne Langer, John Dewey, and others. Langer states that what is being signified in music are not specific and identifiable meanings; instead music is thought to be "an unconsummated symbol" of human psychological processes and feelings (Langer, 1942, p. 195). Although "unconsummated," music does signify states of being and feeling. Music is especially suitable for this purpose because it possesses kinetic and dynamic qualities—expressed through tempo, tension and relaxation, and other devices—that are similar to experiences in life itself. As Langer (1953. p. 27) writes: "The pattern of music is that of the same form worked out in pure, measured sound and silence. Music is the tonal analogue of emotive life."

Langer's version of expressionism is interesting and in many ways profound. However, it is questionable on a number of points. As Monroe Beardsley (1977, p. 361) wonders, "Why should we take the music as referring to anything beyond itself, any more than we take a chair or a mountain that way?" He then points out that "unconsummated" symbolism is close to no symbolism at all. He also maintains that in her later writings Langer significantly moderated her views away from the unconsummated-symbol idea.

Expressionism is closely aligned with John Dewey's pragmatic views of the aesthetic experience. Life is always in flux, he claims. There is a rhythm of struggle and contentment, of equilibrium and disequilibrium. The arts, and especially music, call forth feelings that were generated at some time in a person's experience. The artist, Dewey (1934, p. 15) maintains, "does not shun moments of resistance and tension. He rather cultivates them, not for their own sake, but because of their potentialities, bringing to living consciousness an experience that is unified and total" (1934, p. 15). In other words, the arts express in an intense and indirect way human feelings associated with life. As we become more mature and sophisticated, the patterns of tension and release, become wider, richer, subtler, and more complex.

According to Langer and Dewey, the feelings music expresses are not specific emotions like joy or sadness. Also, the feelings engendered by a musical passage are personal, as are all feelings. One person may listen to the first movement of Mendelssohn's Symphony No. 4 (*Italian*) and say that he or she felt the music was "happy," while another person might use a term like "optimistic." In neither case is the adjective adequate or accurate for what was felt. That doesn't matter to the expressionist, because trying to attach a verbal descriptor to music is unnecessary, and could even be an impediment to enjoying it.

The fact that music arouses or expresses feelings without the need for words is one of its attributes. As Irwin Edman (1939, pp. 108–9) writes:

> The very fact that there is nothing definitive or exclusive in the emotional atmosphere of a given composition will make it all the more accessible as a means of catharsis or relief for the listener. Words are too brittle and chiseled, life too rigid and conventional to exhaust all the infinity of human emotional response. The infinite sinuousness, nuance, and complexity of music enable it to speak in a thousand different accents to a thousand different listeners, and to say with noncommittal and moving intimacy what no language would acknowledge or express and what no situations in life could completely exhaust or make possible.

Dewey states the same thought less romantically: "If all meanings could be adequately expressed by words, the arts of painting and music would not exist" (Dewey, 1934, p. 74). According to the expressionist theory that would be true, but one can argue that there are other reasons for the arts in addition to the expression of meanings.

Two qualifications should be stated about expressionism. It is not believed that the composer or painter vents his or her own personal feelings in the artwork, although that has happened on occasion. Rather, it is the listener or observer whose feelings are aroused. Also, the expressive quality is culture-bound in that "happy" music in an unfamiliar style to us might not strike us as happy; probably persons used to Western music would not have much reaction to it at all.

A variation of expressionist theory that is especially interesting to music educators is that of *absolute expressionism*. This view accepts the value of the formal properties of works of art, but rejects the notion that these properties should be considered apart from the rest of life. It supports enthusiastically the expressionistic view. The relationship between the qualities of the artwork and the qualities of human experience is felt by the perceiver of the work as "significance." Reimer states: "The major function of art is to make objective and therefore accessible the subjective realm of human responsiveness. Art does this by capturing and presenting in its intrinsic qualities the patterns and form of human feeling. . . . Education in the arts, then, can be regarded as the education of feeling" (1989, p. 153).

Although being deeply involved with music is beneficial in many ways, the point about educating feelings is questionable. To say that music arouses feelings is one thing, but to say that it "educates" feelings is quite

another. Virtually every experience in life from eating turnips to studying about the Spanish-American War is accompanied by reactions and
feelings; music is not alone in its feeling-arousal capabilities. Other questions can be raised about the idea of educating feelings. Can we teach
persons what and how to feel? Would that be ethically proper, even if it
were possible? Aren't feelings personal matters over which teachers, and
even parents, can or should exercise little control? Many parents have
said to a son or daughter, "You will like your carrots," and while the
child swallowed a few bites, the dislike of carrots remained unchanged.
Perhaps what the proponents of absolute expressionism mean is that
they want people to become more sensitive and responsive to the qualities present in music and the other arts. That goal is easily supportable
and defensible.

Formalism or Absolutism

While expressionism is concerned about the effect music has on the listener and to some degree the performer, formalism considers only the formal
properties of the work of art without regard to other considerations. The
idea of formalism is expounded ably by Edward Hanslick, the nineteenth-
century aesthetician and promoter of Brahms's music. He writes (1957,
pp. 21, 23): "The ideas which a composer expresses are mainly and primarily of a purely musical nature. . . . Definite feelings and emotions are
unsusceptible of being embodied in music."

The difference between formalism and other theories can be seen in
how proponents of each might describe the same musical work. The formalist might say, "The music *has the qualities* of order and symmetry."
The expressionist might say, "The music *arouses feelings* that can be
described as order and symmetry." The referentialist might say, "The
music *presents the message* of order and symmetry."

The idea of absolutism or formalism, in which sounds are considered in
an antiseptic way without contamination from the other experiences of
life, seems impossible. Humans are not normally able to segment one
aspect of life so clearly from other aspects. To center attention on and
teach an understanding of the musical properties of a work is entirely possible and desirable. There will, however, be feelings and reactions to what
is heard, but precisely what these feelings are or should be, and the degree
to which they can be influenced, cannot be known or controlled.
Therefore, it is more worthwhile for music educators to concentrate on
those aspects of the music experience—structure, rhythm, melody, dynamic changes, and so on—that can be taught. As is pointed out in chapter 8,
such an emphasis is probably the best course of action for promoting positive attitudes.

Unfortunately, formalism has often been associated with the nineteenth-century elitist view of the arts. According to this view, most people are not able to understand or appreciate great artworks. The composer, conductor, critic, and the like are extraordinary persons with superior abilities. It is one of their tasks to interpret and to educate the masses by raising their understanding so that in time they will be able to appreciate the great works. Whether most average persons will ever appreciate such works is doubtful, according to this type of formalistic thinking. The association of formalism with elitist thinking is not required, however. The formal qualities of a work can be examined and appreciated without believing that such experiences are limited to an intellectual elite.

What connections, if any, are there among the three points of view for explaining the value of music and the three philosophies presented in chapter 2? There is no one-to-one relationship in which, for example, referentialism is coupled to the philosophy of rationalism. The reason for the lack of a direct relationship is the fact that referentialism, formalism, and expressionism are attempts to describe a psychological-aesthetic phenomenon. They are not basic philosophical considerations.

There are some instances in which a philosopher has written on aesthetics, notably John Dewey. And there is a strong association between pragmatism and expressionism. Not only is Dewey involved with both, but the experience-centered emphasis of both is clear. The intellectual purity of formalism makes it ripe for association with the philosophy of rationalism. However, aesthetic associations with realism and naturalism are not so easy to establish with confidence.

Other Reasons for Valuing Music

As was pointed out earlier in this chapter, it is likely that there are reasons for listening to music in addition to those that are contained in the referential, expressionistic, and formal viewpoints. Aaron Copland (1957, pp. 9–10) has pointed out two further reasons. One is the sensuous attraction of music. The word "sensuous" means "of or appealing to the senses." An incident involving the American composer Howard Hanson illustrates the impact of the sensuous side of music, even for a brilliant and highly educated composer. He was listening to a performance of an orchestral work by Debussy. As the orchestra sounded one of Debussy's lush chords. Hanson poked the colleague sitting next to him with his elbow and whispered, "What a gorgeous sound!" The rich-sounding chord was sheer sensuous pleasure to Hanson and the other listeners. There is also pleasure in hearing the timbre of various instruments and voices (in a good performance), to say nothing of the peaks and valleys in dynamic levels.

Copland also cites what he calls the "sheerly musical" type of listening. This type appreciates the skill and imagination with which the sounds are organized: what notes are being played, at what speed, in what combination with other notes, on what instruments, in what pitch range, in what form or pattern, and so on. While containing a large dose of formalism, this type of listening also has the element of admiration of the skill and imagination exhibited in the composition. Often when musicians hear a work by Bach, Brahms, or Bartok, they are left with a feeling of awe for the ingeniousness that is being exhibited. Most people enjoy seeing or hearing someone who is highly gifted at what he or she is doing, whether that activity is diving from a springboard, dancing, playing the piano, or composing music.

Any of the several theories or reasons described in these pages can be combined with other reasons, even by the same listener within a span of a few seconds. The human mind has a great capacity for flitting rapidly from one listening approach to another. Virtually no one is a formalist all the time, or even for a few minutes, without also appreciating the qualities of a particular chord or the emotional qualities of a particular passage.

Sometimes people are physically or mentally tired and simply do not want to attend to something requiring concentration. At other times they are satiated with a certain type of music and want to hear something different. Since there are different ways of listening to music, it is not surprising that several of the composers who have established themselves among history's greatest wrote music that seems equally suitable for appreciation of its formal qualities *or* its sensuous qualities *or* its expressive power.

All of this discussion about why music is valuable should not cause anyone to lose sight of this important fact: knowing the reasons *why* people value music is not nearly as significant as realizing that they do value it. Fortunately, no agreement or definitive reason is needed to make music or the study of it worthwhile. The position a teacher takes on the value of music will, however, significantly affect the nature of his or her teaching. It makes quite a difference, for example, whether one is teaching for referential or formal properties!

Characteristics of the Aesthetic Experience

The word "aesthetic" often appears in discussions of music and the fine arts. Sometimes music education is described as part of "aesthetic education." Unfortunately, the word "aesthetic" is easier to use than it is to define. Perhaps it can be clarified best by pointing out the characteristics of an aesthetic experience.

First, an aesthetic experience has no practical or utilitarian purpose. Instead, it is valued for the insight, satisfaction, and enjoyment that it provides. It is an end in itself, and not a means to something more desirable or important.[*] Most experiences in life are motivated by practical considerations. People eat because they need food for energy and health; they work at a job because they need money to buy food and pay the rent; they buy a coat to keep warm; and so on. Listening to music or looking at paintings or pieces of sculpture has no utilitarian purpose. In a practical sense, attending to molecules being bumped around in the air (a crude description of how music reaches our ears) is a silly thing to do. As Ralph Vaughan Williams once said: "Music is the most useless thing in the world; you can't eat it, sit on it, or make love to it. Consider the humble brick, and compare it to a Schubert song. I can think of a thousand uses for the brick, but for which purpose the Schubert song is almost totally inefficient" (Beglarian, 1971, p. 59).

Second, an aesthetic experience involves feelings. There is a reaction to what is seen and heard, just as there is a reaction to nearly everything experienced in life. Most of the time these feelings are not obvious or simple, so that one starts to cry or laugh; they are more subtle than that. However, feeling is always present.

Third, an aesthetic experience involves the intellect. Thought and awareness are necessary, and a person is quite conscious of the object being looked at or listened to. It is not enough just to undergo an emotional interlude, as if one were merely standing under a shower and enjoying the feeling of water running over the skin. The mind is active as it consciously notices the aesthetic object and then relates that object, and the reactions it has stimulated, to previous experience.

Fourth, an aesthetic experience involves a focus of attention. To gain aesthetic satisfaction from looking at a painting, one must center attention on the painting; one must contemplate it—consider it thoughtfully. Whirring by a painting in a gallery while riding in an electric golf cart will not lead to an aesthetic experience of much quality.

Fifth, an aesthetic experience must be experienced. It is almost worthless (and annoying!) to have someone describe a song or painting to you. There is no way to have "secondhand" aesthetic experiences. It is not even possible to cheat on aesthetic experiences—for example, by listening to only the last minute of a symphony. It is possible to look up the answers to math problems or geography quizzes, but that doesn't work with things aesthetic. There are no aesthetic "answers," only experiences.

Sixth, the result of aesthetic experiences is a richer and more meaningful life. It is interesting to consider what the antonym of "aesthetic" is. It is not "ugly" or "crude" or "repulsive" or anything that desirable. Instead it

---

[*]Sometimes it is described as a "terminal" experience, a term that carries some undesirable connotations!

can best be thought of as "anesthetic"—nothingness, no life, no feeling, no humanness.

There are some other, less significant aspects of aesthetic experiences. As is true of most experiences in life, they occur in varying degrees of intensity. Some are rather weak (looking at a refrigerator—not an unsightly object), while others are much stronger (contemplating a painting by Rembrandt). However, they seldom consist of a feeling of being "thunderstruck."

Aestheticians have sometimes questioned whether aesthetic experiences are confined only to art objects. Somehow the question does not seem very important. In any case, if one looks at a painting for the qualities of design and color, then is it not logical to assume that one can look at scenery or trees for their design or color?

The quality of the aesthetic experience depends on the quality of both the object *and* the viewer or listener. The object needs to possess the qualities that encourage aesthetic reactions, and the person contemplating the object must be perceptive and inclined to "drink in" whatever the object has to offer. There is a reciprocal relationship between object and observer.

Aesthetic experiences are not limited to the intelligentsia or a special group of gifted persons. Age, race, and sex make no difference in this regard. However, a person who has benefitted from a good education in music or other fine art is likely to be more sensitive and more inclined to notice thoughtfully, which allows for more and deeper aesthetic experiences. It is true that some people seem to be more aesthetically inclined than others. People appear to vary in this regard just as they differ in how thoughtful they are of other people, how well they like language study, how easily they put on weight, and a hundred other things.

Aesthetic experiences are seldom, if ever, pure. Formalists can almost never achieve the goal of a neat separation of art from life. All of the previous experiences of an individual, plus all the individual's inherent inclinations, affect each experience. For example, some people like simple, clean lines in artworks because consciously or unconsciously they want to lead neat, uncluttered lives. Such qualities are evident in furniture made by the Shakers, members of a religious sect that admired simplicity.

The culture also influences conceptions of what is considered aesthetic. Not only are these differences striking as one compares the different cultures around the world, but even in Western civilization such ideas change with time. The women in Rubens's paintings, done in the early seventeenth century, look as if they were weightlifters in comparison to the clothing models of today. Cultural bias also encourages people to look and listen for different "cues;" this will be discussed in greater detail in chapter 5.

It may seem surprising that the word "beauty" has not come up until now in this discussion of the aesthetic experience, but there are good reasons why. One is that the words "beauty" and "beautiful" have been used so loosely for so long that they now have no clear meaning other than "I like it." Another reason is that beauty is not the only, or even a sizable, consideration in the aesthetic experience. Stravinsky's *The Rite of Spring*, Shakespeare's *King Lear*, and Mathias Grünewald's "The Entombment" on the altar at Isenheim are works with great aesthetic impact, but none of them could accurately be described as "beautiful." There is also a metaphysical problem with the concept of beauty. Some people (realists) say it is inherent in the object, while others agree with David Hume (1711–1766) that "Beauty in things exists in the mind which contemplates them" (Bartlett, 1968, p. 434). In any case, beauty is only one of several responses aroused by art works.

The Aesthetic Mode of Thinking

There is more to aesthetics than immediate experiences and the consideration of particular artistic properties. Aesthetic thinking requires the perception of the properties in combination, in relationship to each other. It calls for looking for large principles such as unity, variation, symmetry or balance, and theme. It is at this macro level that one can best think about "the fine arts" rather than each individual art. The principle of symmetry, for example, can be realized in an *aba* formal pattern and in the roofline of the Parthenon. Like looking down at the ground from an airplane flying at an altitude of 30,000 feet, the large concepts provide a broad perspective that allows for thinking about aesthetic qualities without the encumbrances of the technical aspects of each art.

For the most part, education tries to teach students to think logically and objectively, and it is at least partially successful in its efforts. In both the physical and social sciences the students are taught to analyze problems, look for evidence, and follow certain procedures; in mathematics they are taught the symbols of mathematics and its operations and equations; in language courses they are taught correct forms and symbols for communication in a language. In the arts it is different, or at least it should be different. In the arts students should acquire an inclination, desire, and ability to consider objects for the qualities they possess and to react with feeling to those qualities. Logic, proof, and correctness are not required to perceive qualities or to react with feeling. What is needed is an imaginative, sensitive, and perceiving way of beholding visual objects and listening to aural objects.

A passage from the Book of Isaiah (55:12) can serve to illustrate the difference between cognitive, rational thinking and the type of thinking that has been termed by different writers as "subjective reality," "aesthetic world," "artistic," "poetic," "world of feeling," and the like. In these lines the poet is telling the ancient Israelites how they will feel when they are delivered from the Babylonian captivity.

> *For you shall go out in joy,*
> *and be led forth in peace;*
> *the mountains and the hills before you*
> *shall break forth into singing,*
> *and all the trees of the field*
> *shall clap their hands.*

The ordinary, cognitive way to express the thought of this passage would be to say something like "You will feel very happy when you leave." In contrast, the poet—an inhabitant of the "aesthetic world"—stirs the imagination with metaphors and the rhythmic pattern of the lines and words. The passage is attractive and pleasing, and it is highly effective in getting across the idea of how the Israelites will feel.

Is the poetic way better than the rational way, or vice versa? Neither is superior; they are *different* ways. Each way is valuable, and human beings need both modes of thought. It is rationally correct that the Israelites will feel very happy when freed from Babylon, but it is also true in terms of feelings that they will be so overwhelmed with joy that the trees will seem to "clap their hands" and the mountains and hills "break forth into singing." Both rational and aesthetic modes are vital to life, and therefore should be a part of everyone's education.

The rational and aesthetic modes of thinking are not antithetical. The aesthetic way is not antirational, it is nonrational; the rational way is not anti-aesthetic, it is nonaesthetic. The two modes of thought can and should be present in virtually everyone. Even if one is an artist or musician, that fact does not demand eccentric, irrational behavior, any more than being a scientist requires an unfeeling, mechanistic mentality.

It may be that the need for imagination and feeling is one important reason for the arts, because they relieve tedium and add another dimension to life. After all, to spend an entire lifetime being only rational and ignoring feelings would be dreadful and drab. To do so would mean giving up a large measure of the human characteristic of restless aspiration, which was mentioned earlier in this chapter. However, to try to live without rational thought is undesirable and probably impossible. One might end his or her days on earth by leaping off a cliff trying to "mount up with wings as eagles," to quote another verse from the Book of Isaiah.

Quality in Musical Works

To be in favor of "good" music is about as startling and controversial as being in favor of safe driving and the prevention of forest fires. While nearly everyone is for good music, very few people agree on what constitutes it. Each person thinks he or she knows what good music is, of course; the problem is that sometimes other people don't agree!

Theorists, musicologists, and aestheticians have had a difficult time in developing a consensus on a set of criteria for the evaluation of musical quality. Sometimes certain technical features (rhythmic proportions, melodic contours, chord use allocations, and others) have been identified. Unfortunately, either the criteria have been so specific that some works generally considered good must be eliminated, or they have been so general that they provide little help. A judge in a dog show would find of little value a general set of criteria such as "To be judged as being of championship quality a dog should have two eyes, four legs, and one tail."

The difficulties in developing criteria for quality in music have led some persons to take the view that since no foolproof criteria have been developed, there must be no difference in quality among music works. In other words, all music is of equal artistic value. That position seems at least as untenable as the idea that there are universal and eternal criteria for music. Brahms's Symphony No. 4 is not just another tune, and neither are hundreds of other works that musicians recognize as being of high quality.

Can anything worthwhile be said on the topic of quality in music? To begin with, as will be pointed out in chapter 5, music is a human creation. Therefore, it exhibits the same degree of cultural variation throughout the world as is found in languages, dress, and manners. This fact means that the notion of a universal set of standards for music is untenable. A Mozart piano sonata cannot be compared with a *raga* from India, any more than the athletic prowess of a star baseball player can be compared with that of a championship tennis player.

Evaluations of music must be in terms of comparison of the relative merits of works within the same genre, rather than the assignment according to discrete categories such as "bad" or "good." Very few published works are really incompetently written. Instead, music seems to fall along a continuum that runs from "boring" to "very fascinating."

MEYER'S THEORY. One defensible approach to evaluating musical works that are in similar styles has been developed by Leonard Meyer. His rather lengthy arguments can be summed up in four essential points:

1. Listeners know one (and occasionally more) syntactical style of music. The importance of a sense of pattern can be easily demonstrated. Those who have a sense of the flow of "common practice" harmony in

Western music (which probably includes almost all the readers of this book) would expect the chord progression in example 3.1 to conclude with a tonic chord, and only occasionally with a submediant chord resulting in a deceptive cadence. Ending with a foreign chord such as C#–E–G# would sound syntactically wrong. People have expectations about melodies, too.

Example 3.1

A melody such as that in example 3.2 with its pitches and rhythmic values determined by drawing cards at random,* would probably be thought of as the work of an incompetent or a clown. Music listeners expect the pitches and rhythms of a melody to provide some interest and variety, yet still sound cohesive and unified. Not only are there expectations about the smaller aspects of music, but similar expectancies also exist about music's larger proportions. For example, one anticipates some manipulation of themes in a development section of a work in sonata form and the musical enrichment of the text in an art song.

Example 3.2

2.   Composers *usually* write music that follows the expected musical patterns. The main difference between a composition that is considered

---

*3 = C, 4 = C#, etc. 3 = a quarter note, 4 = a half note, etc. The direction of the pitches generally alternates on each beat. The "system" is *not* copyrighted!

good and of some lasting value and one that is soon forgotten lies in how immediately the tendencies of those patterns are fulfilled. Run-of-the-mill musical works fulfill those expectancies quite promptly and directly, while quality musical works have some interesting but temporary deviations before fulfilling the syntactical expectations.

3.   For reasons rooted in human psychology, people value and find more meaningful experiences that are *not* routine and do *not* occur just about as expected. As Meyer points out (1956, pp. 13–14):

> If, for example, a habitual smoker wants a cigarette and, reaching into his pocket, finds one, there will be no affective response. If the tendency is satisfied without delay, no emotional response will take place. If, however, the man finds no cigarette in his pocket, discovers that there are none in the house, and then remembers that the stores are closed and he cannot purchase any, he will very likely begin to respond in an emotional way. He will feel restless, excited, then irritated, and finally angry.
>
> This brings us to the central thesis of the psychological theory of emotions. Namely: Emotion or affect is aroused when a tendency is arrested or inhibited.

The difference between art music and nonartistic music is the difference in the promptness with which tendencies are fulfilled. Art music deviates in its journey toward points of gratification and travels by a sometimes circuitous route; nonartistic music contains almost no uncertainties in its quick consummation of what is expected.

4.   What does this have to do with maturity and "higher" or more sophisticated thinking? Meyer states (1967, p. 33):

> One aspect of maturity both of the individual and of the culture within which a style arises consists then in the willingness to forgo immediate, and perhaps lesser, gratification for the sake of future ultimate gratification . . . self-imposed tendency inhibition and the willingness to bear uncertainty . . . are signs that the animal is becoming a man.

Children want what they want *immediately*, as anyone can report who has observed them waiting anxiously during the weeks before Christmas. Mature persons, presumably most adults, usually enjoy anticipating the holiday season. They may find the day more meaningful and deeply enjoyable (even if they are glad it comes only once a year!) because of their anticipation, in contrast to just the momentary pleasure of opening presents.

BERLYNE'S RESEARCH.   Berlyne and associates explored immediate and delayed gratification of expectations in music. In a series of experiments they had subjects rate melodic phrases created according to a mathematical formula in terms of complexity-uncertainty and degree of beauty. The subjects correctly ranked the melodies according to complexity as determined

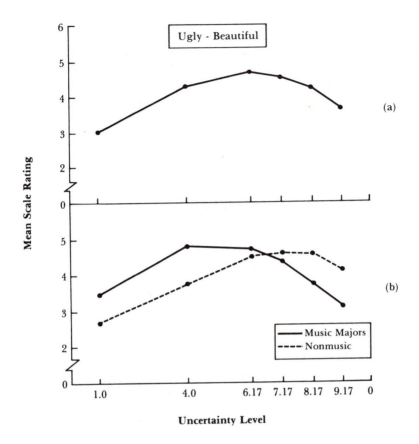

Figure 3.1. From *Studies in the New Experimental Aesthetics*, edited by
D. E. Berlyne, copyright © 1974 Hemisphere Publishing Corporation. Used
by permission.

by the music's mathematical properties. However, the responses on the
degree of beauty formed an inverted U-shaped curve, as can be seen in figure 3.1. The very simple melodies were not considered very beautiful, but
the rating for beauty increased as complexity increased until an optimum
point was reached. Beyond that point, further complexity caused a reduction in the ratings of beauty. As can be seen in figure 3.1, the music-major
subjects had a somewhat reduced liking for complexity-uncertainty (J. B.
Crozier in Berlyne, 1974, pp. 38–46).

The need for a balance between unity and variety expressed by Meyer
and other writers on aesthetics is supported by Berlyne's research. He
write (1974, p. 9):

> The upshot of these hypotheses is that the appeal of a work of art depends on the interplay of two sets of factors, one tending to drive arousal upwards and the other tending to reduce arousal or to keep it within bounds. The idea that aesthetic value requires a combination of two partly opposite and partly complementary factors has cropped up repeatedly over the centuries.

The analogue between people's desire for stability and novelty in their lives and the requirement for both the predictable and the novel in music adds much to the validity of the expressionists' view about the deep psychological significance of music and the fine arts. Music and art do indeed have deep roots in people's psychic nature; they are clearly more than entertainment, recreation, decoration, or frills.

Meyer's and Berlyne's ideas can help to render evaluations of musical quality, but they do not settle everything. A person experienced in music is still required to make an informed judgment about the skill and speed with which tendencies are fulfilled. That task, however, seems much more possible than attempting to apply a set of technical criteria or defending the proposition that there are no differences in quality among musical works. It is possible (but by no means certain) that some time in the future Meyer's ideas can be quantified for more precise comparisons through statistical analysis.

Teaching Music for Its Aesthetic-Musical Qualities

Assuming that all the readers of this chapter are now convinced that aesthetic experiences are a vital part of music education, hold some views as to why this is so, and understand what such experiences are, let us examine the practical aspects of teaching for aesthetic outcomes in the class or rehearsal room. Here are five general guidelines, which if followed lead to a great variety of specific actions.

1. Teaching for aesthetic-musical sensitivity involves much pointing out of the qualitative features of the music and/or many experiences in which students are guided to find such aspects for themselves. The "Air" from Bach's Suite No. 3 for Orchestra (known in one arrangement as "Air for the G String") can serve as an example. Many other works would be equally useful, but the "Air" is slow and clearly presents its patterns, and it contains no programmatic associations or words. (Only the first portion of the melody is presented in figure 3.3.)

Example 3.3

If you were going to teach the aesthetic qualities of this music, just exactly what would you teach? The dates of Bach's life and other historical information? No. The fact that it is in common meter, in the key of D major, and/or with an *aabb* form? No. Such information is generally covered in theory and music history and literature courses, and is of much value to music majors, but does not offer much aesthetic insight or increase aesthetic sensitivity. What, then? The students should be made aware of the qualities and patterns of sounds and their feeling-arousal properties. In Bach's "Air" these properties include the feelings or reactions stimulated by:

- the opening whole note, which is usually played with a crescendo;
- the change of rhythmic motion caused by the several long notes followed by the faster-moving notes;
- the sequential character of the pitches in the third and fourth measures;
- the accented appoggiaturas (circled in measure 3 of example 3.3) in the ascending series of pitches;
- the simple, steady quality of the accompanying bass line that leaps in octaves;
- the contrapuntal, contrasting quality of the second violin and viola parts as they weave in and out, especially while the melody part is sustaining long notes; and
- the timbre of the string instruments.

A quick way to locate the prominent aesthetic features of a musical work is to ask yourself, "What about this piece makes it interesting and attractive to listen to?" It's one thing to like a musical work; everyone can do that without thinking. It is another to analyze what are the features of the music that make it attractive and satisfying. Seven are mentioned in conjunction with Bach's "Air." However, most listeners probably find that the melodic "architecture" and the contrasts of that line with the steady, simple bass line provide the work's main attraction. Those attributes have made it a favorite of listeners for at least two centuries.

Above all, the students should become aware of the gentle sense of "tension" or "energy" increasing and then receding as phrases come and go. It will help them to think more about the qualities of the music if they are asked to decide questions such as when phrases begin and end, which notes seem to be more important in the melody, and what effect some of the accidentals have on the music.

The amount of detail the students should try to notice depends on their background. With younger or less experienced students, the "pointing out" would need to be more general, while advanced students could be asked to consider such points as the musical effect of the thirty-second notes in measures 5 and 6 and the slight syncopation on two of the beats in these measures. Regardless of the background of the students, teachers should seek to have them become thoughtfully, consciously, and affectively involved with the music as it progresses through time.

2.   When teaching the performance of a work, teachers should seek to develop an aesthetic-musical awareness, and not be content with *only* the correct notes played or sung at the correct time. Often the musical qualities of a work are stifled by a nitpicking, "mechanical" approach in rehearsal. The notes end up being performed correctly, but the musical qualities are lost; there is no longer much feeling for or awareness of the work's musical properties. Even when beginning instrumentalists play "Twinkle, Twinkle, Little Star" or "Lightly Row," they can do so with a sense of phrase and musical awareness. Music teachers should not wait months (or years!) for the achievement of technical skills and then think about the musical qualities of the piece. Skill development and musical awareness should increase almost simultaneously.

3.   The information that is provided (and some imparting of useful and valid information is good teaching) should be related as much as possible to the musical sounds. It is fine to teach that Bach's "Air" is in a major key. However, the students should also hear the musical quality of the major mode. It is fine to teach that Bach lived from 1685 to 1750, but that fact should be related to the Baroque period and style of music, with its attention to the outer voices, use of melodic sequence, and the like.

4.   Aesthetic awareness and sensitivity are more easily taught when music of good quality is utilized. The study or performance of any piece of music requires effort on the part of both teacher and students. Dull music is no easier to learn than interesting music; in fact, sometimes it is more difficult. Nor does uninteresting music contain as many of the qualities that the students should learn to notice. Why not use the best music that the students are capable of performing or understanding?

5.   Finally, objective terms should be used in making the students more sensitive to the qualities in music. The goal is to make them more conscious of the nature of the music, and not to be introspective about

their reactions. Therefore, the use of subjective adjectives such as "sad," "gleeful," and "contrite" does not encourage greater attention to the sounds and their organization. Instead, it leads to an inward search for some word to describe how one feels. The quotation from Edman on page 71 explains the futility of trying to affix verbal symbols to music. Also, if a suitable word is decided upon, it applies only for the person who chose it. A work may seem "sad" to one person but "contrite" to another. Therefore, there is little that teachers can do in the way of clarification, discussion, or communication of subjective descriptors.

The Nonmusical Values of Music

From the time of the ancient Greeks and their doctrine of *ethos* through the quadrivium of the medieval universities (both discussed in chapter 1) until at least the 1950s, music in the schools was justified almost entirely on the basis of its nonmusical values. For example, in 1837, when Lowell Mason was given permission to start music instruction in the Boston schools, the subject was justified because it contributed to reading and speech and provided "a recreation, yet not a dissipation of the mind—a respite, yet not a relaxation—its office would thus be to restore the jaded energies, and send back the scholars with invigorated powers to other more laborious duties" (Birge, 1966, p. 43).

The belief that music possesses the power to aid people in ways beyond the art itself did not cease with Lowell Mason. For more than the first half of the twentieth century, nonmusical reasons were almost the only ones offered for including music in school curricula. For example, in 1941 Peter Dykema and Karl Gehrkens, two important people in the development of school music in America, wrote that "the teacher teaches children through the medium of music" (pp. 380–81). The clear implication of their statement is that music exists in the schools to achieve goals beyond the learning of music. In 1991 the report of the National Commission on Music Education, entitled *Growing Up Complete*, devoted a sizable amount of space to the idea that music study contributes to improved performance in school and life (pp. 17–24).

Why is the belief that music has powers beyond itself so durable? Is it because those beliefs are true? Or is it because music educators are searching for irrefutable practical reasons for including in school curricula a subject that they believe in? Or do they think nonmusical reasons are easier to explain to nonmusicians than aesthetic ones? The answer seems to be "all of the above." The matter is not a simple one, however; it contains a number of aspects and issues.

It is clear that music can contribute to an understanding of many other areas of school curricula. This is especially true of the social sciences. The study of Africa or the Middle Ages is not complete without some attention being devoted to the appropriate music for the topics. The enrichment of the study of other subjects by the inclusion of music is something that is not utilized enough, because the teachers of these subjects often lack the knowledge of music needed to effect such enrichment. In addition, music teachers often do not know when various topics are to be taught, so they are unable to offer much help to the teachers of various courses. Communication about such matters between music and other teachers would help to make music a more vital force in the curriculum.

The matter of nonmusical values, however, usually centers on the benefits to individual students. Often the claims for the nonmusical values of music seem to say that just being in music classes or groups produces certain benefits, that something from music class transfers to another area of the curriculum or life. It would be nice if it were only that simple and true, but it isn't. Clearly, the nature of the instruction in music makes a great deal of difference. Just being present in a music class is not enough, and it would be naive to think otherwise. Musical sounds in and of themselves do not cause greater mental powers, improved work habits, or more harmonious interpersonal relations. The research support for such benefits simply doesn't exist. As Karen Wolff points out after her careful review of the extant research on the transfer of learning in music to other subjects (1978, pp. 19, 21):

> The weight of evidence gleaned from the research leads one to believe that there may be measurable effects of music education on the development of cognitive skills and understanding. This seems to be true for both general transfer, i.e., "learning how to learn," and specific transfer. Specific transfer is particularly apparent in its effect on performance in the language arts. . . . While it is true that most of the research related to the nonmusical outcomes of music education has produced positive results, the conclusions drawn generally remain unconvincing. This is due largely to obvious inadequacies in the experimental designs and also to the incomplete and equivocal descriptions of the experiments themselves.

Wolff's summary indicates that music instruction appears more likely to have an effect on young people's learning in the language arts than any other area of the curriculum. Apparently the ability to process sound information related to language or music derives from similar psychoacoustic operations. Casual observation confirms that a much higher percentage than would be expected of students who are in speech correction classes also have problems singing on pitch. Other studies found improved reading scores for elementary school students after a special treatment period involving music (Movesian, 1967; Maze et al., 1967). Related to the processing of sounds is the ability to talk without stuttering or stammering.

Music is helpful in aiding over 92 percent of persons who stutter (Graham, 1975, p. 35).

Some benefits from music study have also been observed in the improved attitudes of students toward school as indicated by a decline in absenteeism (Rodosky, 1974). Some of this benefit may not be so much from music as it is from offering the students an interesting change of activity, a point cited in the 1837 report to the Boston School Committee (Birge, 1966. See pp. 12–13). Often, elementary students are given large doses of study in reading and arithmetic. Many activities, including music, would be a welcome and beneficial change in such situations. Music can be an effective "antimonotony" activity.

Many times the benefits of music participation are related to the non-musical activities of a group—performing before an audience, knowing well a teacher who is a good role model, wearing a band uniform, and the like. Such benefits can be achieved in a variety of ways. Athletics, drama, and other extracurricular activities provide such opportunities in addition to music. Some students find success and satisfaction in athletics, some in special interest clubs, some in student government, and some in music. One study of secondary school principals uncovered the fact that more than 70 percent of the respondents could think of students who would have dropped out of school had it not been for the music and art programs (*The Role of Fine and Performing Arts*, 1990, p. 22). Clearly, the quality of the situation in which music is taught makes an enormous difference in the effectiveness of this benefit. Teachers who eliminate or drive away students are seriously reducing this potential value of music programs.

Every year, *USA Today* features twenty outstanding high school seniors from around the nation who form what it refers to as the "All USA Academic Team." This list, always includes a percentage that is much higher than expected of students who are very active in music, sometimes as many as thirteen out of the twenty (*Soundpost*, 1989, p. 5). This phenomenon is but one example of the fact that high school students who study music tend to be more successful. They score consistently better on college aptitude tests and other measurement tests, and they generally participate more in school activities. For example, in 1989 the Scholastic Aptitude Test (SAT) verbal scores for students who participated in music performance averaged 446, while the verbal scores for students who did not participate in the arts averaged 408 (*Data on Music Education*, 1990, p. 60). In math the comparable scores were 491 for students who studied performance and 467 for students who did not study any art.

Doesn't the fact that music students achieve higher scores on aptitude tests and are generally more successful in school (and therefore presumably in life) *prove* that music study is good for students? The answer is both yes and no. Yes, music is good for all people. But, no, that doesn't mean that it *causes* students to be smarter in school or more successful in other ways. The question is: "Do able students gravitate toward music, or does music cause them to become more able students?" The first part of the question is easier to answer than the second. Able students are often attracted to music. The second half of the question is less certain. What in fact appears to happen is that some students get a "cycle of success" going in which already able and alert students become involved in music. In turn, involvement in music helps them to become even more able and successful. Regardless of whether this cycle of success is the result of attitude or ability or hard work or something else, it seems like one accomplishment by a student fuels another achievement, which in turn fuels another, and so on. Music is one component of that cycle for many, if not most, successful high school students.

Naturally, music educators want to build the strongest possible case for including music in the schools. However, their enthusiasm for claiming nonmusical values should be tempered by three facts:

1. The research evidence supporting most such claims is lacking, with the possible exception of some benefits in language arts and attitudes of students toward school in general.

2. Many curricular and extracurricular areas can better provide a particular benefit. For example, music can contribute to teamwork, but so can playing basketball; music can contribute to making better citizens, but courses in government and related topics normally do a better job in that particular area.

3. Making claims for nonmusical benefits can divert attention away from the fact that music is worth studying regardless of any nonmusical benefits. Biology teachers, for example, do not claim that they teach something greater than a knowledge of biology and science, and music does not need to make such claims either. In fact, unsupportable claims about the nonmusical values of music tend to make music educators appear illogical or uncertain in the eyes of other educators and the public. In the end, such claims may hurt music's status in the schools more than they help.

AVOCATIONAL VALUE. The avocational value of music does not manifest itself until after the students have graduated from high school. While average life expectancy has been increasing, the average workweek has been decreasing. These facts indicate that more time for leisure is available. Music is an important avocational activity in many countries, including America. One list of community orchestras contains over 1,600 entries (American Symphony Orchestra League, 1992), and there are thousands of church choirs and other amateur choral groups. An enormous number of people listen to music, which makes some training in listening an important aspect of music education.

Fortunately, music can be both an art filled with aesthetic rewards *and at the same time*, a contributor to some nonmusical outcomes. The place of music in the schools does not depend on its nonmusical contributions, but its position may be stronger because of some of them.

Clearly, there is more to teaching music than singing or playing through a number of pieces. Questions about the quality and purpose of music are as basic as the nature of life itself, which should be reassuring to music educators. That fact, however, carries with it a number of implications and obligations regarding why music is taught in the schools and how it should be taught. It is in the music classroom where the benefits of synthesizing insights from philosophy and aesthetics are realized. With such understandings teachers can be more confident that what they are teaching has a solid rationale and that their teaching is as effective as possible.

Summary

The chapter opened with a fundamental proposition: Living is more than biological existence. Art and music are manifestations of humanity's fundamental need for more than mere existence, and they represent a desire to achieve and create. This view is supported by the interest people have shown in the arts throughout the ages and in America today.

The question of why people value the arts and listen to music is not easy to answer. Several different views or theories have been offered from time to time to explain this interest. These viewpoints are summarized in table 3.1.

There appear to be reasons for listening to music in addition to those presented in the three viewpoints. Sometimes people simply enjoy the sensuous qualities of music, while at other times they are fascinated by a composer's skill in handling the musical material. Sometimes they are physically or mentally tired, and at other times they just want to hear something different. It appears that no one explanation can account fully for why people listen to music.

The word "aesthetic" is often found in writings on music education. An aesthetic experience has all of the following characteristics:

1. Possesses no practical or utilitarian purpose; it is an end in itself.

2. Involves feelings; there is a reaction to what is heard or seen.

3. Involves intellect; the mind consciously contemplates an object.

4. Focuses or centers attention on an object.

TABLE 3.1
Comparison of Three Viewpoints on Listening to Music

	REFERENTIALISM	EXPRESSIONISM	FORMALISM
Viewpoint	Value of music is in its nonmusical references to ideas, events, or objects.	Music expresses generalized and unidentifiable states of feeling.	Artworks should be considered for their inherent properties without reference to any other matters.
Implications for teaching	Teach students the correct association between musical stimulus and non-musical referent.	Teach students to become more sensitive and responsive to the ebb and flow and similar aspects of music.	Teach students to become more aware of the formal qualities in music—melody, form, timbre, harmony, etc.
Strengths	Useful for associating text and music in vocal music and for very programmatic works.	Encourages listener to be responsive to music, which makes it more meaningful and enjoyable.	Concentrates listener's attention on the musical properties found in a work.
Weaknesses	"Message" is largely guesswork in instrumental works; search for it distracts listener from musical qualities.	Whether music can refer to anything beyond itself is debatable; existence of unidentified states of feeling can be questioned.	Whether people can segment feeling and intellect is debatable; sole attention to formal properties encourages listener to ignore effect of music on feelings.

5. Is experienced; no one can successfully tell another about an aesthetic experience.

6. Makes life fuller and more meaningful.

The quality of an aesthetic experience depends on both the object and the observer. The object needs to possess qualities that encourage contemplation, and the person considering the object must be perceptive of and "opened up" to these qualities. Such experiences have no limits with regard to age, race, or sex. Previous experience and education in the arts may make a difference, however.

An aesthetic mode of thinking is one that considers overall attributes such as variety, unity, and the like. This mode of thought contrasts with the usual logical and factual approach found in other areas of the school curriculum. Both the logical and aesthetic aspects of life are valuable and desirable.

Although everyone seems to favor "good" music, there is little agreement about what constitutes a good work of music. To date, no one has been able to come up with a set of technical standards; at best only general statements are possible. This situation has encouraged some people to conclude that all music is equally good. This conclusion is as hard to defend as the idea that a precise set of criteria can be stated.

The approach of Meyer, supported by Berlyne's research, appears to be the best one yet devised for evaluating works in a similar style. In his view listeners have a sense of what they expect to happen in a musical work. The composer then writes music that follows the expected pattern, but the successful composer includes some deviations and delays in fulfilling the listeners' expectations. The theory is that people value music more that does not progress exactly as anticipated.

Music teachers can encourage the development of aesthetic sensitivity in their students by pointing out the qualities in the music, not allowing for a concern for technical correctness to obscure the aesthetic qualities, relating information about music to the sounds in a musical work, using music of quality, and concentrating on the objective aspects listeners might notice.

The nature and extent of the nonmusical benefits of music study is a complex matter. Although such reasons have traditionally been offered to justify including music in school curricula, the validity of such claims is doubtful. Music appears to correlate positively with language skill and encourages better attitudes toward school. Activities involving music have been valuable to many students, including some who probably would have quit school had they not been in music.

Students who are involved in music score significantly higher on scholastic aptitude tests and other measurement tests, but it is impossible to know whether the abler students select music or music fosters achievement and aptitude. Music teachers should realize that research data supporting the idea of sizable amounts of transfer value resulting from music study are very limited, that usually other subjects are more logical choices to promote particular nonmusical goals, and that the place of music in school curricula does not depend on its nonmusical benefits.

STUDY AND DISCUSSION QUESTIONS

1. What do music and the other fine arts have to do with making people more human?

2. Suppose you had to defend the idea that people value music and the other fine arts. What kinds of evidence could you provide?

3. Which position regarding the values of listening to music is represented by each of the following statements? Be prepared to offer reasons for your choice of position.

   (a) "This musical work stands by itself without being contaminated by worldly matters."

   (b) "In this fugue one can sense the majesty of a great cathedral."

   (c) "A musical work arouses within each person feelings that are too deep and complex to be put in words."

4. Are there reasons other than those proposed by the referentialists, expressionists, and formalists for listening to music? If so, what are those other reasons?

5. What are the characteristics of an aesthetic experience? Which of these characteristics is not true of ordinary, everyday experiences such as mowing a lawn or riding a bicycle?

6. Are the words "aesthetic" and "beautiful" synonymous? Why or why not?

7. How does the "aesthetic mode" of thought differ from the mode of thought used in most academic areas? Is the aesthetic mode superior or inferior to that found in most of the other areas of education?

8. On what basis does Meyer suggest that the evaluation of musical works in a similar style be made? According to his thinking, what quality or qualities indicate greater significance and value in works of music?

9. How likely is it that the following actions of music teachers will increase students' awareness of the aesthetic properties in music? Be prepared to defend your answers.

   (a) Working with the students to achieve a "note perfect" rendition of a song.

   (b) Helping the string players decide which bowing will contribute most to the phrasing of the music.

   (c) Asking the students to write a short paper on the key schemes found in the first movements of Beethoven's thirty-two piano sonatas.

   (d) Asking the students to describe how they feel about the first movement of Schubert's *Unfinished* Symphony.

10. Can a convincing case for music instruction in the schools be built on its transfer benefits to other subjects? Does a good program of study in the arts improve the attitudes of students toward school?

INDIVIDUAL OR CLASS ACTIVITIES

1. Select any piece of music you wish—vocal or instrumental, long or short, old or new. Decide what a teacher could do to make the students more aware of its aesthetic qualities. Be specific about the places in the music that you would point out. Be sure not to list historical or theoretical features; cite only aesthetic ones.

2. Listen to two short works (or portions of larger works) by the same composer or different composers writing in the same style—perhaps the final movement of two Mozart piano sonatas. One of the works should be one that is performed rather often and apparently highly regarded by musicians; the other should be largely ignored by musicians today, presumably because it is not of equivalent quality. Keeping in mind the points made by Meyer regarding musical value, give reasons why the more frequently performed work appears to be of greater value than the other one.

REFERENCES

AMERICAN SYMPHONY ORCHESTRA LEAGUE. (1992). Washington, DC.

BARTLETT, J. (1968). *Familiar quotations* (14th ed.). Boston: Little, Brown.

BEARDSLEY, M. C. (1977). *Aesthetics.* New York: Harcourt Brace Jovanovich.

BEGLARIAN, G. (1971). In *Comprehensive musicianship: An anthology of evolving thought.* Reston, VA: Music Educators National Conference.

BERLYNE, D. E. (1974). *Studies in the new experimental aesthetics.* Washington, DC: Hemisphere Publishing.

BIRGE, E. B. (1966). *The history of public school music in the United States.* Reston, VA: Music Educators National Conference.

COOKE, D. (1959). *The language of music.* London: Oxford University Press.

COPLAND, A. (1957). *What to listen for in music.* New York: McGraw-Hill.

DATA ON MUSIC EDUCATION. (1990). Reston, VA: Music Educators National Conference.

DEWEY, J. (1934). *Art as experience.* New York: G. P. Putnam's Sons.

DU NOÜY, L. (1947). *Human destiny.* New York: New American Library.

DYKEMA, P., & GEHRKENS, K. (1941). *The teaching and administration of high school music.* Evanston, IL: Summy-Birchard.

EDMAN, I. (1939). *Arts and the man.* New York: New American Library.

FINCK, H. T. (1917). *Richard Strauss: The man and his music.* Boston: Little, Brown.

GRAHAM, R. M. (Comp.). (1975). *Music for the exceptional child.* Reston, VA: Music Educators National Conference.

GROWING UP COMPLETE: THE IMPERATIVE FOR MUSIC EDUCATION. (1991). Reston, VA: Music Educators National Conference.

HANSLICK, E. (1957). *The beautiful in music* (G. Cohen, Trans.). Indianapolis: The Liberal Arts Press.

LANGER, S. K. (1942). *Philosophy in a new key.* Cambridge, MA: Harvard University Press.

LANGER, S. K. (1953). *Feeling and form.* New York: Scribner's.

MALM, W. P. (1982). Personal communication.

MAZE, M. M., et al. (1967). *A study of correlations between musicality and reading achievement at the first-grade level in Athens, Georgia.* Unpublished doctoral dissertation, University of Georgia.

MEYER, L. B. (1956). *Emotion and meaning in music.* Chicago: University of Chicago Press.

MEYER, L. B. (1967). *Music, the arts, and ideas.* Chicago: University of Chicago Press.

MOSES, H. E. (1971). Relevance starts with human involvement. *Music Educators Journal, 58* (1), 25.

MOVESIAN, E. A. (1967). *The influence of teaching music reading skills on the development of basic reading skills in the primary grades.* Unpublished doctoral dissertation, University of Southern California.

REIMER, B. (1989). *A philosophy of music education* (2d ed.). Englewood Cliffs, NJ: Prentice-Hall.

RODOSKY, R. (1974). *Arts IMPACT final evaluation report.* Columbus, OH: Columbus Public Schools.

THE ROLE OF THE FINE AND PERFORMING ARTS IN HIGH SCHOOL DROPOUT PREVENTION. (1990). Tallahassee: Florida Department of Education.

SOUNDPOST. (1989). 6(1).

WOLFF, K. I. (1978). The nonmusical outcomes of music education: a review of the literature. *Council for Research in Music Education Bulletin, 55* (Summer), 19.

CHAPTER 4 _____

The Role and Purpose of Music in American Education

CHAPTER 2 provided information about what each of the three philosophical viewpoints (rationalism, empiricism, pragmatism) considers to be the role of schools and education. This chapter examines broad reasons, which are partially derived from the philosophical views, for the establishment and maintenance of education systems and their impact on music education. Although each philosophical viewpoint contributes something to these reasons, the empiricist position is utilized in music more than the others.

The Role of Education

Why does the United States and virtually every other country in the world need a system of schools? A short, quick answer could be: "Because they can't function without it." Every nation seeking to move beyond the primitive, tribal level has discovered that it was necessary to establish an educational system. In spite of the fact that schools cost a great deal of money, occupy a considerable amount of children's time, and have not always been effective and efficient, nations have been unable to devise any other way to fulfill the school's function.

Society's commitment to education is by no means halfhearted. In the United States children are required by law to attend school from the age of six to the age of sixteen or seventeen, and teachers cannot teach without a license indicating that they have had a certain amount and type of training. In fact, "the federal budget for education represents 2 percent of the total budget" (Dillon, 1981, p. 15). (Recent figures have suggested that the budget for education may be even as high as 7 percent.)

Minimum Competencies

The short, quick answer that society is unable to get along without schools is not really satisfactory. It merely raises the same challenging basic question in slightly different words: "*Why* can't it get along without schools?" Well, why? One major reason is the need to educate the younger generation to be able to function in society when they become adults. People need a minimum amount of skill in reading and writing, as well as need to understand how the culture and society function. Furthermore, individuals need to develop some occupational competency. These thoughts are central in countless documents and writings on education. They are described in a wide variety of ways, but the basic underlying commitment is similar: People need to be competent to live in society.

Then why are schools needed to teach the basic competencies? In simpler times and societies the learning of the essentials of life took place in the family or tribe, but as civilization became more complex very few parents had sufficient knowledge, skill, or time to conduct an adequate educational effort for their children. In Western civilization the time has long since passed when the family, except for a very few exceptional parents, could even think about undertaking the education of their children. Skills and knowledge as difficult and diverse as playing the violin, neurosurgery, interpreting tax laws, repairing an automatic transmission on an automobile, or managing a stock feeding farm can rarely be learned within the family. In brief, no institution other than the school has been found that can or will assume the task of providing future citizens with the necessary skills and knowledge.

Usually complex occupational skills cannot be taught in the family or tribal setting; similarly, music cannot be adequately taught in most family situations. Few contemporary American parents have sufficient musical training to be able to help their children much in the study of music. In addition, the help that families provide is limited in terms of the type of music taught. For example, it is fine for a family to learn and sing religious songs together, but such songs represent only a tiny portion of the world of music. Other songs will probably seldom be performed, and besides, the experience would be limited to a small vocal ensemble. A few exceptional families do form small ensembles, but clearly the large ensemble in a family setting is out of the question. It is only the school that can provide the variety and organization required for an adequate education in music. (Incidentally, even in the Suzuki movement, in which parents play an important role, they are taught along with the children.)

The role of education in providing the basic knowledge and competencies to live in society can draw support from the three philosophical viewpoints. Empiricists consider meeting perceived needs to be the heart of their philosophy. Pragmatists are satisfied that the need for a system of education has been demonstrated. Rationalists believe that the high goals of the school can be met only by highly competent and trained teachers.

A Cohesive Society

A second major role of education is the formation of a cohesive society. If a nation or society is going to function well, it needs to be somewhat unified in a democratic way. Not only must it avoid internal strife, but it needs a common language and culture.* The function of language can hardly be overemphasized. Nations with major language differences within their populations—and there are many of them around the world—find the divisions caused by multiple languages to be a serious debilitating factor. The French-English conflict in a country as sophisticated as Canada is a good example of this point. Another example is the conflicts that occurred when the Soviet Union, an organization of countries with different languages and cultures, was disbanded. A more recent illustration of this point would be what has occurred in Yugoslavia.

Given the above examples, it is not surprising that the teaching of a common language and culture is seen as one of the important functions of schools. The need for a common language for the amalgamation of society is well illustrated by the immigrant groups that came to America at the turn of the century from non-English-speaking countries. Many immigrant families would not permit their children to speak the old foreign tongue. Their social halls in the cities had signs posted that read "No Italian spoken here" (or whatever their language had been). These immigrants understood that to become a competent American citizen one had to learn the English language and American culture while preserving one's own heritage. Diversity in a democracy is desirable; it is a source of strength. Educated citizens should possess some ability in more than one language, and many are taught in our schools. The only implication in the reference to a "common language" is that there needs to be a single language of communication that is basic for all citizens.

---

*"Avoid" as used here does not imply suppressing disagreement.

As an important part of culture, music has a role to play in the formation of a cohesive society. It is true that people can get along in a country without knowing anything about its music. However, they will get along *significantly better* if they know about that culture's music; they will be a little better acculturated and a little more a part of the world in which they live. It is true, however, that America is a pluralistic society with a number of subcultures, and the variety of subcultures presents music educators with a special challenge.

Learning from the Past

A third function of school systems is to pass on to the younger generations the culture and learning of the past. The goal is not so much that the past be revered as it is that each generation profit from the experiences of its predecessors. Each generation should not need to rediscover the multiplication table, the typewriter, Mozart's music, the tape recorder, civil and criminal laws, vaccines, nineteenth-century English novels and poetry, and all the other countless accomplishments that have occurred over thousands of years. It is clear that if each generation had to rediscover everything for itself, there would not be very much progress; time would run out long before that generation achieved most of civilization's previous accomplishments.

The reasons for retaining the utilitarian accomplishments of civilization are easy to understand. Virtually everyone realizes that the human race would suffer if it lost the knowledge of anesthesia, the concept of mass production, electricity, and so on. The reasons for retaining culture, with its paintings, buildings, music, books, and dances may not be quite so obvious. However, there is much to learn from the past in cultural matters; that is one reason for retaining such things. Musicians would be set back if we lost, for example, the knowledge of acoustics and equal temperament, and techniques for varying a theme and creating forms, just as painters would be hurt by losing the knowledge of how perspective has been treated and how colors have been achieved and handled.

There is also a need to preserve past accomplishments because they demonstrate human ingenuity and diversity, and provide insight into past mores. We want to know about and admire those persons from the past who demonstrated extraordinary skill in and devotion to their art: the Beethovens, Michelangelos, Rembrandts, Frank Lloyd Wrights, and others. There is much satisfaction in viewing their artistic works as well as realizing the accomplishments they achieved within the limitations of their period.

Rationalists and empiricists probably applaud this goal of education more loudly than pragmatists—who don't strongly believe in looking back.

A Richer Life

The fourth function of schools is one that empiricists would applaud along with the other philosophers. It is to make life as rich and full as possible for each student. In a democratic society such as exists in the United States, the state's function is to "promote the general welfare" of its citizens, to quote a phrase from the Preamble to the Constitution. This simple principle is the antithesis of totalitarian systems, in which the citizens exist to serve the state. Sometimes the analogy to a flower is used to make this point. In a democracy, the roots and stem (the state) exist so that the flowers (the citizens) may flourish, whereas in totalitarian societies the leaves and flowers exist to benefit the stem and the roots. Schools in democratic societies seek to have their students "flourish"; that is, to develop to the fullest extent that their potential and abilities permit. Schools in a democratic society do not just train youngsters to become bricklayers, dentists, pianists, or draftsmen. They seek to educate well-rounded persons who can function happily and successfully in society *and* who have among their occupations bricklaying, dentistry, playing the piano, and drafting. Which point of view is chosen makes a monumental difference in the way in which society and schools function!

The implications of a broader vision of education are important, especially for music education. This view says that the schools should think in terms of how much they can reasonably do for each child, and not be satisfied with only the attainment of some rudimentary skills. An education confined to the "three R's" is analogous to buying an automobile with only an engine, frame, seats, and wheels. It is only the bare minimum, whether it be a car or an education. More is needed if life is to be enriched.

The belief that schools should be more than a training ground for the rudimentary needs of life has strong support among educators and school administrators, and also among the public, *providing that the basic skills areas are also taught satisfactorily.* An example of support from school administrators is the resolutions made by the American Association of School Administrators (AASA). On three occasions it has gone on record in support of music and the other arts as necessary in the school curriculum. The first time was more than sixty-five years ago, in 1927. Another statement was adopted in 1959. A portion of it reads:

> We believe in a well-balanced school curriculum in which music, drama, painting, poetry, sculpture, architecture, and the like are included side by side with other important subjects such as mathematics, history, and science. It is important that pupils, as a part of general education, learn to appreciate, to understand, to create, and to criticize with discrimination those products of the mind, the voice, the hand, and the body which give dignity to the person and exalt the spirit of man. (AASA, 1959, pp. 248–49)

A third statement of support for the arts was adopted on February 25, 1973, by the AASA at its annual business meeting in Atlantic City:

> As school budgets today come under extreme fiscal pressures, trimming or eliminating so-called "peripheral" subject areas from the curriculum appears often to be a financially attractive economy.
>
> The American Association of School Administrators believes that a well-rounded, well-balanced curriculum is essential in the education of American children. We believe that deleting entire subject areas which have value in the total life experience of the individual is shortsighted.
>
> Therefore, AASA recommends that school administrators declare themselves in favor of maintaining a full balanced curriculum at all grade levels, opposing any categorical cuts in the school program. ("Curriculum Balance," 1973, p. 1)

State educational agencies—of Utah, Washington, South Carolina, Florida, and Pennsylvania, to name a few that have done so in recent years—have also expressed strong support of the arts in the schools.

Much has been written in the past few decades about nurturing the uniqueness of the child. Many terms have been employed to verbalize this idea: "self-actualization" and "creative environment" among others. Essentially, such thinkers are saying that an attempt should be made to encourage each child to explore, express, and experiment so that he or she can develop potential abilities to the fullest extent. Certainly, the artistic, aesthetic area is one in which children should be given a chance to test their aptitudes and explore their interests. Music, art, and drama are uniquely suited to allowing for creative expression. When and where music and the other arts are omitted from the curriculum, the children are being deprived—"cheated" may be a better word for it—of a valuable and significant part of an education for living today and in the twenty-first century. Perhaps the American patriot and second president of the United States, John Adams, summarized best the value of the arts in a letter he wrote to his wife, Abigail, during the Revolutionary War: "I must study politics and war, that my sons may have liberty to study mathematics and philosophy, geography, natural history and naval architecture, in order to give their children a right to study painting, poetry, music, architecture, statuary, tapestry, and porcelain" (Adams, 1841).

Music Learning

Music as a discipline involves the three traditional domains of learning: the cognitive, the affective, and the psychomotor (see chapter 9). However, a fourth domain or component of the other three that should be included in educational thought is what could be referred to as the "aesthetic domain." It is an area in which music—in fact all the arts—makes unique contributions to the development of the whole being. It is a domain too often ignored when discussed in educational circles and yet it is a facet of learning that offers much insight into humanistic concepts and has a salutary effect on decisions involving the affective domain. Aesthetic sensitivity contributes to that area of human growth and development that assists in achieving perception of and insight into human feeling and human emotion. Furthermore, it is aesthetic judgment that contributes to one's sense of values in arriving at conclusions that affect a personal life-style and mode of existence. If there is agreement with the above, and then if aesthetics is to be meaningful in an individual's life, the prime aim of music education should be the development of aesthetic judgment and aesthetic value.

Once music became formalized in a social institution such as the schools, it then became necessary to provide a forum where music educators could interact and exchange ideas that would ultimately provide direction and standards for the profession. Thus, MENC evolved (see chapter 1) and became the organization that spoke for the profession. It is therefore appropriate that in discussing aesthetic sensitivity readers should examine the conference's 1970 statement, *Goals and Objectives for Music Education*, to find direction toward achieving this laudable objective of aesthetic awareness. In this document the organization states that "MENC shall conduct programs and activities to build: a vital musical culture [and] an enlightened musical public." These broad aims—"a vital musical culture" and "an enlightened musical public"—may also serve as specific aims for the individual teacher. If one can develop a commitment to artistic values and an aesthetic sense in each individual, then one can realize an enlightened society that will serve a musical culture, which in turn will grow and expand until it becomes vital in the life of all its citizens.

In order to achieve its stated aims MENC has identified four professional goals for developing its programs. They are:

1. Comprehensive music programs in all schools.

2. Involvement of persons of all ages in learning music.

3. Quality preparation of teachers.

4. Use of the most effective techniques and resources in music education.

The Role of Music Education

When all is said and done, the fundamental reason for music teachers in the schools is to educate students in music. That seems simple and straightforward, and in a way it is. However, defining the phrase "educating students in music" in terms of what teachers teach and what students learn is a more complex matter.

First, let's examine what students should learn in music. In 1965 a MENC committee offered a general proposal of what all students should know by the time they completed high school. The committee's efforts resulted in the book *Music in General Education*. In spite of its age and somewhat dated language, its list of goals for music in the schools has proven to be remarkably durable; it is still well worth considering. The eleven desired "musical outcomes" for an individual are stated by the conference as follows:

SKILLS

    I. He will have skill in listening to music. . . .

    II. He will be able to sing. . . .

    III. He will be able to express himself on a musical instrument. . . .

    IV. He will be able to interpret musical notation. . . .

    UNDERSTANDINGS

    V. He will understand the importance of design in music. . . .

    VI. He will relate music to man's historical development. . . .

    VII. He will understand the relationships existing between music and other areas of human endeavor. . . .

VIII. He will understand the place of music in contemporary society. . . .

    ATTITUDES

    IX. He will value music as a means of self-expression. . . .

    X. He will desire to continue his musical experiences. . . .

    XI. He will discriminate with respect to music. . . . (Ernst and Gary, 1965, pp. 4–8). . . .

In 1986 MENC published a revision of *The School Music Program: Description and Standards*. It contains a list of goals that bear a great many similarities to the 1965 list. These goals are still very much alive in the 1993 draft version of the curriculum and assessment standards being developed by MENC under a grant from the National Endowment for the Arts and the U.S. Department of Education. They are:

    1. Ability to make music, alone and with others.

    2. Ability to improvise and create music.

    3. Ability to use the vocabulary and notation of music.

4. Ability to respond to music aesthetically, intellectually, and emotionally.

5. Acquaintance with a wide variety of music, including diverse musical styles and genres.

6. Understanding of the role music has played and continues to play in the lives of human beings.

7. Ability to make aesthetic judgements based on critical listening and analysis.

8. Development of a commitment to music.

9. Support of the musical life of the community and desire to encourage others to do so.

10. Ability to continue musical learning independently. (*The School Music Program: Description and Standards*, 1986, pp. 13–14)

Essentially, the members of the profession must never lose sight of the fact that the school music program is primarily for young people who are in the process of advancing through life. Aims and objectives must therefore focus on the impact they will have on the lives of these students.

It is a false premise to presume that all "music is a universal language." There is too much music from diverse cultures that does not communicate with the established culture. It is, however, correct to conclude that music is a universal form of expression, and that the common bond that enables all persons to cross the barriers created by cultural differences develops through aesthetic growth and aesthetic sensitivity. To achieve this growth and development it is essential that the emphasis in music be focused on auditory discrimination and auditory analysis, not merely musical gymnastics or music organizations. Music is sound, and the utilization of sound is the unique quality that separates music from other art forms.

Individual Benefits Derived Through Music

Every individual requires a form of self-expression. Music meets this need through sound. A performance in music can be expressed on an individual basis, as in solo performance, or it can be expressed through a collective, as in an ensemble. It can be restricted to the confines of one's home or shared in the expanse of a concert hall. It knows no limitations other than one's talent or interest. To deny children the opportunity to express themselves through music is to deny them an important facet of self-expression. Furthermore, as pointed out earlier in this chapter, music is a form of self-expression that requires instruction and guidance if it is to achieve its maximum development. It should not be left to chance, but should be channeled into forms of expression that satisfy each individual's needs.

Another by-product identified with music instruction is what can be referred to as "the discipline of achievement." There is talent in every child; the distinction lies with degrees. It is these varying degrees that separate one individual's musicality from another's. Every child, however, is entitled to the opportunity to develop his or her talent regardless of that degree. It is within the process of developing this talent that one acquires the discipline necessary to realize its growth and fruition. It is true that there are examples of individuals with "natural talent" who have succeeded with little formal training. These individuals, however, are the exceptions, and one cannot help but reflect on how much further they might have developed and how much more they might have achieved musically with some appropriate guidance. There can be no question that even these "naturally talented" individuals worked diligently and were committed to their art in achieving their success. Regardless of one's talent, it cannot be realized in music without effort and application. Herein lies the concept of establishing a discipline and applying effort if one is to realize one's inner latent talent.

Special Issues in Music Education

Several matters appear to affect music education in a different way and to a greater degree than other areas of the school curriculum. Teachers of mathematics, for example, are not affected by calls for "multicultural mathematics," and biology teachers are not involved in presenting "bioformances" around the community. These matters are discussed here without implications regarding order of importance.

MUSIC INSTRUCTION FOR ALL STUDENTS. In 1837 a special committee of the School Committee in Boston reported favorably on Lowell Mason's proposal to include music instruction in the schools. One of the concluding sentences of this report carries this stirring challenge:

> From this place first went out the great principle, that the property of all should be taxed for the education of all. From this place, also, may the example, in this country, first go forth of that education rendered more complete by the introduction by public authority, of vocal music into our system of popular instruction. (Birge, 1966, p. 47)

It is easy to forget more than 150 years later that the idea of education for all students, and subordinately education in music for all students, was revolutionary in the 1820s and 1830s. It is also easy to overlook the fact that it is an idea that still requires the efforts of music educators today. "Music for every child; every child for music" was adopted by MENC about seventy years ago, yet it is far from being achieved. Only twenty years ago it was interpreted to include students in special education programs; even today the nature of many school programs does not encourage minority students or students from low-income families to elect to take music in the secondary schools.

Was Lowell Mason right in his belief that everyone should be educated in music? Does this idea include even students with limited talent and interest? Does it mean a mediocre education in music, especially for the students who are talented and interested? Music educators should be able to answer these and similar questions.

First of all, Mason was right on two counts: (1) all students deserve an education in music and should not be deprived of this aspect of life; and (2) if America is to enjoy a vital culture that includes music, people need to be educated in music. To use a metaphor from the world of gardening, an informed population is the soil in which music can flower.

The matter of talent is misunderstood by most people. Nearly everyone has *some* talent for music. It is the degree of talent that varies. Most people can be taught to sing songs and play simple instruments, as well as to listen somewhat perceptively to music. These skills can be learned by students in the schools.

The misunderstanding about music talent stems from the almost mystical aura that surrounds the topic, complete with its tales about people with perfect pitch and those who sit down at the piano and play pieces without ever having had a lesson. These talents are rare. (See chapter 7 for a more complete discussion of music talent.)

The purpose of music instruction in the schools is to educate all students in music, not to separate the more talented from the less talented. The goal of teaching music in the schools is not to have all graduates become members of the New York Philharmonic or the Robert Shaw Chorale! Music education has not "failed" if a student chooses not to continue in the high school choir or band, providing that he or she has had a worthwhile educational experience in music and has gained a basic education in the subject.

Does the call for music for all students suggest that school music must be a series of mediocre experiences? The answer is no, if music teachers and others do not confuse *equality of opportunity* with *identical experience* for all students. All students deserve a basic education in music, but not all students should be given the *same* education in music, it depends on the interests and abilities of each individual. Randy Mitchell may play trumpet well enough to march with the band, but not play at the level required for membership in a high-quality concert band. It would not be fair or good music education to diminish the concert band by including Randy and others like him who are unable to achieve at the appropriate level.

MUSIC AND THE FINE ARTS. Music enjoys much in common with the other fine arts. They all exist for the richness they provide to life; they all are expressive of deep human feelings. But are they a unit, an academic discipline? No, the differences among the arts are too great for that to be true. Artists deal with space, while musicians deal with time. Both manipulate their particular medium for artistic purposes, but their techniques and skills are vastly different. Courses in each art area must therefore also be different.

EDUCATION VS. ENTERTAINMENT. The fact that people enjoy performances by school music groups is both a boon and a bane for music education. Performances have a number of significant benefits. They give students an opportunity to perform before an audience. They build an awareness of and support for certain portions of the music program. Unfortunately, however, there is a downside to performances as they are currently used in some schools. The basic problem is that entertainment begins to dominate the curriculum, and the educational reasons for including music in the schools seem to become lost. In order to present the best possible performances, music teachers sometimes discourage the less able students from joining an instrumental or choral group, and work excessively on a limited number of pieces. They select music for its audience appeal instead of its educational value and devote most of their energies to the groups that perform publicly, to the detriment of classes that do not perform publicly.

The chief concern where this situation exists is to achieve some reasonable balance between performance and educating musically nonperforming classes. To that end, in 1986 the Standards Committee of MENC developed *Guidelines for Performances of School Music Groups: Expectations and Limitations.* This publication raises a number of issues related to performances and offers some guidelines for various types of performances.

DEVELOPING CULTURE. It is interesting to consider why certain educational artistic associations, including MENC, are awarded tax-exempt status by the Internal Revenue Service. It is not because they are nonprofit. Many other groups and businesses do not make a profit, but they are not eligible for such status. The answer is that in its wisdom, the United States government recognizes the contribution of such associations to the common good. And what is that contribution to common good? It lies in the affects these groups have on building and maintaining culture. Although busy music teachers seldom have time to think about their contribution to culture, the fact is that they are helping to build a better society.

The value of such a society was ably expressed by President John F. Kennedy when he articulated a vision of what he wanted America to become. "I look forward," he said, "to an America which will not be afraid of grace and beauty . . . an America which will reward achievement in the arts as we reward achievement in business or statecraft . . . I look forward to an America which commands respect throughout the world not only for its strength but for its civilization as well" (address, Amherst College, October 26, 1963). It's an awesome task, but one of the goals of music in the schools is to better the quality of American culture.

This fact presents music educators with both obligations and opportunities. It calls for teaching the best music in the best way to the most students possible. On the other hand, it means that music education is to be taken seriously. It is not a frill.

The National Commission on Music Education

The "educational reform" movement of the 1980s showed little concern for the arts in its deliberations. As a result the Music Educators National Conference, along with the National Association of Music Merchants and the National Academy of Recording Arts & Sciences, Inc., organized in 1990 a coalition of educators, performers, composers, retailers, manufacturers, technicians, and publishers to reverse this omission. This coalition was determined to restore educational balance to the reform effort of the 1980s by including the arts. It formed the National Commission on Music Education and held public forums in three cities: Los Angeles, Chicago, and Nashville. The function of these gatherings was to provide an opportunity to exchange ideas, gather information, and sample public opinion at both the local and national level. By that time, a nationally circulated petition had accumulated more than 150,000 signatures in support of this campaign.

At midpoint in this national effort a National Symposium was held in Washington, D.C., on March 6–7, 1990. It was designed to provide an opportunity to address and discuss many of the commission's concerns under the organizing concept "America's Culture at Risk." "The organizers also hoped to offer policy makers and leaders in the arts, business, and education the opportunity to discuss how music and the other arts could make a major contribution to the solution of today's problems in education and society" (National Commission on Music Education, 1991, p. xii).

The message disseminated by the Commission was that "Just as there can be no music without learning, no education is complete without music" (The National Commission on Music Education, 1991, xiii). The Commission's final report, *Growing Up Complete: The Imperative for Music Education*, was presented to members of Congress and the Bush administration. It was "distributed in organizations, major corporations, advocacy groups, and individuals committed to the basic role of music and the other arts in education" (National Commission on Music Education, 1991, xii). The major focus of this document was that music is a part of *basic* education, and it contained specific recommendations designed to make music education an integral part of a child's learning. (As early as 1978 MENC President Klotman selected as the theme for the in-service conference in Chicago "Music is Basic Education.")

Administration and Supervision: Its Function

It is not enough merely to identify aims and objectives in music education. Actually, this is only the initial phase in an ongoing process. If these aims are to be realized, programs need to be implemented and organized with specific objectives that will assure the pursuit and realization of these overall goals. Furthermore, not only do programs and processes need to be established, they also need to be monitored and evaluated to be certain that they are following the appropriate direction. All of these activities require direction and guidance from an assigned person acting in the role of music administrator. It then becomes the major responsibility of that individual to provide the essential musical and educational leadership that can move the program toward its designated goals and objectives. Furthermore, an administrator who is responsible for the music education of large numbers of students needs to have a clearly defined philosophy on which all the music activities will be based. It is this combination—a sense of leadership responsibility guided by a well-thought-out philosophical position—that enables a music administrator to lead the program.

This concept of leadership does not imply that the administrator is the only person responsible for working toward established goals. Everyone in the profession regardless of his or her position should assume a degree of responsibility for achieving the goals identified both by the profession and individual school faculties. What is implied is that the responsibility in a school system for leadership in directing programs toward these goals and aims rests with the administration. It is the chief music administrator who tries to arrange for the necessary conditions that will motivate individuals or groups to overcome any obstacles that might interfere with the realization of the objectives.

Leadership is easy to talk about but difficult to achieve. One must keep in mind that change, and particularly a change of direction, occurs only through changing the behavior of individuals. Many factors are involved in changing peoples' actions and attitudes. There are values, perceptions, understandings of roles, and development or redirection of basic skills. To bring about effective change, teachers must alter one or more of these factors. The responsibility for serving as the catalyst belongs to the administrator—if not directly, at least indirectly.

Priorities need to be determined in relation to their effect on learning and achieving stated goals. Priorities are essential if the administrator is to utilize time and conditions most efficiently. The ability of music administrators to be effective in this role of being catalysts for change is based on how they perceive themselves as leaders in music, both in the school system and the community.

In the final analysis, school music administrators should evaluate their effectiveness in terms of how well the music program has achieved its goals. These goals should have been predetermined through studying needs in consultation with the school, community, and staff members.

True leadership releases the energies and capabilities of the staff members; it does not inhibit and restrict them to petty tasks or limited goals. Too often staff and faculty have been restricted by administrators who are far more preoccupied with their own ego than with progress in the program. Such individuals seek the limelight and not only fail to give appropriate recognition for work done, but also discourage creative activities of others for fear of losing their image as leaders. Fortunately this type of individual represents a small minority of administrators in the music education profession.

Music administrators should focus on the quality of programs rather than the quantity of offerings. Numbers have only limited value. They are important in terms of numbers of students being reached and whether or not expenditures are justified on a cost-per-pupil basis. However, what is even more significant is when the program is shown to have considerable impact on the aesthetic values of the student body and the artistic vitality of the community as a whole.

Funding

A major restriction imposed upon schools is the limitation of funds. Everyone in this nation is interested in improved schools; no one objects to better curricula and expanded experiences. However, the funds available for such educational endeavors are almost always in short supply. The challenge of administration is to determine how they can be utilized most expeditiously to provide the country's young people with the necessary education.

The chief source of funds for the local school system is local taxes. These are the heart of the community's financial base and have direct impact on the school offerings in that community. The second source of income is the state, and in some cases the local tax rate depends on the state formula. A third source of revenue available to boards of education is the federal government. Although funding is still uneven, in recent years the government has assumed a much greater role because of attempts in legislation to equalize education throughout the United States. The amount of such support has varied with the different presidential administrations, but the basic concept continues. Thus, we see that there are three governments responsible for providing the necessary income to maintain schools in our country—local, state, and federal. How this money is actually spent is determined by the local board of education. It is true that sometimes guidelines are attached to funds coming from the state and federal government, but it is the responsibility of the local board of education to see that these guidelines are followed, or that, if they are not, the funds are returned to their source.

Other sources for funding such as foundations, individual contributions, and even local businesses also exist. However, no board of education can build a budget on these extra sources unless the money has already been allocated and given to the local board for distribution. These funds represent a supplementary resource that cannot be considered basic to structuring an annual school budget.

A Rationale for Music in the Schools

In its *The School Music Program: Description and Standards* (1st ed., 1974), MENC offers the following rationale for music in the schools:

> Anthropologists have found no society anywhere that functions without music. In every culture music plays a role not only in the rituals of society but also in the personal lives of its citizens. Modern technological advances and mass communication media have brought music to a position of prominence and made it readily accessible to an eager audience of a magnitude undreamed of only a few decades ago. (p. 3)

This accessibility has made it imperative that educational guidance be given the young to assist them in formulating judgments regarding the use and quality of music. Music serves many functions, and only through education can a perspective be developed that enables one to assess music that is heard under a variety of situations and conditions.

In the second edition of *The School Music Program: Description and Standards* (1986), the Music Educators National Conference expanded its rationale for music in the schools to include the following:

1. Music as an art form requiring a special knowledge and distinct skills is a part of a desirable education for every individual.

2. Transmitting our cultural heritage has long been a basic objective of education.

3. The schools have an obligation to assist each student in realizing his or her musical potential.

4. Music provides a means for self-expression and expressing one's creative ability.

5. Through the study of music, students are better able to comprehend the nature of humankind.

6. Through music, students who may have difficulty in other areas of the curriculum can find success.

7. Music study can "sharpen one's sensitivity, raise one's level of appreciation, and expand one's musical horizons" (p. 13). As student's appreciation and understanding mature, they are able to deal with more sophisticated and complex forms of music.

8. Music is a form of communication. It possesses a symbol system that is most powerful and profound.

9. The study of music teaches young people that there are areas that can be dealt with subjectively. Not every aspect of life can be quantified.

10. Music enhances the quality of life; "it exalts the human spirit" (p. 13).

Summary

All members of a society, if they are to be successful, contributing members of their community, require a minimum amount of skill in reading and writing, as well as an understanding of how the culture and society function. Life today has become so complex that only schools have the capabilities of providing future citizens with the necessary skills and knowledge.

The role of education in providing the basic knowledge and competencies to live in society can draw support from three philosophical schools. Empiricists consider meeting perceived needs to be the essence of their philosophy. Pragmatists are satisfied that the need for a system of education has been demonstrated. Rationalists believe that the high goals of the school can be met only by highly trained, competent teachers.

It is important that music be a part of one's education. Not only does it serve to unify the individual with contemporary culture, but it also gives insight into the cultural practices of the past. Furthermore, it enriches life and helps bring beauty into the daily existence of the individual.

Music as a discipline not only deals with the three domains of learning: the cognitive, the affective, and the psychomotor, but also includes aesthetic values.

The Music Educators National Conference, music education's professional organization, has established in its statement of broad aims that it will conduct programs and activities to build "a vital musical culture—an enlightened musical public." To realize these goals the conference organized a basic comprehensive list of objectives and tasks.

Special issues that keep reappearing in music education are: (1) music instruction for all students; (2) education vs. entertainment; (3) music and the fine arts; and (4) building an American culture.

Because the educational reform movement of the '90s disregarded the arts, a coalition that included representatives from all members of the music community and educators was formed to install the arts as a part of *basic* education. A commission was formed from this group to study the issue, and it published as its final report *Growing Up Complete: The Imperative for Music Education* (National Commission on Music Education, 1991).

It is the function of music administration to provide the essential musical and educational leadership that can move a music program toward its designated goals and objectives. Decisions that guide this direction should be based on a clearly defined philosophy that has been formulated by the profession and individuals to achieve the maximum learning experience for members of a society. Basic funding to support school programs in these endeavors comes from three sources: local taxes, state funding, and federal funding.

Mass media and technological advances in recent years have brought music to a position of prominence and made it accessible to audiences of a magnitude that was inconceivable only a few decades ago. Thus the schools, more than ever before, have a responsibility to assist young people in developing judgments regarding the music that they hear under a variety of conditions.

In 1986 the conference expanded its rational for music in its second edition of *The School Music Program: Description and Standards*.

STUDY AND DISCUSSION QUESTIONS

1. Why has every civilized nation found it necessary to establish a system of schools?

2. Which of the four basic reasons for schools most strongly calls for including music? Why?

3. Are the points noted in MENC's *Goals and Objectives for Music Education* applicable to individual teachers or to the profession of music education? Do these goals have implications for what individual teachers should be engaged in as a part of their work?

4. (a) How do the musical outcomes listed in *Music in General Education* relate to the domains of learning?

   (b) Are any of those musical outcomes more important than others? Are any of them now out of date or no longer valid?

5. What does the phrase "the discipline of achievement" on page 106 mean?

6. (a) What is the main function of the administrator of a school music program?

   (b) What must be changed before changes in a music program can be made?

    (c) What are the characteristics of effective administrators of music programs?

7. What are the sources for funding school music programs?

8. What is the relationship between the idea of enrichment as a major goal of education (pages 101–102) and the idea of the "aesthetic domain" mentioned on pages 102–103?

9. What is your position on the special issues in music education? Defend it.

INDIVIDUAL OR CLASS ACTIVITIES

1. Identify some of the ethnic groups in your class and discuss how music is treated in their ethnic setting (church, home, etc.). Are there any differences, educationally or musically, as to where the emphasis is placed? What are the similarities?

2. Hold a class forum on "why music is basic education" as if it was a debate with an unsupportive board of education or an ultraconservative public official.

SUPPLEMENTARY READINGS

MARK, M. L. (1978.) *Contemporary music education.* New York: Schirmer Books.

PETERS, G. D., & MILLER, R. F. (1982) *Music teaching and learning.* New York: Longman.

REFERENCES

AMERICAN ASSOCIATION OF SCHOOL ADMINISTRATORS. (1959). *Your AASA in 1958–1959: American Association of School Administrators, official report for the year 1958.* Washington, DC: Author.

ADAMS, C. F. (Ed.). (1841). *Letters of John Adams addressed to his wife* (Vol. 2). Boston: Little and Brown.

BIRGE, E. B. (1966). *History of public school music in the United States.* Washington, DC: Music Educators National Conference.

CURRICULUM BALANCE. (1973). Washington, DC: Music Educators National Conference.

DILLON, D. (1981). Maintain representation in Washington. *Music Educators Journal, 68*(4), 42.

ERNST, K., & GARY, C. (Eds.). (1965). *Music in general education.* Washington, DC: Music Educators National Conference.

Music Educators National Conference. (1986). *Guidelines for performances of school music groups: expectations and limitations*. Reston, VA: Author.

Music Educators National Conference, Hoffer, C. (Chair). (1974). *The school music program: Description and standards*. Reston, VA: Author.

Music Educators National Conference, Lehman, P. (Chair). (1986). *The school music program: Descriptions and standards* (2d ed.). Reston, VA: Author.

National Commission on Music Education. (1991). *Growing up complete: The imperative for music education*. Reston, VA: Music Educators National Conference.

5

Sociological Foundations of Music Education

IT IS A FUNDAMENTAL assumption in the social sciences: almost everything human beings do and know is learned after birth. The way humans act, think, talk, and even the way they feel is largely the result of their contacts with other human beings. There is some genetic endowment, to be sure, but mostly it involves physical makeup, biological functions, and probably a few personality tendencies and capacities. According to this sociological view, even the way in which biological functions are fulfilled is culturally determined. For example, everyone needs to eat, but the time, place, and type of food eaten varies greatly among the different cultures of the world.

Nature Versus Nurture

The sociological view about the great importance of the social environment in which a child grows up is not accepted by some scientists. One of the oldest controversies debated in the social sciences has been between those who believe that nurture outstrips nature in determining what a child becomes and those who take the opposite view. Those who stress nurture believe that a baby can be molded into any type of adult, *if* the appropriate conditions are provided. Those who stress the influence of nature through genetic endowment think that the type of environment in which a child is reared makes a limited difference because of the limits and influences of inborn characteristics.

The classic work of the scientists emphasizing genetic endowment was a 1912 account by Henry E. Goddard, who studied the descendants of a Revolutionary War soldier given the pseudonym of Martin Kallikak (Goddard, 1912). Kallikak procreated two family streams, one from a marriage to a "worthy Quakeress" and the other from an affair with a mentally retarded barmaid. From the union with the Quakeress flowed "hundreds of the highest type of human beings," including doctors, lawyers, businessmen, and even college presidents(!). Only two of the nearly 500 "good" Kallikaks ended up with below-average intelligence. The illegitimate son born of the affair with the barmaid was later to be known as "Old Horror" by his friends and neighbors. Apparently some women were not repulsed by "Old Horror," because he fathered two children of his own. According to Goddard this line of "bad" Kallikaks produced "lowest forms of humanity"—horse thieves, prostitutes, alcoholics, and the like. Only forty-six of the more than 480 descendants were thought to have normal intelligence.

In its time Goddard's work was influential. Today it is considered to present an important concept but to be naive in its belief in a single cause as the reason for the differences between the two strains of Kallikak's descendants. It is likely that the Quaker lady and the mentally retarded barmaid offered their children two vastly different environments, which then tended to be perpetuated by their offspring.

There is enough evidence in terms of correlations of intelligence-test data and inheritance to make one ponder, however.[*] Table 5.1 presents a summary of the studies on the correlations between genetic relationships and IQ (Erlenmeyer-Kimling & Jarvik, 1963). As can be seen in the table, the closer two people are, genetically speaking, the more likely they are to possess similar intelligence-test scores. Notice that identical twins reared apart have an average correlation of .75 in the studies conducted. The correlation between foster parent and child is much lower: .20.

Casual observation of children as they mature also confirms that some personality tendencies seem to be inherited; for example, sometimes a child will display personality characteristics of a grandparent who died before the child was born.

The classic writings of the nurture, or "environmentalist," school appeared at approximately the same time as Goddard's espousal of the hereditary point of view. In 1913 John B. Watson began applying the stimulus-response theories of Pavlov to infants. By associating objects made of fur with the banging of a steel bar a few inches from the infant's head.

---

[*]A correlation is a mathematical expression of the degree of relationship between two or more factors. A correlation coefficient of 1.00 indicates a perfect positive relationship, while a—1.00 indicates a negative relationship like a seesaw. A correlation of .00 indicates no relationship between the variables. The values are not percentages and should not be thought of in that sense. A correlation does not necessarily mean causation.

TABLE 5.1
Various IQ Correlations

RELATIONSHIP	NUMBER OF STUDIES	AVERAGE CORRELATION
Unrelated children reared apart	4	–.01
Foster parent and child	3	.20
Unrelated children reared together	5	.24
Siblings reared apart	33	.47
Siblings reared together	36	.55
Identical twins reared apart	4	.75
Identical twins reared together	14	.87
Grandparent and grandchild	3	.27
Parent and child	13	.50

Watson was able within two months to condition a nine-month-old infant named Albert to be terrified by anything resembling fur, even a Santa Claus mask with beard (Watson & Raynor, 1921). Watson was not modest in his claims. "Give me the baby," he asserted, "and I'll make it climb and use its hands in construction of buildings of stone or wood . . . I'll make it a thief, a gunman, or a dope fiend. The possibilities of shaping it in any direction are almost endless. Even gross anatomical differences limit us far less than you may think. . . . Make him a deaf mute, and I will build you a Helen Keller. Men are built, not born" (Watson, 1927).

Today the followers of the behavioral psychology, nurture outlook are perhaps less assertive, but equally convinced that they are right. Chief among contemporary proponents of such thinking is B. F. Skinner and those favoring "behavior modification." The advocates of stimulus-response psychology have demonstrated repeatedly that their ideas work in achieving short-term results. Their effectiveness in achieving comprehensive, long-range goals is open to question, however.

The nature/nurture disagreement also exists with respect to musical talent. The differing concepts of the nature of music talent discussed in chapter 8 have not restrained the proponents of either view very much. The genetic-endowment advocates can cite a number of highly musical families in history, with the Bach family being the most notable. Over a period of about six generations, from 1580 to 1845, more than sixty Bachs were musicians of some sort, and at least thirty-eight of these achieved eminence. However, the Bach family can also be used as an example of the importance of environment. Being a musician was a Bach family tradition. Johann Sebastian's father was a musician who died when Johann was ten. The boy's music training was then taken over by an older brother, Johann Christoph, who was an organist. Carl Seashore, an eminent music psychologist, considered music talent as a collection of innate capacities, and produced tests to measure these capacities. Seashore's view on this has been challenged by those who claim that training and environment alter these abilities significantly (Lundin, 1967, pp. 235–43). The matter will probably never be settled to everyone's satisfaction.

The more important fact is that a child may, depending on the environment in which he or she is raised, turn out to use his or her ability for something constructive *or* something antisocial. Heredity appears to set the potential, but the social environment largely determines the use to which that potential is put.

Whatever the truth may be about the relative importance of nature and nurture in shaping human behavior, the obligation for teachers is clear: *Teach each student as much as possible.* Even if his or her parents are noticeably above (or below) average in mental ability, no one knows what a child's potential is. Research data can only indicate tendencies and probabilities, which may not apply to a particular student. The information on the nature/nurture question is of interest to researchers and teachers, but it should in no way affect the efforts teachers make in classrooms on behalf of their students.

The Process of Socialization

Anna was born in the 1930s, the daughter of an unwed mother. Because in those years illegitmate children were a social disgrace, Anna's grandfather hid her in a small, dark attic, where she had no contact with outsiders. Her mother maintained her physically, but in other ways the child was neglected. She was found by local authorities when she was six years old. At that time she could not walk, talk, or do anything that indicated intelligence. Doctors found her reflexes to be normal, but otherwise she was almost a vegatable, so she was placed in a school for retarded children (Davis, 1949, pp. 204–208).

She died at the age of ten, but during the four years between discovery and death she became a human being. Her eating manners became reasonably acceptable. She learned how to dress herself (except for fastening her clothes), wash her hands and brush her teeth, and use the toilet. She learned to follow directions and helped other children. In addition, she acquired the ability to repeat words and talk in phrases, and she tried to carry on conversations.

Isabelle was also an isolated child, but her situation differed in several ways from Anna's. Her mother was a deaf mute who spent a lot of time with her in her isolated room. After she was discovered at the age of six, Isabelle was given prolonged and expert speech training. Initially, she could only make croaking sounds, and she was afraid and hostile with strangers. Despite her slow start, she was able to surmount her difficulties with language. After the initial breakthrough, she went through the usual stages of learning for children between the ages of one and six, but she did so much more rapidly than normal. Within two and a half months from the time she spoke Isabelle her first word, was saying sentences. Nine months later she could identify words in books, write, add to ten, and tell a brief story. Within another two and a half years she had caught up to the normal levels for children her age. By the age of fourteen she completed sixth grade and had developed a cheerful and energetic personality. Later she completed high school, married, had two children of her own, and led a quite normal life (Davis, 1949, pp. 204–208).

It is unwise, of course, to base assumptions about human behavior on the experiences of just two persons. There is, however, much other evidence of the detrimental effects of isolation from human contact. Another example comes from an Iranian orphanage (before the revolution of 1979) in which children were kept in isolation in separate, soundproof cubicles. Virtually all the children were below normal mentally, in spite of the fact that they came almost entirely from the literate population of Tehran (Dennis, 1960, pp. 47–59). Even physical skill development was impaired. Sixty percent of the children could not sit up alone when they were two years of age, and 85 percent could not walk by the age of four.

Even adults need contact with others. During the Korean War, thirty-eight out of the fifty-nine Air Force men in the POW camps "confessed" to nonexistent U.S. bacteriological attacks on Korea, and some of them collaborated with their captors. To extract such confessions the Korean Communists exerted extreme psychological pressures and kept each prisoner by himself (Kinkead, 1959, pp. 160–61). A study of prisoners in Massachusetts also reported that solitary confinement "gets you thinking backward" (Diesenhouse, 1988, p. 176).

In recent years the view has sometimes been expressed that society and schools are forces that discourage individual uniqueness, and that a person develops best when given a minimum of guidance. The experiences of Anna and Isabelle, of the orphans in Tehran, and of many others contradict this idea. As Amitai Etzioni concludes, "Individuals may all have been made in God's image, but God delegated creation to the community of parents, educators, and neighbors" (1983, p. 28).

Music as Human Behavior

Music is a form of human behavior created by human beings for human beings, just as speaking French, conducting experiments in a laboratory, playing tennis, eating with a knife and fork, writing, showing affection for someone with a kiss, smoking, driving a car, and countless other actions are human behaviors. Therefore, music and the way people use music is subject to the same influences that affect any other human action. Musical behavior are learned, and the way people use music is not preordained.

Music is a social activity in that a number of people must understand what the organized sounds are, and what they are for, or else the sounds are meaningless. Music depends on a consensus among people in a society about what music is. Usually music is founded on a number of traditional elements inherited from previous generations, just as other aspects of culture are passed on from one generation to the next.* Some avant-garde works by John Cage and others have encountered rejection by many listeners because they exceeded society's consensus of what music is.

Sometimes musicians are bothered by the description of music as a form of human behavior. Describing music in that way seems to demean it as an art form, with all the high and lofty sentiments that the word "art" implies. The belief that the arts and music are something extraordinary or above everyday life was prevalent in the nineteenth century, and vestiges of it still exist today. According to this nineteenth-century idea, the composer is a "prophet," an extraordinary person who in some mysterious way receives inspiration and guidance from beyond this world. Therefore, art and music are not made; rather, they are discovered and brought into being by the prophet-genius. The artwork, then, is not *of* human life but *above* human life; it transcends life, which is why the view is often called "transcendentalism." It is the duty of the lay audience to try to understand and appreciate the creations of the prophet-genius, even if full understanding is not possible.

While the transcendental position now seems extreme, one need only look at the writings of Wagner, Schoenberg, and others to sense its basic message. Schoenberg writes: "The composer reveals the inmost essence of the world and utters the most profound wisdom which relatively few people are capable of understanding. . . . The work of art exists even if no one is overwhelmed by it"; he also says that music is "subconsciously received from the Supreme Commander" (1951, pp. 38–39, 111 passim).

Can one reject the extremeness of the transcendentalist view of music and still not think that music is just another human activity? The answer depends on whether the arts and music are extraordinary activities or just ordinary activities. Works of art music *are* human creations, but they *are not* just another creation like the pitchfork or the pepperoni pizza. They are aesthetic objects and experiences, objects valued for their own sake, involving intellectual awareness and human feelings, and making life richer and more meaningful. Therefore, it is possible to consider music as a form of human behavior and yet not strip away its above-ordinary attributes.

---

*Vander Zanden defines culture as "the social heritage of a people; learned patterns for thinking, feeling, and acting that characterize a population or society, including the expression of these patterns in material and nonmaterial ways" (1990, p. 90).

One of the reasons that the arts are sometimes considered as being "higher" than other human activity is the claim that they are "creative." Although we do not often think about the other human endeavors in this way, there are quite a few activities that contain the elements of mystery and invention associated with the creative process; such virtues are not limited to the arts. True, the way in which the human mind can conceive of sounds and create compositions is a mystery, but so is the way in which people can conceive of experiments, draw conclusions from data, and write short stories. The mystery is the awesome and wonderful capabilities of the human mind. The differences between the arts and the sciences with regard to human invention is that the arts have exalted and proclaimed it, while the sciences have taken it for granted and accepted it.

Factors Affecting Musical Behavior

There are literally hundreds of factors that affect the nature and use of music in a particular culture and society. To keep this chapter within reasonable limits, they will be grouped into biological, social, cultural, and technological factors, and only several of the more important aspects of each factor will be discussed.

Biological Factors

The makeup of the human body affects music. For example, if human beings had more or less than ten digits on their hands, the music for piano and organ would be altered accordingly and the mechanisms of clarinets and bassoons would be redesigned. If there were no bass voices or if humans could produce two vocal sounds simultaneously, clearly that would mean different arrangements for choral groups and operas. Nor can humans hear pitches above or below a certain range. Music, therefore, must fall within the physical capabilities of the performers and listeners.

Social Factors

FUNCTIONS OF MUSIC. Music performs a number of functions in society. The anthropologist Allan Merriam (1964, pp. 209–27) discusses ten of them.

1. Emotional expression: the venting of emotions and the expression of ideas.

2. Aesthetic enjoyment: providing the type of experience discussed in chapter 3.

3. Entertainment: The use of music as diversion and amusement is widespread in most societies, including America. In fact, it may be the largest single use of music in America.

4. Communication: not the type made through language, but communication conveying emotions that are understood within a particular society.

5. Symbolic representation: Some symbolization is found in the texts of songs, some in the cultural meaning of the sounds, and some in deep symbolism related to human experience.

6. Physical response: The use of music for dancing and to accompany physical activity is widespread throughout the world.

7. Enforcing conformity to social norms: In many cultures music provides instruction or warnings.

8. Validation of social institutions and religious rituals: The use of music for religious services and state occasions is found in most cultures.

9. Contribution to the continuity and stability of culture: Merriam believes that "music is in a sense a summation activity for the expression of values, a means whereby the heart of the psychology of a culture is exposed" (1964, p. 225).

10. Contribution to the integration of society: Music is often used to draw people together, such as the fight song for a school.

Kaplan (1990, p. 28) lists eight "social" functions of music: as a form of knowledge, collective possession, personal experience, therapy, moral and symbolic force, incidental commodity, symbolic indicator of change, and as a link with the past and future. Honigsheim identifies several functions: ceremonial, entertainment, accompaniment for work, use in the home, concerts, and oratorios (1989, pp. 60–65). Gaston (1968) lists the need for aesthetic experience, the enhancement of religion, communication, emotional expression, rhythmic response, gratification, and the potency of music in the group situation. Clearly there is some overlap of Gaston's list of functions with those of Kaplan, Merriam, and Honigsheim, which is to be expected.

Other classifications and functions can also be named. An important function in contemporary America is as a "sonic background" for nonmusical activities ranging from studying to jogging to shopping in a store. In other instances music is used as a social accoutrement or trapping, in the same manner as is designer clothing or certain makes of automobiles.

Although listening to or participating in music for aesthetic reasons is listed as one function by Merriam, Honigsheim, and Gaston, this can involve other functions. Depending on one's aesthetic views, art music functions to meet a desire that human beings have to represent certain ideas in sound, or to symbolize states of feeling, or to transcend everyday life. In any case, in art music much importance is attached to the organization and character of the sounds. Any effects on the listener in terms of promoting actions or beliefs are largely incidental and irrelevant to the main purpose of the music.

Each use of music that has been described is appropriate to particular times and sets of circumstances. For example, people do not sit around the campfire in the evening and sing Arnold Schoenberg's "Four Pieces for Mixed Chorus" or a chant from a Navajo rain dance, any more than they would wear tuxedos or scuba diving equipment around a campfire. The manner in which the music is performed and the reaction and behavior of the audience also differ according to the purpose of the music. Concert audiences in Europe and America are expected to listen silently and to be intellectually analytical, while in sub-Saharan Africa everyone is expected to clap, dance, or shout along in a musical event. To Africans, music is an integral part of their daily lives, and they deal with it in an active, participatory way.

The roles and functions of music usually become *institutionalized*, a sociological term meaning that something becomes established and organized in the society. There are art councils, symphony and opera societies that oversee the performances of music in concert halls, magazines devoted to certain types of music, companies that produce and/or sell recordings of music, disc jockeys and music commentators, publishers of music and music books, all the performances of music from singing "The Star-Spangled Banner" at ball games to the premiere of a new avantgarde composition, and much more.

Institutions have defined roles for each person. The orchestra conductor has one role, the second-clarinet player another, and the personnel manager another. Many of the institutions related to music overlap with other institutions. Publishing and broadcasting involve business, instruction involves education, and symphony and opera societies involve the social life of the community.

Folkways have also been developed for music and its performance. The conductor shakes hands with the concertmaster after the performance as the audience applauds, but onstage never shakes the hand of the clarinet player or manager. Solo pianists sit with their right side facing the audience, and not their back, which was true until Liszt's time. The country singer doesn't appear on stage wearing a choir robe.

The roles and functions of music have a number of implications for music teachers, three of which will be mentioned here. First, teachers should be aware of the function of the music that is being studied, because such knowledge should affect how it is taught. For example, a purely recreational song such as the American square-dance tune "Cindy" should not receive the same meticulous attention to phrasing and expression as Palestrina's motet *Sicut cervus*. "Cindy" should sound carefree; it loses some of its charm if its performance is too polished. *Sicut cervus* should never sound carefree and unperfected.

Second, the students should be made aware of the different functions of music. Each function calls for a somewhat different mental outlook and manner of listening. One should listen very carefully to a work of Maurice Ravel, but the same concentrated listening is not needed for most popular music. Nor does one listen to the music from a film score in the same way as Sergei Prokofiev's Second Violin Concerto. The film score is designed to be associated with the film; the two were conceived together, and they are more effective when combined. The Violin Concerto is not enhanced by an association with something else.

Third, when teaching music that has nonmusical associations, teachers should include at least some instruction on the nonmusical factors related to the music. For example, the rhythm of some sea chanteys is associated with the motions of pulling a line, and knowing that fact makes the sea chantey more meaningful. The *raga* of India is virtually inseparable from its religious function; in fact, most Indian musicians resist the idea of isolating the *raga* from its cultural and religious context. When music is designed for incorporation with nonmusical factors, it is not appropriate to treat it as though it has been designed for objective contemplation like a work of Western art music.

SOCIAL STRATIFICATION. The sociological term *stratification* means "the structural ranking of individuals and groups; their grading into horizontal layers or strata" (Vander Zanden, 1990, p. 267). It refers to what is usually thought of as *socioeconomic status* (SES) or what is occasionally referred to as *social class*. "Class" is not an accurate term for the phenomenon in America, where people do not inherit social rank by being born into nobility or a particular caste. Social status can change and often it does; social class cannot usually be changed. In fact, a feature of SES in America is the degree of social mobility from one level to another.

Regardless of what it is called, "sociologists generally concur that social stratification in some form and degree is a feature of all societies" (Roach et al., 1969, p. 11). Even in so-called "classless" socialist societies people receive different treatment and esteem. No one is certain about why social stratification exists. One of several causes appears to be differing roles required of people as societies become more complex. Someone or some group of people is needed to care for the sick, clean up the streets, run the affairs of the government or the tribe, and so on. Each of these roles acquires a different value in the eyes of the society.

The classic work on social stratification in America was done in the 1940s by W. Lloyd Warner (Warner, 1960). Since that time, more than a thousand studies have been conducted by sociologists on the topic. Warner devised a rating scheme for SES that considers occupation, income, education, and place of residence. The system produces numerical data that assigns people to one of six levels: upper-upper, lower-upper, upper-middle, lower-middle, upper-lower, and lower-lower.

In 1978 Coleman and Rainwater updated the concept of class structure into one that is largely based on economic circumstances. In this study people ranked one another and themselves according to the following economic descriptions:

1. People who have really "made it."

2. People who are doing very well.

3. People who have achieved the middle-class dream. These people lack luxuries but enjoy the "good life."

4. People who have a comfortable life.

5. People who are just getting by. These persons make up the broad "working class."

6. People who having difficult time.

7. People who are poor.

From time to time polls have been taken in the United States on the prestige ratings for various occupations. Over the years a particular occupation may shift a little in prestige, but in general the professional occupations (doctor, lawyer, research scientist, professor) rank higher than most "white collar" jobs (economist, undertaker, newspaper reporter, insurance agent), which in turn rank well above the jobs that consist of manual labor (mechanic, waiter, janitor, garbage collector). Within occupations subgroups differ in the status accorded them. For example, medical doctors with specializations have more prestige than general practitioners, medical doctors rank higher than dentists, registered nurses higher than practical nurses, and so on.

There is a relationship between the status of an occupation and the income it provides, although this is certainly not always so. A champion prizefighter makes much more than a college president, but is accorded nowhere near the same status. Many manual occupations (plumbers, truck drivers, garbage collectors) make at least as much money as public school teachers, yet they do not have the same status.

There is also a rather high correlation between amount of education and social status, and in turn between education and prestige of occupation. Place of residence (inner-city slum, well-to-do suburb, farm, etc.) is a function of income and the desire of people to live close to others of similar status. Novels and soap operas are replete with stories about persons born on the "wrong side of the tracks," thereby adding popular support to the observations of social scientists.

Social stratification affects just about every aspect of life. Following are some general (*not* uniformly true) facts about certain areas in which SES makes an important difference:

- Upper-class people devote less of their resources to food and housing; the highest tenth spends about 11 percent on food, in contrast to the lowest tenth, which spends over 40 percent (Blumberg, 1980, p. 252).
- Upper-class people have a longer life expectancy (Katz, 1983, pp. 1218–1224) and have lower rates of mental illness (Link, et al., 1986, pp. 242–258).
- Lower-class people consume more "convenience foods," drink more beer, and watch more television (Bridgewater, 1982, pp. 16–20).
- Upper-class people are more likely to attend Episcopalian or Presbyterian churches (Smith, 1984, pp. 19–23).
- Upper-class people are much more likely to vote in elections (McBride, 1988, p. 1).
- Lower-class people experience sexual intercourse at earlier ages (Weinberg & Williams, 1980, pp. 33–48).
- Lower-class people are far more likely to make the "he don't" grammatical error and their pronunciation of words often differs from standard English.
- Upper-class people are far more likely to be interested in tennis and soccer, while lower-class people follow stock car racing and boxing.

A characteristic of upper-SES people that affects musical preference is a willingness to postpone immediate satisfactions in order to gain an ultimate goal, while people in the lower strata generally are not willing to do this. Sociologists term this practice the *deferred gratification pattern* (Schneider & Lysgaard, 1953). For example, the pattern can be seen when a person puts off getting a job immediately after graduation from high school to attend college, with the eventual probability of four years later securing a better paying and more satisfying position.

The promptness of gratification and its vital role in determining the value of musical works was discussed in chapter 3. A person who is willing to defer gratification is logically much more likely to enjoy listening to music that contains an inhibition of expected tendencies, which is characteristic of art music. On the other hand, the person who expects and wants immediate gratification will probably select music that is simple and direct.

The audience for art music, both in terms of concert attendance and purchase of recordings, consists overwhelmingly of college graduates—the upper middle and upper levels of society. In a report synthesizing all available research on arts audiences, DiMaggio, Useem, and Brown reported that 83.4 percent of the audience for classical music had at least attended college, and 63 percent of those had graduated. Furthermore, although they constituted only 25.5 percent of the total employed population, people in professional and managerial positions made up 70.8 percent of the audience (1978, pp. 20, 22). (Although they constituted only 4.1 percent of all employed persons, school and college teachers made up 22.1 percent of the audience—a greater-than-expected ratio exceeded only by artists, performers, and writers.) Similar results were reported in an extensive study conducted by Baumol and Bowen: Blue-collar workers were 60 percent of the working population but only 2 or 3 percent of the arts audience, while people who had done graduate work constituted 5 percent of the working population but 55 percent of the arts audience (1966, p. 96). Apparently the truck driver who attends a symphony concert or buys a recording of Brahms's Fourth Symphony is the exception to the rule. The audience for country music, on the other hand, is largely blue collar.

Another reason for the difference in musical preference among social strata is the cultural reinforcement given within the social group. Although people in lower strata can recognize the various types of music (e.g., they know what a symphony orchestra sounds like), they are not really familiar with such music. As Karl Schuessler (1948) points out, "Socio-economic position operates to channelize experiences in such a way that a given individual tends to form a favorable attitude toward certain kinds of music. . . . Likewise, familiarity affects musical taste, and socio-economic position may cause an individual to be regularly exposed to some kind of music and remain virtually isolated from other kinds," (pp. 330–35). Children grow up hearing the music that their parents play on CD or tape players. In the adolescent years the contact is with music that their friends (usually at the same social level) play and talk about. The tendency to like what one is familiar with operates in the world of music just as it does in other areas of life.

Music preferences are self-reinforcing; that is, one listens to the type of music one likes best, which in turn further strengthens the preference for that kind of music. The school is virtually the only place in which most children in American society hear any art music—a fact that places a special obligation on music educators to do a good job of teaching such music.

A third reason for the differences in music preferences among social levels is what might be called the "comfort" factor. Not only do people like what they are familiar with, but they are also more comfortable and confident with it. The comfort factor not only refers to the qualities of the music itself, but also to the folkways that accompany the performances of the different types of music. A bricklayer may prefer not to attend a symphony concert in an elegant concert hall because he is not quite sure how to act and not confident that his clothes and way of talking are quite right for associating with the "cultured" people who usually attend such concerts. He would be just as comfortable, staying home and listening to music in his living room, sitting in a reclining chair with his shoes off and no worries about whether he "belongs" with the concert-going crowd. In turn, the people who usually attend symphony concerts would not feel comfortable at a performance of soul music or in Nashville's Grand Old Opry house.

Some years ago the Danish State Radio conducted an experiment in which it played on a particular program the same music during two successive weeks. It was a selection of ear-appealing and not-too-difficult classical music (Geiger, 1950, pp. 453–60). The first week the program was introduced as "popular recorded music." The identical program was repeated a week later, only this time it was introduced as "classical music." The size of the listening audience was cut in half, a phenomenon Geiger termed "reverse snobism." Apparently the highbrow trappings and image of concert music are an impediment to concert music for many people, at least in Denmark a generation or two ago.

What are some implications of social stratification for music educators? One is that they need to be understanding of the differences among schools that contain predominantly one SES level of student. For example, the fact that string programs are largely found in schools containing an above-average proportion of college-bound students should not be surprising when one realizes the social level of most college-bound students.

A second implication is an obligation. If school is almost the only place where most students will learn about art music, teachers should do a good job of teaching such music. When planning music courses, they should allow time for an adequate experience with (but not be limited to) art music.

A third implication is that teachers should attempt to make students "comfortable" with art music. The aristocratic trappings associated with such music should be stripped away, and it should be made a logical and natural type of music to perform and study.

A fourth implication is that teachers should attempt to get students to recognize the value of music that does not immediately fulfill expectancies. Sometimes this can be accomplished by telling the students that "it's worth waiting for something that's better," and in other cases it involves having them think of the form and development of an entire piece of music. The students should be interested not only in the current moment of a work, but also in what has taken place previously and what may happen before the music concludes.

Other aspects of social stratification and personal identification will be discussed in chapter 6, which deals with social psychology.

AGE STRATIFICATION. American society is not only stratified in terms of socioeconomic status; there are also groupings according to age level. For a number of reasons American society has great age-level differences. One reason is the longer life span today, which has increased on the average by twenty or thirty years from what it was in the nineteenth century. A second reason is the rapid rate of change in so many aspects of life in this century. Today's young people truly have grown up in a different world from that of their parents and certainly their grandparents. It was only sixty-six years from the first flight by the Wright brothers in 1903 to 1969, when Neil Armstrong walked on the moon, and the first presidential election in which women could vote occurred only in 1920. A third reason for the increase in age-group consciousness is the sheer size of America's population, and especially the population around the age of forty. A fourth reason is the economic power that young people enjoy. Today they are able to buy records, clothes, movie admissions, and cosmetics of their choice—something that was not possible for many of their parents when they were teenagers. Therefore, many businesses cater to the "youth market." A fifth reason is the youth orientation of American society. Everyone is exhorted to think and look young. A sixth reason is the segregation that exists among different age levels in American society. In the nineteenth century the grandparents, parents, and children all lived close together on a farm or in a small town. Today there are retirement communities and nursing homes for the elderly, and young people have the automobile, which can take them away from their homes to gather with others of their own age group.

Many families with teenage children today find that it is unusual for them to all be present for the evening meal because of school or youth activities and part-time jobs; they never are together for lunch during the week, and breakfast is often skipped or eaten "on the run." Seldom do they have any extended contact with each other. One father solved this situation in part by buying a sailboat on which the family liked to spend time, and another father planned summer travel and vacations for the family so that they would be together at least for a few weeks each year, but many families can't or won't make such plans.

For these reasons—and some others that will be discussed in chapter 6—it should not be surprising to see that preferences for different types of music vary according to age. Casual observation confirms that teenagers do not watch the same channels or shows on television or buy the same types of music on recordings; MTV (a cable channel that telecasts music videos) is watched primarily by teenagers. Radio stations and music producers are keenly aware of the different age-level music markets, and they market accordingly.

Dramatic evidence of differing age-level preferences in music was published by the National Assessment of Educational Progress ("A Perspective on the First Music Assessment," 1974, p. 23). Information was gathered from four age groups: nine, thirteen, seventeen, and "young adults" (ages twenty-six–thirty-five). The respondents were asked which type of music they liked the most and which type they liked the least. The results showed that rock music was "most liked" by 32 percent of the nine-year-olds; that figure jumped to 62 percent with seventeen-year-olds, only to plummet to 14 percent with young adults. Instrumental art music and country music experienced the opposite phenomenon. Instrumental art music increased in "most liked" ratings from 5 percent with seventeen-year-olds to 12 percent with young adults, and country music leaped from 5 percent with seventeen-year-olds to 29 percent with young adults. Similar results were reported for the types of music liked least. Rock music had a corresponding increase in its negative percentage from 11 to 25 percent, while instrumental art music improved its negative percentage from 14 to 9 percent.

Unfortunately, for funding reasons the second survey by the National Assessment of Educational Progress did not include young adults, who had to be contacted individually because they were no longer in school. Even more unfortunate is the fact that music has not been included in surveys by the National Assessment since the second assessment in the late 1970s. No one knows what the responses regarding the most- and least-liked music would be today, but it is likely that the four age levels would still differ significantly.

In general, the data from the National Assessment survey are consonant with previous research cited by Farnsworth (1969, pp. 124–25). His summary of several studies concludes that music taste grows more like adult tastes as a young person matures.

The differences among various age groups present music educators with some real challenges. For one, they need to devise ways of breaking down what Rieger (1973) refers to as "the phoniness-stuffiness-jeweled-dowager syndrome," which represents the inaccurate perception that art music is for older people, is something out of date, and has about it an air of stuffiness and false morality. Rieger suggests establishing "beachhead" by letting students "discover the parallels between the music they know and the music they don't know" (p. 31). His suggestion reaffirms what music educators have long known but often seem to forget: Begin where the students are. When teachers have their students draw parallels between art music and popular music, they are achieving another desirable educational outcome: They are diverting attention from thinking about music as being "ours" and "theirs" to thinking about the nature of the musical sounds, which is one of the goals of music education.

ETHNOCENTRISM. Regardless of the culture or subculture into which people are socialized, they tend to think of it as right, true, and good, as the best way of life. This universal tendency is called *ethnocentrism*. The term was coined in the early part of this century by Sumner, who defined it as "that view of things in which one's own group is the center of everything and all others are scaled and rated with reference to it" (1906, p. 13). There is a logical basis for ethnocentrism: People understand their own culture and know how to function in it, so *for them* it is superior. Ethnocentrism applies to groups within societies, as well as societies in their entirety. It is so deeply ingrained that even anthropologists have trouble avoiding it (Bernstein, 1988, p. 74; Geertz, 1988, p. 74).

This sociological view of life, including the arts, means that beauty is indeed "in the eye of the beholder." It is ascribed by people to art and music only to the extent that the objects exhibit properties that are familiar and understood in the particular culture. The wide differences among the types of music found around the world support the idea of the importance of the cultural basis of art and music.

This view of the arts is at odds with the idea that objective or intrinsic qualities within works of art hold the secret to their quality, which is generally the approach in aesthetics and music appreciation courses. Instead of looking for such qualities in artworks, the sociological approach calls for examining the social and psychological processes that have encouraged artists and musicians to create certain kinds of works and their shared convictions about the nature of art works (Mueller, 1958, p. 100). The challenge, according to the sociological view, should be to search for norms and beliefs that exist in the minds of people in a particular culture. For example, a climactic moment in a symphony by Brahms is climactic only to persons familiar with Western art music. They are the ones who have been taught that certain sound patterns are climactic; people from central Africa or China would probably not react to the sounds in that way.

An important action that music teachers can take to avoid ethnocentrism is to teach different listening attitudes and approaches for art and popular music, a point that is made in more detail earlier in this chapter.

Whenever possible, music should be presented to students without the trappings that are often associated with a formal concert or recital. Several types of informal concerts have been tried with much success in various places around the world, including, in Australia, the removal of seats in a concert hall (Hopkins, 1973, pp. 83–84). Once the nonmusical factors that hindered acceptance by young people were removed, a more positive attitude was achieved.

Music teachers should do what they can to relate music, and especially art music, to their students. For example, a former music major and all-American football player named Mike Reid played for a number of years in the defensive front four of the Cincinnati Bengals football team. Occasionally he appeared as a performer with the Cincinnati Symphony. Music teachers should have taken advantage of such events by clipping the newspaper pictures and stories about them and putting them on bulletin boards. Music teachers should also promote appearances of students who perform with the local orchestra so that the young people will realize that art music is not only for people over thirty.

ETHNIC GROUPS. Not only are there differences according to socio-economic status and age, but there are differences in music preference according to race and ethnic background. Such groups have their own musical interests and preferences. For example, many African-Americans like soul and other types of soul music better than the general population; Hispanics prefer Latin-American music and performers more than African Americans and the general population, and so on. This phenomenon can be seen clearly in the three classification used for reporting record sales in *Billboard* magazine. Seldom is the top seller in the "General" list also the top seller in the "Soul" list and/or the "Country" list. The lack of crossover lists has also been confirmed by research data (Hakenen & Wells, 1990, pp. 62, 65). That does happen, but not very often. The ethnic groups add to the complexity of the social stratification and age-level mix. At least thirty-six combinations exist: two for age, three for ethnic grouping, and six for socioeconomic status. Actually, most of the categories are continuous variables, not discrete groupings. American society is complex—very complex!

PLURALISM. The preceding discussion of the various age, social, and ethnic classifications leads to a point that sociologists have long made about American society: It is *pluralistic*. It is not a homogeneous blend of one type of people who know or like one type of music, or one type of food or clothing, or who have the same value system; it is a heterogeneous mixture of many diverse elements. This pluralism is the result of America's large physical size and large population, the varied backgrounds of its peoples, and its tolerance of differences and preferences among individuals and groups of people.

The expressed ideal of American society was for many years that of the great "melting pot" in which all people were blended into a unified nation. To a degree that has happened, especially for the immigrants from Europe who arrived in the eighteenth and nineteenth centuries. However, for several other large ethnic groups this blending (the sociological term for it is "integration," not to be confused with school integration) has occurred only to a limited degree. Nevertheless, it has probably taken place in the United States more than in any other nation of its size and also more than in many small countries. Many nations ranging from the Russian republics to Canada to South Africa to India are racked far more severely by differences in languages and ethnic background than the United States.

Music teachers need to realize that there is not now, and will not be in the foreseeable future, one kind of music for all Americans. Instead, there are a number of somewhat similar musical subcultures with a very small "core" of music that most people know to a limited extent. To realize how small the core of commonly known music is, try naming songs that you can be quite sure most Americans know well enough to sing together without previous rehearsal. After "America" and "The Star-Spangled Banner" the list begins to consist of songs from which people know only phrases.

The pluralism of American culture means that music teachers must try to meet the need for diversity within unity, a task that involves two contradictory goals. To function satisfactorily, the culture requires musical elements that are held in common among its members, just as it is desirable for everyone to speak the same language. Yet there still exists the wide variety of ethnic backgrounds that children bring to school with them. Members of the various cultural groups feel deeply about and rightfully take pride in their art, music, and customs. Music teachers do not and should not want to lose the richness that the music of the Hispanics, African Americans, or Native Americans offer, any more than they want to lose the music of the German, English, or Italian immigrants.

The issue of social and cultural diversity has grown more intense in recent years. The tension between "To each his own" and "e pluribus unum" ("one out of many," the motto used on the Great Seal of the United States of America) makes decisions about what to teach in music classes more subject to scrutiny and outside pressures. This matter is discussed more fully in chapter 10, which deals with curriculum and subject matter content.

Cultural Factors

Everyone grows up in a particular cultural setting with all the attendant beliefs, social practices, and viewpoints. People are not born with ideas about economics, religion and ethics, politics, and the arts; such things are learned. The process of learning one's culture is termed *enculturation*, or sometimes, *socialization*. Without such a process, there would be chaos.

The type and form of individuals' convictions depend on the particular culture or subculture into which they are born. A child growing up in India in a Hindu family will practice vegetarianism; eat with the first two fingers and thumb of the right hand; accept a marriage partner arranged for by the parents; speak Hindi or another of the fourteen major language groups of the country; often sit on his or her haunches; believe in reincarnation; think that things change but do not improve; and assume that Indian art, music, and dance are the right and appropriate expressions of those art forms.

CULTURAL STANDARDS. Although social scientists may study the formation of the arts and customs of a culture, there is no way in which they can be evaluated and verified in a scientific sense. It is not possible to establish scientifically that Indian classical dance is superior or inferior to traditional Western ballet, or that the sari worn by Indian women is more or less beautiful than a Western dress. The reason for this circumstance is the fact that *qualities* cannot accurately be transformed into *quantities*. A beauty pageant winner's height and weight are quantities, and can be compared to the quantitative data of other women. However, the qualities of her beauty could not be so compared. Furthermore, whether she would be lovelier weighing 110, 150, or 190 pounds is a qualitative judgment that is largely the result of one's cultural bias. Whatever norms and standards exist for quality in the arts or other areas are cultural and exist primarily in the minds of the people of that culture. In contrast, the properties examined by physical scientists can be checked against nature, and these observations are not influenced by culture. For example, pure water boils at a certain temperature and altitude regardless of time or place.

The implications of the difference between social-cultural phenomena and physical-science phenomena are enormous. There is a space here to examine only a few of them that are of special importance to music educators. One implication is that once tastes and preferences are established in a culture or subculture, they are nonrational in the sense that their rightness or quality cannot be demonstrated in a rational, scientific sense. The Latin proverb *De gustibus non disputandem est* ("There is no disputing tastes") is true; there is no use arguing about preferences. They exist for a particular group of people at a particular time and place.

Aesthetic preferences and ideological and ethical convictions are ends in themselves; they are "terminal experiences," to use a phrase mentioned previously. As is true of other convictions and preferences that all of us hold, criticism of them is not welcomed; instead, we seek to reinforce them. When we like a certain type of music, we listen to that type and largely ignore other types, and we get together with like-minded people to listen to and praise our preferred music.

Since there is no way to test them in terms of their contribution to achieving some goal, changes in preferences and convictions cannot be considered "progress." The refrigerator replaced the ice box, which had previously replaced the preservation of food with spices. The refrigerator was an improvement. However, Beethoven did not replace Mozart, and neither of these composers was supplanted by Bartók. Instead, each composer created something different—a change, but not an improvement. The chants of the primitives were as expressive to them as Bach's *B Minor Mass* and Stravinsky's *Symphony of Psalms* are to us.

This fact causes artworks to accumulate, while in most areas of life outdated objects and practices are discarded. No astronomy professor spends much time teaching the geocentric view of the universe; the belief that the earth is the center of the universe has long since been discarded. However, in music courses students will still perform and study Palestrina,

Monteverdi, J. S. Bach, and a host of other "out-of-date" composers. And with good reason! Their music stands as worthwhile in itself; its value does not depend on what was composed previously or will be composed in the future.

MASS TASTE. With the growing sense of democracy in Western civilization, have the "elite" or "aristocratic" or "mandarin" tastes yielded over the past two centuries to mass tastes? Alexis de Tocqueville, the French aristocrat who in the 1830s studied and wrote brilliantly about life in America, predicted that "the taste for intellectual enjoyments will descend, step by step, even to those who, in aristocratic societies, seem to have neither the time nor ability to indulge in them" (1956, p. 162). Twentieth-century writers such as Alvin Toffler are more optimistic: "A major step toward democratization has, indeed, been taken." As a result, "the rise of a mass public for the arts can, in its way, be compared with the rise of mass literacy in the eighteenth century in England" (1965, pp. 34, 51).

Some writers have attempted to describe the differences between "high culture" and "mass culture." According to Bantock (1968), high culture is "legitimized" by the dominant cultural group, while mass or popular culture is manufactured for the mass market. Mass culture is marked by a separation between those who create it and those who consume it. This process of creating the popular culture, sometimes referred to as the "massification hypothesis" (Fox & Wince, 1975), is seen by some critics as revealing a lack of integrity in the quest for the lowest common denominator.

Vulliamy (1977) outlines the application of the massification hypothesis to music:

(a) High culture ('serious' music) is not subject to commercial pressures; commercial gain must inevitably lead to inartistic works.

(b) High culture ('serious' music) results from the unique creative potential of the artist.

(c) Mass culture ('popular' music) is produced solely for a mass market. Its commercial nature therefore leads to standardization of the product. This in turn denies the possibility of creativity to the artist.

(d) Mass culture ('popular' music) is a homogeneous category whilst high culture ('serious' music) is subdivided into many different types with strict boundaries.

(e) Mass culture ('popular' music) inhibits the growth of high culture ('serious' music) mainly due to the former's sheer quantity in the mass media.

(f) Mass culture ('popular' music) is imposed from above and the audience (teenagers) are therefore exploited. (p. 191–92)

This massification hypothesis has by no means met with full acceptance. Fox and Wince (1975) studied the musical preferences of sociology students according to nine styles of music, from which the researchers identified five factors or "taste cultures." These were analyzed with the researchers controlling for seven demographic factors including sex, age, and religious preference. The results did not support the mass culture idea. Instead, they indicate a diverse pattern. Robinson and Hirsch (1969) provide further evidence of the diversity of taste. Hirsch (1971) concludes: "The stratified teenage audience is an aggregate of individuals who form distinct popular music subcultures" (p. 379).

Analysts and critics have failed to agree on whether the present public for the arts is mass or elite. Part of the reason for this disagreement is a matter of definition about what counts as art. Is it only what is seen in art galleries and heard in concert halls or does it include films, crafts, and jazz? Also at issue is who is considered the public. Does it mean only the consistent consumers, or do persons who attend a pops concert once a year also count?

There is little doubt that the political and economic power has shifted gradually from the rich to the middle-class majority, which comprises a greater number of citizens who vote and pay taxes. For example, no longer is it possible for a few families to subsidize an orchestra or opera company or support a composer; today such financial help must come from a communitywide arts council or state and federal funds. This shift of power is one that most people applaud. However, the question remains: "Have our political and social gains been detrimental to the quality of our arts?"

Sociologically speaking, culture is culture, and all forms of it are accepted without qualitative judgment. No attempt is made to grade different cultures, any more than a chemist tries to evaluate whether barium is an inherently better element than sodium. The sociological view is, of course, not the only way to consider the question. It can be established through an analytical process like the one advocated by Leonard Meyer (described in chapter 3) that there are differences in music in terms of intricacy, subtlety, and intellectual appeal. Mendelssohn's *Elijah* is a more intellectually complex work than the popular song "Pretty Woman," just as *canard à l'orange* (duck with orange sauce) is a more sophisticated food than Kentucky Fried Chicken, and Arthur Miller's *Death of a Salesman* is a more intellectually appealing drama than a typical television sitcom. To the degree that the prevailing mass taste in artworks is less intellectually appealing, quality has been diminished, even though the gains in terms of a more equitable society have been worth it.

There is a corollary question that should be considered. Has the democratizing process raised the general level of understanding and appreciation, so that the average level of culture is somewhat "higher" or more intellectually challenging than it was before? There is simply no way to answer this question objectively, but there are scraps of evidence here and there indicating that the level of understanding has become somewhat greater. There is a tendency for musicians today to think of the "good old days" back in the eighteenth and nineteenth centuries as a time when everyone just loved art music. Not so. Letters from Mozart to his father complained how the supposedly aristocratic people in the audience talked while his music was being played (Turner, 1938, p. 271). Liszt tried to play a complete Beethoven sonata at one of his performances, but the audience became restless, so he inserted some short, lighter pieces between the movements of the sonata (Loesser, 1954, p. 378). History contains many instances of composers having difficulty finding publishers for works that are considered masterpieces today, and often the composers received very little money for their efforts. Even great musicians have seldom been really appreciated, and it is doubtful if art music has ever been understood and appreciated by more than a rather small minority of the population. Today, however, largely because of the massive efforts at education, which includes some instruction in music, and the dissemination of music by radio and recording, more people probably know more music, including art music, than ever before.

It should also be remembered that there always seem to be differing degrees of interest and levels of taste in music, just as there are differing degrees of interest in baseball, photography, and politics. Not everyone is going to desire what musicians think is the "best" music, because if the taste of a majority of the population moved "up" to Bach, Bartók, and Brahms, then the musicians would probably find a new "best" to which they would want the mass of people to move "up."

Technological Factors

Technology is a part of a culture, but because it has had such an impact on music it is discussed separately in this chapter. Throughout the ages people have made musical instruments from the materials that were available: shells, horns of animals, woods, and metals. As technological knowledge of acoustics and mechanics increased, musical instruments also changed. For example, the piano would be a quite different instrument if it did not have an iron frame and steel strings. Music was affected significantly at the beginning of the sixteenth century when scores could be printed instead of copied by hand, because accurate versions could be reproduced rather easily. Even the current ease of travel influences the course of music in that it allows musicians from various places to hear music, which in turn brings about a wider knowledge of all kinds of music. However, the most significant technological development has been the mass availability of music through broadcasting and recordings, a topic that merits special attention.

MASS AVAILABILITY OF MUSIC. In the eighteenth century the Esterházy family could ask Haydn to create music whenever they wanted it. Few people during that age were rich enough to join the circle of privileged listeners or to maintain their own resident composer and orchestra. Today we can buy for less than twenty dollars two Haydn symphonies on a superb compact disc performed by one of the world's fine orchestras.

No other technological changes have had such an impact on the world of music as electro-acoustical reproduction. Not only did it have a devastating, impact on the employment of commercial and theater musicians (and encourage many of them to go into teaching music in the schools), it affected greatly the way people listen, what they listen to, their need to perform music, and the way music is marketed. It should also affect the way music is taught.

The fact that there is music virtually everywhere has encouraged people *not* to listen to it. They simply cannot give concentrated attention to all the music they hear each day, and often the conditions under which the music is heard are not conducive to careful listening. So people learn to ignore much of what they hear, just as they overlook sounds of traffic, a clock ticking, and so on. The fact that people acquire the habit of not listening carefully to music is perhaps the most detrimental effect of its mass availability.

The pervasiveness of recorded popular music in today's society has also encouraged the development of listening expectations that are generally at odds with those required for art music. For one thing, popular music is often reproduced at loud dynamic levels. In comparison, the restrained dynamics of some art music works must seem rather pale to many people.

Second, there is a difference in the time dimension for the listener. Most popular music states its ideas clearly in the first thirty or forty measures. There is virtually no thematic development and the entire piece is usually over in less than three minutes. So the longer time frame of many works of art music is incomprehensible and even irritating to the person who has established a faster "time clock" for music. To that person, the gradual nursing of a motive by a composer such as Sibelius must be something like watching a slow-motion film of an athletic contest.

Third, most popular music does not present imaginative or refined treatment of the musical material. Some of it is deliberately primitive and crude, a characteristic that is boasted about in the advertising of some rock groups. Listeners, therefore, learn not to listen for skillful composition. When they do hear music with subtle or complex nuances, they don't apprehend them and consequently find such music lacking in vitality.

Fourth, much popular music is associated with physical and visual activity. A musical performance by a rock group often includes lighting effects and much movement by the performers. The audience does not expect or even accept only listening in the usual concert-behavior sense. They clap, dance, and/or sing along. While involvement is desirable in some aspects, it does interfere with hearing the music carefully. If one claps and dances through Debussy's String Quartet, he or she will miss much that the music has to offer.

There are some additional liabilities of the mass availability of music. When the contact most people have with music is through recordings or radio, usually it becomes largely a passive matter of accepting what someone else has done. This type of experience is less of a personal expression, and is therefore less meaningful. It is analogous to buying and sending a printed birthday card instead of writing a personal letter of good wishes for the occasion.

Most of the music that people hear today is produced by someone else and presented by some electro-acoustical means. In previous centuries this was not so. Every performance was a live performance; if music was desired, the people themselves or someone they knew had to make it. For example, people often accompanied themselves at square dances by singing or playing a fiddle; without their own efforts there would have been no music.

The change from live to recorded music has greatly reduced the importance of public performances. Although there are a few highly publicized rock festivals, popular music exists primarily on recordings, not in printed music or at concerts. Some performers of popular music almost never perform in public. On the other hand, in spite of high ticket prices, the long distances that many people must travel to the place of performance, and the elitist atmosphere of the concert hall, art music concerts still continue to draw an audience, which is a testimony of a sort to the genre's vitality and value.

Most of the music we hear today, both art and popular, is not heard in its "pure" form. It is manipulated and altered by recording techniques and amplification equipment. A fourth party—the electronic technician—has been added to the traditional progression from composer to performer to listener. The involvement of technology with music is not new or necessarily undesirable, but it does raise questions about the authenticity of what is heard. Especially in popular music there is a great difference between the actual sound of the singer's voice and what comes out of the loudspeaker. Some recordings are as much the product of the recording engineer as they are of the performer listed on the label. Also, the enriched sounds of a recording can discourage or confuse people when they listen to a live performance. The unamplified live performance may appear dull by comparison, and the sounds and timbres may seem false.

IMPLICATIONS FOR TEACHING. The mass availability of music should affect what music teachers do in class and rehearsal rooms. One thing they should do is try to develop in their students two approaches toward music listening. One approach consists of keen attention to and contemplation of the sounds. This is required for music in which the sounds are handled in a complex, subtle, and sophisticated manner. This approach is learned only through persistent effort and attention to detail. The other approach is one that consists of casual attention to the sounds. It is an acceptable mode of listening for most commercial, popular music, and it is usually learned without much help or effort. In brief, the basis of the two approaches to music listening is that some music must be listened to carefully if the listener is to appreciate its intricacies, while other music is structured simply enough to be grasped without much effort. Unless music teachers are able to impart this distinction to their students, the vast majority of them will continue with their usual approach of listening in a halfhearted, careless manner.

The categorizing of music into the two types can be challenged on the grounds that it does not accurately account for every piece. This is true; not every piece of music falls neatly into a category. But the great majority do. One need only look over the list of best-selling records in *Billboard* magazine to realize that the few popular music groups that manipulate sound in a more subtle and sophisticated manner represent only a small portion of the popular music field. They are the exception, not the rule.

When one no longer needs to play or sing in order to have music, the type of music education given should change somewhat (but not entirely!). The skills associated with music making—music reading, singing methods, and so on—are not as significant in the classroom as they were in the past, but definitely should not be dropped. Instead, listening to music becomes more significant and some effort should be devoted to teaching listening techniques. Teachers repeatedly exhort their students to listen carefully, of course. This is fine, but many students do not know how to listen carefully, or what to listen for. They need a type of "ear training" designed for nonmusicians. In recent years some books and materials for this purpose have been published, but there is still much work to be done.

Music teachers should encourage live music making, because without such efforts that activity will become even less common than it is today. Most predictions are partly self-fulfilling in that people tend to take actions that make the predictions come true. If it is prophesied that performing music is fading, teachers may be tempted to stop teaching and encouraging music making. As hinted in the preceding paragraph, a sizable reduction in the activities of singing, music reading, or playing should be avoided. Experience with actual performance is still an excellent means of fostering an understanding of music, as well as being a satisfying activity in itself.

Because youth is action-oriented, music teachers need to be imaginative in devising active techniques for presenting music. Audiovisual equipment is one potential resource. Electronic equipment with feedback of the student's responses and performance offers opportunities that have hardly been touched by music educators. Computer-assisted instruction is another approach that is in embryonic stages. Music teachers also need to work harder at incorporating the music activities of young people that take place outside of school into the school music program. The sale of millions of electronic keyboards each year provides music teachers with an improved chance to relate the music instruction received in school with music making at home.

It is seldom possible for teachers to control sociological factors to the degree they can manage other aspects of teaching. Culture, social stratification, ethnocentrism, and technological changes are all facts of life, and they very much influence what happens in music class and rehearsal rooms. However, music educators can influence some sociological conditions and in other instances take them into consideration in their teaching.

Summary

This chapter explored a number of sociological concepts and their implications for teaching music. The specific ideas discussed included:

1. Nature/nurture: the relative influence on human behavior of inborn qualities versus the effect of what is learned after birth. Both appear to be significant, but a teacher's obligation still remains to teach each student as well as, and as much as, possible.

2. Socialization: the process by which the young learn how to live in society. This process is essential for people to acquire the characteristics that mark them as human, which is a major reason for education.

3. Music as a human behavior: the idea that music is something that people learn, just as they learn many other things in their lives. Music is of this world, so to speak, not somewhere out in the cosmos.

4. Functions of music: the concept that music fulfills different needs and roles in human life. These roles include emotional expression, aesthetic enjoyment, entertainment, and maintenance of the cohesiveness of society.

5. Social stratification: the mental construct of differing levels within society, and its effect on what people do. These differences significantly affect music preferences and the use of music.

6. Age stratification: how being in a particular age group affects a person's actions and interests. These differences are especially important to music teaching in the secondary schools.

7. Ethnocentrism: the tendency of people to view things using their own group as the standard. It is typical to think that one's own society or group is superior.

8. Pluralism: the concept that society is made up of many different groups with different interests and styles of life. The pluralism of American society makes it necessary for music teachers to try to meet the need for diversity within unity.

9. Cultural standards: the fact that such standards are largely qualitative and cannot be defined in a rational way. They exist, and in a sense are their own justification for being.

10. Mass taste: the question of whether the increased democratization of Western society has lowered the quality of the fine arts. The answer to this question is complex and unclear.

11. The effect of technology on music and music teaching: the mass availability of music is something new in human existence, and it has greatly affected how people experience music, and, in turn, how music should be taught.

STUDY AND DISCUSSION QUESTIONS

1. What evidence is there to support the belief that environment largely determines a person's attributes? What evidence is there to support the idea that heredity largely determines a person's attributes?

2. What is socialization, as the term is used sociologically? What implications does this process have for the learning of music?

3. What are some of the social functions of music? How do such functions differ from the aesthetic, artistic function of music?

4. How should the role or function of a musical work affect what a music teacher does with it?

5. What is the "deferred gratification pattern"? How does it affect musical preferences?

6. How does socioeconomic status affect the kinds of music people know and like?

7. What implications do the age-level differences in musical preferences and knowledge have for music teachers in the schools?

8. What does the term *pluralism* mean? What implications does the pluralistic nature of American society have for music educators?

9. Why is it rather logical that people adopt at least a somewhat ethnocentric view of culture and music?

10. What important point is contained in the phrase "There is no disputing tastes"? What are some implications of that point for music educators?

11. What are some ways in which technological advances in reproducing music should influence (or have influenced) how music is taught?

INDIVIDUAL OR CLASS ACTIVITIES

1. Observe and analyze the social (*not* musical or aesthetic) aspects of one situation in which music is performed and/or listened to. Situations that might be studied could include a string quartet recital, the performance of an anthem by a church choir during a worship service, the music performed at a school dance, or the music used for a graduation ceremony. Describe how the social aspects you identify influence the type of music used, the type of audience or participants, the response of the audience or performers, the manner in which the music is performed, and so on.

2. Divide the class into two groups. One group can represent the view that music and the other fine arts are "above" or better than everyday life; the other group should represent the view that music and the arts are a part of life, or at least should be a part of life. Each group should develop some reasons to support its position, as well as be able to refute the claims of the other group. Support can come from scholarly writings, research findings, or logical thinking.

REFERENCES

BANTOCK, G. H. (1968). *Culture, industrialization and education.* London: Routledge & Kegan Paul.

BAUMOL, W., & BOWEN, W. (1966). *The performing arts: The economic dilemma.* Cambridge, MA: M.I.T. Press.

BERNSTEIN, R. (1988, May 11). Anthropologist, retracing steps after 3 decades, is shocked to change. *New York Times*, p. 74.

BLUMBERG, P. (1980). *Inequality in the age of decline.* New York: Oxford University Press.

BRIDGEWATER, C. A. (1982, May). Consumer psychology. *Psychology Today*, pp. 16–20.

COLEMAN, R. D., & RAINWATER, L. (1978). *Social standing in America.* New York: Basic Books.

DAVIS, K. (1949). *Human society.* New York: Macmillan.

DENNIS, W. (1960). Causes of retardation among institutional children: Iran. *Journal of Genetic Psychology, 96,* 47–59.

DIESENHOUSE, S. (1988, April 19). Inmates are wary of person ruling. *New York Times,* p. 176.

DIMAGGIO, P., USEEM, M., & BROWN, P. (1978). *Audience studies of the performing arts and museums: a critical review* (Research Report No. 9). Washington, DC: National Endowment for the Arts.

ERLENMEYER-KIMLING, L., & JARVIK, L. F. (1963). Genetics and intelligence: A review. *Science, 142,* 1477–1478.

ETZIONI, A. (1983). *An immodest agenda.* New York: McGraw-Hill.

FARNSWORTH, P. R. (1969). *The social psychology of music* (2d ed.). Ames: Iowa State Press.

FOX, W. S., & WINCE, M. H. (1975). Music taste cultures and taste publics. *Youth and Society, 7,* 192–224.

GASTON, E. T. (1968). Factors contributing to responses in music. In E. T. Gaston (Ed.), *Music therapy.* Lawrence, KS: Allen Press.

GEERTZ, C. (1988). *Works and lives: The anthropologist as author.* Stanford, CA: Stanford University Press.

GEIGER, T. (1950). A radio test of musical taste. *Public Opinion Quarterly, 14,* 453–460.

GODDARD, H. E. (1912). *The Kallikak family.* New York: Macmillan.

HAKENEN, E. A., & WELLO, A. (1990). Adolescent music marginals: who likes metal, jazz, country, and classical. *Popular Music and Society, 14*(4), 62, 65.

HIRSCH, P. (1971). *The structure of the popular music industry.* Ann Arbor: Survey Research Center, University of Michigan.

HONIGSHEIM, P. (1989). *Sociology and music* (2d ed.). (K. P. Etzkorn, Ed.). New Brunswick, NJ: Transaction Press.

HOPKINS, J. (1973). Tomorrow's audience. In E. Kraus (Ed.), *International Music Educators yearbook.* Mainz, Germany: B. Schott's Söhne.

KAPLAN, M. (1990). *The arts: a social perspective.* Rutherford, NJ: Fairleigh Dickinson Press.

KATZ, S. (1983). Adult life expectancy. *New England Journal of Medicine, 309,* 1218–1224.

KINKEAD, E. (1959). *In every war but one.* New York: W.W. Norton.

LINK, B. G., DOHRENWEND, B. P., & SKODOL, A. E. (1986). Socio-economic status and schizophrenia. *American Sociological Review, 51,* 242–258.

LOESSER, A. (1954). *Men, women and pianos: a social history* (2d ed.). New York: Simon and Schuster.

LUNDIN, R. W. (1967). *An objective psychology of music* (2d ed.). New York: Ronald Press.

McBride, N. C. (1988, May 5). Not only do rich get richer, they vote more, too. *Christian Science Monitor*, p. 1.

Merriam, A. (1964). *The anthropology of music*. Evanston, IL: Northwestern University Press.

Mueller, J. H. (1958). Music and education: A sociological approach. In T. Madison (Ed.), *Basic concepts in music education*. Chicago: National Society for the Study of Education.

A perspective on the first music assessment (Report 03-MU-02). (1974). Denver: National Assessment of Education Progress.

Rieger, J. (1973). Overcoming the phoniness-stuffiness-jeweled dowager syndrome with young people. *Music Educators Journal, 59*(9), 29–31.

Roach, J. L., Cross, L., & Grusslin, O. R. (1969). *Social stratification in the United States*. Englewood Cliffs, NJ: Prentice-Hall.

Robinson, J. P., & Hirsch, P. M. (1969). *Teenage response to rock and roll protest songs*. Paper presented at the annual meeting of the American Sociological Association, San Francisco.

Schneider, L., & Lysgaard, S. (1953). The deferred gratification pattern. *American Sociological Review, 18*, 330–335.

Schoenberg, A. (1951). *Style and idea*. London: Williams and Norgate.

Schuessler, K. F. (1948). Social backgrounds and musical taste. *American Sociological Review, 13*.

Smith, T. W. (1984). America's religious mosaic. *American Demographics, 6*, 19–23.

Sumner, W. G. (1906). *Folkways* (3rd ed.). Boston: Ginn.

Tocqueville, A. de (1956). *Democracy in America*. New York: New American Library.

Toffler, A. (1965). *The culture consumers*. Baltimore: Penguin.

Turner, W. J. (1938). *Mozart: The man and his music*. New York: Knopf.

Vander Zanden, J. W. (1990). *The social experience*. New York: McGraw-Hill.

Vulliamy, G. (1977). Music and the mass culture debate. In J. Shepherd, P. Virden, G. Vulliamy, & T. Wishart (Eds.), *Whose music? A sociology of music languages*. London: Latimer.

Warner, W. L. (1960). *Social class in America*. New York: Harper and Brothers.

Watson, J. B. (1927). The behaviorist looks at instincts. *Harper's Magazine*.

Watson, J. B., & Raynor, R. (1921). Conditioned emotional reactions. *Journal of Experimental Psychology, 3*(8).

Weinberg, M. S., & Williams, C. J. (1980). Sexual embourgeoisment? Social class and sexual activity: 1938–1970. *American Sociological Review, 45*, 33–48.

6

Social Psychological Foundations of Music Education

SOCIAL PSYCHOLOGY is an academic discipline that studies human behavior. Like the other social sciences, it assumes that much of what humans do is the result of social conditioning and acculturation. It emphasizes the inter-action between society and the individual, while sociology concentrates on interactions among groups. Social psychologists, for example, are more likely to be interested in how individuals acquire musical preferences, and sociologists more inclined to study the roles of music in a society. The line between sociology and social psychology is not a clear one, however, and in more than one university the sociology and psychology departments have each laid claim to the discipline.

A number of social psychological factors very much affect what music teachers are able to accomplish. In fact, this chapter can only scratch the surface of those aspects that influence music education.

Self-Image

At about the turn of the twentieth century Charles Horton Cooley (1902, pp. 102–3) coined the phrase "looking-glass self" to describe the process of discovering the nature of one's self from the reactions of others. He described three parts in the development of the looking-glass self. One is our perception of how we look to others; the second part is our perception of their judgment of how we look; and the third part is our feelings about these perceived judgments. Suppose that you thought of yourself as of at least average attractiveness; that would constitute the first aspect of the looking-glass self. In such a case you would think that others would find you reasonably attractive—the second aspect. Yet, suppose also that every time you asked someone of the opposite sex for a date, you were given lame excuses and turned down. This situation would begin to give you the impression that something was rather undesirable about you, perhaps your appearance, or perhaps—the manufacturers of toilet articles and grooming aids thrive on doubts about such things—something about your breath or teeth or hair. In any case, doubts would begin to well up in your mind, which would alter your original impression about your attractiveness to others—a revision of the second part of the looking-glass self. The third part of the looking-glass self, the part concerned with feelings about the judgments of others, would also be involved, and in this example its reactions would probably be unhappy ones.

George Herbert Mead (1934, part 3, pp. 140–41) pointed out another aspect of self-image, which he labeled the "generalized other." In this aspect of self-image a person looks at himself or herself as though he or she was another person, and judges his or her actions and appearance according to the opinions of the generalized other. This notion is an extension of Cooley's looking-glass self in that the generalized other develops positions partly from perceptions gained about what others think. An example of Mead's generalized other can be seen when a little girl plays with a doll. She can do this only if she puts herself in the role of another person, usually her mother. The individual is never really alone, according to Mead, because he or she is always responding inwardly to a pattern of behavior attributed to other people. There are always present the social expectations of others, which is the subject of the "Peanuts" cartoon (figure 6.1).

The generalized other is concerned with self-respect and personal identity. Identity permits an individual to distinguish those elements or characteristics that make him or her different from others. Self-respect concerns a person's perception of how he or she is rated by others, especially others the person regards with esteem.

SELF-SERVING BIAS. There is a tendency for all of us to hold a self-serving bias that protects our self-image. As Whitely and Frieze (1985, pp. 608–16; 1986 pp. 35–51) point out, people attribute their successes to their ability and effort; at the same time, they attribute their failures to external factors such as bad luck and the inherent "impossible" nature of the problem. For example, athletes explain their victories by hard work

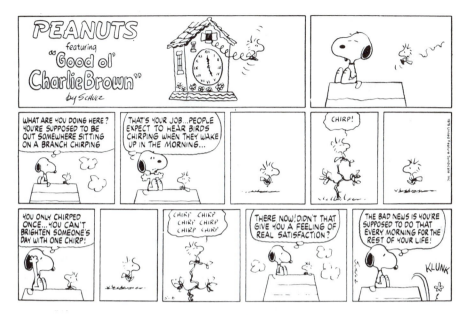

Figure 6.1. PEANUTS reprinted by permission of UFS, Inc.

and skill, but blame their defeats on bad breaks, poor officiating, and the other team's superhuman efforts (Mullen & Riordan, 1988, pp. 3–22). As Ross and Fletcher state, "The need to view oneself in a favorable way following a success or failure . . . may be one of the best established, most often replicated, findings in social psychology" (1985, p. 73).

The tendency to be self-serving affects how people view their abilities in relation to others. For example, business managers see themselves as offering more encouragement of openness and innovation (Hollander, 1985, p. 485). High school seniors taking the Scholastic Aptitude Test are sometimes asked: "How [do] you feel you compare with others your own age in certain areas of ability?" Seventy percent rated themselves as above average in "leadership ability"; 2 percent rated themselves as below average. In "ability to get along with others," *zero* percent rated themselves as below average, 60 percent placed themselves in the top 10 percent, and 25 percent viewed themselves as in the top 1 percent (Myers, 1990, p. 84). One wonders what the responses would be if such questions were asked of music educators regarding their teaching abilities! Unfortunately, no such study is available. Apparently Garrison Keillor's weekly observation about his fictitious town of Lake Wobegon on his radio show "Prairie Home Companion" is true: "All the children are above average."

The tendency of humans to hold a self-serving bias explains at least part of the difficulties encountered in evaluating teachers for merit pay and rating the performances of music students and groups. Because teaching and musical performance contain a heavy element of subjectivity, they trigger more self-serving biases due to their potential for flexibility in defining what good teaching or performing is. The fact that evaluations of success in teaching or performing music sometimes conclude with disputes and feelings of unfairness should not be surprising. Indeed, it would be much more surprising if there were no such disagreements, given the nature of human nature to be self-serving.

Formation of Self-Image

How is self-image formed? It is an extremely complex process, which may be an intellectual way of saying that no one really knows. Probably it is not the simple phenomenon of trying to model oneself after someone who is admired. It is more likely a process of observing actions and appearances that one likes, and then forming a composite of them into the desired image, with adjustments according to one's capabilities and characteristics. Still unanswered, however, is the matter of why certain characteristics are liked and others aren't. The family has a strong influence, but it is only one factor. Contacts with others outside the family are certainly important, too, but many other influences are present, including what is seen in movies and television and in advertisements.

Music educators can probably influence the formation of self-image only to a limited degree, but they can at least have some effect. They can attempt to associate music with desired self-image.

The suggestion to make music a part of an esteemed self-image should not be misconstrued to mean that it should be given snob appeal. Snobbery is an attitude of "I am better than most other people are," which is rather different from the idea of a person thinking of himself or herself as an informed, able, and honorable person. Snobbery excludes most persons; the goal of developing educated and upstanding people is for everybody. What music teachers subtly need to develop in their students is the idea that they should—to put it in the vernacular—be neither snobs nor slobs.

Associating music, especially art music, with a positive self-image motivates a person to learn about music and become more involved with it. People try to be the kind of person they hope to be; "This above all; to thine own self be true" is the way Shakespeare expressed it in *Hamlet*. Actually it is somewhat of a "chicken-egg" situation regarding which comes first: Does a positive self-image lead to learning about music, or does a knowledge and understanding of music lead to a better self-image? Probably it works both ways. In any case, music teachers who motivate students through an attitude of "You don't want to be ignorant" are on firm ground from the standpoint of social psychology.

Another way to influence self-image is to borrow a technique used by clothing and liquor advertising in attempting to form an association in the students' minds between art music and social status. The slogan "Dress for success" may be shallow and misleading, but it does seem to help sell quality clothing. Liquor ads never show winos sleeping in doorways in the slums of a city. Instead, they give their product an elegant image with pictures of elegant-looking people and slogans like "It's downright upright." The slogan "Music is downright upright" will not by itself put music in everyone's self-image, but such an appeal is a step in the right direction.

Also important is the reduction of any age, social class, or ethnic gaps between the students and music. A number of ideas for achieving this were offered in chapter 5.

Music and Self-Image

The phenomenon of the self-image has an important effect on preferences. Perhaps the relationship between self-image and preference can be more easily explained in terms of clothing than music, because most of the readers of this book are so close to music that it is difficult to be objective about it. In a clothing store one's generalized other is actively engaged as one stands before a mirror trying to decide which clothes to buy. Although we seldom articulate it, we want our appearance to give a certain impression, which is partly the result of what others expect of us and partly what we want others to think of us. Items of clothing are bought or rejected because they look young or old, cheap or expensive, flashy or conservative, and so on.

Music, clothes, styles of speech, cars, and many other things are often treated by people as accouterments as identifying trappings. They are seen as contributing to the image a person wants to present. The man who wears a tie at work and the woman who puts on stockings both have a self-image that is likely to be associated with listening to art music, because art music is likely to be viewed as part of the image of being "educated," "cultured," "informed," "not tacky," and the like. A person who has a different self-image might avoid using correct English in some situations, wear work boots and no tie, and avoid listening to symphonies or operas. Self-image is also related to the concept of social class discussed in chapter 5, although this is not always so.

Conformity

Almost everyone has seen how people tend to follow or accept what others do or think. For example, when someone on a street stares up into the sky, other people tend to begin looking up also. This tendency to rely on others for the verification of observations and for decisions on what actions to take is termed *conformity*.

Conformity has been tested in the psychological laboratory by Sherif, Asch, and others. Asch's work (1952) is especially interesting. He constructed a simple experiment in which the subjects were shown two cards containing a total of four lines, which are shown in figure 6.2. The subjects were asked to choose the line on the first card that was most similar in length to the line on the second card. As can be seen in the figure, the B line on the right card is exactly the same length as the X line on the left card, while the other two are rather different in length. A small group of subjects was shown the cards and responded verbally, one after another giving their judgments about the length of the lines. When everyone had responded, another set of cards was shown, and so on.

For the first several cards there was no problem; everyone answered correctly. However, this situation was soon to change. The first subject had been coached to give an incorrect answer at this point. He looked carefully at the lines, and then gave the wrong answer. The next three subjects, who had also been coached, gave the same answer as the first subject. When it was time for the fifth subject to respond, he was quite disturbed. It was clear that the others were wrong in their answers. The uncoached participant faced a difficult choice: either disagree with the unanimous opinion of what appeared to be normal and intelligent people or give an answer that seemed wrong. The results? Over the course of many experiments and many trials in each experiment, subjects went against the evidence of their own eyes and gave the incorrect answer provided by others about 35 percent of the time. Some persons were not swayed by the opin-

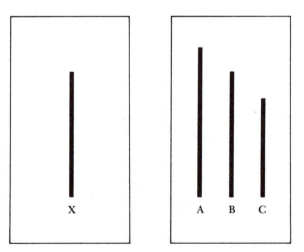

Figure 6.2. Cards for Asch's conformity experiments. Copyright © Solomon E. Asch. Used by permission.

ions of others, but overall an incorrect response was given about one time in three.

Similar experiments have been tried by other psychologists using variations of the Asch model. Inglefield found this phenomenon among musical judgments of ninth-grade students (1968, pp. 175–76). In his experiment, the participants indicated musical preferences by pushing buttons on a small box. The equipment also purported to show the preferences of the other subjects. However, the responses provided were not the actual ones; false ones had been substituted to test the effect of a need for conformity on the subjects. In a replication of the Asch design, Radocy also (1975) conducted a study in which college music majors altered their reported perceptions of pitch and loudness.

The human tendency to determine attitudes, actions, and in a sense reality from others can also be seen in many other ways. One more example will suffice here. Latané and Darley (1968) have studied the phenomenon in which persons obviously in need of help were ignored by large numbers of people. The most famous such case is the widely publicized murder of Kitty Genovese, which was made into a television drama. Thirty-eight people saw her screaming, but no one helped or even called the police.

It is impossible, of course, to replicate such situations for experimental purposes, but Latané and Rodin (1969) tried several approaches. In one experiment subjects were put in a room either alone or with other subjects. Smoke was then induced into the room through the ventilation system. When subjects were alone, they usually reported the smoke promptly; 50 percent reported it after two minutes and 75 percent within six minutes. However, when other people were present, there was a strong tendency not to report the smoke at all; the range of reporting varied between 10 and 38 percent, depending on the circumstances. While humans are not quite like the Norwegian lemmings that sometimes follow one another in a death procession into the sea, they are strongly influenced by what others do, even to the extent of ignoring their senses and consciences.

Why Conformity?

What encourages people to conform? There are two basic reasons. One is that following the accepted behavior of the group leads to one's own acceptance in the group. The tendency "to go along" with the groups is therefore strong, especially if the action is seen as a rather minor matter. Who cares which hand you shake hands with, or the style of the handshake? People who deviate from accepted practice or beliefs face disapproval or even rejection (Schacter, 1951; pp. 190–207; Miller & Anderson, 1979, pp. 354–63).

The other reason for conforming is for information or confirmation. A novice concert-goer may look around before applauding to find out how and when to applaud. Clapping at the wrong time or yelling out "One more time!" at a chamber music recital can be embarrassing. Sometimes when a person sees something highly unusual, he or she will ask someone, "Did you see that?" People want to be reassured that their senses and sensibilities are not deceiving them.

What factors influence how conformist a person is? One is the confidence that one has in the opinion of others. It is not easy to argue with the opinions of an expert like Itzhak Perlman as to how the Tchaikovsky Violin Concerto should be performed. Even though you may be a good violinist, you are going to give his views very serious consideration. In one study Radocy (1976) played paired excerpts from what were actually the same recordings, but bogus information was provided to one group of listeners. The evaluations were significantly affected by whether the subjects thought the music was performed by renowned performers or performers who were unknown (such as graduate students). The degree of unanimity has an important effect on whether people conform or not. Once the unanimity of the group is punctured, the group's influence is weakened (Asch, 1955, pp. 31–35; Morris & Miller, 1975, pp. 215–23). The more cohesive the group is, which usually means limits on the size of the group, the greater the tendency for its members to conform (Crandall, 1988, pp. 588–98). Finally, the less secure a person is, the more likely he or she is to conform to the group's views.

Adolescent Conformity

Because youngsters at twelve and thirteen years of age are undergoing so many changes so rapidly, it is natural that they feel less than secure in what they are doing. It is probably this sense of insecurity that more than anything else encourages the high degree of conformity found among adolescents (figure 6.3). Both casual observation and psychological research confirm this fact, as can be seen in figure 6.4 (Sprinthall & Sprinthall, 1977, p. 209). One of the authors recalls when "all" (that was what he was told) the girls in his daughter's seventh-grade class began wearing clog shoes. The first day his daughter wore them she came home from school with the tops of her feet raw and bleeding slightly. In spite of this, she still pleaded for the chance to wear them again the next day and claimed that her feet didn't *really* hurt. Such is the power of conformity at that age.

If conformist behavior is strong enough to cause adolescents to wear uncomfortable shoes, it certainly is strong enough to affect their musical interests. It is not possible to predict what styles of music will be the favorites of teenagers in the future, but it can be assumed that the styles

Figure 6.3. Reprinted with special permission of King Features Syndicate.

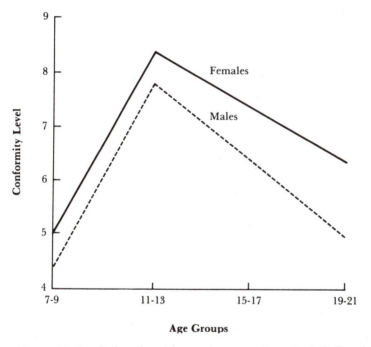

Age Groups

Figure 6.4. Level of conformity at various ages. From Sprinthall and Sprinthall, *Educational Psychology: A Developmental Approach*, p. 209. Copyright © 1977 Addison-Wesley, Reading, MA. Used by permission.

will be adopted with a high degree of homogeneity. Not only does conformist behavior influence the music that teenagers talk about, buy, and play for their friends and at school dances; it also carries over to their private listening. As David Riesman (1954, p. 189) points out:

> When he [the teenager] listens to music, even if no one else is around, he lis-
> tens in a context of imaginary "others"—his listening is indeed often an
> effort to establish connection with them. In general what he perceives in the
> mass media is framed by his perception of the peer group to which he
> belongs. These groups not only rate the tunes but select for their members in
> more subtle ways what is to be "heard" in each tune. It is the pressure of
> conformity with the group that invites and compels the individual to have
> recourse to the media both in order to learn from them what the group
> expects and to identify with the group by sharing a common focus for atten-
> tion and talk.

The importance of peer groups to teenagers can work both for and against quality music education. It is positive that once the music program becomes "the thing to be in," it can grow and achieve phenomenally. The trick is to get the trend moving in the right direction, because it can just as easily go in the wrong direction. There are no sure means by which this can be accomplished. In general, it appears that successful music classes and groups in the eyes of the students stand the best chance of being regarded favorably, with the phrase "in the eyes of the students" being crucial. What teenagers regard as "successful" may differ considerably from what music teachers think is successful. The teacher may want a high rating in contests and esteem from his or her colleagues, but what most students want more than that is recognition and praise from their peers. Along with music of artistic quality, one choral director who was aware of this need among adolescents included in every program one or two num-bers that were very likely to win over the students in the audience. Usually these numbers were entertaining, popular, or semipopular ones, and they were often staged or danced to. Through these numbers the young per-formers could receive the applause and recognition they wanted from the student body.

Another way to influence teenagers favorably toward music is to let the students feel that the class or group is theirs as much as the teacher's. This may mean letting students decide on which of two numbers they will per-form, asking students to write and deliver the commentary on the music at a program, asking them to invest in the organization by supplying part of the uniform, and so on.

Conformity and Music Learning

Of course, conformity affects the musical behavior of people other than adolescents. Human beings learn from observing how other people respond, and what they respond to, when hearing music. In many situa-tions around the world the audience does not passively listen as it does in a concert hall here; instead it participates by clapping, singing, and shouting out words of encouragement to the performers. Each of the uses of music

described in chapter 5 has its concomitant mode of behavior for both performers and listeners.

How we react to music is learned from others, usually vicariously. If
music is being played in a room and everyone is talking and otherwise
ignoring the sounds, one gains the idea that the music is not to be contem-
plated carefully. If the listeners in the room are "grooving" and swooning
over the music, thereby giving the impression that they are being trans-
ported to ecstatic realms, it is easy to get the idea that this is how one
should react. There are certain situations in which people talk and largely
ignore music, while at other times they listen carefully, and such distinc-
tions are learned.

Roles and Expectations

Rarely is William Shakespeare thought of as a social psychologist, even if
he did possess a number of social psychological insights. In *As You Like It*
the character of Jaques recites these lines:

> *All the world's a stage,*
> *And all the men and women merely players:*
> *They have their exits and their entrances;*
> *And one man in his time plays many parts. . . .*
> —(*Macmillan Dictionary of Quotations*, 1989, p. 520)

Indeed, the actor playing Jaques has one role, Shakespeare had another,
the stage manager another, and so on. And each person must carry out his
or her role if the drama is to be successful.

Actually, all of us play a number of different roles — a mother or
father, teacher or other professional, a student, sometimes a member of a
group and sometimes a leader in that group, amateur athlete, spouse, and
many more. The more clearly a role is defined, the more effectively it is
carried out. The actor who delivers Shakespeare's words has less trouble
carrying out his role than the manager of the theater company, which is a
job that entails a wide variety of activities ranging from handling finances
to solving personnel problems.

Sometimes one role conflicts with another, which is termed *interrole
conflict*. The theater manager may have to spend many extra hours at the
job, which reduces the time spent with family or on outside activities.
Although occupying several roles has disadvantages in terms of some conflicts, it has at least one advantage. A person's sense of self-worth is less
threatened by problems in any given area (Linville, 1987). The theater
manager who does not do a good job of it can still think, for example:
"Well, I am a good parent (or student, or athlete), at least."

Within limits people generally do what they are expected to do by others and/or themselves. These expectations are not spelled out in "orders of the day," but rather are gained vicariously from contacts with other people. Informally children learn that they are expected to be kind to animals, earn a living someday, eat with a fork and spoon, yell only under certain conditions, keep their hair combed, shake hands when meeting someone, and so on. In music, expectations affect everything from concert manners to singing ability to choice of instrument. The importance of expectations is humorously illustrated in figure 6.1.

An American educator-friend of one of the authors spent two years working as a consultant to the Korean educational system. When he returned to the United States, he expressed a number of very favorable impressions about the children and people of Korea (Hedges, 1965). One of his observations was: "I never encountered a Korean child who couldn't sing quite well," and he went on to tell how impressed he was with the singing in the classrooms he had visited. Similar reports have been given by educators who visited Hungarian schools, and especially the Singing Schools, in which music receives special attention. If one can believe the sources available to us today, in Elizabethan England any gentleman worthy of his velvet cape was expected to be able to sing madrigals at sight, and apparently most of them could do so. Even a madrigal composer as important as Thomas Morley was not exempted from the requirement. He described, in 1597, his discomfort as a dinner guest.

> But supper being ended, and music books, according to the custom, being brought to the table, the mistress of the house presented me with a part, earnestly requesting me to sing: but when, after many excuses, I protested unfeignedly that I could not, everyone began to wonder; yes, some whispered to others, demanding how I was brought up! (Ariès. 1962, p. 79)

In contemporary America there is a folk axiom of sorts that says that girls can sing and boys can't do so nearly as well. Anyone who has heard men sing at a Rotary or Kiwanis club meeting has witnessed how well the men fulfill the expectation of poor singing.

Four of the examples in the preceding paragraphs demonstrate the power of expectation in music. Expectations work in a positive sense with the Korean and Hungarian children. Undoubtedly there are some Korean and Hungarian children who don't sing very well, but they have learned to do enough to be acceptable as singers, largely because it is expected that they do so.

Do teacher's expectations of students' work have a significant impact on whether they learn or not? It is clear that the evaluations of teachers are correlated with the achievement of students. Teachers rate students higher who do well. But are those high ratings *caused by* or *the cause of* student performance? The answer to that question is by no means clear.

To test the idea, Rosenthal and Jacobson (1968) randomly selected children, who were then described to teachers in terms of bogus information as being on the verge of a spurt of intellectual growth. The subsequent improvement in designated students' academic work appeared to suggest that the problem of low achievement was largely the result of low teacher expectations. But further studies and analysis have tempered this conclusion. Even by Rosenthal's own count, in only 36 percent of the hundreds of studies available on this question do teachers' expectations make a significant difference (Rosenthal, 1985, 1987). Apparently, it's not a simple matter of what teachers expect. The expectations teachers have sometimes have a significant effect on learning, but sometimes they do not.

Does the reverse situation also apply? Do student expectations affect how well they learn? Does a teacher with a strong reputation as a successful teacher cause him or her to be a more successful teacher? To a degree, the answers to these questions seem to be yes. Feldman and Prohaska (1979) and Jamieson, Lydon, Stewart, and Zanna (1987) have demonstrated that such expectations affect both the students and the teacher.

Expectations are not only based on academic or intellectual capabilities. Whether or not it is valid or sensible, there also exist in America differing musical expectations according to sex, an example of which is the singing in men's club meetings recently mentioned. In an article that contains some reminiscences about his youth, Max Kaplan (1970 pp. 39–42), a writer on sociology and music education, tells how when he grew up in a city ghetto he would sneak through the alleys to his violin lessons, because any boy who played the violin was ridiculed as a sissy by his peers.

Abeles and Porter (1978) sampled the opinions of adults about what instrument they would like their son or daughter to play. The clarinet, flute, and violin were preferred for the daughters, and drums, trombone, and trumpet for the sons. In another study discussed in their 1978 article, Abeles and Porter attempted to find out at what age gender/instrument associations first appear. Children from kindergarten through fifth grade were shown pictures of instruments and asked to state preferences. The preferences were not strong in young children, but after grade 3 they become rather well established. The boys selected "masculine" instruments and the girls "feminine" instruments, just as the adults had done. Griswold and Chronback (1981, pp. 57–62) and Holt (1991, pp. 54–55) conducted replications of the studies by Abeles and Porter. Their studies indicate little change in gender associations since 1978. A study by Brandenberg (1991, p. 36) found that the electric keyboard was favored by males, while the piano was favored by females.

Other sex differences among American children with regard to musical ability and interest have tended to support the notion that music is more for girls than boys, except for the playing of certain instruments (*Music Technical Report*, 1975, pp. 11–124).

The expectations of a society regarding interest and ability in music have an enormous effect on what music teachers can accomplish. Imagine how much more they could teach if American society provided the support that exists in Korea and Hungary! Unfortunately for music teachers in America, changes in roles and expectations happen with the speed of a glacier; they do change, but only over a long period of time. Music teachers can, however, encourage the process of change a little bit. For one thing, the suggestions for incorporating music into a desirable self-image that were presented earlier in this chapter will help.

Most of the encouragement of change cannot be done directly in the instructional process, but must occur in society at large. To the extent that music becomes more vital in our culture, the task of music teachers in the schools is made easier. It is for this reason (among others) that music educators should work with arts councils, the music industry and music merchants, and the mass media to promote music in every possible way. The results of such cooperation are seldom visible in the immediate future, but in the long run it is bound to help. Not all the efforts at improving the attitudes of American society toward music will be fruitful, however. As John Wanamaker, founder of the largest and most successful department store in Philadelphia, is reported to have said: "Half of the money I spend on advertising is wasted, and the trouble is I don't know which half" (Adams, 1969, p. 9). Wanamaker apparently thought—correctly—that half being wasted was better than nothing being gained.

Competition/Cooperation

Competition enjoys a long history in the world of music. Handel endured much from competitive singers; two sopranos actually got into a hair-pulling fight onstage one night while members of the royal family, including Princess Caroline, were in the audience. To prove his drawing power at the box office, Liszt scheduled a performance at the same time as a rival pianist named Thalberg was giving a concert across the street. Music contests have traditionally been important in music, and competitions are held in many places in the world to help launch the careers of young performers.

Cooperation has existed for a long time in music too, but it rarely receives the attention that competition does. Any ensemble must work together to make music, as is inherent in the definition of the word *ensemble* in the French language. Students work together in music classes most of the time, and in some situations they help each other learn music.

Competition is a situation in which a few people win and lots of people lose. Often there is only one winner, which prompted the late Vince Lombardi, renowned professional football coach, to say: "Wanting to win is the only thing" (*Macmillan Dictionary of Quotations*, 1989, p. 590). In contrast, cooperative efforts are designed so that, if all goes well, everyone benefits.

If cooperation benefits everyone, and competition benefits only one or a few persons, why is there so much competition in music, especially at the secondary school level? According to Kohn (1986) in his thought-provoking book, *No Contest: The Case Against Competition*, the answer lies in the prevalence of several "myths" about competition in American society, which is fueled by Americans' excessive attention to football, basketball, and baseball. One myth is that competition is a part of human nature. Kohn claims this is incorrect. As is true of so many human attributes, competitive behavior is learned. It is no more natural than racial prejudice or a subordinate status for women, both of which were thought to be natural throughout much of human history.

The second myth cited by Kohn is the belief that competition motivates people to do their best. Sometimes this appears to be true, but more often it is not the case. There is a sizable amount of research that fails to support the idea that competition provides motivation. Indeed, in complex tasks such as creating piano sonatas or solving complicated problems, competition is detrimental. The myth that competition motivates is fostered by the attention given to individuals in athletic competitions, especially events like the Olympic Games. These events receive a lot of "hype" in the media, and the stories of the athletes' long, lonely hours of training and practice are treated as glorious struggles. Of course, the many losers in these events are ignored and quickly forgotten.

The third myth about competition cited by Kohn is that it builds character. This myth exists primarily because people fail to distinguish between *competition* and *competence* — the meeting of a minimum standard of performance is some area. The gaining of competence builds self-esteem and character, but the defeating of someone often does not contribute to a person's character. Why is competition usually not helpful here? First, its goal is winning, not being competent. In other words, attention is diverted from the gaining of competency to coming out on top. Second, winning becomes paramount even if one has to break a few rules to do so, as has been demonstrated repeatedly over the years in the recruiting of college football and basketball players and the use of performance-enhancing drugs by athletes. Third, competition among music groups can draw attention away from the lasting joys of making and knowing music to defeating someone. Once the competitive situation no longer exists, a person's primary reason for being involved in music also ceases to exist.

A fourth reason why competition is not helpful is the number of persons it "discards." As Martin Maehr points out: "There is a tendency in music education to place elites and regulars on the same track, designing the system in such a way that most will inevitably fall by the wayside with only the cream of the crop surviving. Competitions, contests, and recitals all seem to revolve around that end. . . . One does not create enduring motivational patterns by showing people that they are incompetent. Insofar as an activity is structured to do that, it will be a motivational failure for the large majority of the participants" (1983, p. 10).

If winning means that you will be a hero and losing means you will be humiliated, you will usually decide that the risk is not worth it and will avoid getting into a competitive situation. Some people learn from the repeated failures in an activity that a particular activity is not for them. For example, after throwing mostly gutter balls when bowling, one is inclined to avoid bowling.

Fortunately, competition and cooperation need not be two mutually exclusive paths to learning in music. The answer to the problem that stems from this dichotomy appears to lie in devoting attention to gaining competency and using cooperative efforts to achieve it. By doing this, attention is shifted from defeating someone else to the acquiring of skills and knowledge. In this way, everyone "wins."

If the idea of competency is to be successful in motivating students, music teachers need to decide what constitutes competency at varying levels and in varying situations in music. What is satisfactory accomplishment for a first-year instrumental class is clearly not satisfactory for a high school band or orchestra; what is acceptable or a select choir should be quite different from what is acceptable achievement for a general music class.

Next, music teachers need to educate their students about what is expected in terms of competency for a particular class or group. Not only is such information required during the year the class or group exists in school, it is also valuable for the years following high school when no music teachers will be around to tell former students how a piece of music is to be performed or listened to.

The basic idea of competency is the meeting of objectives for the individual or group. Even in professional football, which is certainly a highly competitive situation, the coaches often give each player a rating for his performance in the previous game. Presumably that rating is the same whether the team won or lost, because it involves playing to the player's potential.

To a degree, the festival systems found in many states for secondary school performing groups approach the idea of competency. Instead of a contest in which a single winner is decided in various categories ("best trumpeter," "best band from a Class A high school," for example), these festivals have adjudicators rate groups according to a standard of performing competency. Theoretically, all bands or choral groups could receive a "I" rating. The standard is somewhat vague, however, because it exists only in the minds of the adjudicators, each of whom has a somewhat different standard. In practice, the goal of standardized competency evaluations is further diluted by the way directors, students, and the public view them. Too often a "I" rating is confused with winning first place, and successful directors seldom go out of their way to clarify this misunderstanding! Nevertheless, the festival idea with ratings rather than rankings is a step in the right direction.

Music teachers, especially directors of performing groups at the secondary school level, can take actions that tend to focus more attention on competency and cooperation. Such actions could include:

- Rotating the seating placements occasionally in ensembles
- Listing the students' names in printed programs in alphabetical order rather than according to chair placement
- Grading on accomplishment rather than in comparison to the other students
- Emphasizing accomplishment, especially of musical goals, instead of winning contests
- Educating the students, parents, school administrators, and the community about what constitutes success for a performing group
- Encouraging students to help each other learn

Undoubtedly, actions in addition to these are possible. The main goal should be an attitude that emphasizes learning more than winning. When that exists, appropriate actions will follow.

Leadership

Leadership involves a complex relationship between an individual and a group. Theoretically, a leader causes or enables the group to achieve certain results — a good performance of music, the defeat of an enemy, the successful launching of a sales campaign. Why some people are effective leaders, and others are not, is an interesting question. And it is an important one, too, because music teachers are often required to assume leadership positions.

Is there a set of characteristics that make a person a leader, regardless of the nature of the group or the situation? Social psychologists have largely rejected the "great leader" theory in which a certain set of characteristics assures a powerful leader. Why? Because leadership takes place in a particular setting at a particular time. History is filled with leaders who failed miserably in one situation but are acclaimed for their leadership on another setting. For example, Ulysses S. Grant led the Union army to victory in the Civil War, but later became one of the nation's most unsuccessful presidents.

What are some of the circumstances that affect leadership? First, there is the nature of the task. If the goal is the achievement of a certain task, then someone will be required who gives orders and focuses the attention of the group on that task. Conducting an orchestra is a clear example of task-oriented leadership. The idea of a leaderless orchestra was tried in the Soviet Union in the 1920s, because it was thought that having one person in a superior position to the other musicians contradicted the communistic ideal of social equality (Schwarz, 1972, pp. 46–47). The orchestra with no conductor was soon abandoned, however, because it lacked the galvanizing effect of a leader who established a uniform interpretation and standard of performance.

If the situation calls for bringing people together so that they can work out what should be done, then someone will be needed who delegates authority and involves people in the decision-making process. Many university administrators tend to be enablers who try to bring the disparate elements of a faculty together to provide an effective education for the students. Studies by Smith and Tayeb (1989) indicate that a combination of these two styles of leadership tends to be most effective. Successful leaders do a good job of overseeing tasks and yet are sensitive to individual and group needs.

A second factor affecting leadership is the sophistication of the group. A speech that is highly effective at a professional conference of well-educated people would probably fall flat in a political campaign. A third factor is the expectations of the group. Some groups expect to be involved in making decisions. A leader who fails to involve them will probably be considered dictatorial and will receive little cooperation or support. Other groups want an authoritarian leader who tells them what to do; a leader who does not give orders is seen as weak and indecisive.

A fourth factor affecting leadership concerns the position a person holds. Many persons become leaders by virtue of assignment to a leadership role. For example, a person may be appointed district supervisor of music, which designates him or her as the leader in that curricular area for the school district. An appointment to a leadership position doesn't automatically make a person into a real leader, but such a position does offer him or her a far better chance to become one. This role of leadership was discussed in chapter 4.

In recent years researchers have reexamined the characteristics of leaders. While they still reject the "great leader" concept, they do find some common features among effective leaders (Bennis, 1984, pp. 64–71; House & Singh, 1987). One characteristic they found is a sense of vision, a sense of what the group could accomplish. Second is the ability to communicate that vision to the group. Third is the ability to inspire the group to take the desired actions to turn the vision into a reality. These abilities can be thought of as "dreamer-schemer-cheerleader." To be able to do this, leaders need to be confident about their views and their ability to lead the group. Furthermore, the group needs to respect both professionally and personally the person who is going to lead them. It would be almost impossible for performers to take seriously a conductor who doesn't know an oboe from a bassoon or can't name the notes in the alto and tenor clefs. It is difficult for the members of a group to work effectively for a leader who they can't trust or in other ways find personally undesirable.

In a sense, the position of teacher in the schools involves leadership. Only qualified persons are licensed to teach. In addition, teaching is a task-oriented situation in which the goal is learning by the students. Although it is task-oriented, teacher-leaders are more successful when they are sensitive to the needs and feelings of the students. Because they have much more knowledge and skill in music than their students, teachers should be able to gain the respect of the students in terms of professional capabilities. The teacher is a local expert in music.

Teachers also have an opportunity for leadership beyond their school classes and rehearsals. They are, or should be, leaders for music in their communities. They can contribute to music-making efforts in church choirs and community bands and orchestras. They can also promote music and the arts through working with organizations such as arts councils. By doing so, music teachers can become leaders in promoting lifelong learning in music.

Part of being a leader is thinking of oneself as a leader, and not as just another teacher meeting the requirements of a job. Music teachers should think of themselves as leading a process in which students learn music. They should also think of themselves as leaders for music in their communities. The opportunity for leadership is therefore present for all music educators, but it is up to each individual to make the most of that opportunity.

Feelings of Self-Confidence

An area that becomes very important in the adolescent years is the feeling of confidence that one can operate in the adult world. Such a feeling tends to accompany physical maturation. A child's confidence is boosted when he or she becomes as tall as one or both parents, and can drive a car and do many other of the same things as adults. Sometimes teenagers get a bit carried away with their newfound abilities, leading to the observation attributed to Mark Twain (Flesch, 1966, p. 16): "When I was a boy of 14, my father was so ignorant I could hardly stand to have the old man around. But when I got to be 21, I was astonished at how much he had learned in seven years." It is vitally important for young people to gain self-confidence in meeting the challenges of, the adult world; it is a necessary part of growing up and developing a desirable self-image.

Not only do adolescents want to be able to do the same things that adults do, but they need to find a few areas in which they can excel over adults. Often teenagers develop some slang words that their parents don't know, learn some dances that older people can't do (and if the dance can shock some of the older generation, that is all the better), dress in ways that differ from their parents, and know some music that older people don't know. They want a music that is "theirs," that is different from the out-of-date music popular five or ten years ago. Part of the desire for a music of their own is related to the group identification factor mentioned in chapter 5, but partly it is a result of the need to establish feelings of self-confidence.

If one of the reasons for the existence of a "youth music" is the need for something that is theirs and not part of the adult world, this fact has some implications for music educators. One implication is that music teachers should not attempt to preempt teenagers' musical "turf." In other words, the latest pop music should not become the main fare for the performing organizations or the general music classes. As is pointed out in the chapter on curriculum, a balance among types of music is needed in school music classes.

A second implication concerns the teacher's role. The truth is that adult music teachers (roughly anyone over twenty years of age) seldom do a good job (in the eyes of the students) of teaching the currently popular music, even though the teachers may think they do. Some school music teachers may have been good performers of pop music back in their college days, but the pop music styles change so rapidly that it is difficult to avoid obsolescence. Furthermore, as Cutietta (1991, p. 28) points out, pop music is rarely performed authentically in the schools.

A third implication is that teachers should not deride or criticize the currently popular music. It is not "trash" any more than pop music was a generation or two ago. It has a useful place in the scheme of things. True, it generally was not created for artistic purposes, but that fact is true of much of the music in the world. Students want music teachers who are tolerant toward pop music, just as the teachers want the students to really give art music a fair chance. As was pointed out in chapter 5, "There is no disputing tastes."

There is also some question about whether "youth music" should be studied in the same analytical way used to study a Bach fugue, for example. Some teachers who have tried an analytical approach report that, much to their surprise, some students did not like the idea. These students appeared to fear that objective analysis would ruin a piece for them. In addition, the usual analytical procedures for studying music are not appropriate for pop music (Cutietta, 1991, p. 28).

Music teachers should try to strike a balance between being too interested in current pop music and ignoring or denigrating it. Many features of pop music can be used for comparison purposes in teaching various aspects of music. Also, music teachers should try to teach their students the place and role of pop music in the world of music as a whole.

Attitudes

One of the most important goals of music education is the development of positive attitudes toward music. Not only do music teachers want students to know music, they also want them to have favorable feelings toward it and eventually to act in accord with those feelings. A teacher can "win the battle but lose the war" if the students are taught cognitive knowledge and listening skills but end up disliking music and avoiding it whenever they can. And unlike learning in reading, writing, and arithmetic, students can avoid music after class is over by *not* buying recordings, attending concerts, or singing in church choirs. Therefore, the affective component of music education is very important.

How are attitudes formed? There are three not necessarily contradictory views on the matter. One is that attitudes are learned through the process of association and reinforcement. A student who wins a medal for a trumpet solo will gain a more positive attitude toward music than one who doesn't, and therefore will have pleasant associations with the instrument. A second view holds that attitude situations often present conflicting factors, and that the individual adopts the position that maximizes his or her benefits—the idea of "When in Rome, do as the Romans do." This view of attitude development probably does not apply as much to music as it does to matters of belief about politics or economics. A third view of attitude formation is that people seek consistency in what they encounter, and therefore like those things that fit with what they know and understand, and dislike those that don't. For example, some people dislike tone-row music because it contains no singable melodies and thus doesn't fit their understanding of music.

The development of feelings toward one's country can serve as an example of attitude formation. Early in life a child is told that he or she is an American. The name of the country is learned and positive things are heard about it. At school the songs sung about America include words such as "great," "good," "strong," "beautiful," "bountiful," "rich," and so on. When a child says something positive about America, usually people smile and agree; negative statements draw the opposite reaction, at least in most segments of American society. A child soon realizes that parents, teachers, and friends think America is a good place; by the process of imitation and reinforcement he or she tends to accept this view. Furthermore, a child tends to be exposed to only one view of America. Almost everyone he or she encounters holds the same view. Once that attitude is somewhat established, negative statements about America are rejected because they don't fit in with the person's previous knowledge. Furthermore, it is usually in an American's best interest to hold favorable attitudes toward our country. The individual is then seen by other Americans as trustworthy and possessing common sense; the opposite is thought of those who hold deviant views.

The same process that affects the development of attitudes toward the country also operates in the case of music. There is the important early exposure, largely through the family, and the reinforcement (or lack of it), and later in life the selective exposure, a fact confirmed by Schuessler's research cited in chapter 5. The differences between the formation of attitudes about one's country and about music are: (1) musical preferences carry no moral overtones, while beliefs about country do, and (2) musical preferences are quite heterogeneous. Friends and relatives usually smile and say nice things when a child sings a song in a pleasing manner, but what the child sings and the way he or she sings it may differ depending on the social and/or ethnic group.

Factors Affecting Attitude Formation

The acquisition of attitudes is affected by a number of conditions. If there be truth in the statement "I know what I like," there is also truth in the words "I like what I know." This principle has been uncovered repeatedly by social scientists. In one study Zajonc (1968) showed subjects a number of Turkish words, with some words shown more often than others. The subjects were then asked to guess the meanings of the words. There was a strong tendency for them to give positive meanings to words they had seen more often. A similar experiment was conducted by Zajonc on pictures of faces that were projected on a screen.

Similarity also affects attitude formation. It is probably easier to encourage a more positive attitude toward art music in a person who already likes Broadway musicals and other semiclassical music than it is to do so with a devoted lover of country music. People can change, but usually it is gradual, evolutionary change rather than radical, revolutionary change.

People are more willing to consider changing attitudes if they like the person who is urging the change. A friend is more convincing than a stranger; an attractive teacher with a pleasing personality is more effective in changing attitudes than a teacher who is grouchy and unattractive. This phenomenon is true partly because the association between the liked teacher and what is being taught is more pleasant, which encourages a positive reaction.

There is a tendency to conform in matters of attitude just as there is in other things. If all your friends like a particular piece of music, the chances are greatly increased that you will also like it. Usually people respect the judgments of their friends, and therefore are less likely to disagree with them, and the desire to avoid tension in the group encourages an acceptance of their preferences.

The objective evidence for the importance of family and early contacts in attitude formation can be seen in a number of ways. One study, for example, found that when both parents favored the same political party, only 10 percent of the high-school-age children had the opposite preference (Jennings & Niemi, 1968).

Music Instruction and Attitude Formation

The implications for music teachers seem clear for attitude formation in music: Seize upon every opportunity to make students familiar with the music that it is hoped they will learn to like. The more they hear a piece, the greater the chances are that they will like it.

Usually attitudes are not learned by direct teaching procedures such as those a teacher might use in instructing students to read notes in the bass clef or memorizing the year of J. S. Bach's birth. "Attitudes are caught, not taught" is a more accurate description of this aspect of the learning process. In fact, attitudes seem to resist being affected by direct methods such as "Now, you *will* enjoy this song!" Instead, students notice how others react, how the teacher acts, whether the music seems to agree with previously held beliefs about music, and a host of other factors.

In terms of winning students over to art music, perhaps one of the best music teachers one of the authors has ever observed was not a music specialist, but rather a fifth-grade classroom teacher. She was fond of art music and promoted it at every opportunity. She often played recordings of Brahms and Mozart during study periods and other quiet times. Although this practice does seem to violate the idea of listening with concentrated attention, it was highly effective in developing positive attitudes in her students. In addition, the teacher was an attractive and sensitive person whom the students liked; she was a good role model. Also, as a classroom teacher her opportunities to influence students were not limited to two thirty-minute sessions each week (which, by the way, is a good reason for involving classroom teachers in some aspects of the music instruction in the elementary schools).

There is also the clear implication for music teachers that the learning of music should occur under pleasant circumstances so that positive asssociations can be formed. True, some students will tolerate a great deal of carping criticism and insults and still like music, but the majority will try to avoid such treatment, and in doing so may avoid music. If the situation is one of constant pressure to maintain a first chair or a first-division rating in a contest, that will not encourage positive attitudes toward music either.

The old axiom about starting where the students are is implied again by the research findings on attitude formation. By utilizing music that the students know and pointing out the similarities between it and other music, it is made less strange and new to the students, which in turn increases the chances of positive attitudes being formed toward it.

Creativity

> When I am, as it were, completely myself, entirely alone, and of good cheer—say, travelling in a carriage, or walking after a good meal, or during the night when I cannot sleep; it is on such occasions that my ideas flow best and most abundantly. When and how they come, I know not; nor can I force them. Those ideas that please me I retain in memory, and am accustomed, as I have been told, to hum them to myself. (Mozart, in E. Holmes, *The Life of Mozart*, 1979, p. 317)

Because it is used to indicate so many different things, the word "creative" has lost much of its meaning. At most, it implies that creative behavior is not deliberate imitation of something that already exists. For example, making an exact copy of a painting is not a creative act.

Stating what creativity is not, however, is not an adequate definition. Part of the problem in defining creativity may be that the word is employed for activities as different as finding an economical way to make gas and oil from coal and composing string quartets. Similar mental efforts are required for the two tasks, to be sure, but there are also significant differences. Making gasification economically feasible is a more scientific, quantitative problem than creating a new quartet.

Another part of the problem of defining creativity lies in the likelihood that it has several aspects, and therefore should not be defined as a single entity. This point was developed by J. P. Guilford, whose structure of intellect is presented in chapter 7. Guilford's traits can be grouped into what he calls a "factor," which is a cluster of interacting traits. The formation of traits into factors has yielded one that he sees as primarily responsible for what is generally termed creativity. The traits are labeled *fluency*, *flexibility*, and *originality*. Fluency is the ease with which people can make associations of words or ideas. Researchers evaluate fluency through the use of word-association and idea-association tests.

Flexibility involves changing procedures to solve a problem. This trait is often evaluated by giving the subjects puzzlers or riddles. One such puzzler asks about a farmer who must transport a chicken, grain, and a wolf across a river, which would be a bit of a problem. He can't leave the chicken alone with the grain because the chicken will eat it; he can't leave the wolf and the chicken together because the wolf would enjoy the chicken for lunch; and he can carry only one at a time in his boat. For those readers who wish to check their flexibility factor, the solution to the problem appears at the bottom of this page.[*] When the solution is worked out or explained in the test situation, researchers present a change in the puzzler. For example, suppose that while the farmer is transporting the chicken on the first trip, a second wolf appears on the bank toward which he is headed. The second question would give some information about how spontaneous the subject is in terms of flexibility.

Originality is a trait involving the ability to think in unusual ways, to see relationships that others have not seen, and to think of new and different uses for ideas and objects. The evaluation of originality is done partly by asking subjects to describe different uses for familiar objects. If a subject says that a shoe can be worn on the foot, that would be a conventional, or *convergent*, response and would not rate high in terms of originality. If the subject responds by saying that the shoe could be used to bail water out of a sinking canoe or could be eaten if one were starving, these would be unconventional, or *divergent*, answers and would rate high in terms of originality.

The term *divergent thinking*, by the way, has often come to be synonymous with creativity for many psychologists and educators. The implication is that creative thinking must necessarily be different from other kinds of thinking. Such an implication has been questioned by some psychologists and educators, especially in terms of validity: Do tests of divergent thinking really identify creative persons? In one experiment Piers, Daniels, and Quackenbush (1960) administered such tests to seventh and eighth graders, and then compared the results with ratings of creativity for each subject by the subjects' teachers. The ratings did not agree at all with the test scores. In fact, the three separate ratings of creativity by the teachers for each student did not agree with each other. The researchers concluded that the results were partly "due to vagueness and variability in the popular conception of what is meant by creativity."

The relationship, if any, between creative behavior and psychotic behavior has aroused the curiosity of psychologists since the analytical efforts of Sigmund Freud. There appear to be some similarities. Freud (1947) believed that artists are more likely to involve what he termed "primary processes," and he thought he saw in the works of Leonardo da Vinci signs of infant disturbances that accounted for his later obsession with work and for some of his artistic themes. Also, the lower brain centers of artists are more "opened up." However, there is a very significant difference between psychotic and creative behavior: Artistic behavior is controlled but psychotic behavior is not; it lacks the order, self-questioning, and processing that is needed for creating works of art.

---

[*]Answer: The farmer takes the chicken across first, leaving the grain and wolf together, then brings the wolf across and takes the chicken back. Next he leaves the chicken and takes the grain, and then on the last trip picks up the chicken.

Are there other aspects of what might be termed "the creative personality"? Probably. Barron (1969) studied a group of writers who had been classified as "highly creative" or "average" by authorities in the field. The highly creative group scored higher on both the test questions indicating neurosis and psychosis and the questions involving ego: self-confidence, responsibility, independence, and the like.

John Gardner in *Self-Renewal* (1963, pp. 35–39) cites four traits of creative persons: (1) openness—a receptivity to all the sights, sounds, and ideas that one encounters and to one's own inner feelings; (2) independence—the ability to be free from social pressures and to question assumptions; (3) flexibility—the willingness to try ideas and the ability to tolerate internal conflict and to suspend final judgment; and (4) the capacity to find order in experience—"Every great creative performance since the initial one [the creation of the universe] has been in some measure a bringing of order out of chaos."

Components of Creativity

Margery Vaughan (1973, pp. 34–37) has identified four stages in creative behavior. The first is *acquisitional* or *precreative*, in which basic information and skills are acquired and assimilated. The second is *combinational*, in which ideas are shuffled and alternatives considered. It is at this stage that divergent thinking can begin to appear. The third stage is *developmental*, in which insights and intuitions bring forth significant new ideas and products. The fourth stage is *synergistic*, in which the individual's creative efforts combine with needs and desires of the society to produce a work that is both unique to the creator and accessible to the society as a whole.

Sylvia Farnham-Diggory (1972, pp. 512–24) lists three major aspects of the creative process. The first is the *intuition of an order*—the belief that an organization of elements is possible. The second is *combinational play and self-testing*. In this aspect trial organizations are attempted. The third is *styles of ordering*, or what Jerome Bruner (1964, pp. 93–94) refers to as "puzzle forms." He writes: "Much of what we speak of as discovery consists of knowing how to impose a workable kind of form on various kinds of difficulties. A small but crucial part of discovery of the highest order is to invent and develop effective models or 'puzzle forms.' " The creative solution, Farnham-Diggory points out (1972, p. 524), is characterized by what is termed *effective surprise*. In other words, the solution is not only novel, but also useful and appropriate to the situation. Some effective solutions may be predictable because they associate things that have been associated before; some consist of ordering elements of a specific problem in a new and fresh way, as when one composes music; and some consist of connecting different aspects of life in new ways.

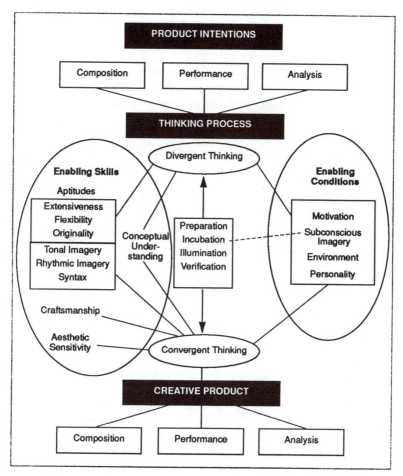

Figure 6.5. Webster's *Model of creative thinking in music.*

Webster (1990) presents a model for creative thinking in music that accounts for the skills, conditions, and various thought processes (figure 6.5). As the model indicates, creativity in music is a complex matter.

In Webster's model the word "imagery" refers to the ability to imagine various aspects of sounds in the mind. The box in the center of the figure presents the stages involved in the creative process as Webster envisages them.

It is surprising to read the matter-of-fact way in which composers speak about the supposedly different and mysterious process of creating music, as is evident in Mozart's remarks on page 172. He writes in his letters about pleasing audiences in words not too different from a modern-day songwriter who is worrying about a new pop tune that is being released. Some of Mozart's works were thrown together in a very short time, including the overture for *Don Giovanni*, which was completed only a day before it was first performed on opening night (Turner, 1938, pp. 346–47). In fact, the idea of a composer giving a little of his psyche to the world in his musical works did not appear until the nineteenth century. Bach and Mozart considered themselves master craftsmen in the art of music, which they certainly were. In the twentieth century the romantic view of composing has been reduced. Aaron Copland (1957, p. 21) writes: "He [the layman] forgets that composing to a composer is like fulfilling a natural function. It is like eating or sleeping. It is something that the composer happens to have been born to do; and, because of that, it loses the character of a special virtue in the composer's eyes."

Virtually every creative effort contains large doses of existing ideas and practices. For example, many people consider Beethoven the epitome of a creative and original composer. Yet most of what he used had been developed by his predecessors. The system of notation had been developed, as had the instruments, the orchestra, the system of tuning, sonata and rondo forms, tertian harmony, common-practice harmonic progressions, techniques of writing counterpoint (with which, according to one of his teachers, Beethoven had some trouble), *sforzandi*, augmented sixth chords, and so on. What Beethoven contributed was the final 3 or 5 percent (the amounts here only represent an idea, and are in no sense actual quantities). Why, then, is he so highly esteemed? Because that final 3 or 5 percent is so difficult to achieve; almost no one has been or is able to do as well. Most merely mortal musicians can hardly add half a percent, no matter how hard they try.

Factors Contributing to Creativity

One trait of many creative people that is seldom mentioned is plain hard work. The creation of a novel or concerto is a mighty labor. Someone has said that talent is 10 percent inspiration and 90 percent perspiration, and that notion is probably correct. Beethoven's messy manuscripts and Michelangelo's stiff neck from years of work on the Sistine Chapel ceiling are two bits of evidence among hundreds of possibilities of the devotion and effort required for such great creations.

A creative artist's place in history can be helped by (but does not depend on) being in the right place at the right time.[*] Beethoven had the good fortune to live during the time of transition from the Classical to

---

[*]Some people do not agree with the idea that the age produces great people; they prefer to think that great people make for the accomplishments of an age. It is a bit of a "chicken-egg" causation question.

Romantic styles, which encouraged a balance in his music between objectivity and subjectivity. Would he have been as well known today if he had been born seventy-five years later? No one knows, of course, but it is quite possible that he would have been merely a good composer, not the great one that he is considered today. Sometimes there is a fortuitous match of personality and the age in which the person lived. Brahms's rational tendencies were a good balance for the subjective romanticism of his time. Had he lived in the Classical era, his music might have become hopelessly academic.

Sometimes technological or cultural developments help or hinder creative talents. The fact that many jazz artists' renditions were preserved on recordings allowed their accomplishments to be heard and appreciated again and again, whereas a hundred years ago those efforts would have passed into oblivion. There may have been some great improvisors back in the centuries before a system of notation was developed; we will never really know.

Values of Creativity

There is little dispute about the value of creative efforts by the Beethovens, Edisons, and Leonardo da Vincis of this world. Their works represent significant contributions to the betterment and enrichment of humankind. What about the value of creativity for most of us, and especially for youngsters in schools? Is a child struggling with the melody bells somehow to be compared with the great Beethoven? Are the sloppily painted paper plates that children bring home for Mother's Day as valuable as the paintings of a Monet or a Picasso?

From an artistic point of view the tune on the melody bells and the designs on the paper plate are of virtually no value. However, creative activities in music and the other arts are included not because teachers hope that great works of art will result; instead, creative activities are undertaken because the act of creating is itself of value to the students. One value of creative efforts for the students is that they allow and encourage individuals to try out their own musical ideas. In attempting to create music, an individual is expressing himself or herself and gaining an enriching experience in life. Although music is not the only area of the school in which students are enriched and have the opportunity to express themselves, it is a logical area for such activity, and creative activity is an important aspect of the art of music. Being educated in music is not only learning to reproduce or listen to what others have done.

A second value of creativity is the motivation it provides. One's own personal efforts are especially meaningful. The paper that fifth-grader Lisa writes on "What I Did Last Summer" means more to her than if she merely copies what someone else writes on the topic. If the paper is read in class, she will discover that when the others read their papers there will be a tendency for her attention to wander. But when her paper is read, her attention will be intense.

A third value of creative activity for school students is that through it the students learn music better. When a person is in the process of creating some music, be it a one-measure-long ostinato using only two pitches or a cantata for chorus and soloists, the mind is going through much trial-and-error in thinking about the sounds that will best express the person's intentions. People who are creating must think intently about sounds and their organization in a way that they never do when studying what someone else has done.

There may be some artistic benefits, too, of creative efforts by school students. It is not in the products that they create at the moment, but maybe, just maybe the experiences will encourage a potential Prokofiev or Brahms, so that future generations will be enriched by some great new works. The possibility of developing outstanding composers for the future is not the main reason for providing creative experiences in school music classes, however. It is a desirable bonus for an activity that music teachers should undertake anyway.

Fostering Creativity

The question of how best to promote creativity in schools and society is an especially interesting one, because it is possible to build a rather logical and defensible case for two contradictory approaches. Surprising as it may seem, it is not unreasonable to argue that creativity is fostered best when people are subject to restrictions and demands. When J. S. Bach was a boy, a portion of his music education consisted of copying parts from scores, which has to be among the more uncreative tasks in this world. Composers under the patronage system in the Baroque and Classical periods had to produce most of their music "on demand"; Haydn's contract with the Esterházy family specifically required him to appear (wearing white stockings!) each day to await his orders. Many film buffs think that one of the most creative periods of film was in the 1920s, with the silent comedies and their "sight gags" and other techniques. These films were created under what one would think would be a serious restriction: no sound. After World War II the natives of Trinidad and other islands in the West Indies took the empty oil drums left behind by the U.S. Navy and used them to create the vibrant steel bands. Their success with the oil drums causes one to wonder if the results would have been nearly as interesting if the Navy had left behind some band instruments and instruction books. Maybe the old saying "Necessity is the mother of invention" is true. Perhaps requirements and restrictions compel people to be creative.

When studying the lives of composers, one is struck by how many great composers were discouraged by their families from following a career in music—Dvořák, Berlioz, Handel, Tchaikovsky, Stravinsky, and several more. Could it be that discouragement by the parents actually motivated the child to demonstrate that he was right? Or was it that true interest and talent cannot be discouraged or blocked? No one knows, but history contains many examples of great creative talents who had to overcome enormous obstacles and who were creative in uncreative environments.

There is other evidence that suggests that structure (or restrictions, depending on how you want to look at it) is not harmful to creativity, and in fact may contribute to it. There is something a bit overwhelming about being able to compose anything you want with absolutely no guidelines, and this must be especially true of elementary school children when they are asked to create music. Perhaps one of the reasons for the success of the Orff-*Schulwerk* is the fact that it approaches creative efforts within a high degree of structure; in the early stages a limited number of pitches are permitted within a certain rhythmic context, and only gradually are the students given more freedom in what they are allowed to use. Working within a structure or system is what happens in the world of music outside of the school. When a jazz player improvises, he or she follows the tonal and rhythmic patterns expected for that style, and the same is true of improvisation in non-Western music. People do not improvise and create music "out of thin air." They are grounded in a style system, and then make small permutations within that system.

It is also possible to build a good case for giving creative talent encouragement and freedom, which is the way most people assume is best. Many successful composers were encouraged and in some cases "pushed" into music by their parents. At times, either circumstances or environment has brought forth a flowering of some aspect of the arts, as with the English poets of the eighteenth century, the Flemish-Dutch painters of the seventeenth century, the Italian composers of the sixteenth and seventeenth centuries, and the German-Austrian composers of the eighteenth and nineteenth centuries. No one fully knows why such flowerings occur, but something in the society must have encouraged them. There is also some experimental evidence by Paul Torrance (1970) and others that procedures designed to encourage creativity in classrooms do in fact result in more creativity as measured by the tests presently available. As is true of other areas of the curriculum, teachers usually achieve at least to some degree what they try to teach.

Effective teaching for the development of creative abilities requires more than a one-shot exposure, which is true of nearly every significant aspect of music education. Creative efforts appear to be more a matter of a mental inclination and outlook than of technique, although techniques are certainly desirable. Outlooks and inclinations require a variety of experiences over a long period of time.

It is also important for music teachers to realize that creativity in music is largely an individual matter. Even in folk music few songs have been created "by committee," that is, by a group of people marching into battle or sitting around a campfire (Nettl, 1973, pp. 5–6). Anyone who has tried to write even a short verbal statement in a committee situation knows how difficult and frustrating that process is, and the result usually reflects the difficulty. In such situations the whole is not equal to the sum of its parts. Sometimes composers do in fact collaborate with others, but usually each person has a different function to fulfill, as when a librettist and composer work on an opera. Sometimes it is claimed that an elementary school classroom has "composed" a song. Actually what often happens is that the teacher points out some possibilities, and the children either formally or informally render a group opinion as to which possibility they prefer. Also, almost no class-composed song has earned a permanent place in the musical repertoire!

There seems to be little that can be said for certain about fostering creativity in terms of specific classroom procedures. Rather, it is the establishment of the right atmosphere that appears to be more significant. Meichenbaum (1975) has been successful in having subjects talk themselves into becoming more creative. Much of the conversation that is recommended consists simply of encouragement: "Break away from the obvious," "Let ideas flow," "Good—you're getting it," and similar statements. In creative learning and teaching, what a teacher *is* is perhaps far more important than what he or she *does*. The teacher needs to let the students know that new and different products, as long as they are genuine attempts and not just perverse or senseless, are not only tolerated but welcomed. Coming up with something different involves a certain amount of psychological risk; students need to feel assured that their creative attempts will not be denigrated.

The interactions of individuals with society have an important impact on the culture, which in turn affects the efforts of music teachers. If there were no attitudes or self-images, no conformist behavior, or no competitive situations, music educators would find their work very different from what it is today. Because teachers can build on some of these social psychological factors, and because in other instances they can reduce the detrimental effects of other factors, music educators would be more effective in their planning and teaching if they applied information drawn from social psychology.

Summary

This chapter discussed a number of concepts from the field of social psychology and their implications for music teachers. The specific ideas presented included:

1. Self-image: the perception of how one looks to others, one's perception of their judgments of oneself, and one's feelings about those perceptions. Also included in self-image is the idea of the "generalized other," in which responses are guided by the perceived expectations and opinions of other people. A self-serving bias operates in most people to preserve self-image when it is challenged. Self-image affects the kind of music people like and the nature of their involvement with it. For many people music is one way of projecting a certain image and associating themselves with a group or idea.

2. Conformity: the human tendency to follow or accept the actions of others. People's musical activities, especially those of teenagers, also have a tendency to conform. The degree of conformity is influenced by such factors as the confidence one has in the other people, the degree of agreement among them, and the feelings of security and self-confidence held by the individual.

3. Role: the concept that people generally do what is expected that they will do. Such expectations can make an important difference in how well students learn in music classes. Role expectations show up clearly, for example, in the differences between boys and girls in the selection of musical instruments.

4. Competition/cooperation: the idea of a few people winning at the expense of others vs. the idea of working together to achieve some task so that everyone "wins" to some degree. Competition receives much attention in school music. However, its educational and psychological benefits are mixed. Competency is a more appropriate goal for school students, with cooperative activities being one means of achieving it. In order for students to learn, and thereby become competent, music teachers need to make the criteria for accomplishment clear and reduce elements of competition in their classes.

5. Leadership: the concept of guiding a group in the achievement of a task. Most effective leaders possess a sense of vision, the ability to communicate that vision, and an ability to inspire people to take action. However, leaders function in a particular situation, and different situations call for different qualities and abilities. Because of their specialized training, all music educators should exercise some degree of leadership in school systems and their communities.

6. Self-confidence: the need for teenagers to feel capable in their emerging adult status. Adolescents need to develop self-confidence in dealing with the adult world. One manifestation of this desire is knowing some music that their elders don't know, which, in turn, encourages the development of a "youth music." Music teachers need to understand why their role may be limited in working with this music.

7. Attitudes: the favorable or unfavorable disposition toward something. The encourging of positive attitudes toward music is an important and complex matter. Generally, attitudes are formed through association, reinforcement, and the desire for consistency, but the ease with which attitudes are changed depends on factors such as familiarity (the more, the better), similarity, disposition toward the person suggesting the change, and conformity.

8. Creativity: forming something that is not a conscious imitation of something else. The matter of creativity appears to be a highly complex one; it appears to be a combination of several traits such as fluency, flexibility, and originality. The mark of creative behavior, in contrast to deviant or psychotic behavior, is the bringing to the creation a sense of order and organization. There is little agreement on how best to encourage creativity. Evidence can be presented indicating that, at least in the initial stages, much structure is better, but other evidence suggests that encouragement and much freedom are more effective. It appears that creating is largely an individual undertaking, not a group effort.

STUDY AND DISCUSSION QUESTIONS

1. (a) How does the "looking-glass self" guide a person's actions with regard to music?

   (b) How can music teachers influence the musical self-image of their students?

2. (a) How does conformity influence a person's actions with regard to music?

   (b) What can music teachers do to take advantage of the tendency toward conformity among adolescents?

3. In what ways do the expectations of society affect how people are involved with music?

4. (a) According to Kohn, what are the three myths about competition?

   (b) Why is competence a more appropriate goal than competition for school music groups?

5. Although psychologists have largely rejected the "great leader" theory of leadership, they find some features in common among successful leaders. What are those attributes?

6. Teenagers possess a desire for a type of music that their elders don't know very well. What are the psychological reasons for this desire?

7. (a) Why are favorable attitudes toward music an important goal of school music instruction?

   (b) What factors affect the attitudes that students form?

   (c) What steps can music teachers take to increase the chances that favorable attitudes will be formed?

8. (a) What is creativity?

   (b) What traits appear to be related to creativity?

   (c) What evidence is there that learning to work within a strict structure is the best way to encourage creativity?

   (d) What evidence is there that learning without any restrictions is the best way to encourage creativity?

   (e) Why should all students be encouraged to attempt creative activities?

   (f) What are some procedures music teachers can employ to encourage creativity in music classes?

INDIVIDUAL OR CLASS ACTIVITIES

1. Class members can examine the advertisements in popular magazines and select three for analysis. For each ad selected, they should decide the type of self-image to which it is attempting to appeal. Students should be prepared to offer reasons for their analysis.

2. Each class member can report on one or two instances in which a person's or a group's attitude toward music was affected in some way. Situations that might be considered could include a children's concert, a director criticizing the members of a performing group, or the teaching of a difficult passage in a piece of music. In each instance an attempt should be made to analyze why the attitude was affected in addition to how it was affected.

3. Divide the class into two groups. One group can represent the view that creativity is best encouraged by eliminating all structure and restrictions from the situation; the other group should represent the view that creativity is best developed, initially at least, by providing

much structure and few options. Each group should develop some reasons to support its position and be prepared to refute the claims of the other group. Support can come from scholarly writings and research, as well as case histories of people who are usually identified as being creative.

REFERENCES

ABELES, H. F., & PORTER, S. Y. (1978). The sex-stereotyping of musical instruments. *Journal of Research in Music Education, 26*(2), 65–75.

ADAMS, A. K. (Ed.). (1969). *The home book humorous quotations.* New York: Dodd, Mead.

ARIES, P. (1962). *Centuries of childhood: A social history of family life.* London: Jonathan Cape.

ASCH, S. E. (1952). *Social psychology.* Englewood Cliffs, NJ: Prentice-Hall.

ASCH, S. E. (1955, November). Opinions and social pressure, *Scientific American,* pp. 31–35.

BARRON, F. (1969). *Creative person and process.* New York: Holt, Rinehart.

BENNIS, W. (1984). Transformative power and leadership. In T. J. Sergiovani & J. E. Corbally (Eds.), *Leadership and Organizational Culture* (pp. 64–77). Urbana: University of Illinois Press.

BRANDENBURG, N. A. (1991, September). Sex stereotypes and student preferences. *The School Music News, 55*(1), 32–39.

BRUNER, J. (1964). *On knowing: Essays for the left hand.* Cambridge, MA: Harvard University Press.

COOLEY, C. H. (1902). *The nature of human nature.* New York Scribner's.

COPLAND, A. (1957). *What to listen for in music* (rev. ed.). New York: McGraw-Hill.

CRANDALL, C. S. (1988). Social contagion of binge eating. *Journal of Personality and Social Psychology, 55,* 588–98

CUTIETTA, R. A. (1991). Popular music: An ongoing challenge. *Music Educators Journal, 77*(8), 28.

FARNHAM-DIGGORY, S. (1972). *Cognitive processes in education.* New York: Harper and Row.

FELDMAN, R. S., & PROHASKA, T. (1979). The student as Pygmalion: Effect of student expectations on the teacher. *Journal of Educational Psychology, 74,* 485–93.

FLESCH, R. (Ed.). (1966). *The new book of unusual quotations.* New York: Harper and Row.

FREUD, S. (1947). *Leonardo da Vinci.* New York: Vintage Books.

GARDNER, J. W. (1963). *Self-renewal.* New York: Harper and Row.

GRISWOLD, P. A., & CHRONBACK, D. A. (1981). Sex-role associations of music instruments and occupations by gender and major. *Journal of Research in Music Education, 29*, 57–62.

HEDGES, W. (1965). Personal Communication.

HOLLANDER, E. P. (1985). Leadership and power. In G. Lindzey & E. Aronson (Eds.), *The handbook of social psychology* (3rd. ed., p. 485). New York: Random House.

HOLMES, E. (1979). *The life of Mozart.* New York: Da Capo Press.

HOLT, C. B. (1991). Sex-role associations of music instruments and occupations by gender and major: A replication study *Georgia Music News, 52*, 54–55.

HOUSE, R. J., & SINGH, J. V. (1987). Organizational behavior: some new directions for I/O psychology. *Annual Review of Psychology, 38*, 669–718

INGLEFIELD, H. G. (1968). *The relationship of selected personality variables to conformity behavior in the musical preferences of adolescents when exposed to peer group leader influence.* Unpublished doctoral dissertation, Ohio State University.

JAMIESON, D. W., LYDON, J. E., STEWART, G., & ZANNA, M. P. (1987). Pygmalion revisited: new evidence for student expectancy effects in the classroom. *Journal of Education Psychology, 79*, 416–66.

JENNINGS, M. K., & NIEMI, R. G. (1968). The transmission of political values from parent to child. *American Political Science Review, 62*, 169–84.

KAPLAN, M. (1970). We have much to learn from the inner city. *Music Educator's Journal, 56*(5), 39–42.

KOHN, A. (1986). *No contest: The case against competition.* Boston: Houghton-Mifflin.

LATANÉ, B., and DARLEY, J. (1968). Group inhibition of bystander intervention in emergencies. *Journal of Personality and Social Psychology, 10*, 215–21.

LATANÉ B., and RODIN, J. (1969). A lady in distress: Inhibiting effects of friends and strangers on bystander intervention. *Journal of Experimental Social Psychology, 5*, 189–202.

LINVILLE, P. W. (1987). Self-complexity as a cognitive buffer against stress-related illness and depression. *Journal of Personality and Social Psychology, 52*, 663–76.

MACMILLAN DICTIONARY OF QUOTATIONS. (1989). New York: Macmillan.

MAEHR, M. L. (1983). The developing of continuing interests in music. In *Motivation and creativity.* Reston, VA: Music Educators National Conference, pp. 5–11.

MEAD, G. H. (1934). *Mind, self and society.* Chicago: University of Chicago Press.

MEICHENBAUM, D. (1975). Enhancing creativity by modifying what subjects say to themselves. *AREA Journal, 12*(2).

MILLER, C. E., & ANDERSON, P. D. (1979). Group decision rules and the rejection of deviates, *Social Psychology Quarterly, 42*, 354–63.

MORRIS, W. N., & MILLER, R. S. (1975). The effects of consensus-breaking and consensus-preempting partners on reduction of conformity. *Journal of Experimental Psychology, 11,* 215–23.

MULLEN, B., & RIORDAN, C. A. (1988). Self-serving attributions for performance on naturalistic settings: A meta-analytic review. *Journal of Applied Psychology, 18,* 3–22.

MUSIC TECHNICAL REPORT (03-MU-21). (1975). Denver: Education Commission of the States, pp. 11–123.

MYERS, D. G. (1990). *Social Psychology* (3rd. ed, p. 84). New York: McGraw-Hill.

NETTL, B. (1973). *Folk and traditional music of the Western continents* (2d ed.). Englewood Cliffs, NJ: Prentice-Hall.

PIERS, E. V., DANIELS, J. M., & QUAKENBUSH, J. F. (1960). The identification of creativity in adolescents, *Journal of Educational Psychology, 51,* 346–56.

RADOCY, R. E. (1975). A naive minority of one and deliberate majority mismatches of tonal stimuli. *Journal of Research in Music Education, 23*(2), 120–33.

RADOCY, R. E. (1976). Effect of authority figures basis on changing judgments of music events. *Journal of Research in Music Education, 24*(3), 119–28.

RIESMAN, D. (1954). *Individualism reconsidered.* Glencoe, IL: Free Press.

ROSENTHAL, R. (1985). From unconscious experimenter bias to teacher expectancy effects. In J. B. Dusek, V. C. Hall, & W. J. Meyer (Eds.), *Teacher expectancies.* Hillsdale, NJ: Erlbaum, pp. 37–65.

ROSENTHAL, R. (1987, December). Pygmalion effects: Existence, magnitude, and social importance. *Educational Researcher,* pp. 37–41.

ROSENTHAL, R., & JACOBSON, L. (1968). *Pygmalion in the classroom: Teacher expectation and pupils' intellectual development* (Vol. 2). New York: Holt, Rinehart, p. 73.

ROSS, M., & FLETCHER, G. J. O. (1985). Attribution and social perception. In G. Lindzey & E. Aronson (Eds.), *The handbook of social psychology* (3rd ed, p. 73). New York: Random House.

SCHACTER, S. (1951). Deviation, rejection, and communication. *Journal of Abnormal and Social Psychology, 46,* 190–207.

SCHWARZ, B. (1972). *Music and musical life in Soviet Russia.* Bloomington: Indiana University Press.

SMITH, P. B., & TAYEB, M. (1989). Organizational structure and processes. In M. Bond (Ed.), *The cross-cultural challenge to social psychology.* Newbury Park, CA: Sage.

SPRINTHALL, R. C., & SPRINTHALL, N. A. (1977). *Educational psychology* (rev. ed.), Reading, MA: Addison-Wesley.

TORRANCE, E. P. (1970). *Encouraging creativity in the classroom.* Dubuque, IA: W. C. Brown.

TURNER, W. J. (1938). *Mozart: the man and his music.* New York: Knopf.

VAUGHMAN, M. M. (1973). Cultivating creative behavior. *Music Educators Journal,* 59(8), 34–37.

WEBSTER, P. R. (1990). Creativity as creative thinking. *Music Educators Journal,* 78(9), 22–28.

WHITLEY, B. E., JR., & FRIEZE, I. H. (1985). Children's causal attributions for success and failure in achievement settings: A meta-analysis. *Journal of Educational Psychology, 77,* 608–16.

WHITLEY, B. E., JR., & FRIEZE, I. H. (1986). Measuring causal attributions for success and failure: A meta-analysis of the effects of question wording style. *Basic and Applied Social Psychology, 7,* 35–51.

ZAJONC, R. (1968). Attitudinal effects of mere exposure. *Journal of Personality and Social Psychology Monographs, 9.*

CHAPTER 7

Psychological Foundations of Music Education

MUCH OF THE INFORMATION contained in this chapter is organized under topics concerned with factors that influence learning or stages of the learning process such as child development and motivation. Sometimes within the same section theories and research results will be reported that represent different psychological positions. To help the reader identify material representing distinct schools of thought and to add continuity across the subsections of this chapter, the chapter begins with a brief overview of the dominant psychological schools of learning theories and theorists.

Theoretical Positions

An examination of individual theorists' positions suggests that two distinct approaches dominate the field. These can be labeled the *behaviorist* approach, exemplified by the writings of B. F. Skinner and Robert Keller, and the *cognitive* school, exemplified by the writings of Jerome Bruner and David Ausubel. Behaviorism (sometimes referred to as the stimulus-response theory) has historical roots in the early part of the twentieth century with the theoretical and experimental work of Watson, Thorndike, and Spence. Contemporary behaviorism seems to be more descriptively pragmatic and less theoretical. It is primarily based on the work of Skinner. The cognitive school seems historically related to, although not a direct descendant of, Gestalt psychology. The work of psychologists such as Wertheimer, Köhler, and Koffka in the first half of this century form the foundation for the work of more contemporary cognitivists such as Bruner and Ausubel. A more detailed historical perspective of these two schools of thought may be gained by examining Hilgard and Bower's *Theories of Learning* (1981) or Hill's *Learning: A Survey of Psychological Interpretations* (1971).

These two approaches differ not only in their basic premises but also in the different aspects of the learning process they tend to emphasize. The research of the behaviorists has tended to focus on simple learning situations. Topics such as classical and operant conditioning, rote verbal learning, and discrimination learning are typical of their research. The cognitivists have tended to focus on more complex learning areas such as information processing, concept formation, and problem-solving. As each school has expanded its focus of interest, additional conflicts between the two positions have arisen. The behaviorists have sought to apply their explanations of simple behaviors to more complex learning situations, while members of the cognitive school have extended their theories of complex learning to simpler behaviors. It is in these extensions that differences between the two schools of thought are highlighted.

Representatives of these two psychological viewpoints also tend to approach the problem of explaining learning differently. Behaviorists consider the observable response and the observable environment to be appropriate objects of study. Cognitivists attempt to analyze the conscious experience to determine principles governing different psychological processes such as remembering and forgetting.

The Behaviorists

Behaviorists describe learning as the development of a "bond" or association between a stimulus and a behavior or response. As mentioned earlier, the behaviorist school has produced what seem to be reasonable explanations for simple learning processes such as Pavlov's classical conditioning, but has had more difficulty in providing satisfactory explanations of thought processes that involve symbols. In their attempts to explain complex behaviors they have developed the concepts of *stimulus generalization* and *mediational process*. Stimulus generalization occurs when similar stimuli evoke the same response. For example, music played by *any* brass instrument will produce listener responses similar to that produced by music played on a trumpet. "Mediational process" may be conceived of as an *internal* series of associations or stimulus-response bonds that occur between the presentation of an environmental factor and an observable response. According to behaviorists, these mediating responses may help lead to or prohibit finding the solution to a problem. For example, beginning violinists first learn a specific fingering sequence for certain musical phrases. This sequence is usually affected by their stage of technical development, so their initial attempts will likely be limited to "first position." As they become more technically proficient, more options become available for fingering the same passage. The young student, though, will probably demonstrate a preference for first-position fingering solutions because habits have been formed that may *mediate* against the most efficient fingering solution.

The Cognitivists

Cognitivists view the mind as being comprised of several sets of different processes or operations. The process of incorporating new experiences or information into an individual's cognitive structure gives them meaning (Ausubel, 1968). Cognitivists view the human nervous system as a data-processing and storage mechanism. New information is retained by an individual by classifying the new stimulus into categories that already exist in the person's mind. In the cognitivists' view the mind consists of hierarchical structures of concepts and subconcepts. The process of forgetting may be explained, from this viewpoint, as the lost specificity of the new knowledge (e.g., clarinet timbre), leaving only the generalized category (e.g., a sound produced by a musical instrument) in which it was placed.

Cognitivists have been interested in the ways that new knowledge is acquired so that it can be easily integrated with previously stored information and be resistant to forgetting. Different viewpoints within the cognitive school exist on this question. Jerome Bruner has advocated an approach to new knowledge acquisition called *discovery learning*, in which students play an active role in organizing the material to be learned. On the other hand, David Ausubel has advocated a pedagogical strategy he calls *reception learning*, in which the material to be learned has been organized in advance by the instructor. These two approaches will be discussed in detail later in the chapter. It should be noted at this point, however, that most theorists agree that new knowledge needs to be organized either by the teacher or the student to facilitate its acquisition and retention.

Those who model human information processing on computers, such as Simon and Feiganbaum, represent a subgroup of cognitive psychologists. Their work, based on the principles of information theory, provides a means by which theories of learning may be tested. Although their investigations have tended to focus on inputs and outputs, which is a somewhat behavioristic focus, the processes that they stimulate tend to be similar to those of interest to the cognitive school. For example, in 1963 Feigenbaum described the development of a computer program called EPAM (Elementary Perceiver and Memorizer) that simulated human remembering. The greatest contribution of this school may be as the intermediate validators of the theoretical propositions of others.

OTHER POSITIONS. There has been important work done by individuals or groups of learning theorists and researchers that does not neatly fit into the two categories described above. Jean Piaget is an example of a theorist whose breadth of work in the area of child development, seems to overlap both the cognitive and behaviorist schools.

Carl Rogers's and Abraham Maslow's theories are based primarily on their observations as clinical or counseling psychologists and can also be adapted to the teaching-learning situation by considering the teacher as the counselor and the student as a client (Hunt & Sullivan, 1974). Both theories are developmental and emphasize individual potential. Maslow discusses a hierarchy of needs, and he states that when individuals' basic needs (such as safety, love, and self-esteem) are met, they are motivated primarily by what he refers to as "self-actualization," "defined as ongoing actualization of potentials, capacities, and talents, as fulfillment of mission, as a fuller knowledge of, and acceptance of the person's own intrinsic nature, as an increasing trend toward unity, integration or synergy within the person" (Maslow, 1968, p. 25). Rogers focuses on the development of a "fully functioning person." Both men question whether individual potentials can be reached in conventional school settings. Maslow's theories have been often cited by music educators because of the view that music is one area that is likely to be pursued by the self-actualized individual: "A musician must make music, an artist must paint, a poet must write if he is to be ultimately at peace with himself" (Maslow, 1954, p. 91). Both Rogers's and Maslow's theories on motivation will be explored later in this chapter.

Several psychologists have presented theoretical structures that attempt to describe the mind as being comprised of several capacities. Guilford, in his 1956 article "Structure of the Intellect," presents a three-dimensional 120-cell description of intellectual ability. Of the three dimensions that Guilford proposes—contents, products, and operations (see figure 7.1)—the dimension of operations is most relevant to a discussion of learning. Guilford divides this dimension into five operations: (1) cognition, (2) memory, (3) convergent thinking, (4) divergent thinking, and (5) evaluation. Several of these operations will be examined in later sections of the book. Guilford's work has been criticized at times because the same technique (factor analysis) was employed to generate and verify the structure. The model does have interesting pedagogical implications, because it suggests that instructional material should be focused quite specifically on the development of these separate intellectual abilities.

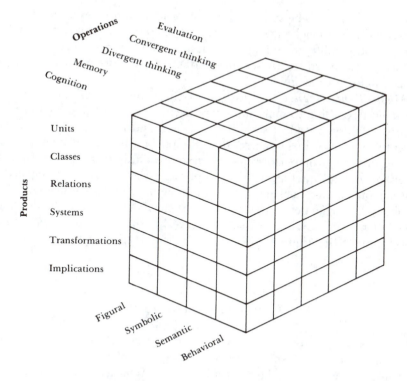

Figure 7.1. Guilford's Model. From J. P. Guilford, *The Nature of Human Intelligence*, p. 63. Copyright © 1967 McGraw-Hill, New York. Used by permission.

Howard Gardner's book *Frames of Mind* (1983) presents a theory of multiple intelligences comprised of seven different components. Gardner describes these intelligences as potentially useful scientific constructs that may not be empirically verifiable entities. *Linguistic intelligence* is a sensitivity to the meaning and order of words. Poets and translators are examples of individuals with high linguistic intelligence. *Logical-mathematical intelligence* is an ability to handle chains of reasoning and to recognize patterns and order. Mathematicians and scientists possess a high level of this intelligence. Athletes, dancers and surgeons all are likely to have high degrees of *Bodily-kinesthetic intelligence*, which is defined as skilled bodily performance, including a well-honed sense of timing and the ability to handle objects adroitly. *Spacial intelligence*, the ability to perceive the world accurately and re-create or transform aspects of that world, is characteristic of those who achieve success as sculptors, architects, and painters. *Interpersonal intelligence* is the ability to understand people and relationships. Individuals with careers as politicians, religious leaders, and teachers are likely to be strong in this dimension. *Intrapersonal intelligence* is described as a heightened awareness of oneself and others, particularly one's emotional life, including fears, desires, and competencies. This intelligence would be strong in persons who are social workers or psychological counselors, for example.

Musical intelligence is also one of the intelligences identified by Gardner. According to him, music intelligence may emerge early in life. It is primarily comprised of sensitivity to pitch and rhythm and to a lesser extent timbre. Gardner suggests that different musical roles such as composing, listening, or performing may require different types or different levels of musical intelligence. He emphasizes that musical intelligence is distinct and cannot be assimilated within linguistic or logical-mathematical thinking. Unfortunately, because of our society's hierarchies, the development of musical intelligence seldom receives the same attention as the development of other intelligences, particularly linguistic and logical-mathematical.

Child Development

The characteristics of the children sitting in a general music class, band, orchestra, or chorus should influence significantly the type of music instruction they receive. How do they think? What type of instruction is best suited for them? It should be clear to the most naive music teacher that music instruction materials that "work" for first graders may not be equally effective for fifth-grade students. However, *how* to present the same concepts effectively to students of different ages may not be so clear.

Developmental psychology (or child development) can provide some guidelines for music teachers. It can provide a foundation for making curriculum decisions and developing instructional materials and techniques.

Two aspects of curriculum planning seem especially affected by the level of development of students for whom instruction is being planned. First, the sequencing of instructional material should be undertaken with an understanding of how children at various stages of development organize information. Instructional material should be presented in sequences that are integrated and well structured to allow students to build upon previously acquired concepts. Second, the curriculum designer should consider the style of instructional material so that it will be most effective for children who at different ages may process information in different ways. Thus, the readiness of the child to accept the instruction, the characteristics of the instructional material, and the sequence in which it is presented constantly interact in the educational environment, and should be considered when a teacher is planning *what* and *how* to teach to *whom*.

The Swiss psychologist Jean Piaget has had a great impact on child development theory and research in this country. Although other psychologists like Bruner have offered other viewpoints, their positions are often considered in terms of how they relate to Piaget's positions rather than as independent propositions. As Piaget's ideas on child development have become widely known, they have occasionally been criticized. However, the testing of his positions has generally resulted in support for his ideas. Therefore, this section will primarily focus on Piagetian theories of development.

Piaget's Stage Theory

Piaget presents a four-stage theoretical structure for understanding developmental process of children. The first stage, the *sensorimotor stage*, precedes the appearance of language. The *preoperational stage* lasts approximately from age two to age seven; the *concrete operational thought* stage lasts, according to Piaget, from ages seven to eleven, while the final phase, that of *formal operational thought*, is found in children from ages eleven to sixteen. It is important to note at this point that children move through these four stages in a precise order, not at precise time intervals, and that they do not completely abandon previous problem-solving modes as they move into a new stage. Instead, they simply tend to rely on the new mode of problem solving because they find it more efficient.

According to Piaget, the processes of *accommodation* and *assimilation* provide the energy that keeps the individual interacting with the environment. These processes will be discussed in greater detail in the section of this chapter on motivation, but a brief explanation at this point is needed. Piaget uses the term "assimilation" to refer to the integration of a new bit of information into one's mode of interacting with the environment. "Accommodation" is the adjusting of the individual's mode to this new object or bit of reality. Piaget suggests that this cycle of assimilation-accommodation is the basic force that moves children through the developmental stages described below. (For a more in-depth examination of Piaget perspectives see Modgil, Modgil, & Brown [1983]).

THE SENSORIMOTOR STAGE. The sensorimotor stage of intellectual development is characterized by children interacting with their environment through their senses. Children at this stage tend to rely on *what is*; that is, if an object cannot be apprehended through one of the senses (e.g., they cannot see it), then it does not exist. Gradually children develop the ability to form images of objects not physically present, and they may develop a primitive means-ends awareness, realizing that if they shake the hand holding a rattle it will cause a sound. Piaget labels these strategies that children employ to interact with their environment sensorimotor *schemas*.

As children pass through the sensorimotor stage, they learn to differentiate and integrate objects and events in their environment. In order to know the environment they must actively interact with it; they cannot be told what it is like, but must rely on firsthand information. This way of knowing, which is characteristic of young children, has several implications for the teaching of music. How are children to understand best the musical concept of tone quality? Can teachers describe for them how a clarinet sounds? What sounds would the children have in their mental repertoire to associate with your description? Children must have first-hand experiences if teachers expect them to differentiate and integrate with their musical environment. This requires that children's initial experiences with music be dominated by sounds: sounds of their own singing and playing, and sounds that they hear by listening. It is necessary for children first to build a repertory of musical sounds, a foundation upon which they can develop the more complex processes characteristic of musical intelligence.

As schools or other institutions become increasingly responsible for the education of very young children, an understanding of their musical potential and behavior becomes increasingly important. This is evident from an examination of the substantial amount of research that has been conducted with preschool children in general and specifically in music. Several generalizations can be made from this body of studies: (1) children generally begin to react to music as early as eighteen months, although other apparent musical behaviors may be exhibited earlier; (2) young children progress from imitating words, to singing melodic fragments (ages two to three), to producing whole songs at about the age of three to four; (3) children during the early stages of development (ages two to three) have a greater tendency for free improvisatory and unstructured note-play, which gradually develops with the incorporation of diatonic intervals and then disappears into a preference for exact imitation; (4) as children move through this period they become increasingly better at organizing their songs tonally and metrically according to rules, although they apparently are not reflectively aware of these rules; and (5) children between the ages of five and ten become reflectively aware of these rules, which in Piagetian terms is a change from preoperational to operational thinking. (See Scott-Kassner [1992] for a review of this research).

THE PREOPERATIONAL STAGE. The mode of "thinking" or informational processing in young children is more cumbersome and limiting than that of adults. An important characteristic of adult thinking processes is the capacity to store images. Children in the stage of preoperational thought acquire this skill, which is most clearly evidenced with the appearance of language. By means of language the world can be represented through symbols that can be stored in the mind. The beginning of imagery also allows children to fantasize, which Piaget suggests is an important aspect of development in this stage.

Preoperational thought only provides children with limited tools to deal with their environment. The children's interactions with the world still tend to be dominated by the senses, particularly the visual and tactile ones. The inability of children in this stage to "conserve" (that is, to resolve logically conflicting perceptual and conceptual information) illustrates this point. One classic conservation experiment test the ability of the child to understand that the same amount of liquid in a tall, thin glass will look different in a short, fat glass. The child who cannot resolve this perceptual-conceptual conflict (that is, who cannot conserve the volume of the water as the shape changes) will always conclude that there is more liquid in the tall thin glass because the liquid goes up higher. A conservation of musical meter experiment might have children first being taught to distinguish between duple and triple meter while listening to and/or performing examples in which the rhythm and pulse were the same (e.g., $\frac{2}{4}$ ♩♩|♩♩, $\frac{3}{4}$ ♩♩♩|♩♩♩). The children then would be asked to correctly label the meter of new examples in which the durational values of the notes were altered (e.g., $\frac{2}{4}$ ♫♫|♩♫, $\frac{3}{4}$ ♩♩|♩♩). Children able to correctly label these new examples would be able to conserve the concept of meter.

As they move through this stage they begin to develop the ability to classify items by common attributes, such as making a sound. Most of the progress made during this stage is related to language acquisition. So if a child is handicapped in verbal development, he or she may suffer a serious developmental lag.

As has been implied, the main difficulty children have at this stage of development is related to resolving perceptual and conceptual conflicts. Musical activities with children of this age should be planned with this in mind. Children should be provided with opportunities to discriminate among different examples of musical elements. Musical material developed for children in this stage should rely on visual and tactile cues, since children's learning interactions are dominated by these senses. The presentation of musical ideas should be done with the minimum of distractors so that the children can focus on the concept being developed. For example, when teachers are selecting material to help their students develop the concept of conjunct and disjunct melodic movement, they should take care that all the examples selected to illustrate conjunct movement are not also in a minor key, and that the rhythmic complexity of the examples does not distract the students from the concept being developed.

THE CONCRETE OPERATIONAL STAGE. There are several differences between the cognitive processing abilities of the preoperational child and those of the concrete operational child. The ability to conserve is acquired

during the concrete operational stage. Children in this stage of development can comprehend that the contents of a can of white modeling clay in
the shape of a ball will weigh as much as the contents of a can of blue
modeling clay in the shape of a cigar of the same size. They may even be
able to identify the same melody when it is played at different tempos or
by different instruments.

A ten-year-old will have a greater capacity to perform mentally complex
actions, such as taking a field trip to a children's concert, than a five-year-
old. The concrete operational child can place characteristics of phenomena
on continuums (e.g., loud-louder-loudest), while the preoperational child
tends to classify characteristics in dichotomies (e.g. loud-not loud). The
five-year-old will probably have difficulty in solving problems that require
a simultaneous understanding of a part of the whole and the whole. For
example, the question "If the first sixteen measures of a piece comprised
of sixty-four measures are repeated, how much longer is the entire piece?"
is more likely to be answered correctly by a ten-year-old listener than a
five-year-old.

Because the transition from the preoperational stage occurs typically
while the child is in school, there has been considerable interest by educators in identifying how and when this change takes place. Much of this
interest has focused on the ability of the child to conserve. In music education, several studies have focused on conservation-type musical tasks
(Pflederer, 1964; Zimmerman & Sechrest, 1968; Serafine, 1975; Webster
& Zimmerman, 1983). The results of these studies have tended to support
Piaget's view of child development; that is, younger children (five years
old) were generally unable to conserve musical elements, while older children (eight years old) were able to do so.

Sloboda (1985) questions whether much of the work done in music
under the Piagetian label conservation is in fact conservation. He prefers
to say that children around the age of eight ". . . are capable of perceiving
and remembering invariant aspects of otherwise different patterns" (p.
210). While he distinguishes this behavior from conservation, he states
that it is of profound psychological interest and that it shares with conservation the "increasing awareness by children of the possibility of going
behind surface perceptual features in their search for underlying patterns
and structures" (p. 210).

Serafine's research (1988) supports the importance of the period
between ages five and ten or eleven to the development of musical understandings. She states that musical "processes are generally well in place in
human cognition by the age of ten or eleven years . . . " and that they "are
not strongly in evidence earlier at around five years of age" (p. 224). She
suggests that there is a rapid period of growth in musical understanding
between the age of eight and ages ten or eleven. Another conclusion she
reaches is that these changes in understanding "are not dependent on

intensive formal tuition in the interim." In her work she compared the performance on certain cognitive musical tasks of children who had received Suzuki training with those who had not received any formal instrumental training. For a majority of the musical processes investigated, the two groups performed at a similar level. While urging caution in interpreting her findings, Serafine does suggest that what children do need during this period of rapid growth in musical understanding is exposure to music rather than intensive training. She states that "typical school experiences with music may well be part of the normal, everyday experiences that contribute to the acquisition of the processes in question" (p. 229).

An important result of these and other studies was the establishment of a developmental sequence of musical concept formation. Children first seem to develop the ability to form musical concepts about volume, and then in this order: timbre, tempo, duration, pitch, and harmony (Zimmerman, 1981, p. 52). These findings have clear implications for the elementary school music teacher regarding the sequence of presentation of musical concepts.

THE FORMAL OPERATIONAL STAGE. How does the cognitive processing of twelve-year-olds differ from that of seven-year-olds? Children entering the final stage of Piaget's structure, that of formal operational thought, are better able to solve problems. Adolescents are able systematically to review and evaluate different solutions and decide on a strategy to solve a problem. Seven-year-olds are more likely to arrive at one solution without reviewing other possibilities. While children under ten are focused primarily on the present, fourteen-year-olds are able to hypothesize about the future. Generally adolescents are more preoccupied by thought than are concrete-operational children. Adolescents can evaluate statements solely on the basis of their consistency or logic rather than their correspondence with a concrete empirical world. Adolescents can deal with abstractions and are no longer encumbered by a dependence on reality. Seven-year-olds make their decisions through intuition. They are highly imaginative and have difficulty distinguishing dreams from reality. The ten-year-old is more interested in facts. The music teacher working with kindergarten children is likely to find that the use of images, such as running and walking notes, will help reinforce musical concepts. Middle-school music teachers will find that their students are more eager to understand the rules of music notation uncluttered by such "distractions."

The middle-school music teacher is interacting with students who have developed most of the basic thought processes of adults. Such students are complex individuals with frequent interactions between their physical, personal-emotional, and intellectual facets. The individuality of each child is developing rapidly; value systems are being formed, and future goals established. It would seem at this stage of development that the musical uniqueness of each child is important to consider. Music programs should try to meet the individual needs of each child, and varied ways of interacting with music should be provided.

Other Points of View on Child Development

Other psychologists have views of child development that do not differ significantly from Piaget's. Jerome Bruner seemingly does not propose a structure as rigid as Piaget's three stages. His position on cognitive growth focuses on three different modes of cognitive processing that are related to early, middle, and late stages of development: *enactive, iconic,* and *symbolic.* In the enactive mode, actions are represented through motor patterns. For example, a clarinet teacher may easily be able to show a student how to finger a note by doing so on an instrument, and yet the teacher may have difficulty in verbalizing the fingering pattern in a way a child can understand. Young children, according to Bruner, tend to represent their environment in their muscles. Bruner suggests that young children primarily employ the enactive mode to process information. This position seems quite similar to the sensorimotor schemas of Piaget. Some music educators have advocated the use of Jaques Dalcroze's eurhythmics. The use of such techniques helps develop the *enactive representation* abilities of children, thus providing them with a means of conceptualizing their environment.

Bruner suggests that as children develop they move from relying exclusively on enactive representation to the use of iconic representation, which is defined by Bruner as representing the environment through images. When children are relying primarily on iconic representations, they can easily be victims of perceptual illusions, as can children in the preoperational stage of Piaget. The symbolic mode of representation is the most sophisticated in Bruner's scheme, and seems to be analogous to Piaget's concrete operational stage of thought.

Differences do exist between Bruner's and Piaget's views of cognitive development other than the naming of stages. Bruner views language training as a catalyst in assisting children to employ symbolic representation, while Piaget places less importance on language acquisition, viewing it as simply an outgrowth of the developmental process.

Robert Gagné, another educational psychologist interested in the developmental process, further emphasizes the difference between a rather passive or developmental approach to cognitive growth and a more active approach. Gagné takes exception to Piagetian theory, which he says suggests that learning plays a minor role in developmental change. He also disagrees with the idea that there is not much teachers can do to change the rate at which children progress through Piaget's stages. Gagné is concerned that if educators emphasize development, teachers will not present material until children are "ready." He advocates a more active role for teachers, having them present material to assist children in progressing through the developmental process.

Gagné's position seems to be a rather extreme interpretation and application of Piaget's ideas. What seems appropriate for the music teacher would be a middle ground: that is, being sensitive to the dominant processing mode of children at different stages of development, while planning instructional material that will enable students to move into the next level of processing.

Implications of Child Development Theory for Music Teaching

Music educators since the 1960s have demonstrated an interest in child development theory. Zimmerman (who first published as Pflederer), Petzold (1963), Serafine (1988), Shuter-Dyson (1981), and others have published important research exploring children's early musical development. In 1985 MENC published a summary of research in the field, *The Young Child and Music.*

Concurrently, and yet somewhat independently of this research effort, came the integration into American music education of music curricula that incorporated several principles of recent child development theory. The use of movement as a basis for representing musical concepts seems to be an important aspect of the Kodály method, the Orff approach, the Dalcroze technique, the Carabo-Cone method, and others. This emphasis on movement is supported both in Piaget's and Bruner's positions on the importance of sensorimotor schemes and enactive representation in early learning. Children who can experience physically a rhythm, melody, or musical form will be more likely to label and classify it correctly when their symbolic skills become more sophisticated.

One implication of the research on musical development relates to this experiencing-labeling problem. When do children understand a musical concept? Must they be able to describe music verbally before they conceive it, as is expected of adults? Studies by Hair (1977), Scott (1979), and Webster and Schlentrich (1979) have focused on this problem. Their investigations suggest that music teachers should strive to develop alternative means for children to demonstrate musical concepts, because children's verbal abilities probably limit their ability to communicate their understandings.

A final important implication, mentioned previously, is the identification of a developmental sequence for introducing musical concepts. Zimmerman (1981, p. 52) states that more than a decade of research suggests "a development sequence pervades the findings in musical concept formation, with concepts appearing to develop in the following order: volume, timbre, tempo, duration, pitch, and harmony."

Cognitive Processes

As the developmental psychology literature suggests, children at various stages are limited in understanding their environment by the information-processing modes they have available. Adult learners, however, may select from several different processing strategies the mode most suitable for the learning problem presented. In adult learners this selection will probably be governed by the characteristics of the task they need to do. If a college music major is asked to sing a single pitch being played on the piano, he or she is likely to use a different strategy or process than if asked to listen to an eight-measure melody once and then sing its tonal center. Another strategy may be used when memorizing a sonata for performance, and still another when asked to give an example of a piece that contains a tone row. In each of these tasks a different set or series of mental steps is needed. These sets of actions may be thought of as *programs*, which may be employed whenever similar tasks are presented. This section will explore some of these human programs.

Recently, educational institutions have spent much time and money on examining the outcomes of schooling. Educational activities such as setting behavioral objectives, assessing accountability, competency testing, marching-band contests, and the National Assessment of Educational Progress all support the notion that educators are very concerned with the *products* of education. Of course, most teachers will realize that this is not actually the case. Educators should focus also on the *process* of education; the products are indicators of how successful the process is. Directors of performing ensembles obviously are concerned about the quality of the spring concert, but their success in producing a musical performance is closely related to their understanding of the processes that enable their students to play or sing musically. If band directors, for example, do not help their students to play with breath support and correct embouchure, their bands are not likely to produce as musical a product.

Two Types of Processes

The processes that are employed by students to achieve the desired educational product vary, but they seem to represent two distinct types. Either the teacher may supply the sequence of steps to solve the problem or students may be left to develop their own problem-solving strategies. In the first approach students apply formal rules, or what are termed *algorithms*. In the second approach students develop personal rules, or what are called *heuristics*. Some instrumental music teachers may demand that all of their students develop a performance skill in the same manner, while other teachers may assist each student in developing his or her own solution to the performing problem.

Type 1. Signal Learning. A particular stimulus (a black dot on the third line of the treble staff) always elicits a particular response (the depression of the second valve of a trumpet).

Type 2. Stimulus-Response. More complex than signal learning—what is often referred to as operant conditioning. The notated B appears; the trumpet player responds by depressing the second valve; and the correct pitch is produced, thus rewarding the behavior and increasing the likelihood of that particular response to that particular stimulus.

Type 3. Chaining. Stimulus-response units are connected into sequences. A short notated phrase produces a sequence of valve depressing and lip movement by the trumpet player, which produces the correct sequence of pitches.

Type 4. Verbal Association. This is a subdivision of chaining. A musical parallel may be the discovery by a flute player that fingerings for notes in one octave may be similar or identical to fingerings for notes in a different octave. Thus the fingering for E, first line treble staff, is chained to the fingering for E, top space treble staff, as well as to the notation symbol for each note.

Type 5. Multiple Discrimination. Stimulus-response chains may work in combination. An instrumentalist may discriminate between one sequence of notes (a B-flat major scale) and another (a B-flat melodic minor scale) when sight-reading a composition, and employ the correct sequence of fingerings learned when practicing scale etudes.

Type 6. Concept Learning. Sets of multiple discriminations come together under a verbal label such as "major scale."

Type 7. Principle Learning. This is a chain of concepts such as the rules that govern the construction of various musical modes on different starting pitches.

Type 8. Problem Solving. The process of combining principles into novel, higher-order principles.

Figure 7.2. Gagné's learning hierarchy. Adapted from R. M. Gagné, *The Conditions of Learning*. New York: Holt, Rinehart and Winston, 1965.

There has been much debate over which approach is most valuable. Educators who support the heuristic approach assert it provides learners with a flexible, enduring process for solving problems. The debate seems to have been temporarily won in some subject areas by those who favor the heuristic approach. The recent interest by educators on issues such as reflective thinking and problem solving suggests a more heuristic than algorithmic approach to education.

The design of an instructional program often reveals the type of problem-solving strategy that is to be emphasized. Gagné's eight-category hierarchical theory of learning (see figure 7.2, p. 203) represents a pedagogical philosophy that would yield a rigid sequence of activities to which all students would adhere. Students progress from one level of the hierarchy to the next, but no provision is made for the skipping of steps or the return to a previous level, so a rigid formal instructional program results. Linear programmed instruction (see chapter 8), as advocated by Skinner, would also yield a static instructional sequence.

Instructional programs that emphasize the heuristic processing approach are more flexible in their design. The basic component of these programs would be the feedback loop (see figure 7.3). With feedback loops students continue to evaluate their progress toward an objective and receive instructional programs that enable them to progress. Most programs of the human mind contain several feedback loops, with the number depending upon the complexity of the operation, but single-loop programs do exist. For example, the concertmaster tuning his violin to the pitch provided by the oboist is testing (comparing) and operating (making adjustments to the string) until he or she is satisfied with the tuning and goes on to adjust the other strings.

Programs employing natural learning strategies are less organized. Because they are learner-oriented rather than content-oriented, they tend to be less stable. It is more difficult to make generalizations about these programs, because learners may differ in the strategies they employ to solve the same problem. The objective of describing these programs has generated considerable interest in the psychological community, and it has resulted in the identification of the components of a few general human programs.

The use of the term *program* to identify these processes has been borrowed from computer scientists, because they have been involved in the modeling of several basic programs used by the mind. Other labels have been employed to identify these processes, including "schemas," "func-

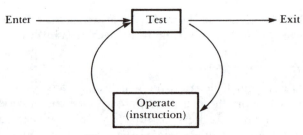

Figure 7.3. Feedback loop.

tional systems," and "cognitive maps." Regardless of what label is used or what objective the process has, most programs used by the mind have common components. These human programs are *goal-oriented*; the program is implemented to achieve some objective. To achieve this goal, *operations* in the form of mental activities are performed involving the *elements* or contents of the field or discipline involved. The operations are performed within the *rules* or constraints of the program. Operations result in new *states of knowledge*, which then may be subjected to testing by comparison with the goal to determine if the goal has been achieved. For example, children in a music class are working toward developing a concept of meter (the goal). As the children listen to a variety of examples (the content) labeled by the teacher as being either duple or triple meter, they begin to identify attributes of the pieces that enable them to distinguish between duple and triple meter (operations). The teacher selects only examples in simple meter (constraint). At the end of the instructional sequence many of the children are able to label new examples of duple and triple meter correctly, thus reaching a new state of knowledge.

The identification of the goal and the evaluation of an individual's current state often initiate the program cycle. The value and type of goal may dictate which program is employed to reach it. Goals may differ and can be categorized (e.g., social, achievement), but the value placed on the goal may determine whether the program is initiated at all. For example, members of an ensemble may attend concert rehearsals for different reasons. They may gain a rewarding aesthetic experience from performing, or they may be determined to master a particularly difficult passage, or they may enjoy the social interaction that the group provides. If the director is to be successful in preparing the group for the concert, the students must value these different types of goals sufficiently to attend the extra after-school rehearsals that the director schedules.

Some Human Systems For Information Processing

The rest of this section will explore four human programs and their possible applications to music learning. Programs for scanning and holding information, remembering, concept formation, and problem solving will be reviewed.

SCANNING AND HOLDING PROGRAMS. When teaching a new piece, choral directors will often sing a short phrase—"It should sound like this"—and ask their students to mimic their performance: "Now you do it just as I did." What mental processes, what human programs enable the choir members to sing the model back to the instructor? First, we must realize that the instructor's performance represents a complex multidimensional stimulus. The director may ask the students to focus on a particular aspect of the model—"Listen to the dotted quarter and eighth note in measure 3"—which should reduce the amount of information that needs to be retained.

One general characteristic of *scanning and holding programs* is that they are selective in the information that is retained. Because a large amount of information available would be likely to overload the system, only highlights or general outlines of a stimulus are held. Which aspects of the stimulus are retained depends on the instructions provided prior to the presentation of the information. This provides a preparatory mental *set* to aid the student in the retention of important information.

There are limits to the amount of information that can be held temporarily before it is either lost or moved to a more permanent storage mode. The number of individual elements or pieces of information that can be stored temporarily in *short-term memory* is thought to be about seven, plus or minus two (Miller, 1956). If the information exceeds the limitations of short-term memory, then it is reorganized and moved to *long-term memory*. This reorganization process is called *recoding*. For example, when music history students are preparing for a test on the Classical period, they may first focus on the important events in the life of Mozart, essentially working with a few bits of information. These events may then be tied together so that periods of Mozart's life may be thought of as a unit. Eventually the time periods become larger so that an entire sequence of events that constitute Mozart's life are integrated in long-term memory. While students being exposed to the life of Mozart for the first time are likely to begin this task with isolated events such as the date of his birth, more experienced students will work with larger chunks, such as his trips to Italy.

A diagram of the scanning and holding process is presented in figure 7.4.

Research on scanning and holding programs has yielded information on the components of the programs that may have pedagogical implications. The screening of the aspects of the information to be retained seems to work in a minimum effort-maximum efficiency manner. The smallest amount of information possible is retained. Only information that is necessary to distinguish the stimulus (in the sense of identifying unique objects) is collected. The more familiar the stimulus is, the fewer bits of information are needed for it to be held and the easier the material is to process and recode. This suggests, for example, that the more familiar pianists become with piano literature, the more efficient they will be at memorizing pieces—that is, placing them in long-term memory.

LONG-TERM MEMORY PROGRAMS. The process of remembering, or long-term memory, has two critical aspects: *recoding* and *retrieving*. Recoding is the component of remembering that transfers information from short-term memory into long-term memory. The manner in which recoding takes

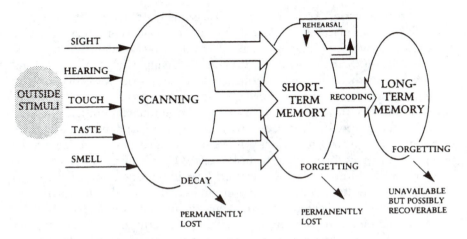

Figure 7.4. Scanning and holding programs.

place is critical to the ease or difficulty with which the material will later be retrieved. Information that has been organized and stored systematically can be much more readily retrieved than information that has not. The amount of information to be stored may also play an important role in the remembering process; thus, the more condensed the information is, the more likely it is to be retrieved.

Since the main task in long-term memory is retrieval, that has been the focus of researchers interested in the topic. The characteristics of the material to be stored that enhance retrieval are the same as those that improve scanning and holding. The use of *retrieval cues* will greatly increase the ability of the learner to retain large amounts of information. These cues serve as a framework upon which more detailed information can be stored. For example, one assignment music educators often require of students involves naming the lines and spaces of the treble staff. To facilitate this memorizing process the teacher may suggest the use of retrieval cues such as the sentence "*Every good boy does fine*," in which the first letter of each word names the lines of the treble staff from bottom to top, and the word FACE, in which each letter of the word names the spaces in order from bottom to top. Other teaching strategies for this task can be and are employed, but this particular approach is not uncommon. When faced with the task of recalling this information on a test, children have the nine separate bits of information organized into two meaningful forms.

Forgetting may be simply thought of as a breakdown in the retrieval system. The mind's storage facilities are analogous to a file cabinet. When the cabinet is new, each bit of information is placed in its own "folder." As new information arrives it may be placed in a new folder or integrated into existing folders. As the cabinet becomes full, individual file folders contain an increasing variety of information. Occasionally, items may get misfiled; that is, they get placed in a folder that at the moment seems the appropriate place but proves to be inappropriate when the item is needed. When people have a lot on their minds, it is analogous to having a full file cabinet, and items that at the time are not critical may be stored in places where they cannot be retrieved quickly, if ever. Mental rehearsals, which are calisthenics for the retrieval system, help ensure that forgetting will not take place.

For the piano student faced with the task of remembering a large amount of information, such as a movement of a sonata, there seem to be several strategies for making the task easier. Organizing the information to be memorized into phrases or sections, providing a network of cues such as the opening few notes of a section, and condensing the information to be memorized into melodic contours and the like all should assist in memorizing the piece. In addition, research on long-term memory has suggested that active rehearsal, like verbal repetitions, rather than passive rehearsal, thinking about the material to be memorized, facilities the long-term memory process.

CONCEPT FORMATION. As was suggested in the preceding section on long-term memory, the manner in which incoming information is organized is an important factor in the retention of the information. The organization of incoming information—that is, *concept formation*—has been of particular interest to theorists, researchers, and practitioners of education.

A concept may be thought of as a group or cluster of similar phenomena. Meter, orchestra, music stand, Classical style, timbre, and woodwind, for example, are all concepts for which specific exemplars exist. Music education over the past two decades has produced a considerable amount of literature on the teaching of music concepts. This material has focused on the presentation of organized aspects of musical knowledge rather than the isolated facts. The general thesis of this approach has been that systematized knowledge base provides a foundation on which other musical information can be linked and will provide for easier recall of the information. For example, instrumental music teachers may at times want their students to develop the concept of good tone quality on their instruments. This desire implies that the teachers hope to enable their students to integrate the infinite possibilities of timbre for different pitches in different ranges and loudness levels into a generalized concept of good tone quality.

Advanced clarinetists are capable of producing what listeners might call a clarinet-like sound. Listeners have developed this concept of "clarinetness" by having been exposed to a variety of clarinet tones as well as those of other instruments and by classifying these sounds in the appropriate categories. The importance of the ability to conceptualize can be illustrated by the large number of different timbres the clarinetist is capable of producing. Human beings cannot possibly store each unique timbre but instead must form a generalization (e.g., throat tones) based on similar characteristics of the sounds. These characteristics that are selected to be used in the classification process are called *criterial attributes.* Criterial attributes are used to integrate as well as discriminate among pieces of incoming information. Individuals may very well employ different criterial attributes to form similar concepts based on their experiences with the items being classified. For example, clarinetists might classify clarinet timbres differently than other musicians. Some studies (e.g., Bruner, 1964) have suggested that the dominant classification schemes employed by learners may differ at different ages, so an adult learner's concept of woodwind timbre is likely to differ from a child's.

Concepts formed employing criterial attributes may be depicted as tree-like structures, with the trunk serving as the broadest classification category, and the branches representing concepts that get narrower as they become more distant from the trunk (see figure 7.5, p. 210).

Educators concerned with concept formation have developed strategies to facilitate the process. One major question regarding such teaching strategies is concerned with who should organize the incoming elements—the teacher or the students. Advocates of the *discovery approach* to concept formation suggest that all the elements of the concept, such as timbres of all the woodwind instruments, be presented at once, with the learner being primarily responsible for identifying the criterial attributes and consequently identifying the concept. Promoters of the *reception method* of concept formation recommend that the material be previously organized by the instructor. Studies conducted in this area (Huttenlocher, 1962; Hunt, 1965) seem to indicate that the reception approach is most effective for young learners (preformal operational thinking), while the discovery method is more efficient for adult learners.

PROBLEM SOLVING, CRITICAL THINKING, AND METACOGNITION. Musicians who have to prepare a piece for performance often have an image of how the final product should sound. They may read through the piece to identify difficult passages and get a feel for the amount of work that will be required to get the piece in shape. Systematic practicing that focuses on the most difficult passages may follow, during which the performer continually compares her or his efforts with the imagined model. The constraints of limited practice time, the general level of previously acquired skill, the limitations of the instrument being played, the availability of other musicians with whom to consult, and other factors all affect the ability of the performer to prepare the piece. The final human program to be examined in this section is one that is employed when solving problems like the one just described. It involves goal identification, assessment of current status, the initiation of operations toward the goal, and assessments of the progress made.

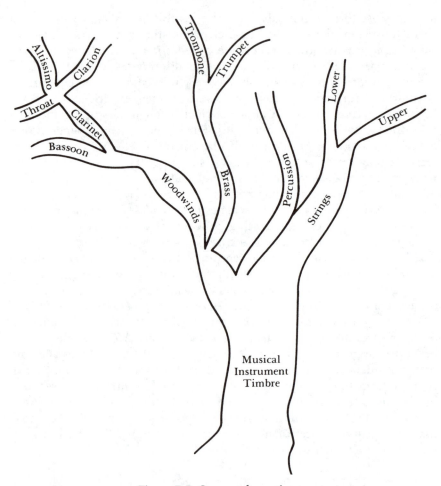

Figure 7.5. Concept formation.

The successful solution of a problem may involve several of the learner's abilities. Is the learner capable of recognizing when the components necessary to solve the problem are available? Is the learner capable of identifying and employing elements in his or her situation in new ways to solve problems, or is the learner's concept of the use of an object tied to its original purpose? Research suggests that these abilities interact with an individual's problem-solving programs, so the clarinetist who realizes that a rubber band may substitute for a broken spring is likely to be a better problem solver.

The problem-solving program is employed frequently. The more generalized the program, the more easily it can be applied to the different types of problems that confront the learner. A general problem-solving strategy has been proposed by Polya (1945). First, the problem must be understood; second, a plan must be devised for solving the problem; third, the plan must be carried out; and fourth, the solution must be examined.

Recently, literature in both general education and music education has often referred to the process of problem solving as "critical thinking." There seems to be a consensus among writers using the term that critical thinking involves developing discriminating evaluative skills. Critical thinking is a process that involves deliberation, and is sometimes referred to as higher-order thinking, referring to the upper (higher) levels of Bloom's cognitive taxonomy (see chapter 8). A curriculum based on critical thinking can be distinguished from one that does not stimulate critical thinking by the opportunity students have for active mental involvement in their learning. Teaching strategies that emphasize giving facts and stimulating the recall of facts do not develop critical thinking skills. Instruction that provides students with the opportunity to work through, debate, challenge information, find support for their perspectives, and establish criteria by which they will use to judge enables students to thinking critically.

Swartz (1987) suggests that critical thinking skills must be developed across different subject areas and that separate programs in critical thinking should be established. However, such programs must emphasize the integration of teaching for critical thinking into the entire curriculum, so that as areas like science and history develop materials and strategies for developing critical thinking, music instruction cannot be ignored.

Pogonowski (1989a) recommends approaches to developing critical thinking in music listening. Lecturing alone is not sufficient to develop critical thinking. It must be supplemented with classroom interactions that encourage analysis, synthesis, and evaluation of content. She suggests that by using broadly conceived questions such as "What are the predominant musical characteristics of the work?" to stimulate classroom dialogue, students can develop perspectives on the work and evaluate perspectives offered by other members of the class. Such "thought-provoking questions" must take place in an environment in which students feel nurtured and not at risk for offering their points of view.

Metacognition is an area of research and theorizing in psychology that has also received an increasing amount of attention in education since the early 1970s. Yussen (1985) describes metacognition as "thoughts about cognition, or thinking about thinking" (p. 253). Examples of metacognition include the contemplation of which strategy to use to memorize a list of the style characteristics of different periods of music history, the consideration of whether one understands the interpretation one's teacher has just described, and the consideration of what conditions will produce the fewest distractions while one is trying to listen critically to the first movement of a symphony.

Metacognitive skills are characteristic of the mature, independent learner. Individuals with metacognitive skills are learners who are not tied to formal instructional modes such as a teacher or a book. Rather, they are able to develop strategies for learning on their own. As one of the goals of music instruction is to develop independent musicians—individuals who can continue to learn music after they leave the formal instructional setting—it is important for music teachers to assist their students in developing metacognitive skills in music.

To enable students to become aware of their metacognitive skills in music, several writers on the subject such as Alvarez (1989), Pogonowski (1989b), and Welsbacher (1989) recommend having students examine their own thought processes by asking them "why," "how" and "what" questions. Music teachers who want to develop metacognitive skills in their students need to step back from "spooning out" information and instead assist students in discovering their own strategies for learning. Teachers need to ask students to report how they arrived at a particular response, emphasizing that recognizing the processes employed to arrive at an answer are as important as the answer.

This section has briefly reviewed a few general human information processing programs. Most of the research on which descriptions of these systems are based did not involve the processing of musical information. Is the processing of musical information unique? How does it differ from the processing of verbal information? These are major questions that need to be explored before music educators can readily adopt the systems discussed above. At the present time, however, there is little known about the processing of musical information.

Motivation

"How can I get my students to practice more?" "My seventh-grade general music class won't listen to anything I play for them." "My chorus takes ten minutes to settle down before we can start rehearsals." Each of these statements illustrates a need for a change of behavior. These types of perplexing problems frequently confront teachers and are often critical in determining the success of a music education program. These situations all describe problems with *motivation*. Motivation may be thought of as the energy that a learner employs when changing a behavior. Although at times teachers feel it is impossible to motivate certain students, it is likely that motivation problems are simply a matter of the teacher identifying or supplying the right type of "fuel" for a particular student's "engine."

Some behaviors like eating or sleeping seem to require little motivation, while others such as practicing scales may require more. Physiological motives such as hunger, which are critical to the survival of the species, are often labeled "primary drives." Both primary and secondary drives may be thought of as intrinsic motivators. Intrinsic motivators function without observable rewards. Extrinsic motivators pair observable rewards with the task to be accomplished. While intrinsic motivation has tended to be explored by the members of the cognitive school, extrinsic motivators have been of interest primarily to behavioral learning theorists. This section will focus on intrinsic motivation, while a section of chapter 8 will examine extrinsic motivation in music education applications.

Intrinsic motivators include both primary biological drives and secondary psychological drives. Primary drives such as pain, hunger, and thirst are thought to be inborn and are instrumental in the acquisition of basic survival skills. People acquire certain competencies and work toward accomplishing certain objectives to reduce drives. In primitive times these included the skills of hunting, foraging, and transportation of food, while in contemporary society these may be thought to include budgeting, shopping, and cooking.

Secondary, or psychological, drives tend to be of more interest to educators, since teachers are not allowed to starve or inflict pain on students in order to facilitate learning. Rather than being inborn, these secondary drives are probably acquired, although the acquisition is likely not to be in a formal educational setting. Psychological drives include fear, love, frustration, curiosity, the need for stimulation, the need for achievement, and others idiosyncratically defined by researchers and theorists, such as Maslow's "self-actualization."

Competence and Achievement Motivation

White (1959) proposes a psychological drive that he labels "competence." Competence motivation is an intrinsic need to master one's environment: for example, performing a technically difficult passage of music. A young child's interactions with the environment probably fulfill a need to explore and experiment. Gradually, children become capable of dealing with their environment to the extent that they exhibit some control over it. Thus, competent adults possess the skills to manipulate their environment as well as the confidence to do so. Teachers can influence the development of students' competence by the manner in which they provide directions for them, reward them, and evaluate them. Accordingly, music teachers should provide students with the opportunity to make decisions regarding their own achievement. They should not *excessively* reward students, and they should set realistic goals and standards for each individual. These strategies will be likely to produce a confident, skilled learner, one characterized by self-assurance and a willingness to take risks.

McClelland's theory of achievement motivation (1955) is similar to White's competence motivation theory. In addition to the notions of competence theory, McClelland's theory adds a standard of evaluation (doing a *good* job) and an emotional component (a sense of satisfaction). Much research on the theory of achievement motivation has been conducted over the past three or four decades. The results suggest that a student's need to achieve can be appreciably affected by formal and informal environmental factors, such as the learner's ego-involvement or pride in the learning task, family influences, and cultural influences.

Nicholls's (1982) "task-involvement" theory contrasts two psychological states associated with mastering a task. He believes that there are important motivation differences between learners who have high "ego-involvement" and those who have high "task-involvement." Ego-involved students "focus on themselves rather than the task—they are more consciously self-evaluative—and competence is indicated by performance that is superior to that of others" (Nicholls, 1982, p. 2). Task-involved learners "focus on the task rather than themselves and learning or performing is an end itself . . . thus task-involved students 'feel competent' if they achieve their personal best, if they make real gains in mastery. . . . Ego-involved individuals 'have to' beat someone else" (Nichols, 1982, p. 2). Thus, the sense of competition that is often developed in musical ensembles is likely to be successful in motivating *some* performers to high levels, but may generate problems for other members of the group, as pointed out in chapter 6.

Maehr's theory of "personal investment" seems to readily apply to several music learning scenarios. His perspective is designed to take a broader view of motivation by addressing social motives other than the need for achievement. He suggests that motivation can be understood in terms of "personal investment."

Maehr believes that the meaning of a situation to a person is the primary determinant of personal investment. This meaning is determined for a particular situation by three related ways: (1) beliefs about self, (2) perceived goals of the behavior, and (3) possibilities for action. What an individual sees as possible actions can also be tempered by social acceptability or social norms, so that while a student may have a "good ear" and find it easy to play an instrument, he or she may not choose to play if the idea of music making is not reinforced by the student's friends. On the other hand, research has shown (e.g., Maehr, 1983) that people tend to seek out tasks that help develop their recognized abilities.

Maehr emphasizes the importance of goals he identifies as task-goals, those that involve attempts to master a task because one has become absorbed in the task or because one is trying to demonstrate competence to oneself. Teachers who encourage the development of a task-goal orientation develop students' independent, self-initiated learning skills. Several factors can influence students' ability to develop such learning skills. Personal past experiences can be a factor, such as when a student's sense of competence is influenced by past successes and failures (e.g., someone who has been told he or she can't sing may feel less competent in terms of singing ability.) Peer expectations will also influence which tasks students may attempt. Features of a task such as the manner in which the task is to be evaluated can also effect motivation. External evaluation tends to reduce intrinsic interest.

The results of research on task and ego involvement seem to suggest that for many learners the development of task involvement is critical in sustaining motivation. Fortunately for teachers of music, this may be easier than for teachers of algebra, as music has a high degree of appeal.

The concepts of level of aspiration (Lewin, 1951) and fear of failure (Atkinson, 1965) also are closely related to the theory of achievement motivation. Levels of aspiration are examined by sampling students' goals. If students are allowed to construct their own goals, a higher degree of personal involvement is generated. If a student experiences early success, higher goals are likely to be established, with additional commitment to their completion. The expectation of eventual success may be an important factor in achievement motivation, and this expectancy will probably be high as long as the means for reaching a goal are available.

In addition to aspiration, fear of failure influences achievement motivation. Lack of success in reaching identified objectives may cause emotional problems in the learner, including anxiety, depression, frustration, and unrealistic expectations. Students' susceptibility to these problems will be affected by their environment both in and out of the classroom. In a study of motivation in music, Asmus (1989) concludes that the teacher may be the most important component in the motivation equation. The music teacher can assist students in avoiding problems by considering their family and cultural backgrounds when helping them to establish realistic goals. Good teachers are able to guide their students, indicating their present position or starting point, their final destination, and alternative routes to their goals as well as providing subgoals along the route that will allow for measurement of how much of the total distance has been traveled. For the instrumental music teacher, for example, the choice of whether to use a beginning method book with thirty pages or with sixty pages should be influenced by these factors.

Self-motivating Learning Cycles

Corno and Rohrkemper (1985) have made an important contribution in the area of intrinsic motivation with their "self-regulation" theory. Self-regulated learning is the highest form of cognitive engagement that students can use to learn. It requires that a systematic effort be made by students to develop an understanding of new material, to manipulate the network of ideas they already possess related to the content, and to monitor their progress in acquiring the new information.

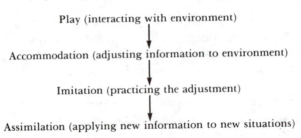

Play (interacting with environment)

Accommodation (adjusting information to environment)

Imitation (practicing the adjustment)

Assimilation (applying new information to new situations)

Figure 7.6. Piaget's self-motivating learning cycle. Adapted from J. Flavell, *The developmental psychology of Jean Piaget*. New York: D. Van Nostrand Co., 1963.

Corno and Rohrkemper suggest that teachers can aid students in developing self-regulated learning skills by employing teaching/learning strategies that foster intrinsic motivation. Such strategies include using a variety of activities and teaching methods, providing for student choice to reinforce individual differences, having teacher-student and student-student discussions of the content, pursuing topics in sufficient depth so that significant networks of knowledge and understandings can be developed, and providing feedback that is "timely, informative, encouraging and oriented toward private support of learning rather than public comparison of performance" (Good & Brophy, 1990, p. 368). Corno and Rohrkemper also recommend that as students gradually develop self-regulated learning abilities, teachers should withdraw supports that were initially necessary to establish the motivation, and instead provide opportunities for students to work with increasing autonomy.

Piaget has also proposed a self-motivating learning cycle in his "equilibrium theory." He proposes that the processes of assimilating, or taking in new information, and accommodating this information to our environment are the engine that motivates learners to seek new knowledge. His self-motivating learning cycle is shown in figure 7.6.

Equilibrium theory suggests that while children are interacting with their environment, new ways of interacting are discovered that require adjustment through practice so that they may become part of the way they deal with the environment. As new means of interacting are adopted, the environment is once again disturbed and so the process is renewed. Piaget suggests that this is self-continuing because the individual seeks equilibrium. The cycle may be thought of simply as practice → expand → practice.

These self-motivating learning styles have much appeal to the educator. The teacher with a class of self-motivated students may be in an educator's nirvana. However, self-motivated students are probably made, not born, so the teacher can do much toward reaching this ideal.

It is relatively easy to conjure up examples of self-motivating learning cycles in music instruction. Beginning instrumentalists, after being shown how to finger just a few notes, proudly come to their next lesson playing their favorite tunes, which they have "discovered" on their instruments. The third-grader, after a lesson on musical form, brings in five of his or her own records and identifies the structure of each of the songs employing his or her own idiosyncratic symbols. Both of these examples illustrate informal learning situations that are outside the music classroom.

Humanistic Motivation

Abraham Maslow and Carl Rogers have similar approaches to the question of motivation (Hunt & Sullivan, 1974). Both focus on personality aspects of the learner rather than the learner's interaction with the learning problem. The approach is often labeled "humanistic."

Maslow's conception of motivation involves a hierarchy of needs: for physiological well-being, for safety, for "belongingness" and love, for esteem, for self-actualization. He suggests that once the needs at a lower level are gratified the individual then becomes concerned with needs at the next higher level. When a need is gratified, it disappears. Thus, once students are recognized in front of their peers for their skill in accomplishing a difficult task, their need for esteem disappears. Maslow's theory suggests that healthy individuals—those whose lower-level needs have been gratified—continue to be motivated by self-actualization. He describes self-actualization as fulfillment of one's potentials or mission or trend toward unity within the individual. According to Maslow, the self-actualizing person is more likely to have a "peak experience," which he or she defines as an intensely pleasurable insight.

Carl Rogers's position was developed from a counseling environment and focuses on the importance of a learner being self-aware, that is, being in touch with himself or herself. Rogers is concerned that learners function in an accepting environment, one in which they are able to become more self-aware, to grow, and to develop. An accepting learning environment is student-centered and is sensitive to a student's feelings. It is created by actions of teachers that convey to students an acceptance of each of them as a person and provide for an environment in which each student can grow into a fully functioning person.

A major point of agreement between Rogers and Maslow is on the matter of choice. Both concur that learners must make their own decisions. Both feel strongly that fulfilled, self-actualizing learners will make correct choices. This last point suggests that less-directive instruction will be more successful. Not only will students feel strongly regarding the opportunity to make a choice, but they will also make the right choice—for them. This requires that alternatives not be laden with penalties, and suggests a maximum amount of teacher flexibility so that trial experiences with different alternatives may enable the learners to make informed choices.

The ease of applying Maslow's and Rogers's ideas to music teaching and learning depends on the specific music teaching situation. In the general music class, for example, providing opportunities for students to make choices does not seem difficult. The promotion of personalized learning strategies for general music would seem to conform to the directives suggested by these humanistic theorists. The performing program seems to provide for fewer individual choices, particularly in large ensembles; yet the successful director may be able to provide opportunities for some individual choices in ensembles and can provide opportunities in smaller performing groups for individual decision-making.

The different cognitive views of motivation seem very similar. All of the theories are concerned with what individuals believe about why they are engaging in a task, the difficulty of the task, expectations concerning the level of performance, and the probable consequences of that performance. All the theories agree that motivation is optimized when people believe that they are engaging in tasks for their own (internal) reasons rather than external ones; when they view the task as moderately challenging, but still feel capable of succeeding; and when they focus on the task itself, rather than focusing on how others will evaluate their performance.

To be successful, teachers must be able to motivate their students. All the intrinsic motivation theories reviewed here support the notion that each student needs to be treated as an individual. Music teachers, therefore, must strive to assess what type of motivation is best suited for each individual student.

Contextual Factors

Hunt and Sullivan (1974) suggest that there are two categories of factors that affect learning: (1) characteristics of the learner, such as socio-economic class, and (2) the setting in which the learning takes place. A variety of questions regarding the teaching-learning process may be examined by investigations in these two areas. They include questions such as: "Is the school a positive place to be?" "Does the class eagerly await their weekly visit from the music teacher?" "Does a trombone player in the band often forget to bring her instrument to school on rehearsal days?"

Kurt Lewin's "field theory" provides one theoretical framework in which to view the educational context. The young musician who must decide whether to continue practicing or to respond to friends' pleas for a right-fielder for a pick-up baseball game may have an "approach-approach conflict," according to Lewin (see figure 7.7).

Lewin describes an individual's psychological context as "life space" (represented in figure 7.7), in which various forces, either conscious or unconscious, are either attractive or unattractive. In the example above, if

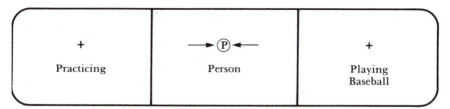

Figure 7.7. Lewin's life space.

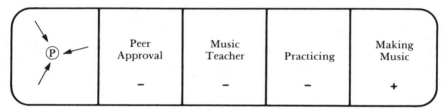

Figure 7.8. Music student's life space.

both practicing and baseball are attractive alternatives, the student has an approach-approach conflict; he or she wants to do both but must choose. Lewin's life space can include more than just momentary decision-making and may include a physical area, event, activity, or group membership. Life spaces can be used to represent various factors that can help clarify reasons for a child's behavior (figure 7.8).

If a music student's life space becomes too negative and full of unattractive alternatives, the young person may leave the field by daydreaming, forgetting to bring his or her instrument to rehearsal, or dropping out.

There are many different aspects of the educational environment that can affect the learning process. Hunt and Sullivan (1974, pp. 89–90) suggest the following taxonomy to help in identifying these factors:

1. *Cultural setting*: includes national and community elements and values.

2. *Current school setting*: includes culture of the school, class values, rural-urban-suburban locale.

3. *School characteristics (or classroom characteristics)*: includes size of school; number, age, and sex of students; number, age, and sex of teachers; physical characteristics, for example, open architecture.

4. *School organization (or classroom organization)*: includes power relations, decision-making patterns, division of labor, communication patterns, relations among staff, relations among students, peer influence, etc.

5. *Personal characteristics of teachers*: includes teacher characteristics specifically oriented toward the teaching function, such as personality structure, religious attitudes, social attitudes, philosophy of life, etc.

6. *Student-oriented teacher attitudes*: includes education goals, concepts about the teacher role and the student role, attitudes toward teaching, acceptance or rejection of student, etc.

7. *Teacher behavior*: includes teaching practices, specific teaching techniques, response to student behaviors, changes in teaching strategies, etc.

This list helps to demonstrate the complexity of the "life space" in which the teaching-learning process takes place. Educational researchers have attempted to isolate different variables cited above in hopes of finding cause-effect relationships with student achievement.

Teachers, of course, heavily influence the context in which the student learns. A series of studies (e.g., Lippitt & White, 1943) by some of Lewin's students examined the effects of democratic, authoritarian, and laissez-faire teachers on social climate and productivity of students. In general it was found that democratically operated classrooms were more motivating, produced more originality, and were more group-minded than the other classes, although they produced somewhat less work than the autocratic classes. The authoritarian class generated more hostility, more dependence on the teacher, fewer individual differences, and more dropouts, while students in the laissez-faire social climate produced less work, and work of poorer quality, than either of the other two groups.

A synthesis of the literature on teaching behavior (Rosenshine & Furst, 1971) suggests that there are five dimensions that are positively related to student achievement: clarity, variability, enthusiasm, task orientation, and student opportunity to learn material.

Another investigation (Abeles, 1975), dealing specifically with the characteristics of ensemble directors, indicates factors that helped distinguish effective from less effective directors. These included: (1) planning ability and familiarity with the literature; (2) ability to execute plans by establishing rapport with the ensemble members and communicating precisely the outcomes desired; and (3) focus on outcomes of the rehearsal in areas other than performance.

Other studies have examined the personality characteristics of music teachers (e.g. Krueger, 1976) and their relationship to various measures of success, including student ratings of instructors and student achievement. The results of these studies are not sufficiently consistent to warrant many generalizations. In addition, most studies conducted in this area have employed different personality measures and different categories of music teachers, which further limits their generalizability.

It is important to remember that as Hunt and Sullivan emphasize, the educational context *and* the characteristics of the learner both affect learning. Other sections of this chapter have focused on some attributes of students (e.g., need for achievement). Other chapters discuss learner characteristics such as socioeconomic status.

Knowledge of the interaction of situational and student characteristics may hold the key to designing successful education systems. For example, what happens when a child of high socioeconomic status is placed in a musical ensemble that is organized like a military unit? Does the same behavior result with the child of low socioeconomic status? Why are music teachers with quite different personalities equally successful? Would they be just as successful working in a different community or school, or with different students?

Research on the influences of contextual factors has yet to provide many answers, but should help sensitize teachers to the importance of this area in designing effective learning strategies.

The Home and Family

Schools are populated by an increasing number of children who come from "disadvantaged" families, families who are at the lowest 20 percent of the socioeconomic spectrum. In the United States, most disadvantaged families are white, and a large proportion of them are rural, even though much attention in relation to the disadvantaged in schools has focused on minority children in urban schools (Good & Brophy, 1990). Disadvantaged children often have difficulty in schools because of nutritional, health, and life-experience deficits. Programs such as Project Head Start were instituted as efforts to help reduce these deficits, but have had limited success.

Because the home environment plays such a critical role in the success of children in school, generations of disadvantaged adults pass their problems on to their children. It is not, as often stereotyped, that disadvantaged parents have values that are contrary to those helpful for success in school, but that they often lack the resources or experiences to know how to nurture their children's intellect. Several studies (e.g., Clark, 1983) suggest that it is relevant knowledge and experience, and not financial resources, that provide a positive home environment for nurturing cognitive growth. Parents who provide a supportive environment interact at length with their children in ways that stimulate thinking. They answer children's questions, encourage exploratory efforts, and assist them in assimilating new experiences. They practice activities such as reading newspapers and books, conversing about current events, listening selectively and attentively to music, participating in social and political organizations, being active in musical groups, visiting museums, and attending concerts.

Parents may not even be aware of the importance of providing this kind of stimulating environment at home and/or may not know what it is or how to create it. In school, the children of such parents are more likely to be successful with teachers who are warm and who establish personal interactions with them, but who still hold high expectations for their progress, require them to perform up to their capacities, and move them along at the most rapid pace possible (Good & Brophy, 1990, 58n). Music instruction naturally has many of the attributes that can help disadvantaged students to succeed. Music teachers often establish close strong relationships with their students, and can encourage students individually to maximize their skills and efforts. Many disadvantaged children may find a link to the rest of school through music instruction.

Musical Ability

One characteristic of learners that is of particular interest to music teachers is that of music ability. Questions such as "Are any of my students musically gifted?" or "Will instruction in music be a waste of time?" may frequently cross the minds of music teachers as they prepare material for a new group of students. All these questions focus on the psychological construct of musical ability.

It is important to remember that notions like intelligence, personality, and music ability are constructs that provide a means of discussing issues without being encumbered by articulating all the different behaviors that constitute the construct (see chapter 11). Thus, constructs can be defined at two levels: (1) by relating them to other constructs—for example, "that characteristic, or those characteristics, which distinguish 'musical' persons from 'unmusical' persons" (Bentley, 1966, p. 13); or (2) by describing the way they are measured, such as scores on the Musical Aptitude Profile (Gordon, 1965).

The definition of music ability has occupied the attention of music psychologists for well over half a century. Considerable debate over the correct term to employ when referring to music ability has been generated. Radocy and Boyle (1988, p. 295) suggest that terms like "talent" and "musicality" are imprecise. They also suggest that "musical capacity" should be used to refer to ability possessed through genetic endowment or maturation; "musical aptitude," to refer to ability possessed through capacity plus informal environmental factors; and "musical ability," to refer to capacity, environmental factors, and formal instruction. So music educators are primarily concerned with musical ability.

The development of tests to measure musical ability has not been neglected. More than a dozen music aptitude tests have been published since *Seashore Measures of Musical Talent* in 1919. The tests vary considerably in the musical behaviors they elect to examine (see chapter 9), and thus have generated much controversy. Broad constructs such as musical ability or intelligence cannot help but generate conflicting definitions based on different test developers' views of the constructs.

These different perspectives on musical ability have generated different theoretical schools regarding its nature. There are two main camps, with a third somewhat in between the other two. The theory of specifics maintains that music ability is not a single trait, but rather consists of several unrelated talents. It was first described by Seashore. His test of talents reflects this position as it assesses the ability to perceive the basic aspects of sound (i.e., pitch, time, intensity, and timbre). The theory of specifics has had several other proponents, including Schoen (1940) and more recently Bentley (1966).

If the theory of specifics represents one end of a continuum of theories of the nature of musical ability, the position of music psychologists such as Mursell (1937) and Wing (1941) represents the other end. These theorists believe that music ability is a single ability. At various times this position has been labeled the "omnibus" theory or the theory of a general musical ability. In contrast to the theory of specifics, this omnibus position is somewhat of a Gestalt approach, which claims that the whole is greater than the sum of its parts.

Shuter (1968) suggests the existence of an in-between theoretical position as exemplified by the research of Holmstrom (1963). This position organizes the nature of musical ability into a few group factors (e.g., general intelligence level, pitch perception skills), each of which is composed of several elements similar to those articulated by the theory of specifics.

Advocates for each of these three theoretical positions can cite research in support of their positions. In some cases they may even make reference to the same study but provide different interpretations of the results.

Although the structure or nature of musical ability has been the focus of considerable attention, it has not generated such intense debate as the question of music ability's source. The issue that has served as a focal point for the controversy is the question of how one comes to possess musical ability or abilities. Are they for the most part inherited or are they primarily developed by environmental influences? The resolution of this question, frequently referred to as the nature-nurture controversy, could have sizeable impact on music education, because if musical ability was shown to be innate, music teachers might choose to exclude some students from their classes. If musical ability was shown to be environmentally influenced, teachers could argue that all children should have music instruction. The assumption of these two positions is that music ability is *either* innate *or* environmentally determined, rather than some proportional product of both positions (Gordon, 1971).

This debate has somewhat paralleled a similar debate over the inheritability of intelligence. Carl Seashore (1919) again was one of the first to articulate one of the positions. His support of the inheritance of musical ability was buttressed by several other early music psychologists such as Schoen (1940) and Revesz (1953), who based their position primarily on the early development of high levels of musical skill by prodigies. Champions of the environmental position include Farnsworth (1969) and Lundin (1967). The relative acceptance by the profession of either the nature or nurture position has varied throughout this century and has tended to parallel the intelligence issue. In the first part of the century the innate-ability position was generally accepted; in the fifties positions that seemed to completely exclude any genetic influence gained popularity.

Some contemporary views of human intellect suggest a strong genetic component, which can be influenced by changes in the environment. Experts in genetics suggest that environmental influences can modify scores on IQ tests by as much as twenty-five points (average IQ scores are usually 100) (Good & Brophy, 1990, p. 590). This suggests that two children with similar genes for music ability could ultimately differ considerably in music achievement if one were to grow up in a minimally musically stimulating environment and one grew up in a maximally musically stimulating environment. This view seems to be reinforced by several studies (e.g., Gordon, 1968) that report that music aptitude seems to be relatively stable after age ten but may fluctuate in younger children—which possibly indicates that such aptitude may be affected by early exposure to music (Gordon, 1971).

Nevertheless, the search for genetic predictors of music ability continues, as illustrated by an article written in 1975 (Scheid & Eccles) that suggests that postmortem examinations of brains may show enlarged *plana temporale* in persons who possessed high musical ability. The question of nature-nurture contributions to musical ability is not likely to be resolved in the near future, since satisfactory research strategies have yet to be developed to isolate the environmental and genetic factors. Unless more mothers and fathers of identical twins are willing to sacrifice their children to science, this intriguing question may remain unanswered.

Several hypotheses have been offered regarding the relationship of characteristics such as sex, race, and intelligence to music ability. Recent studies suggest that while social stereotypes may affect sexual and racial roles in music, no differences in music ability exist as a function of sex or race.

The relationship of intelligence and musical ability is not as clear-cut. Frequently cases of musical idiot-savants (i.e., people with below-normal intelligence but a high level of musical talent) are cited to support the existence of a low relationship between intelligence and music ability, and some studies have reported low correlations between scores on music aptitude tests and intelligence tests. After examining the literature, Radocy and Boyle conclude that "all highly musical people appear to be highly intelligent, but not all highly intelligent people are musical" (1988, p. 303). The clarification of this relationship will continue to attract the attention of researchers in the future.

Summary

Two theoretical positions dominate the psychology of learning. The cognitive school has sought to develop theories to explain complex mental processes such as concept formation. The behavioral school, exemplified by the work of Skinner, has focused on developing practical explanations for simple learning problems. The cognitive school is more theoretically oriented, while the behavioral school has a more applied emphasis. Several other psychologists, who are not easily categorized as belonging to one school or the other, have also made important contributions to our understanding of the learning process. These include Piaget (child development), Gardner, J. P. Guilford (structure of the intellect), and Rogers and Maslow (humanistic psychology).

Piaget's stage theory has had much influence on child development theory and research in this country. He presents a four-stage development theory consisting of a sensorimotor stage, preoperational stage, concrete operational thought stage, and formal operational thought stage. As children progress through these stages they become better equipped to interact with their environment. In the sensorimotor stage children's intellectual development is dominated by their senses. During the preoperational period children acquire the ability to store images and work with symbols (language). The concrete operational stage is characterized by the ability to "conserve." During the formal operational stage children are able to deal with abstractions and are no longer encumbered by a dependence on reality. Several music educators have demonstrated an interest in child development theories and have published research studies exploring the applications of these theories to music learning. Results of these studies have suggested that music concept formation seems to develop in this order: volume, timbre, tempo, duration, pitch, and harmony.

Cognitive psychologists attempt to develop explanations for complex mental processes. These processes or sets of actions may be thought of as human programs. Some programs have dictated sequences of steps, or *algorithms*. Programs in which students develop their own problem-solving strategies are called "*heuristic*." Gagné's eight-category hierarchical theory of learning is an example of an algorithm. Heuristic programs are more flexible and contain feedback loops.

Four human systems for processing information are scanning and holding, remembering, concept formation, and problem solving. Scanning and holding programs enable learners to retain highlights of a stimulus in short-term memory. The preparatory mental set that learners have prior to the presentation of the information can strongly influence the students' retention ability. Students' ability to retain information for long periods of time depends on their remembering programs. Recoding and retrieving information from long-term memory are the critical aspects of the remembering process.

The manner in which the contents of long-term memory are organized is an important factor in retrieving information. The organization of information into concepts can aid students in remembering and acquiring new knowledge. Concept formation is essentially a classification process, and concepts are often hierarchical. Stimuli with similar characteristics are grouped together according to criterial attributes. Psychologists who advocate a discovery approach recommend that the student be responsible for organizing new incoming information, while those who promote reception learning recommend that the material to be presented be organized by the instructor. Retrieval cues, such as acronyms, can also assist in remembering.

Problem-solving programs involve the identification of goals, the determination of current status, the initiation of operations toward the goal, and assessments of the progress made. Learners' abilities to identify elements in their environment that can be useful in solving problems are related to problem-solving success.

Student motivation problems can be understood by successfully identifying the intrinsic and/or extrinsic needs or drives of individual students. Cognitive psychologists have been primarily concerned with describing intrinsic motivators. Theoretical constructs presented by the cognitivists to explain intrinsic motivation have included White's competence motivation, and McClelland's achievement motivation, which adds an evaluative and emotional component to competence motivation. Factors influencing motivation as described by these theories include ego and task involvement, levels of aspiration, and fear of failure.

Piaget's four-step cycle of self-motivation emphasizes a process called "accommodation" (adjusting information to the environment) and a process labeled "assimilation" (applying new information to new situations).

Humanistic psychologists such as Rogers and Maslow emphasize the importance of the personality characteristics of the learner in their approaches to motivation. Maslow presents a hierarchy of needs and suggests that when basic needs are satisfied, individuals continue to be motivated by self-actualization. Rogers's position emphasizes the importance of the learner being self-aware. Both agree that providing choices for students in the learning environment should enhance motivation.

Lewin's field theory provides a framework in which the educational context can be examined. Factors that can influence the educational environment include cultural setting, school setting, school or classroom characteristics, school or classroom organization, personal characteristics of teachers, teacher attitudes toward students, and teacher behavior. Research has indicated that characteristics of teachers (e.g., democratic vs. authoritarian) can influence the social climate of the classroom and the productivity of students.

The home and family also play an important role in education. Disadvantaged children's circumstances may present difficulties that must be overcome by teachers to assist the disadvantaged child to learn.

The nature and assessment of music ability has interested music psychologists and educators for more than fifty years. Theorists concerned with the structure of music ability have debated whether it is a general trait or whether it is composed of several more specific abilities (e.g., pitch perception, timbre perception). A more intense debate regarding music ability has focused on the question "Is music ability inherited?" Research on both these issues does not seem to have completely resolved either question.

STUDY AND DISCUSSION QUESTIONS

1. How might a behaviorist middle-school general music teacher organize a lesson on the features of African music? How might a cognitivist middle-school general music teacher organize such a lesson?

2. In what way does the development of the students affect the planning of what they should learn in music classes?

3. What principles should music teachers follow in teaching children who are at the preoperational stage?

4. In what order does it appear that children develop the ability to form musical concepts?

5. What is the relationship between concepts and the verbal designations of the concepts? Can one exist without the other? Is there a sequence for the learning of one before the other?

6. What is the basic difference between the heuristic and algorithmic approaches to learning?

7. A theory teacher wants to have the students learn about chord functions—tonic, dominant, and so on. Describe how the teacher might do this in terms of:

   (a) goal

   (b) operations

   (c) elements

   (d) constraints

8. What are the differences between how people remember information for short periods of time and for a long period of time? What implications do these differences have for the teaching of music?

9. What is the function of criterial attributes in the forming of concepts?

10. How might a teacher take advantage of the students' desire for competence? Of Piaget's equilibrium theory?

11. What is the most recent thinking of psychologists regarding whether music ability is inherited or developed? What is the relationship between intelligence and musical ability?

12. How do Gagné's and Piaget's views differ on the question of maturation vs. development?

INDIVIDUAL OR CLASS ACTIVITIES

1. In order to explore music concept formation, have pairs of individuals in the class play a word-association game. Student 1 in each pair will start the game by presenting a word that represents a broad music concept, such as "symphony." (These words can be preselected by the instructor.) Student 2 must respond within two seconds with the first word that comes to mind—for example, "Beethoven." Student 1 then presents the new word (i.e., Beethoven), to which student 2 again must respond (e.g. "Eroica"). This continues until student 2 fails to respond within the two-second limit. At that point the roles are reversed: student 2 becomes the presenter and is given a different concept to start the game, and student 1 becomes the respondent. Several pairs of students can be selected prior to the game and asked to leave the room while each of the other pairs plays. This allows the class to compare responses of different pairs to the same concepts. The responses can be recorded and discussed in class.

2. Select a musical concept such as tonality and discuss how such a concept could be taught to students who are in the preoperational stage, the concrete operational stage, and the formal operational stage.

3. Ask each student in the class to respond on a slip of paper "yes" or "no" to the question: "Were you born with musical talent?" Discuss the results of the survey.

SUPPLEMENTARY READINGS

DAVIDSON, L., & SCRIPP, L. (1992). Surveying the coordinates of cognitive skills in music. In R. Colwell (Ed.), *Handbook of research on music teaching and learning* (pp. 392–413). New York: Schirmer Books.

HARGREAVES, D. J., & ZIMMERMAN, M. P. (1992). Developmental theories of music learning. In R. Colwell (Ed.), *Handbook of research on music teaching and learning* (pp. 377–91). New York: Schirmer Books.

THOMAS, N. G. (1992). Motivation. In R. Colwell (Ed.), *Handbook of research on music teaching and learning* (pp. 425–36). New York: Schirmer Books.

TUNKS, T. W. (1992). The transfer of music learning. In R. Colwell (Ed.), *Handbook of research on music teaching and learning* (pp. 437–48). New York: Schirmer Books.

REFERENCES

ABELES, H. F. (1975). Development of a form for the evaluation of ensemble directors by college students. *Journal of Band Research, 12* (1), 12–17.

ALVAREZ, B. (1989). Musical thinking and the young child. In E. Boardman (Ed.), *Dimensions of Musical thinking* (pp. 57–64). Reston. Reston, VA: Music Educators National Conference.

ASMUS, E. P. (1989). The effect of music teachers on students' motivation to achieve in music. *Canadian Journal of Research in Music Education, 30,* 14–21.

ATKINSON, J. W. (1965). The mainsprings of achievement-oriented activity. In J. W. Krumboltz (Ed.), *Learning and the educational process* (pp. 25–66). Chicago: Rand McNally.

AUSUBEL, D. P. (1968). *Educational psychology: a cognitive view.* New York: Holt, Rinehart.

BENTLEY, A. (1966). *Musical ability in children and its measurement.* New York: October House.

BRUNER, J. S. (1964). The course of cognitive growth. *American Psychologist, 19,* 1–15.

CLARK, R. (1983). *Family life and school achievement: Why poor black children suceed or fail.* Chicago: University of Chicago Press.

CORNO, L., & ROHRKEMPER, M. (1985). Self-regulated learning. In C. Ames & R. Ames. (Eds.), *Research on motivation in education* (Vol. 2, pp. 101–35). Orlando, FL: Academic Press.

FARNSWORTH, P. R. (1969). *The social psychology of music* (2d ed.). Ames: Iowa State Press.

FEIGENBAUM, E. A. (1963). The simulation of verbal learning behavior. In E. A. Feigenbaum & J. Feldman (Eds.), *Computers and thought* (pp. 68–91). New York: McGraw-Hill.

GARDNER, H. (1983). *Frames of Mind.* New York: Basic Books.

GOOD, T. L., & BROPHY, J. E. (1990). *Educational psychology: A realistic approach* (4th ed.). New York: Longman.

GORDON, E. E. (1965). *Musical aptitude profile.* Boston: Houghton Mifflin.

GORDON, E. E. (1968). A study of the efficiency of general intelligence and musical aptitude tests in predicting achievement in music. *Bulletin of the Council for Research in Music Education, 13*, 40–45.

GORDON, E. E. (1971). *The psychology of music teaching.* Englewood Cliffs, NJ: Prentice-Hall.

GUILFORD, J. P. (1956). The structure of the intellect. *Psychological Bulletin, 53*, 267–93.

HAIR, H. I. (1977). Discrimination of tonal direction on verbal and nonverbal tasks by first-grade children. *Journal of Research in Music Education, 25*(3), 197–210.

HILGARD, E. L., & BOWER, G. H. (1981). *Theories of learning* (5th ed.). Englewood Cliffs, NJ: Prentice-Hall.

HILL, W. F. (1971). *Learning: a survey of psychological interpretations* (rev. ed.). Scranton, PA: Chandler.

HOLMSTROM, L. G. (1963). *Musicality and prognosis.* Uppsala, Sweden: Almqvist and Wiksells.

HUNT, D. E. (1965). Selection and reception conditions in grammar and concept learning. *Journal of Verbal Learning and Verbal Behavior, 4*, 1–16.

HUNT, D. E., & SULLIVAN, E. V. (1974). *Between psychology and education.* Hinsdale, IL: Dryden.

HUTTENLOCHER, J. (1962). Effects of manipulation of attributes on efficiency of concept formation. *Psychological Reports, 10*(1), 12–19.

KRUEGER, R. J. (1976). An investigation of personality and music teaching success. *Bulletin of the Council for Research in Music Education, 47*, 16–25.

LEWIN, K. (1951). *Field theory in social science.* New York: Harper and Brothers.

LIPPITT, R., & WHITE, R. (1943). The 'social climate' of children's groups. In R. G. Barker, J. S. Kounin, & H. F. Wright (Eds.), *Child behavior and development.* New York: McGraw-Hill.

LUNDIN, R. W. (1967). *An objective psychology of music* (2d ed.). New York: Ronald.

MAEHR, M. L. (1983). The development of continuing interests in music. In *Ann Arbor Symposium on the Application of Psychology to Music Teaching and Learning: Motivation and Creativity* (pp. 5–12). Reston, VA: Music Educators National Conference.

MASLOW, A. H. (1954). *Motivation and Personality.* New York: Harper and Brothers.

MASLOW, A. H. (1968). Some education of the humanistic psychologist. *Harvard Educational Review, 38*(3), 685–96.

MCCLELLAND, D. (1955). *Studies in motivation.* New York: Appleton.

MILLER, G. A. (1956). The magical number seven, plus or minus two: Some limits on our capacity for processing information. *Psychological Review, 63*, 81–97.

MODGIL, S., MODGIL, C., & BROWN, G. (Eds.). (1983). *Jean Piaget: An interdiciplinary critique*. London: Routledge and Kegan Paul.

MURSELL, J. L. (1937). *The psychology of music*. New York: W.W. Norton.

MUSIC EDUCATORS NATIONAL CONFERENCE. (1985). *The young child and music*. Reston, VA: Author.

NICHOLLS, J. G. (1982). Task-involvement in music. In *National Symposium on the Application of Psychology to the Teaching and Learning of Music* (pp. 1–4). Ann Arbor, MI.

PETZOLD, R. (1963). The development of auditory perception of music sounds by children in the first six grades. *Journal of Research in Music Education, 11*(3), 21–54.

PFLEDERER, M. (1964). The response of children to musical tasks embodying Piaget's principle of conservation. *Journal of Research in Music Education, 12*.

POGONOWSKI, L. (1989a). Critical thinking and music listening. *Music Educators Journal, 76*(1), 35–38.

POGONOWSKI, L. (1989b). Metacognition: A dimension of musical thinking. In E. Boardman (Ed.), *Dimensions of Musical Thinking* (pp. 9–20). Reston, VA: Music Educators National Conference.

POLYA, G. (1945). *How to solve it: A new aspect of mathematical method*. Princeton, NJ: Princeton University Press.

RADOCY, R. E., & BOYLE, J. D. (1988). *Psychological foundations of musical behavior* (2d ed.). Springfield, IL: Charles C. Thomas.

REVESZ, G. (1953). *Introduction to the psychology of music*. London: Longmans, Green.

ROSENSHINE, B., & FURST, N. (1971). Research on teacher performance criteria. In B. O. Smith (Ed.), *Research in teacher education*. Englewood Cliffs, NJ: Prentice-Hall.

SCHEID, P., & ECCLES, J. C. (1975). Music and speech: Artistic functions of the human brain. *Psychology of Music, 3*(1), 21–35.

SCHOEN, M. (1940). *The psychology of Music*. New York: Ronald Press.

SCOTT, C. R. (1979). Pitch concept formation in preschool children. *Bulletin of the Council for Research in Music Education, 59*, 87–93.

SCOTT-KASSNER, C. (1992). Research on music in early childhood. In R. Colwell (Ed.), *Handbook of research on music teaching and learning* (pp. 633–50). New York: Schirmer Books.

SEASHORE, C. E. (1919). *The psychology of musical talent*. New York: Silver Burdett.

SERAFINE, M. L. (1975). *A measure of meter conservation in music*. Unpublished doctoral dissertation, University of Florida, Gainesville.

SERAFINE, M. L. (1988). *Music as cognition: The development of thought in sound*. New York: Columbia University Press.

SHUTER, R. (1968). *The psychology of musical ability*. London: Methuen.

SHUTER-DYSON, R., & GABRIEL, C. (1981). *The psychology of musical ability* (2d ed.). New York: Methuen.

SLOBODA, J. A. (1985). *The musical mind: The cognitive psychology of music.* Oxford: Clarendon.

SWARTZ, R. J. (1987). Critical thinking, the curriculum and the problem of transfer. In D. N. Perkins, J. Lochhead, & J. C. Bishop (Eds.), *Thinking: The second international conference* (pp. 72–91). Hillsdale, NJ: Erlbaum.

WEBSTER, P., & SCHLENTRICH, I. (1979). Pitch discrimination of tonal direction by preschool children on verbal and nonverbal tasks. Indianapolis, IN: Music Educators National Conference, North Central Divisional Convention

WEBSTER, P., & ZIMMERMAN, M. P. (1983). Conservation of rhythm and tonal patterns of second- through sixth-grade children. *Bulletin of the Council for Research in Music Education, 73*, 28–49.

WELSBACHER, B. (1989). Musical thinking in the special education classroom. In E. Boardman (Ed.), *Dimensions of Musical Thinking*. Reston, VA: Music Educators National Conference.

WHITE, R. W. (1959). Motivation reconsidered: The concept of competence. *Psychological Review, 66*, 297–333.

WING, H. D. (1941). A factorial study of musical tests. *British Journal of Psychology, 31*, 341–55.

YUSSEN, S. R. (1985). The role of metacognition in contemporary theories of cognitive development. In D. L. Forrest-Pressley, G. E. MacKinnon, & T. G. Waller (Eds.), *Metacognition, cognition, and human performance: Vol. 1. Theoretical Perspectives*. Orlando, FL: Academic Press.

ZIMMERMAN, M. P. (1981). Child development and music education. In *Documentary report of the Ann Arbor Symposium* (pp. 49–55). Reston VA: Music Educators National Conference.

ZIMMERMAN, M. P., & SECHREST, L. (1968). How children conceptually organize musical sounds. (Cooperative Research Project No. 5-025). Evanston, IL: Northwestern University.

CHAPTER 8

Applications of Psychology to Music Teaching

WHILE IT IS IMPORTANT to understand the theoretical basis of learning, it is equally important to be able to apply these theories and principles to the teaching and learning of music. MENC has recognized both the importance of having a sound theoretical base and the need to have theories translated into applications by sponsoring a series of symposia on the applications of psychology to the teaching and learning of music. These three meetings, often referred to as the Ann Arbor Symposia, took place at various times between 1979 and 1981. The symposia were organized around the issues presented in chapters 6 and 7, such as cognitive processing, child development, motivation, and creativity. Many of these theoretical issues have been applied in the music classroom. These applications are outgrowths of both the cognitive and behaviorist perspectives but at times are difficult to categorize, because they frequently represent combinations of theoretical positions from both of these psychological traditions.

Taxonomies of Educational Objectives

The first application described in this chapter illustrates this overlapping phenomenon well. Bloom's *Taxonomy of Educational Objectives,*

Cognitive Domain (1956) describes a hierarchy of cognitive processes similar to the human programs, such as problem solving, described in chapter 7, although Bloom's taxonomy focuses on the *products* of these processes rather than the processes themselves. The taxonomy, however, has been primarily used as a means of classifying behavioral objectives that have as their foundation the principles of the behaviorist tradition. Thus, as educators have attempted to solve practical learning problems, they have tended to look for solutions that work—a clinical approach—rather than to adhere to a particular psychological tradition. The differences in the activities of the educator, the educational psychologist, and the psychologist center on the different goals of their disciplines. Chapter 7 focused on the first half of a continuum from the more laboratory-oriented interests of psychologists to the field interests of the teacher. This chapter focuses on the last half.

The Cognitive Domain

Bloom's taxonomy was developed primarily to facilitate communication among educators. It provides teachers with a means of examining curriculum, organizing, and assessing instructional objectives. Thus, when teachers are asked to develop a curriculum, the taxonomy can provide differing levels of comprehensiveness and complexity in educational outcomes for them to consider. The taxonomy can assist curriculum committees in specifying objectives and planning strategies for evaluating objectives. Using the taxonomy will also help increase the precision with which educators can describe objectives, thus providing a better basis for assessment and instruction.

> For example, some teachers believe their students should "really understand," others desire their students to "internalize knowledge," still others want their students to "grasp the core or essence" or "comprehend." Do they all mean the same thing? Specifically, what does a student do who "really understands" which he does not do when he does not understand? Through reference to taxonomy as a set of standard classifications, teachers should be able to define such nebulous terms. (Bloom, 1956, p. 1)

The taxonomy provides a hierarchy of mental skills employed by students when they process cognitive information. Rather than focusing on the processes, the taxonomy suggests products that can be used as indicators of the process involved. The behaviors categorized at the higher levels of the taxonomy are thought to be more complex than those categorized at the lower levels. The organization of the taxonomy by complexity is based on the principle that the more complex behaviors are built from integrating several of the simpler behaviors. Therefore, for students to demonstrate behaviors at the higher levels of the taxonomy, it is necessary

TABLE 8.1

Major Categories of Bloom's Taxonomy of the Cognitive Domain (Adapted from Gronlund, N. E., & Linn, R. L., *Measurement and Evaluation in Teaching*, 6th ed. New York: Macmillan, 1990)

1. *Knowledge.* The knowledge level involves the recall of previously learned material. The information retrieved is generally in the form in which it was learned, although minor alterations of the material may have occurred. A variety of material may be retrieved, from specific bits of information or facts to theories and generalizations. Knowledge is the lowest level of the cognitive domain.

2. *Comprehension.* At the comprehension level students, in addition to simply recalling material, are able to grasp the meaning of the material. This ability can be demonstrated by translation—placing the original material in a new form that still communicates the original meaning; interpretation—the explanation or summarization of a communication; and extrapolation—the extension of trends or tendencies indicated in the original message.

3. *Application.* Students who are able to employ generalizations, abstractions, or rules of procedure to particular and concrete situations are demonstrating behavior at the application level of the taxonomy. At this level not only must the previously learned material be remembered and understood, but it must also be applied.

4. *Analysis.* Analysis involves the identification and organization of the components of the material so that the ideas contained in it can be made more explicit. The focus at this level of the taxonomy is on the form as well as the content of the material. This additional ability to gain information from the structure of a communication represents a higher level of processing than comprehension and application.

5. *Synthesis.* Synthesis requires students to put together elements or parts to form a new whole. This involves working with previously identified components and combining them in a way that is unique and not previously apparent. This ability may be demonstrated by producing a unique communication, a plan, or a set of operations or abstract relations. The emphasis at this level is on creative behavior.

6. *Evaluation.* Evaluation involves the ability to make judgments regarding the effectiveness of material and methods for given purposes. These judgments may employ internal evidence such as logical consistency or external criteria. It is assumed that the evaluation process requires all the behaviors of the previous levels of the domain, plus the ability to make judgments based on clearly articulated criteria.

for them to have the knowledge and understanding that serve as the building blocks for the more complex behaviors. An abbreviated form of the cognitive taxonomy appears in table 8.1.

The following questions, developed for an instructional unit on meter, illustrate an application of the taxonomy to music learning. When attempting to respond to each of the examples, students would be likely to employ different modes of processing. As you read through each item, try to evaluate the thought process you employ to arrive at the answer.

Question 1. A musical piece that is organized into rhythmic units of three pulses is said to be in:

(a) duple meter

(b) triple meter

(c) uneven meter

(d) waltz time

Question 2. Listen to the following short piece. (The instructor plays the first eight measures of "Peter's Theme" from *Peter and the Wolf*.) The meter of the piece is:

(a) duple meter

(b) triple meter

(c) uneven meter

(d) waltz time

Question 3. Ms. MacMillion is in her first year as the high school band director in Holdenville. The principal has asked her to have the concert band play for the graduation ceremony. She needs to select music for the procession as the students enter the auditorium. Listen to the three following examples. Which of the three would you recommend *not* be included for the processional?
(The instructor plays)

(a) Example 1 (Sousa: "Stars and Stripes Forever")

(b) Example 2 (Williams: "Theme from Star Wars")

(c) Example 3 (Tchaikovsky: "Waltz of the Flowers")

(d) Both Examples 1 and 3

Question 1 is intended to be at the *knowledge* level. Test items at this level emphasize simple retrieval programs. For this item it is expected that students were previously presented with definitions of both duple and triple meter, and thus it simply recalls information previously stored. The ability of students to answer this question correctly should depend primarily on their recording, long-term-memory-retrieval system and little else.

Question 2 examines the ability of students to *analyze*. A correct response to this item depends on a more complex system than is necessary for question 1. Students must be able to analyze the sounds, select from them the ones that determine meter, and then employ the correct label. If this system breaks down at any point, the student is unlikely to produce the correct response.

The third question requires students to employ a complex cognitive process as well as an evaluative process. Students must employ a variety of criteria (including meter) in order to decide on the correct answer. To derive the answer to the third item, students are not simply expected to quickly apply a subjective opinion, but evaluate how well each piece satisfies carefully a selected set of criteria. Not only the students need to evaluate each circumstance to determine what criteria are appropriate to apply, but they must also evaluate each item in light of these criteria.

As suggested previously, the cognitive taxonomy is organized as a hierarchy, with each successively higher level requiring the skills of the previous level. The hierarchy is organized by complexity; that is, higher levels of the taxonomy require more complex thought processes.

The ability of teachers to evaluate the thought processes employed by their students when performing instructional tasks is likely to be related to effective instruction. By examining goals, curriculum, and assessment strategies in terms of Bloom's taxonomy, music teachers are likely to provide more systematic and effective instruction.

The Affective Domain

Many of the objectives of education emphasize an emotional attitude or a degree commitment. These *affective objectives* are present in most disciplines but seem to be more important to areas such as the arts. Such objectives include the interests, appreciations, attitudes, and values of the student.

The affective outcomes of instruction clearly do not receive the same priority as do the cognitive outcomes of instruction in today's schools. To some extent this is as true in music as in other disciplines, and yet the music education profession has tended to cite goals that seem to include the affective domain as a primary support for including music in the schools.

There are several reasons for this emphasis on cognitive behavior. Our technological society requires people with cognitive skills, and to some extent the time spent by teachers focusing on the development of cognitive skills leaves less time to focus on other ares.

In addition, it is difficult for a democratic society to accept education in the affective domain as an appropriate province of the schools. The fear that uniform value systems dictated by a bureaucracy will lead to a controlled society serves as fuel for this view. In music education this has been reflected by urging music teachers not to impose their own musical tastes on their students.

Another fact that has contributed to the neglect of affective outcomes is the perceived difficulty in stating and assessing objectives in this area.

TABLE 8.2
Categories of Krathwohl's Taxonomy of the Affective Domain
(Adapted from Gronlond, N.E., & Linn, R. L., *Measurement and Evaluation*
***in Teaching,* 6th ed. New York: Macmillan, 1990)**

1. *Receiving.* Such behavior is characterized by a willingness to attend. This involves behaviors such as being aware of phenomena or stimuli and being willing to take notice of them. "Capturing" a student's attention illustrates this level. AS the lowest level in the affective domain, it is a prerequisite behavior for the other levels.

2. *Responding.* At the responding bevel the student is not only aware of stimuli, but is interacting with them. This may take the form of complying with a set of rules, seeking out additional information on a topic, or finding pleasure in participating in an activity. It is at this level of the domain that the behavior of "being interested in a phenomenon" would be classified.

3. *Valuing.* A student who demonstrates valuing behavior is one who has attached worth or value to an object, phenomenon, or behavior. Although this is an internalized process, it must be sufficiently consistent to produce observable behavior. This level of the domain may be demonstrated by the mere acceptance of a value as well as a stronger commitment to a position, group, or cause. Behaviors such as expressing an attitude toward or appreciation of an object, phenomenon, or event would be classified in the category.

4. *Organization.* The interrelating of values and the beginning of an organized value system are behaviors that characterize this level of the affective domain. This level includes consideration of the consistency and stability of values and beliefs that evolves into a value complex. The formation of such a system requires that conflicts between values be resolved, yielding a complex that is internally consistent. As such systems develop, they provide the learner with a philosophy of life on which to base decisions.

5. *Characterization by a value or value complex.* At this level of the domain the students' behavior reflects a consistency. This characteristic behavior or life style is due to the internalization of a value or value system to the extent that it is readily observable. While at the organizational level the students are developing a philosophy of life, at the characterization level they are truly living it.

The well-developed techniques employed to measure the products of cognitive processes, such as multiple-choice tests, are not successful in measuring affective behaviors. Such behaviors may develop slowly, suggesting that testing at the end of a semester may be inappropriate. A problem of equal importance is that the terminology typically employed to describe affective outcomes (e.g., "appreciate music") does not readily lend itself to observable changes in behavior that can be easily measured. Chapter 9 explores the difficulties in measuring affective behaviors in greater detail.

With the development of the taxonomy of educational objectives in the affective domain (Krathwohl, Bloom, & Massia, 1967), terminology is more readily available that can be used to state objectives in behavioral terms and therefore provide direction for assessing affective outcomes. An abbreviated form of this taxonomy is found in table 8.2.

The taxonomy is organized in a hierarchy based on internalization defined as "acceptance by the individual of the attitudes, codes, principles, or sanctions that become a part of himself in forming value judgments or in determining his conduct" (Good, 1959, p. 296). The lower levels of the taxonomy (e.g. receiving, responding) represent rather weak commitments that may be easily changed and may be of relatively short duration. The middle levels of the taxonomy (e.g., valuing, organization) represent relatively more stable commitments. The behavior that characterizes these levels tends to be more resistant to change and is likely to be more lasting. As values become completely internalized, the behaviors reflecting these values become consistent and characteristic of the individual. They are difficult, if not impossible, to alter.

The following statements in table 8.3 illustrate behaviors at different levels of the affective domain:

TABLE 8.3

---

1. If I was listening to the radio and this piece came on, I would not change the station.

2. I enjoy singing this song.

3. I would like to play this recording for some of my friends.

4. I would probably like pieces of other composers who wrote in this style better than other works by the composer of this selection.

5. I enjoy playing in the community band and never miss a rehearsal.

These statements are ordered to illustrate lower to higher levels of the affective domain. No attempt is made to place the statements at specific levels, because it is difficult to obtain a consensus for such attempts at classification. This probably results from the overlapping of the taxonomy's categories, and the fact that the same behavior may demonstrate different levels of internalization.

As suggested above, the affective outcomes of music education are important. The development of aesthetic sensitivity to music (discussed in chapter 3), frequently suggested as the primary goal of music instruction, clearly has a major affective component. The ability of music teachers to meet this goal to some extent relies on their ability to develop and assess affective behaviors. If teachers do not assess the affective outcomes of their curriculum, they have no guidelines to determine the effectiveness of the curriculum and no evidence on which to base modifications.

TABLE 8.4.

Categories of the Psychomotor Domain (Adapted from Simpson, 1966)

1.0 *Perception*: the process of becoming aware of objects, qualities, or relations by use of the sense organs.
   1.1 *Sensory stimulation*: impingement of a stimulus upon one or more of the sense organs.
   1.2 *Cue selection*: deciding what cues to respond to in meeting the requirements of a task (ability to distinguish among sensory stimuli).
   1.3 *Translation*: determining the meaning of the cues for action.

2.0 *Set*: preparatory adjustment or readiness for a particular kind of action or experience.
   2.1 *Mental set*: readiness to perform a motor act (cognitive awareness).
   2.2 *Physical set*: having made the anatomical adjustments necessary for a motor act.
   2.3 *Emotional set*: readiness in terms of favorable attitude.

3.0 *Guided response*: overt behavioral action under the guidance of an instructor.
   3.1 *Imitation*: execution of an act in response to another person performing the act.
   3.2 *Trial and error*: trying various responses until an appropriate response is achieved.

4.0 *Mechanism*: habitual learned response.

5.0 *Complex overt response*: smooth and efficient performance of a complex motor act.
   5.1 *Resolution of uncertainty*: knowledge of the sequence; proceeding with confidence.
   5.2 *Automatic performance*: ability to perform a finely coordinated motor skill with much ease and muscle control.

6.0 *Adaptation*: ability to change a performance to make it more suitable.

7.0 *Origination*: ability to develop new skills.

The Psychomotor Domain

The area of skill development, or what Bloom and others refer to as the *psychomotor domain*, often has lower priority with educators than the other two areas previously discussed. This situation exists primarily because of the low priority that schools have generally placed on the development of psychomotor skills. The authors of the taxonomies for the cognitive and affective domains stated: "Although we recognize the existence of this domain (psychomotor), we find so little done about it in secondary schools or colleges, that we do not believe the development of a

TABLE 8.5

---

1. The student is supporting the violin sufficiently with the left shoulder and chin so that the left hand is free to move along the neck.

2. The student is able to echo clap the rhythmic pattern (♩ ♫ ♩ ♩) accurately.

3. The clarinetist performs the solo at "letter B" with an acceptable interpretation.

---

classification of these objectives would be very useful at present" (Bloom, 1956, p. 7).

Of course, for those involved in areas of instruction such as music, psychomotor behaviors play an important, if not dominant, role. In 1964 a professor of home economics at the University of Illinois, Elizabeth Simpson, initiated the task of developing a taxonomy of psychomotor behavior. It appears in table 8.4.

This taxonomy, although not formally related to the other two taxonomies, has been rather widely accepted. The taxonomy is organized by complexity; that is, objectives classified at the lower levels are generally easier to carry out than those at the upper levels. The taxonomy is also thought to represent a hierarchy, with upper-level behaviors requiring the skills contained in the lower levels. The items in table 8.5, which might appear on a rating scale of music performance, illustrate different levels of the psychomotor domain.

The first item illustrates a relatively simple psychomotor task and thus is thought to be representative of the category of physical set (level 2.2). It should be pointed out that the simplicity of the task will vary according to the physical maturity of the student (e.g., a four-year-old Suzuki violin student vs. a college music education major in a string techniques class).

The second item illustrates the level of imitation (level 3.1). A considerable amount of music performance instruction employs techniques of imitation. Frequently, applied-music teachers will play a passage to illustrate a stylistic point that is difficult to verbalize, and often ensemble directors will sing a rhythm to clarify a section of a piece. At times the behavior being imitated may be relatively simple, as suggested by the second item. But at other times teachers may ask students to imitate their tone quality or interpretation of a passage, both of which require considerably more complex behaviors.

The final item in the table represents a complex overt response (level 5.0), and probably the subcategory of automatic performance (level 5.2). In playing a well-learned solo the student must integrate all the aspects of the performance, such as rhythmic accuracy, accurate intonation, good tone quality, and expression—which is clearly is clearly a complex behavior.

Using the Taxonomies

Although the taxonomies were initially conceived of as an aid to develop-ing assessment procedures (see chapter 9), they can also play an important role in the development of course content. A teacher involved in planning instruction can refer to the taxonomies as a source for the types of processes and products to expect from students. The taxonomies can also assist the curriculum developer by providing a means of organizing the outcomes of instruction.

The taxonomies' value to the course developer/teacher does not lie in the skill of the teacher in categorizing goals of a curriculum according to various levels. That is not an easy task, and complete agreement among educators as to the level of a particular objective can seldom be achieved. The hierarchical nature of the taxonomies may be of more value as a con-stant reminder to teachers that the eventual goals of much instruction lie at the upper levels of the taxonomies.

The Overlap of the Taxonomies

Most instruction produces outcomes in more than one domain. People's thoughts and actions are seldom, that compartmentalized. The study of music literature not only produces new knowledge regarding the literature, it also is likely to influence the attitude of students toward the music stud-ied. Orchestral students learning a new piece not only acquire new psy-chomotor behaviors, but, also new insight and attitudes.

Singer (1972) highlighted the relationship between psychomotor behav-ior and cognitive and affective behavior. Singer stresses that emotions such as anxiety and tension all affect the performance of motor skills, and that attitudes, such as the desire to be successful, probably influence the improvement of performance tasks through practice.

Although Singer points out that intelligence is thought to have a posi-tive but low relationship to motor skill, cognitive behavior does play an important role in the development of motor behavior. The relationship between motor skill and cognitive ability is complex. Different types of motor skill require different amounts of cognition. Low levels of motor skill require little thought. Some complex motor activities, e.g., slam-dunking a basketball, may require little involvement of the cognitive domain, while others, such as playing a piano concerto, require a greater involvement. The area of knowledge of results (or *feedback*) is critical to the student developing and refining motor skills. Students vary in their ability to sense when their performance is getting closer to a model perfor-mance. The importance of students' ability to process the various types of feedback present during motor behavior (e.g., verbal, auditory, tactile) and make decisions to alter their performance on the basis of this information cannot be over-emphasized.

Many applied-music teachers spend part of their instructional time providing verbal feedback to aid students in refining their performance. Certain types of psychomotor behavior, such as diving or gymnastics, rely heavily on videotape feedback. Some music educators have attempted to develop additional sources of feedback, such as real-time graphic representations of pitch and rhythm, to aid the student in developing performance skills. Musicians have long recognized the interrelationship of the cognitive and psychomotor domain.

One additional overlapping of the domains occurs when instructors employ objectives in one area to help reach objectives in a second area. An obvious example of this type of overlapping is the traditional music-appreciation class. The instruction in such classes is based on the premise that pursuing cognitive objectives in the history and literature of music will influence the affective behavior (appreciation) of the students. The domains come much closer together at the higher levels. Playing Weber's "Concertino" on clarinet requires thinking about phrasing, communicating feelings, and possessing sophisticated motor skills. Other illustrations of the interaction of the cognitive and affective domains appear in chapter 6 in the section on attitude formation.

Stating Music Objectives Behaviorally

Some educators (e.g., Keller, 1980) suggest that the educational process in the past has focused too much on the presentation of material rather than on changes in students' behavior or the outcomes of instruction. Those who subscribe to this position, disciples of the behaviorist learning school, have employed a variety of strategies in attempts to refocus the educational process. One of their strategies, which may have had the greatest impact on education in the last two decades, is the clear articulation of the outcomes of instruction through the use of well-defined behavioral objectives.

Behavioral objectives are important because they represent the first step of an instructional system advocated by many educators. This instructional sequence (a systems approach), which is outlined below, can serve as the organizing focus for most of the behaviorist strategies that have impacted on education.

An Instructional System

1. *Stating educational objectives*: A clear description of what the student is expected to be able to do after the instructional process is critical to the

system, because without it teachers have no means to determine what the educational process accomplished.

2. *Developing instructional material to assist the student in meeting the objectives*: Instructional material cannot be developed until the purpose of the material has been identified. The development of the material is also important to the effectiveness of the instructional process.

3. *Assessment of the students' success in reaching the stated objectives*: This step has two functions. In addition to providing teachers with information regarding the progress of individual students, it provides the teacher with information on the effectiveness of the materials and methods. The assessment process will be explored more fully in the next chapter.

4. *Revising the instructional materials based on the results of the assessment process*: The monitoring and modification aspects of this system are critical to the success of the system. The ability of the system to be dynamic and the willingness of the teachers involved in the instructional process to make revisions based on objective information is highlighted by many behaviorists as the major characteristic of effective instructional systems.

From Goals to Behavioral Objectives

Behavioral objectives for music instruction are not, or at least should not be, generated spontaneously as music teachers write lesson plans for tomorrow's class. They are based on a well-developed curriculum, which is jointly guided by the goals of the profession as articulated in documents such as *The School Music Program: Description and Standards* (Music Educators National Conference, 1986) and the goals of the particular school system. While school-system and profession-generated curriculum guides provide broad to relatively specific directions for instruction, each music teacher in the classroom needs to see that the objectives are met. To do this, music teachers must develop sequences of instruction that enable their students to acquire the knowledge, skills, and attitudes articulated in curriculum guides. The first step in this process is for music teachers to translate curricular goals into classroom behavioral objectives. In some cases curriculum guides provide statements of objectives in behavioral terms. In such situations teachers must break down long-term behavioral outcomes into sequences of specific music objectives. Table 8.6 illustrates specific behavioral objectives based on broader statements of goals.

A Format for Behavioral Statements of the Outcomes of Music Instruction

Behavioral objectives must be precise, clear, and unambiguous. Ambiguity in such objectives for music leads to difficulty in designing effective

TABLE 8.6

Long-Range Goals	Unit Objective	Behavioral Objectives
1. The student identifies sounds of specific musical instruments.	1. The student identifies instruments in solo settings.	1. Given an aural example of an accompanied solo by one of the basic instruments of the band or orchestra, and pictures of at least three instruments, the student indicates the solo instrument.
2. The student identifies beat.	2. The student differentiates regular from irregular beat.	2. Given two aural examples, one with a steady beat and one without, the student indicates which example has the steady beat.
3. The student identifies the tendency of certain sequential tones to resolve.	3. The student identifies the tonic as a point of resolution in a diatonic scale.	3. Given two aural examples, one containing first seven notes of a diatonic scale, the other containing all eight notes, the student indicates the eight note scale as having a greater feeling of finality.
4. The student identifies harmonic intervals.	4. The student identifies harmonic intervals within a one-octave scale.	4. Given notated examples of intervals contained within one octave, the student classifies each interval.
5. The student identifies stylistic . characteristics of various music periods	5. The student identifies the outstanding traits of given historical periods.	5. Given a list of period characteristics including at least four of the Classical period, the student indicates two of the four as describing the classical period.
6. The student exhibits a positive attitude toward music.	6. The student demonstrates enjoyment of music activities.	6. The student voluntarily attends concerts when available.
7. The student improvises on a given theme.	7. The student improvises a rhythmic accompaniment to a familiar melody.	7. Given a performance of a familiar melody, the student improvises a rhythm accompaniment to it, maintaining the meter and tempo, but creating a rhythm pattern different from the melodic rhythm.

Source: Florida Department of Education, *The Florida Catalog of Music Objectives* (Tallahassee: Florida Dept. of Education, 1974).

245

instructional materials and problems in developing measures of assessment that reflect the outcomes of the instruction.

Although authors sometimes disagree on the specific format of behavioral objectives, almost all agree that they must contain:

1. *A verb*: This describes a performance, action, or operation, that is, some behavior or product that is *observable*.

2. *A statement of conditions under which the behavior occurs*: This component is of course important to the standardization of the objective (e.g., performance on "open-book" and "closed-book" tests is likely to differ considerably).

3. *The standard of quality that the performance must reach*: The acceptability or unacceptability of a performance must be carefully regulated. Playing a scale at $\downarrow$ = 60 is quite a different activity than playing the same scale at $\downarrow$ = 120.

4. *The learner*: Some (but not all) writers strongly feel that statements of objectives must include who is producing the behavior. Those advocating this position argue that many objectives that imply rather than state the subject are ambiguous and do not reinforce the focus of behavioral objectives on the behavior of students rather than teachers.

Table 8.6 illustrates examples of music objectives that regional and local educational units can employ as instructional objectives to organize instruction.

Using Behavioral Objectives: Pros and Cons

The use of instructional objectives has had some impact on music education. The most visible results have been at the professional-association and educational-organization levels (e.g., state departments of education, school boards). As with many movements in education, the instructional objectives movement has probably affected music classroom instruction to some extent, but the degree of impact is difficult to assess.

Some educators believe that stating objectives behaviorally limits the outcomes of education, particularly in the area of the arts. Elliot Eisner in his 1979 book *The Educational Imagination* describes the advantages and limitations of behavioral objectives. He suggests that behaviorally stated objectives belong in the school curriculum, particularly when specific skills or competencies are being developed (e.g., playing a three-octave major scale). On the other hand, he also believes that behaviorally stated objectives are limiting in the following ways:

1. *The language used to state them is limiting.* "For much of our experience, discursive language performs rather well. But for the subtleties of human experience, for our knowledge of human feeling, for modes of conception and understanding that are qualitative, discourse falls far short. . . . How would one describe the qualities of a late Beethoven quartet in pre-

cise, unambiguous, measurable terms? . . . To expect all of our educational aspirations to be either verbally describable or measurable is to expect too little" (p. 98).

2. *The application of standards is difficult in certain areas of education.* For tasks such as naming a state capital or long division, "standards are specifiable and applicable by anyone or by any machine that 'knows' the rules through which the standards are to be applied" (p. 99). But what about the aesthetic quality of a symphony or the rhetorical force of a patriotic speech? Although judgments can be made about them, they cannot be subjected to standards. "It is not to say that one can have no criteria through which to appraise them. Judgments can say much about such qualities, not by the mechanical application of prespecified standards, but by comparison of the qualities in question to a whole range of criteria that teachers or others making the judgment already possess. . . . Judgments about such qualities are not will-of-the-wisp, cavalier, irresponsible conclusions, they are complex appraisals that use an extraordinarily wide range of knowledge to arrive at what, on balance, is a warranted human judgment" (p. 99).

3. *Not all the outcomes of education can be prespecified in advance.* "[prespecification] is rooted in the kind of rationality that has guided much of Western technology. The means-ends model of thinking has for so long dominated our thinking that we have come to believe that not to have clearly defined purposes for our activities is to court irrationality or, at the least, to be professionally irresponsible. Yet, life in classrooms, like that outside them, is seldom neat or linear. . . . Many of our most productive activities take the form of exploration or play. In such activities, the task is not one of arriving at a preformed objective but rather to act, often with a sense of abandon, wonder, curiosity. Out of such activity rules may be formed and objectives may be created" (p. 100).

To compensate for these limitations, Eisner proposes several strategies for specifying the goals of education. He identifies two types of objectives and one kind of "outcome" for this purpose. First, he suggests the continued use of behavioral objectives, but in addition he proposes the use of what he calls *problem-solving objectives.* With such objectives students are given a problem, such as to design a structure using only toothpicks and glue that will support two pounds, or to provide traditional alto, tenor and bass parts given an eight-measure melody. In these examples, "the problem is posed and the criteria that need to be achieved to resolve the problem are fairly clear. But the forms of its solution are virtually infinite" (p. 101).

Eisner points out that these type of problems are common. Often scientists, engineers, or designers are asked to create several products or solutions, or develop several designs, so potential consumers can compare alternatives and decide which is best. The ensemble director selecting and ordering pieces for the annual spring program requires similar problem-solving strategies. "In such situations the potential answers are not known beforehand. What is known is the problem; what constitutes appropriate solutions remains to be seen after the work has been done" (p. 102). Problem-solving objectives engage the higher mental processes described in Bloom's taxonomy, while behaviorally stated objectives often focus on the lower levels of the taxonomy.

The educational outcomes Eisner identifies are *expressive outcomes*. Expressive outcomes occur after an educational activity. The activity is planned to be a fertile experience for generating personal development in the student, but the consequences of the activity are not predictable for each student. Parents often engage in such informal education with their children. Taking the kids to a zoo, on a family vacation to the Grand Canyon, or on the Staten Island ferry to see New York City's harbor are all examples of this. Parents do these things because they are enjoyable, and they expect that something good for their children will come from them, not because they have specific educational objectives in mind. Field trips to a museum, opera, or drum and bugle corps competition are experiences that will likely produce both expected (e.g., students will be able to identify the characters in the opera) and a wide variety of unanticipated learning (e.g., a twirling flag that is dropped can be picked up very quickly). Eisner emphasizes that even in eras when accountability is stressed, "there must be room in school for activities that promise to be fruitful, even though the teacher might not be able to say what specifically the students will learn or experience" (p. 104).

Eisner states that both behavioral objectives and problem-solving objectives follow the traditional means-ends approach to planning; that is, the objectives are stated prior to the educational experience. "What one is seeking is to have students engage in activities that are sufficiently rich to allow for a wide, productive range of educationally valuable outcomes" (p. 104).

While these different approaches to assessment may be particularly applicable for music curriculum, they have not yet had much impact on the field.

Popham (1969, p. 49), in citing arguments against behavioral objectives, states: "In certain subject areas, such as fine arts and the humanities, it is more difficult to identify measurable pupil behaviors. Yet, because it is difficult in certain subject fields to identify measurable pupil behaviors, those subject specialists should not be allowed to escape this responsibility. Teachers in the fields of art and music often claim that it is next to impossible to identify acceptable works of art in precise terms—but they do it all the time. In instance after instance the art teacher does make a judgment regarding the acceptability of pupil-produced artwork. What the art teacher is reluctant to do is put his evaluative criteria on the line. He has such criteria. He must have to make his judgments. But he is loath to describe them in terms that anyone can see."

Any English teacher, for example, will tell you how difficult it is to make a valid judgment of a pupil's essay response. Yet criteria lurk whenever this teacher does make a judgment, and these criteria must be made explicit. No one who really understands education has ever argued that instruction is a simple task. It is even more difficult in such areas as the arts and humanities. As a noted art educator observed several years ago, art educators must quickly get to the business of specifying "tentative, but clearly defined criteria" by which they can judge their learners' artistic efforts.

Although it should be clear from the statements in the preceding section that behaviorally stated objectives are a valuable tool of the music teacher, they are not be appropriate in every music learning situation. Certain music learning outcomes cannot be precisely described before they occur. Alternative approaches such as problem-solving objectives and expressive outcomes can be valuable particularly in circumstances when behavioral objectives seem to serve only as a constraint to possibilities.

Accountability

The belief that schools are responsible for the education of their students is generally related to clearly stated outcomes of instruction. School systems, individual schools, and curriculum areas, including music, are often charged by school boards to evaluate systematically the effectiveness of the instructional program (see chapter 10 for a discussion of program evaluation). These efforts are often grouped under the label *accountability*, and, when behavioral objectives are used to define the outcomes of instruction, are another outgrowth of behaviorism.

The demands for accountability in schools are often strongest during periods in which the public loses confidence in the schools. During the 1960s and early 1970s, and again in the mid-1980s, many people, for whatever reasons, believed that the educational system was not meeting the expectations of society. A related social phenomenon during this time was the apparent vulnerability of various bureaucracies and the eagerness of individuals to have more input into organizations that had significant impacts on their lives. It was also a time of general economic belt-tightening, which gave the impetus for a closer scrutiny of how money (particularly tax revenue) was being distributed. Although these factors served as catalysts for the accountability movement, the particular nature of accountability that developed during this period was defined by the impact of instruction objectives and a general *systems approach* to education advocated by behaviorists.

During the early 1990s, the educational reform movement that had begun in the mid-1980s focused on a system for the development of standards. This proposed system included the development of content standards and assessment instruments to measure students' success with regard to these standards. The recommendations for such a system combined the establishment of standards with means of assessing them in a way that strongly suggested principles of behaviorism.

The general notion of accountability in education regarding standards and their assessment impacted the educational system in several ways. School boards were held accountable to the public for the general philosophical direction and efficiency of the system; school administrators were held accountable for the efficient management of the system; and teachers were held accountable for the learning of their pupils.

As suggested earlier, accountability as defined in the early 1970s was based on a systems approach. Various authors (Cooksey, 1974; Labuta, 1974) list various components of accountability. These generally include statements of goals and instructional objectives and an extensive assessment component, frequently including pre-tests to determine the current status of the students and criterion-referenced post-tests to determine if the students have reached the stated objectives. (*Criterion-referenced tests* are tests in which a student's results are compared with performance expectations rather than with the results of other students, i.e., *norm-referenced* tests.) Other factors important to educational accountability include aspects of the educational system that are expected to assist the students in reaching the instructional objectives—such as teachers and instructional materials—and the cost of these aspects.

Accountability is not accepted with open arms by most educators. It is viewed by many teachers as an idea that is being imposed on the educational process. Colwell states, though, that "in those states where music educators have considered accountability an opportunity, programs have been strengthened. In states where music educators have avoided the accountability issue, or have argued that benefits from the study of music cannot be evaluated, the weaker music programs are found" (1974, p. 2). Labuta also suggests there are dangers in not jumping on the bandwagon: "If music is not to become peripheral to public education, we must develop accountable programs that will receive adequate resources and support" (1974, p. 8).

Individualized Music Instruction

Educators have become increasingly aware of the need to provide for individual differences among their students. This awareness has been prompted by several factors including:

1. An increasing sophistication of educational psychologists in identifying personal factors, such as cognitive style, that affect achievement;

2. An increasing knowledge of child development and maturation rates;

3. An increasing ethnic and racial pluralism in the school population; and

4. An increasing awareness of the ineffectiveness of mass instructional strategies.

Several education movements, especially the competency-based education approach of the late 1960s and early 1970s, promoted individualized instruction. One such movement was "open education," which was mentioned in chapter 2, and which directly altered the traditional learning environment, demanding considerable flexibility in both the physical structure and procedures of the school. A comparison of open education with a more traditional educational approach follows:

> Where the conventional school is one-dimensional in nature and singular in approach, the flexible school offers opportunities for alternatives and multi-dimensional approaches.
> Where the conventional school is graded, the flexible school is nongraded.
> Where the conventional school imposes prescribed standards of material to be covered, the flexible school is continuous-progress oriented and based on a careful analysis of the learner, his readiness to learn, his readiness to learn, his competency at a given time, his learning style, his desire, and many other individual needs that are exclusively resident in him.
> Where the conventional school imposes learning from above, the flexible school contends that the child is the source of learning, and that the teacher is the caretaker of the environment wherein the child can become his own painstaking teacher.
> Where the conventional school is made of segmented classrooms, the flexible school offers a noncentralized environment. It offers free movement to explore under the guidance of a particular teacher or a differentiated staff committed to a whole manner of approaches of approaches to individualized instruction. It is a learner-centered school. (Hillson, 1975, p. 5)

As with other movements that affect education in general, music education professionals have responded to the demands such innovations place on conventional music instructional programs. One response was MENC's publication of *Individualized Instruction in Music* (Meske & Rinehart, 1975), which includes a general rationale for open education, several sections of general suggestions for applications to music instruction, and examples of materials suitable for the open music classroom.

The challenge that individualization brings for music educators may be more unique than for other educators. Music instruction in the schools has become to some extent intertwined with the notion of group instruction; much music making requires groups of performers. Music instruction also includes diverse activities such as conducting bands and listening to records, which are necessary to meet diverse objectives. Music instruction is typically (and to some extent ideally) physically isolated from the rest of the school's instructional program. All of these as well as other factors required music educators to seek innovative and diverse solutions to the demands of individualization.

Many individualized music instructional programs focused on the general music class. This has probably happened for two reasons: (1) the open education movement had more impact on the elementary school than on the secondary school, and (2) general music instruction is more readily adapted to individualized strategies than performing ensemble programs. It should be noted, however, that individualized instructional units in performance areas that are frequently integrated into the general music programs (the guitar and recorder, for example) were developed as part of open education in general music.

Many open education classrooms made use of learning centers. The learning center is a physically separate area in which a particular instructional unit is located. In an elementary school class, learning areas may be structured by subject areas such as math, science, and music. In a music room different aspects and levels of the music program such as singing, listening, and composing may each be located at a different center.

The requirements of music instruction, which often includes sound production, make the establishment of music learning centers somewhat more problematic when contrasted with other more passive subject areas. Solutions to this problem frequently employ some type of technological resource such as tape recorders, phonographs, headphones, or more specialized audio and video equipment. Computer-assisted instruction and programmed instruction can be employed as well.

One important characteristic of much individualized instructional material is that it is self-pacing, which requires each instructional unit to inform the learner of the type of level of criterion that will help determine when the material has been sufficiently mastered. Some instructional units do this in a formal way by means of the successful completion of tests. Other units, such as those focusing on the development of music compositional skills, employ less formal strategies of assessment. Nevertheless, individualization requires carefully constructed systematic (as in the systems approach) instructional units, which force the music teachers to consider carefully each step in the instructional process. When teachers can no longer depend on their ability to improvise when a learning roadblock is reached, much more care is needed to ensure that such roadblocks occur less frequently.

Individualized instruction in music has taken many forms; although the term has been used generically, the different types tend to differ in the manner by which they systematize learning. Programmed instruction (PI) and computer-based instruction (CBI) are one branch of the individualized instruction tree; they will be discussed in a separate section. Another approach to to individualization is called "personalized systematic instruction" (PSI), or sometimes referred to as the "Keller plan" after its developer, Fred Keller.

Greer stresses the difference of the PSI model of learning from the general system-approach model previously described. This difference focuses on the assignment of the responsibility for learning, which Greer suggests is placed on the student in the generalized systems approach, while in the PSI model "the teacher (within his or her power) is responsible for the student attaining the stated goals" (1980, p. 9).

Greer identifies seven components of the PSI model:

(a) The model focuses on the actions and reactions (behaviors) of the learner in terms of the instructional objectives.

(b) The learning tasks are analyzed behaviorally and categorically by hierarchies.

(c) Learning rates and levels are systematically monitored and preserved in numerical terms.

(d) Strategies of teaching are based on scientifically derived principles of learning.

(e) Actual teacher techniques are derived from principles and systematically practiced by the teacher in the classroom and rehearsal hall.

(f) Strategies, principles, and techniques, as well as student learning, are preserved systematically, and there is an explicit system of accountability.

(g) The teacher is responsible, within her or his power, for student learning. (p. 9)

The major distinguishing feature of the PSI approach seems to be the constant monitoring of a student's skill and knowledge level and the *personalized* tailoring of instruction based upon these achievement assessments. This evaluation component is an important aspect of all types of individualized instruction, and is examined in detail in chapter 9.

Interest in individualized instruction continues today, although some of the programs that promoted its use such as open education have faded from the education agenda. To some extent, the technological advances provided by personal computers and related technology such as MIDI (Musical Instrument Digital Interface) have maintained, and in some areas increased, interest in individualizing music instruction.

Programmed and Computer-Based Instruction

One way to achieve individualized instruction is to provide each student with his or her own tutor. Although this might prove ideal in Utopia, it is too expensive to be a reasonable prescription for improving today's educational system. Since a personal tutorial system cannot be implemented, alternatives that provide some of the advantages of such a system have been sought after and developed. The development of self-instructional materials seems to flourish, particularly at times when large student/teacher ratios force teachers to pay less attention to individual student needs, or when technological advances make suitable tools available to educators.

Self-instructional materials such as those that may be classified as programmed instruction (PI) or computer-based instruction (CBI) have a strong lineage in the behaviorist school, particularly B. F. Skinner. These strategies emphasize an active response to a stimulus. They employ a structured, systemized approach to instruction as described earlier in this chapter, and they place considerable emphasis on the importance of overt responses and immediate reinforcement, which is described in detail in the following section.

PI and CBI materials generally have the following characteristics:

1. They employ a systems approach.
2. They proceed in small steps.
3. The materials are carefully sequenced.
4. The student receives immediate feedback.
5. The student works at his/her own pace.

The primary distinction between PI and CBI lies in the mode of presentation, with CBI utilizing computers to present instructional materials and to monitor progress, while PI generally employs textbook presentations.

Linear vs. Branching Programs

In developing material for automated instruction, the pace of the material is a critical factor in the program's success. The program must start with information easily integrated with a student's existing knowledge. The instruction then proceeds in small steps or increments, particularly in the early stages of the program, to ensure that the student experiences initial success.

After the initial stages, the pace of the instruction may quicken and proceed in different ways, depending on what type of programming is being employed. Although there are many individual styles of programs, two broad divisions, linear and branching, are the types most frequently employed.

Linear programming was developed by B. F. Skinner. In it, every student proceeds thought each unit or frame of material. The steps are small enough so that students respond correctly. The students are required to give an overt response, usually a fill-in-the-blank type of answer, and are given immediate feedback. Regardless of the student's success rate, every student proceeds through every frame until the units are completed. Skinner felt that this approach was particularly effective with new material.

Linear programmed instruction has been criticized for not providing the flexibility required by individual differences in learning rates. Critics suggest that linear programming is particularly cumbersome for fast learners, who may quickly become bored with material that proceeds slowly in small steps.

Branching programs are designed to provide more flexibility for the individual learner. The form of the programs is typically alternating sequences of information blocks and multiple-choice questions. When students respond correctly to a question they are directed to proceed to new material. Should students respond incorrectly, they are then directed to additional frames that provide an explanation of why the designated answer is incorrect and provide additional instructional material to assist in the learning of the information. Sophisticated branching programs may have a special series of frames for each incorrect response. Figure 8.1 (p. 256) illustrates how such programs might be designed.

Studies (e.g., Carlsen, 1964) that have compared these two strategies of programming have generally found both to be equally effective. It can be argued that both strategies are needed, since branching provides for individual differences and linear programming assists in the acquisition of new material.

The mechanics of implementing the two different approaches to programming dictate quite different delivery systems. Linear programming seems well suited for presentation in a book format. Examples of various strategies in designing programmed texts are readily found and illustrate a variety of techniques for presenting information, formats for responding, and feedback procedures such as sliding bookmark-like cards down the side of the page to reveal answers. Branching programs have been employed occasionally in textbook formats (e.g., Mager, 1962), but are clearly somewhat encumbered by the rigidity of bound pages.

Music Instruction with Computers

The computer can be an extremely flexible delivery system. It is able to present both linear programs and branching programs, but it may be most effective employing other individualized approaches to music instruction.

There are five primary ways that computer music instruction may be organized. The most frequently used strategy is the *tutorial*, which often employs either linear or branching program instruction. Tutorials typically

CONTEXT — Conducting

TOPIC — Score-Reading

OBJECTIVE — Given a full orchestral score and a tape recorded performance of the work, to indicate with 100% accuracy the point on the written score at which the tape performance stops.

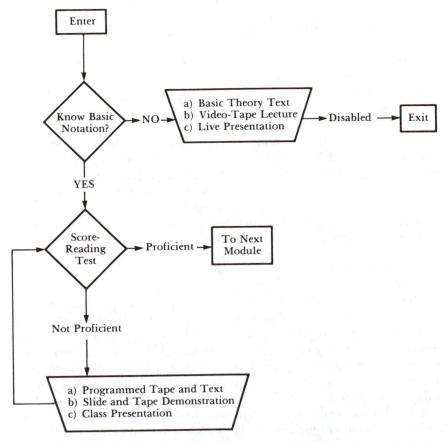

Figure 8.1. A branching program flow chart.

present both information to the learner and then test the learner's acquisition of the knowledge. There are a substantial number of such programs available for music instruction. Many of these programs focus on learning basic music knowledge such as notational information or names, dates, and repertory of composers. Tutorials can provide feedback to the learner and remediation depending on the sophistication of the program. Most tutorials provide for student interaction with the program; that is, the student must actively respond to questions. When students are successful in responding, their responses are often greeted by positive verbal feedback on the monitor (e.g., "great job") and in many music programs reinforcing music feedback (e.g., a trumpet-like fanfare). Good tutorial software keeps track of student responses so that both the student and the instructor can monitor progress. Tutorials are particularly effective in developing factual knowledge (e.g., music terms); simple discriminations, like simple ear training problems; and understanding of rules (e.g., counterpoint). Tutorials are often very time-consuming to develop and tend to focus on acquiring cognitive skills at the lower levels of Bloom's taxonomy.

Another common mode of computer music instruction is *drill and practice*. Drill and practice programs provide the learner with the opportunity to perform and receive feedback on the performance, and in some cases also provide remediation. They are the computer version of workbooks. Drill and practice programs do not teach new concepts; instead, they reinforce previously learned concepts or skills. This type of software has been widely used in music education to develop aural skills. It can be particularly effective in this area because computers can present the instructional materials at different levels. Many drill and practice programs allow either the teacher or the student to set the difficulty level of the practice items. Some even adjust the difficulty level of the items depending on the success of the learner on previous items. This capability for structuring practice and simultaneously tailoring it to the individual is the main strength of drill and practice software, particularly in the area of ear-training where students often progress at widely different rates. Drill and practice programs provide good opportunities for structured practice and for refining skills. The computer has infinite patience, far more than a theory graduate assistant playing melodic dictation examples over and over again! The quality of drill and practice is directly related to the effectiveness of the remedial aspect of the program. Good drill and practice software analyzes student responses and determines the area or areas of weakness, and then provides additional practice on those weakness.

Computer games are also often very motivational and can be a valuable instructional tool. Instructional games let students practice skills. Consequently, in some ways they serve similar purposes to drill and practice programs. Instructional games and drill and practice programs differ on the competence level required of the learner to participate effectively. For instructional games, students need to be relatively fluent with the skill being utilized, while drill and practice programs help develop that fluency. To be thought of as a game, the software must provide some type of competition. In some computer games the computer is the opponent. In others, it is another student, and in some cases, students compete against their own previous performance. Another characteristic of game software is that there is an emphasis on keeping track of successes; scoring is involved and often a time constraint is established. High levels of motivation are often associated with computer games. This motivation is often enhanced with interesting graphics and sound. If designed effectively, games can be an attractive way to present what otherwise might be uninteresting but important information. Care should be taken when using them, however. Sometimes students can become distracted by games that are too graphically stimulating, and some games may provide equally motivating reinforcers for the wrong answers as for the right answers. Teachers should have specific goals for such software and integrate the programs carefully with other instructional strategies.

Computer simulations are designed to explore skills and concepts without the risk, expense, or time required to perform the real activity. One area in which simulations have been used extensively is in airplane pilot training, where complex mechanical devices simulate a variety of flight conditions and provide pitch and roll feedback. There are in fact several flight simulation computer programs available for desktop computers. Simulations have also been used effectively in educational settings like medical education, where computer programs allow students to explore a cadaver's anatomy without the expense and "feel" of the real experience. Other computer programs allow high school students who are drop-out risks to explore different "real-world" job scenarios based upon the educational decisions they make. One popular piece of software for personal computers allows users to create their own "living planet" based on the Gaia theory of the evolution of the Earth. Effective simulations provide rich scenarios with clear choices for learners that lead to plausible consequences. The simulation programs are quite believable, provide reasonable responses to the student's decisions, and revise the set of circumstances the student faces based upon those decisions. The advantage of simulations is that they provide students with the opportunity to engage in thinking at the higher levels of Bloom's taxonomy.

At present there are few music instruction simulation programs. One simulation has been used for developing an understanding of research methods in music (Abeles, 1979), but it is oriented toward graduate/professional education. There are several areas in music education, though, in which one might envision computer simulations being developed. In music teacher education, computers might simulate instructional scenarios such as those found in teaching a heterogeneous beginning woodwind class. Such scenarios could be rich with broken reeds, forgotten instruments and books, and unique combinations of instruments. Simulations might also be developed for younger general music students in which learners could select their own instrumentation for a particular piece and explore how different instrumentations affect how the piece sounds.

The computer has already become an important tool for the working musician. *Tool programs*, such as those that allow musicians to compose or arrange music on the computer and then play it back, do not have to be limited to use by professionals, however. They can also be used for instructional purposes. Such programs, while primarily designed to assist in production, can, with the help of an imaginative teacher, become important educational tools. Good tool programs provide many options for the user and are easy to use initially (i.e., user-friendly). They should not require a semester-long course or the reading of a 500-page manual to get started, but teachers must expect that they will need to feel comfortable with the program before they use it with their students. (Teachers should also expect that some of their students will soon become more sophisticated with the program than themselves.) Two common examples of types of tool software for music instruction are sequencing programs and printing programs. Sequencing software lets students input "sequences" of melodies and harmonies, either through the computer keyboard or a MIDI instrument. The student is then able to modify what was input until he or she is satisfied with the result; in other words, it allows students to compose. Sequencing software can therefore be used to give students experiences generating and organizing sounds. These experiences can be quite simple or very sophisticated. Music-printing software prints in traditional notation what has been sequenced or inputted directly.

There are several advantages to employing tool software in music instruction.

1. The software is used by working musicians, so the student learns to use tools that are used in the real world of music making.

2. Tool programs do not come with a specified instructional sequence, which means that teachers are free to design their own.

3. Many tool programs can be used at a variety of instructional levels, from elementary school through college.

Tool programs used for instructional purposes require more instructor input than other computer instructional programs, such as tutorials. Teachers should provide the goals and objectives for the instructional experiences, as well as the specific directions on how to use the software.

In the last two decades of the twentieth century, technology has played an increasingly important role in the workplace, in the school, and in the home. It has a well-established role in professional music making, and it is becoming increasingly important in school music instruction. It is imperative for music teachers to keep up with the potential of technology for improving music instruction.

A Behavioral Approach to Music Instruction

It is clear from an examination of the research journals in music education that a considerable amount of interest in the application of behavior modification techniques to music instruction exists. It is difficult, however, to assess the extent to which these strategies have found their way into the music classroom. The behavior modification approach appeals to teachers because of its emphasis on direct application and its focus on solving specific problem behaviors. In addition, its techniques seem easy to learn and apply.

Behavior modification techniques have developed out of a branch of behaviorist psychology called "operant psychology." Clearly, B. F. Skinner is the most significant figure in this movement, although the earliest applications of conditioning principles can be traced to Pavlov and Watson. Operant psychology has tended to focus on the use of reinforcers as a means of increasing or decreasing the probability of responses with which the reinforcer is paired. In operant psychology, "contingencies" are established; that is, the occurrence of the reinforcer depends on the response or behavior. If a contingent reinforcer increases the frequency of a response, it is labeled a "positive reinforcer"; if a contingent reinforcer decreases the frequency of a response, it is labeled "punishment" (actually "positive punishment"). Much of the research in operant psychology has focused on the characteristics of the reinforcer.

As suggested in the section on motivation in chapter 7, some reinforcers are primary (e.g., food, warmth) and others are secondary: they are learned or conditioned. Much operant psychological research has been done with animals employing primary reinforcers. (There is nothing more useless to an operant psychologist than a sated rat.) However, because primary reinforcers can generally not be manipulated by educators, behavior modification studies in education have focused on secondary reinforcers: tangible items such as money and candy or social reinforcers such as the teacher's attention and praise. It should also be pointed out that secondary reinforcers may not be practical for the long term in school applications of behavioral theory. Most applications in music have tended to employ verbal reinforcers, particularly in large ensemble situations or in types of activities like listening.

In addition to focusing on the type of reinforcer employed, much effort has been devoted to examining schedules of reinforcement—the frequency with which the reinforcer is paired with the response. A reinforcement may be given every time a response occurs. If reinforcements are made after a given number of responses, the reinforcement schedule is said to be a "ratio schedule"; if reinforcements are made after a given passage of time, the schedule is labeled an "interval schedule." Either type of schedule can be "fixed" or "variable." When reinforcers are administered after a specified number of responses or a specific time period, the schedule is said to be fixed. When the reinforcer is administered at varying intervals or after varying numbers of responses, the schedule is variable.

If a teacher wishes to increase the frequency of a particular behavior, such as band members warming up softly while sitting in their appropriate chairs before a rehearsal begins, and the behavior already occurs, then the teacher must identify and apply an effective positive reinforcer like verbal praise. If the behavior does not exist in a particular student's repertory of prerehearsal activity, the teacher may try a technique called "modeling," in which the desired behavior is demonstrated for the student. Once an approximation of the desired behavior is part of the student's repertoire, it is systematically reinforced, or shaped, until the desired behavior is achieved.

The approach just described seems relatively simple, but several problems may affect its implementation. It is frequently difficult for teachers to identify effective reinforcers. What may serve as a reinforcer for one band member may not be effective for another. In some cases actions taken to decrease the occurrence of a behavior—for instance, verbally criticizing a student for talking while the ensemble director is working with another section—may in fact increase the frequency of the behavior if the student finds the attention she or he is receiving to be rewarding. This fact suggests that the principles of behavior modification cannot be applied haphazardly but must be carefully and systematically coordinated.

Systematic observation of the learning environment and quantification of observable behaviors are necessary if such techniques are to be applied in the music classroom. By employing observation and quantification, instructors will be able to identify the frequency of occurrence of desired and undesired behaviors. They may also be able to identify the antecedent events that might precipitate a certain behavior, as well as the environmental events that follow the behavior and possibly serve to reinforce it.

Thus, a sequence for applying behavior modification techniques in the music classroom might include the following steps:

1. Select the behavior to be modified and identify the desired or goal behavior.

2. Observe the frequency of the behavior and its antecedents and possible reinforcing events.

3. Plan a program to alter the behavior and monitor the change.

4. Remove the program and monitor to see if the goal behavior is maintained.

For example, in many band rehearsals students frequently doodle on their instruments while the director is trying to rehearse a different section of the group. If the director wishes to eliminate this behavior, he or she might ask a colleague or student teacher to record how often this doodling occurs and any events that generally precede or succeed it. In lieu of a human observer the director might make an audiotape or videotape recording of the rehearsals and at a later time complete an observational form while listening to or viewing the tape. After analyzing the observational record it may be decided that a possible strategy for decreasing doodling is to praise students who are not doodling. The director might then attempt to praise in a systematic way the students who are sitting quietly when another section of the band is rehearsing. It is generally considered necessary to record both the director's and students' behavior during this period in order to observe if the undesirable behavior diminishes. Once appropriate rehearsal behavior is established, occasional systematic observational records should be collected to evaluate the maintenance of the behavior.

Because of the systematic nature of behavior modification techniques, research on the effectiveness of these strategies is frequently a built-in component. Typical behavioral research studies first employ careful observation to collect data on the frequency of the "target" behavior in a natural, unaltered environment. This period of data collection is usually referred to as "baseline." During the next time period the "treatment," or contingent reinforcer, is introduced. After a specified period of time the contingent reinforcer is withdrawn. This period in which the reinforcer is withdrawn is again labeled "baseline." Observation of the frequency of the target behavior is recorded during all periods of the study. Frequently in studies that employ such behavioral research strategies, the contingent reinforcer is again introduced. Such research designs are often called "reversal designs" and are represented symbolically as ABAB designs. Their results are typically graphed to display the results of the imposition and withdrawal of the contingent reinforcer (see figure 8.2).

Of particular interest to music educators are studies employing behavior modification strategies that have focused on music learning problems or that employed music as a reinforcer for other behaviors.

In general, studies (Madsen, Greer, & Madsen, 1975; Madsen & Prickett, 1987) have shown that music is an effective reinforcer for academic behaviors like math or verbal learning, as well as social behaviors like attentiveness. These studies suggest that music—either music listening or music performance, or even videotaped music instruction—is as effective at motivating a variety of target behaviors as are other reinforcers like candy.

Some studies have examined the effect of behavior modification strategies in music instructional situations. These studies indicate that

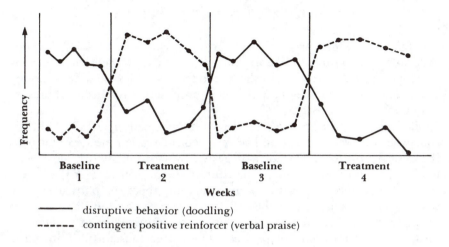

Figure 8.2. Hypothetical data on frequency of doodling.

behavioral strategies may alter musical preferences, reduce disruptive behavior in music instructional situations, increase the amount of time students practice, and reduce instrumental music performance anxiety. Kuhn (1975) examined the effect of teacher approval and disapproval during music instruction. Four groups of fifth-graders were formed. Two of the four groups were taught in such a way that the proportion of teacher's comments expressing approval or disapproval—for both academic and social behavior—was manipulated. (Sample comments were: "John, number 7 is correct," and "Sally is doing her work quietly at her desk; that's good.") Group 1 received 80 percent approvals, while Group 2 received only 20 percent approvals. Group 3 received the music instructional material but no feedback, and Group 4 received regular music-class instruction. The results indicated that the four groups did not differ on music achievement test scores or on a measure of attitude toward the class as a result of the different treatments. The groups did, however, differ on a measure of attentiveness, with the group receiving 80 percent approvals being more attentive than the other three groups.

It seems clear from the extensive number of investigations using behavioral procedures in music classes that such approaches are becoming well established, at least in the music education research community. For, as Madsen et al. (1975, p. 23) suggest, "Behavior modification methodology provides a way for teachers to diagnose, promote more effective strategies, and insure specification of behaviors that can be manipulated and tested in order to expedite students' learning."

Gordon's Learning Theory

Several of the popular music education methods (e.g., Orff, Suzuki, Dalcroze, Kodály) have a theoretical basis. Generally these are positions developed by the proponent of the method and are idiosyncratic, although often parallels can be seen between these proposals and traditional presentations of learning theory.

The learning theory presented by Edwin Gordon (1988, 1990) is somewhat different in that he has spent considerable time describing his theoretical positions. Methods suggested by Gordon's work have been guided by his theories rather than intertwined with it. His work also seems clearly linked to that of general learning theorists, particularly the work of Gagné and Piaget. The key component to Gordon's approach to music learning is sequencing. He divides his approaches to sequencing music learning into two major areas, sequencing music skills and music content. The music skills sequencing hierarchy (table 8.7) appears to be the most important.

Gordon's believes that there are two related aspects to learning music skills: discrimination and inference. He has developed hierarchies for each of these subareas that are similar to the Gagné hierarchy (see figure 7.2). Like Gagné, Gordon proposes a sequence of learning in which students progress from one level of the hierarchy to the next. While such a sequence appears rigid, in practice teachers probably would move back and forth among the levels as individual students progress through different levels. Walters (1992) identifies three important characteristics of Gordon's proposals: (1) teaching opposing classifications of the same dimension somewhat at the same time, for example, staccato and legato; (2) providing sequences of tonal and rhythm patterns at levels from easy to difficult to guide instruction; and (3) teaching different dimensions of music (e.g., melody and harmony) in isolation from each other (p. 542).

Walters characterizes Gordon's and Gagné's positions as "part" rather than "whole" learning approaches; that is, students focus on an aspect of the content rather than the integrated whole. Walters recommends a "whole-part-whole" learning sequence, which consists of an overview of the whole followed by the study of the parts, leading to a greater understanding of the whole (p. 543). Such an approach utilizes strategies for learning both the whole and the parts.

Summary

The taxonomies of educational objectives present teachers with a means of examining curriculum and developing tests to measure the outcomes of

TABLE 8.7.
Gordon's Skill-Learning Hierarchy Briefly Interpreted

Discrimination Learning: A Subhierarchy Featuring Rote Learning	
Aural/oral	—hearing/moving, chanting, singing
Verbal association	—associating words, tonal syllables, and rhythm syllables with sound
Partial synthesis	—recognizing characteristics of wholes (series of patterns rather than isolated patterns) that are heard
Symbolic association (reading, writing)	—associating syllables and sounds with music notation
Composite synthesis reading, writing	—recognizing characteristics of wholes (series of patterns rather than isolated patterns) that are seen in notation and translated to sound in audiation

Inference Learning: A Subhierarchy Featuring Conceptual Learning	
Generalization (aural/oral, verbal, symbolic)	—identifying the unfamiliar on the basis of similarities to and differences from the familiar
Creativity/improvisation (aural/oral, symbolic)	—using skill and content learned at lower levels of learning to improvise and create music
Theoretical understanding (aural/oral, verbal, symbolic)	—learning the mechanics of music notation

Source: D. L. Walters (1992). "Sequencing for Efficient Learning." In R. Colwell (Ed.), *Handbook of Research on Music Teaching and Learning* (p. 542). New York: Schirmer Books.

instruction for three broad types of learning: cognitive, affective, and psychomotor. The cognitive domain is organized into six categories: knowledge, comprehension, application, analysis, synthesis, and evaluation. This taxonomy is hierarchical, with the lower levels of the taxonomy being less complex than the higher levels.

The affective domain organizes outcomes of instruction such as students' interests, attitudes, and values, which are very important in arts education. There has not been as much emphasis on the affective domain by educators as there has been on the cognitive domain. The levels of the affective domain are: receiving, responding, valuing, organization, and characterization by a value or value complex. This taxonomy is a hierarchy based on internalization and commitment.

The psychomotor domain has received even less attention by researchers, yet for music instruction it is very important. This taxonomy, which is a hierarchy organized by complexity, is divided into seven categories: perception, set, guided response, mechanism, complex overt response, adaptation, and origination.

The three domains of learning do not fit neatly into isolated compartments. Attitudes affect cognitive learning, and knowledge affects motor skill development.

Behavioral objectives are an important first step in a systems approach to instruction. This four-stage approach is: stating educational objectives, developing instructional materials, assessing students' progress, and revising instructional materials according to the assessment. Behavioral objectives are based on goals developed by curriculum planners. Statements of behavioral objectives should contain a verb, a statement of conditions under which the behavior occurs, and the standard of quality that the performance must reach.

The instructional objectives movement has had considerable impact on the music education profession, although behavioral objectives are not universally accepted by music educators. Eisner proposes that in addition to behavioral objectives, educators should also employ problem-solving objectives and expressive outcomes to guide curriculum planning.

One related outgrowth of instructional objectives has been educational accountability. School boards, school administrators, and teachers are expected to be responsible for—accountable for—their role in the educational system. Educational accountability may be thought of as a legislated systems approach to education, since more than forty states have laws requiring accountability.

Individualized instruction can also be linked to the systems approach to education. "Open education" helped stimulate interest in individualized instruction among music educators, and such instruction underwent considerable development in general music classes during the period 1965–1975. One approach to individualization is called "personalized systematic instruction" (PSI). PSI is similar to the general systems approach, but in the PSI model the responsibility for attaining the stated goals of instruction is placed with the teacher rather than the student.

Programmed instruction (PI) and computer-based instruction (CBI) are also ways in which music educators have individualized instruction. These approaches can employ either a linear or branching strategy to organize the presentation of materials. In linear programs every student proceeds through each frame, while in branching programs the sequencing of material depends on the students' performance. Computer music instruction can be organized in five different ways. Tutorial programs present information and test acquisition of it. Drill and Practice programs give students the chance to practice developing skills. Computer instructional games also provide practice in a motivating format. Computer simulations allow students to practice higher-order thinking skills, and with careful planning by teachers, tool programs can provide interesting, creative experiences for students.

The application of behavioral techniques in the music classroom is based on the work of B. F. Skinner and others in the area of operant psychology. The applications of these techniques to music teaching are well grounded in research, much of which has focused on the pairing of reinforcers with the occurrence of desired behaviors. Research studies in this area often employ "reversal designs" that alternate periods of baseline with treatment periods. In general these studies have shown that music can be an effective reinforcer for academic behaviors such as verbal learning and that behavioral techniques can be used to reduce disruptive behavior in instructional settings such as ensemble rehearsals.

Edwin Gordon has developed a music learning theory that focuses on sequential learning. His skills sequence hierarchy has two components, discrimination learning and interference learning.

STUDY AND DISCUSSION QUESTIONS

1. The upper levels of the cognitive taxonomy are more complex than the lower levels. In what way is each successive level more complex?

2. Compare the "instructional system" described on page 243 with the description of the common components of human programs as described in chapter 7, page 204.

3. Why is assessment in the affective domain more difficult than in the cognitive domain?

4. In what ways to the upper levels of the taxonomy for the psychomotor domain differ from the lower levels?

5. In what ways are the cognitive, affective, and psychomotor taxonomies useful to music teachers?

6. What are the essential components of an educational objective that is stated in behavioral terms?

7. Identify at least three weakness of behavioral objectives.

8. How has the interest in individualized instruction in the field of music education been demonstrated?

9. What is the main difference between personalized systematic instruction (PSI), on the one hand, and programmed instruction (PI) and computer-based instruction (CBI), on the other?

10. (a) What are the five characteristics that programmed and CBI material have in common?

(b) What is the basic difference between programmed material in a linear design and programmed material in a branching design?

(c) What, in general, have been the results of studies comparing PI and CBI material with more traditional approaches?

11. In what ways can computers be used most effectively to aid music instruction?

12. (a) What are the strengths of behavior modification in managing students in music classes?

(b) What are the limitations of behavior modification?

13. What are the basic steps in applying behavior modification to both academic and social situations in music classrooms?

14. Compare the quotation of Hillson on page 251 with the quotation of Butler found in chapter 2, page 55.

INDIVIDUAL OR CLASS ACTIVITIES

1. Write two questions for each of the three domains that test different levels of the domain. Then read several of the questions to the class and ask the members of the class to independently classify the questions by level and domain. Discuss disagreements in student classifications.

2. Locate a programmed music text or an instructional computer program in music, and report to the class on the type of program employed, the appropriateness of the material for different age levels, and the general appeal of the material.

3. Take the following long-range goals and develop unit and behavioral objectives for each:

(a) The student analyzes the use of timbre in orchestration.

(b) The student identifies meter.

(c) The student identifies tension in melodic line.

(d) The student identifies music of other cultures.

(e) The student performs note values accurately.

SUPPLEMENTARY READINGS

HIGGINS, W. (1992). Technology. In R. Colwell (Ed.), *Handbook of research on music teaching and learning* (pp. 480–97). New York: Schirmer Books.

MADSEN, C. K., & PRICKETT, C. A. (1987). *Applications of research in music behavior*. Tuscaloosa: University of Alabama Press.

WALTERS, D. (1992). Sequencing for efficient learning. In R. Colwell (Ed.), *Handbook of research on music teaching and learning* (pp. 535–45). New York: Schirmer Books.

REFERENCES

ABELES, H. F. (1979). Using an EXPER SIM (Experimental Simulation) model in teaching graduate research courses in music education. Paper presented at the Indiana University Computer Network Conference. Gary, IN.

BLOOM, B. S. (1956). *Taxonomy of educational objectives: Handbook 1. Cognitive domain*. New York: David McKay.

CARLSEN, J. C. (1964). Programmed learning in melodic dictation. *Journal of Research in Music Education, 12*(2), 139–148.

COLWELL, R. (1974, Spring). Editor's note. *Bulletin of the Council for Research in Music Education, 36,* 2–6.

COOKSEY, J. M. (1974, Spring). An accountability report for music education. *Bulletin of the Council for Research in Music Education, 36,* 6–64.

EISNER, E. (1979). *The educational imagination: On the design and evaluation of school programs*. New York: Macmillan.

FLORIDA DEPARTMENT OF EDUCATION (1974). *Florida catalog of music objectives*. Tallahassee, FL: Author.

GOOD, C. V. (1959). *Dictionary of education* (2d ed.). New York: McGraw-Hill.

GORDON, E. (1988). *Learning sequences in music: Skill, content, and patterns*. Chicago: G. I. A.

GORDON, E. (1990). *A music learning theory for newborn and young children*. Chicago: G. I. A.

GREER, R. D. (1980). *Design for music learning*. New York: Teachers College Press.

GRONLUND, N. E., & LINN, R. L. (1990). *Measurement and evaluation in teaching* (6th ed.). New York: Macmillan.

HILLSON, M. (1975). Forces for change. In R. B. Meske & C. Rhinehart (Eds.), *Individualized instruction in music* (pp. 29–43). Reston, VA: Music Educators National Conference.

KELLER, F. S. (1980). Foreword. In R. D. Greer (Ed.), *Design for music learning*. New York: Teachers College Press.

KRATHWOHL, D. R., BLOOM, B. S., & MASIA, B. B. (1964). *Taxonomy of educational objectives: Handbook 2. Affective domain*. New York: David McKay.

KUHN, T. L. (1975). The effect of teacher approval and disapproval on attentiveness, musical achievement, and attitude of fifth-grade students. In C. K. Madsen, R. D. Greer, & C. H. Madsen (Eds.), *Research in music behavior* (pp. 40–48). New York: Teachers College Press.

LABUTA, J. A. (1974). *Guide to accountability in music instruction*. West Nyack, NY: Parker.

MADSEN, C. K., GREER, R.D., & MADSEN, C. H. (1975). *Research in music behavior*. New York: Teachers College Press.

MADSEN, C. K., & PRICKETT, C. A. (1987). *Applications of research in music behavior*. Tuscaloosa: University of Alabama Press.

MAGER, R. F. (1962). *Preparing instructional objectives*. Palo Alto, CA: Fearon.

MESKE, R. B., & RHINEHART, C. (1975). *Individualized instruction in music*. Reston, VA: Music Educators National Conference.

MUSIC EDUCATORS NATIONAL CONFERENCE (1986). *The school music program: description and standards* (2nd ed.). Reston, VA: Music Educators National Conference.

POPHAM, J. W. (1969). *Instructional objectives*. Chicago: Rand McNally.

SIMPSON, E. (1966). *The classification of educational objectives*. (Report No. OE5-85-104). Washington, DC: United States Office of Education.

SINGER, R. N. (1972). The psychomotor domain: General considerations. In *The psychomotor domain* (pp. 2–19). Washington, DC: Gryhon.

WALTERS, D. (1922). Sequencing for efficient learning. In R. Colwell (Ed.), *Handbook of research on music teaching and learning* (pp. 535–45). New York: Schirmer Books.

9

Curriculum

As was mentioned in chapter 2, people's views on the importance of curriculum and subject-matter content vary according to their philosophical and educational beliefs. Some educators think that what is taught in a course is of the utmost importance, while others think that it hardly matters; what is important to them is the process. Regardless of an individual's point of view, at some time or another most music educators must be able to say *what* it is they are trying to teach. Boards of education, taxpayers, and students searching through a college catalog all expect teachers to be teaching their students *something*. In this sense, then, the topic of curriculum is an important one to all music teachers, and to many of us, it is an essential and significant part of the process of education.

Definitions of Curriculum

There are many ways to perceive or define a curriculum. Trained evaluators or administrators view the curriculum as an area of ongoing activities that are actually occurring in the classroom, rather than thinking of it as a static, established course of study. This administrative perspective is sometimes defined as an "operational" curriculum. It is true that courses of study are necessary to describe the various activities planned for the classroom, but the real concern for those responsible is to determine what is occurring in the individual classes to promote learning—learning that is based on formulated objectives and desired competencies, and not just what appears in a guide.

Another view found in the literature promotes what might be referred to as an "ideal" curriculum, or what should be offered, as opposed to a "clinical" view of what is actually offered. This "ideal" usually is a mental construct that may or may not exist. It is usually developed under scholarly conditions and is a result of what curriculum theorists and planners believe the exemplary course of study should be.

Concerned citizens often have other expectations and values regarding the curriculum. State departments of education, commercial interests, school board policymakers, and pressure groups of parents, political groups, or other special-interest groups have viewpoints that represent what is referred to as the "formal" curriculum.

At the same time, teachers' values and attitudes provide still another perspective on the curriculum. Their view reflects what they think they should be teaching compared with what they actually teach. The inference here is that teachers "adapt the formal curriculum because they perceive that their students have certain unique needs and/or interests" (Klein, Tye, & Wright, 1979, p. 245). Too often, however, teachers disregard these differences and attempt to conform to a given curriculum, which is called by some writers the "instructional" curriculum. It is described as follows: "Originally we called this the 'perceived' curriculum because we felt that teachers' perceptions are so significant. However, we realized that *all* perspectives—societal, parental, students', teachers', etc.—are perceptions. Thus, we adopted the term 'instructional,' although we acknowledge its imprecision" (Klein et al., 1979, p. 246).

To formalize the various views for analysis and study, Klein et al. (1979) organized the design shown in figure 9.1. Note that (A) represents the various viewpoints that describe different curricula. Each viewpoint is directly affected by the variable factors (B) and the qualitative factors (C). At the same time, the way in which one utilizes the variable will be determined by his or her philosophy (A) and the qualitative factors (C).

A composite of these views would define a curriculum as a set of planned experiences. The very nature of it suggests that the manner in which these experiences are presented be varied according to the students in the classroom as well as the conditions that change within a school on a day-to-day basis. The activities are affected by such qualitative factors as how one perceives the curriculum, and this is reflected in the individual's description.

A curriculum is influenced by where the decision-making power resides. For example, if it is the responsibility of a fine arts department head or a music teacher, the approach to the nature and appropriateness of the offerings may vary from that of an overall curriculum coordinator who is the final authority in these matters (see C2 in the design). Attitudes of teachers, curriculum specialists, administrators, and the public—as well as facilitators and obstacles—will all have an impact on the quality of a pro-

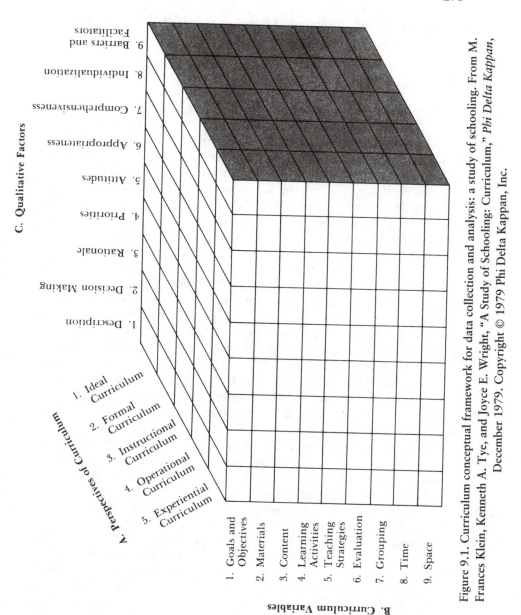

Figure 9.1. Curriculum conceptual framework for data collection and analysis: a study of schooling. From M. Frances Klein, Kenneth A. Tye, and Joyce E. Wright, "A Study of Schooling: Curriculum," *Phi Delta Kappan,* December 1979. Copyright © 1979 Phi Delta Kappan, Inc.

gram being offered. These considerations are all in direct proportion to what ultimately constitutes a curriculum as it is being offered in a school.

Determining Curriculum Content

The responsibility for education in American society lies with the community, which receives its mandate from the state. The aspirations and goals of the people who constitute the local community are responsible for the broad aims that determine the education of their youth. The elected board of education and its employed administrators are authorized to initiate the necessary process that will enable the school to achieve these aims. Teachers, by virtue of their role in the classroom, participate in this process and implement the procedures designed to achieve these goals and aims.

The forces that affect the educational aims and objectives of the community and school are diverse and complex. At times they may even be conflicting influences. These are community pressure groups, school administrators, government agencies, teachers groups, and teachers. Because school administrators are not sufficiently knowledgeable about every subject in the curriculum, teachers in specialized areas such as music can provide guidance and leadership when appropriate. Where this condition of conflict exists, music educators may recommend what is needed to provide the desired education in music. To assist in this situation, MENC has published two editions of its report, *The School Music Program: Description and Standards* (1974, 1986). In situations where a music supervisor exists, he or she may represent the teacher in these deliberations.

After considering the total needs in a school system, school administrators should try to make a fair and equitable decision as to how well the recommendations of the music teacher or music supervisor can be implemented. It is incumbent upon music teachers to inform administrators of their needs; otherwise, administrators will assume that all is satisfactory and will probably continue to proceed without any change.

The detailed daily decisions that determine classroom activities are also the responsibility of the individual music teacher. With the exception of the music supervisor, administrators are usually far too busy to oversee such matters; in fact, it is generally impossible for them to do so considering the size of most school staffs. Music teachers are better trained and better equipped in their specialized discipline to make decisions affecting music classes.

Curriculum Models

There are three basic models that one may find or utilize in planning a curriculum, and each one is governed by a particular philosophical perspective. They extend from maximum to minimum control over student outcomes and fall into the following categories:

1. Linear/control mode.
2. Consensus model.
3. Dialogue/freedom mode.

In the linear/control model based on realism or empiricism the *essential task* of teaching is to enable students to perform precisely delineated responses. It is based on the identification of purposes of curricula by experts. Evaluation of the outcomes of the objectives of this model would be based on pretesting and post-testing of students.

The consensus model (based on pragmatism) is structured on identifying needs and concerns of students. In this model the teacher's role is to guide students into gaining understandings, values, and skills through group planning. Evaluation in this model is done cooperatively.

In the third model, the dialogue/freedom model (based on naturalism), which has the minimum control over student outcomes, the teacher serves as a facilitator and guide. The student is the center of decision making, and evaluation rests with the student.

Curriculum Development

Before anyone becomes involved in developing a curriculum for music, he or she needs to understand the fundamental nature of the art of music. This is essential, because courses of study and curriculum guides should concern themselves with organizing and developing experiences that lead students to acquire the essence of this art form. Furthermore, not only should educators involved in curriculum development understand the fundamental nature of music, they should also be able to articulate an educational philosophy in support of the art of music. The students who will be affected by this curriculum must be ensured an in-depth understanding of each musical experience that is commensurate with their individual growth and development.

When constructing or examining a curriculum or course, one must begin with the existing music objectives for the total music education program (if any have previously been developed), the various activities that are provided in classes designed to achieve these objectives, and how appropriate they are to the students' level of musical development. This construction task involves organizing music experiences and selecting teaching materials. How this is done will depend on one's philosophical perspective as indicated earlier in the three models describing curriculum development. It is in this context that the curriculum is conceived as a totality dealing with the selection of desired musical and educational goals and the way in which the experiences are organized to achieve these goals.

As in all education, these goals should be based on developing musical literacy and sensitivity. In music, literacy and sensitivity should include the ability to analyze what one hears or sees; to perform in some medium that one enjoys; and to organize sounds in the expressive manner that one chooses, as long as such expressivity is in the appropriate style and character of the particular musical idiom being performed. When these objectives are attained, it is hoped that individuals will become actively engaged in the community's musical life. People with such an education will be able to make valid judgments of the available musical opportunities. It is for this reason that music education seeks to develop musically educated individuals and to build a vital musical culture.

Music requires special interest and special training. As a result, music teachers too often confine their attention to a small portion of the total music program: the publicly visible performing groups. It is only natural for each teacher to think of his or her specialty as being of prime importance and to be less concerned about what goes on in the rest of the music curriculum. However, it is essential that each teacher be concerned about and support all aspects of the music curriculum. When any single part of the total school music program suffers, it is bound to have some effect on other areas of the program.

When they begin the process of curriculum development, teachers should not be frustrated and confused by the proliferation of ideas. It is normal for each suggestion to open up vistas for further ideas. Curriculum planners are confronted with questions about what are appropriate ends and means, how they are related to established goals, what should be the content of particular courses, what approaches should be used, and many other factors that infringe on one another in developing a curriculum. One must be certain that there is no confusion about means and ends. Such questions concern themselves with the methods that one follows to achieve ends. The purpose of this discussion is what should be the content of a course.

In building a curriculum or course, one has to be concerned with both short-range and long-range goals. Short-range goals are the immediate concern of the individual music teacher planning a lesson, while long-range goals concern those in administration and supervision of the music curriculum, as well as classroom teachers, in planning for future directions. Teacher and faculty committees often concern themselves with both. It is easy to understand that the pressure of too many performances by performing groups infringes on teachers' efforts in the rehearsal room so that they may be less concerned about long-range objectives than they should be. Curriculum development should look beyond the next concert or the next lesson, however. Teachers should develop long-range plans that include specific statements about the information and skills to be acquired during each year or each level of development, in both performing groups and in general music classes. Such planning gives a music program better direction than merely going from concert to concert or deciding how to entertain best the audiences or students in general music classes.

In the final analysis, the successful music program is one that offers a balance and variety of experiences. Traditionally, music educators have classified music courses either as performing or as academic classes. There is nothing wrong with this distinction, since in each case the methods of teaching will differ. However, at no time should one be exclusive of the other. In other words, academic classes in music should involve some performance of music, if only in the classroom. Performing groups should concern themselves with gaining an understanding and analysis of the music being performed.

All music teachers should be interested in the course content of music classes. It is the responsibility of the supervisors and the curriculum specialists to see that the program is implemented or to provide the necessary leadership to organize opportunities for selection of content, but essentially everyone, including teachers, accepts responsibility for helping to select the musical offerings in a total curriculum. Under these conditions, the program is far more effective. Generally, district and state guides that focus on objectives are utilized in most communities where supervision is not available, and where teachers therefore are not provided with the necessary guidance. Where this occurs, teachers must assume responsibility for organizing class experiences and selecting the necessary music and learning activities if these guides are to be useful.

Selecting Courses and Content

In determining which musical activities should be included in the school offerings, one has to establish certain priorities and make choices. There is no question that a case can be made for virtually every music class or group that exists. However, given the limitations that one has to comply with in a school music setting, guidelines need to be established to give curriculum planners a basis for making choices. The most important aspects of a music program are those that offer the greatest variety of experiences, as well as the broadest scope of musical literature. It is not only the quantity of offerings but also the quality of these offerings that determines the success of a school music program. Quality involves music both as an academic discipline and as an art form. It needs to concern itself with lasting values, not just immediate satisfaction. (Much music, e.g., commercials, is written to sell a product or an idea, with little concern for artistic values.) If music is to receive public support, curriculum planners need to construct school programs that emphasize music as an art form of lasting value, rather than being satisfied with experiences of limited value that only provide short-term satisfaction.

Every child should have a general, broad musical experience before embarking on his or her choice of specialized activities. Without it, most students would not be able to make intelligent choices. It is for this reason that the foundation of a successful school music program resides in the general music program in the elementary and middle or junior high schools. Using the analogy of a tree, the general music program is like the trunk, with the performing groups such as chorus, orchestra, and band, or even literature or theory classes in secondary schools, as the branches. From each branch extend twigs such as the marching band, stage band, or show choir, which are adjuncts to the more basic organizations.* These groups have a limited, specialized repertoire that consists of only a partial segment of the total music literature. For this reason, membership in these special groups should be restricted to those individuals who are members of the broader-based ensembles. Unless students have a broader experience with music, they will have a restricted music education that too often does not sustain them throughout the rest of their maturing musical life.

Anyone involved in deciding what should be taught in music classes has some difficult decisions to make. Because there is never enough time to cover even a small portion of what could be included, the content of a course must be carefully selected. The following guidelines may help in the selection process.

EDUCATIONAL. This guideline is simple-sounding: The students should gain information, skills, or attitudes that they did not have prior to the class or course and probably would not acquire without having enrolled. While the guideline sounds simple, it is highly important; otherwise the class is largely a waste of time for the students. Just as children do not go to school to learn how to ride a bicycle, they do not attend school to learn things they already know or will learn without attending school. Most of what is learned in school music classes should consist of information or skills that would not be learned elsewhere.

VALID. Music is an established academic discipline—a field of study. Music teachers should ask themselves, "Is what is being taught a legitimate portion of the field of music? Would most trained musicians (performers, musicologists, teachers) recognize and accept this content as a part of the field?" For example, some makers of electronic organs have devised ingenious ways of presenting music in unconventional notation, such as color

---

*(James Mursell was probably the first music educator to use this analogy.)

coding, that works well for simple songs. However, no music theorist, symphony musician, or musicologist uses such systems in studying or playing music. Such systems have to be unlearned if the beginner is to progress. They are therefore not valid in the field of music as it is generally understood.

The guideline of validity is a logical one. Why teach something under the name of music that is not really part of the music field? It is neither logical nor honest to transform a subject in this way, even in the hope of aiding learning, and especially when the so-called skill will need to be unlearned in a music setting.

FUNDAMENTAL. Students should learn the basic ideas of a subject, not just factual minutiae. Knowing the keys of Haydn's symphonies is not nearly as useful as understanding how he develops themes. Fundamental learning is essential for a comprehension of the subject, and such learning has wider application for the students. For example, knowing the keys of Haydn's symphonies applies only to Haydn's music, but does not help in understanding how Haydn and other composers develop thematic material.

REPRESENTATIVE. Students need to be given a well-balanced idea of the type of music pertinent to the course they are taking. The high school choral director who spends most of the time on Broadway musicals is not providing a representative sample of the world of choral music, and neither is the director who concentrates exclusively on Palestrina. Music teachers should maintain a chart categorizing types of music and musical activities that cover all significant periods in music. By checking what they have taught in the appropriate categories, they can see whether or not they have involved their students with some music in each significant category.

CONTEMPORARY. Music classes should definitely include contemporary works. A course should not stop with music written in a style that is fifty or a hundred years old.

RELEVANT. The interests and needs of the students should be considered so that what is taught relates to them. It is unrewarding for everyone for a music teacher to concentrate on proper diction when singing a song if the students cannot see the point of the song or why the words have to be sung in a certain way. Making subject matter relevant is probably as much a matter of the *way* something is taught as of *what* is taught. Topics have no inherent relevance; a topic that is important and interesting to one person often couldn't matter less to another. Relevance is present when a subject is given meaning through a teacher's skill in organizing it.

Sometimes the interests of the students and the need for valid subject matter appear to be in conflict. Teachers interested in subject matter wonder, "What good is a subject that has lost its integrity and character?" Teachers interested in relevance wonder, "What good is a subject that seems meaningless and worthless to the students?" Both views have fair claim for the attention of music teachers, and the two viewpoints need not be mutually exclusive. Combining these two concerns is one of the challenges of teaching.

LEARNABLE. It is useless to teach something that is beyond the students' capabilities. While it might be nice to have one's middle-school singers perform Brahms's *German Requiem*, that work is far beyond the vocal abilities of middle-school singers. Whatever is covered should be learnable by most of the students. In some cases, this guideline calls for the adjustment of the content so that the students can grasp the basic ideas. For example, the concept of form in music can be introduced in the primary grades by analyzing same and different phrases, but teaching the sonata form with its modulations and thematic development should be delayed until much later.

In the final analysis, music education should be concerned not so much with the organization of a list of course titles as with what are the essentials for providing a quality education for students in music. Designing what should be taught requires thoughtful attention to subject-matter validity, to the relationship between each selection and the vast body of music, and to the relevancy of subject matter to student needs and interests. It is important that music teachers realize that they are teaching a subject that is extremely important to human development, and that the students are in music classes to learn music.

Subject Matter Content in Music

At first glance, the subject-matter content of music seems simple enough. It consists of songs and other pieces of music and skills in performing music. But is that all? Clearly, it is not. Figure 9.2 divides the subject-matter content of music into *activities* (what people do with music) and *outcomes* (what people gain from being educated in music). This division between activities and outcomes is a close parallel to the distinction between means and ends. Performing, reading, listening, analyzing/describing, and creating can be means or ways of achieving the desired outcomes of making, understanding, and valuing music, which are the major outcomes of music education.

The same musical activity (for example, singing a song) may be either an activity (singing the song contributes to the students' understanding of that piece of music and their valuing of it) *or* an outcome (learning to sing better), *depending on the purpose for which the activity was undertaken.* Although it may seem like hairsplitting, the particular purpose does make a

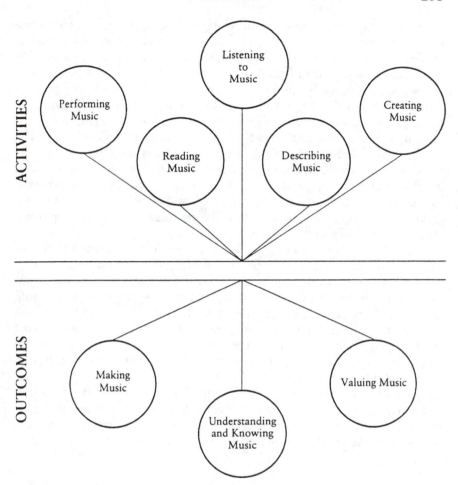

Figure 9.2. The subject matter of music. From Charles R. Hoffer, *Teaching Music in the Secondary Schools*, fourth edition, p. 54.

difference in what happens in a music class. If singing a song is an activity, then the emphasis is on the understandings and values that result from the activity. In that case, the teacher would, for example, ask the students to notice rhythmic or melodic patterns and talk about the cultural setting from which the song came. If singing a song is the main outcome, then the focus of the teaching is on the improvement of singing skill. In that case, the teacher might work on proper breathing techniques and the clear pronunciation of the words.

Although the circles in figure 9.2 are drawn to indicate discrete categories, the categories are not neat and clearcut. For example, listening is an activity that helps performers to play or sing better, enables them to know and understand music more thoroughly, and contributes to the enjoyment and valuing of music. In addition, listening contributes (at least to some extent) to performing, reading, analyzing, and creating music. The interrelatedness of the various parts of figure 9.2 is indicated by the converging of the lines in the middle.

Each of the activities and outcomes represents a broad and complex mental construct. Understanding music, for example, is much more than information and concepts. It includes the syntax of music of particular musical styles. For people in the Americas and Europe (and increasingly the rest of the world, it seems), that syntax is the common practice style developed in the seventeenth and eighteenth centuries. A sense of syntax is so crucial to the understanding of a type of music that in the case of young children, the acquisition of a sense of syntax may well be the important thing they can learn in those years.

The relative importance of different activities and outcomes will, of course, vary according to the age and musical experience of the students, as well as with the nature of the class. Learning to sing songs is important in the primary grades; devoting a large amount of attention to learning about the historical or cultural context of the song is not an effective use of time at that level. Students in an instrumental music class should devote most of their efforts to learning to play their instruments, while students in music theory class should be gaining an understanding of the structure of music and skill in creating it.

Whether or not music teachers agree fully with the structure of the subject matter content as presented in figure 9.2, the fact remains that they should have a clear idea about the subject matter content they seek to have their students learn. It is a topic that merits much careful attention.

Guides and Courses of Study

A *curriculum guide* is printed material that is collated for the purpose of providing a faculty with some direction on what to teach. It can serve in several different capacities.

1. It may be a sourcebook for teachers to advise them as to goals and objectives, and it may even contain some suggestions on how to achieve these goals. This type of guide can and probably should contain information about when and how to secure essential materials like audiovisual equipment as well as how to handle the distribution of equipment.

2. A guide may also be used as an aid for in-service training and staff development for music and/or classroom teachers.

3. Occasionally guides serve to promote good public relations by informing the administration, board members, and interested citizens about the role of music and what is taught in music. Guides need not be confined to one of these specific roles, but may serve in combinations of the above functions.

4. Guides can also be sources of information for the public or even for school officials. They can provide school principals with some means of understanding better the kind of program that is desirable for their school. In fact, anyone wishing to know what a school's music curriculum offers should be able to find that information by examining that school system's music guide. In this sense, guides are not only informative but can perform a valuable public relations function.

Guides should not only list the educational activities in the curriculum; they should state the school's beliefs about music education. Furthermore, they should include the goals and objectives for a specific music course.

Curriculum guides are not hard and fast directives. They are publications that give guidance and direction to a school's music program. They should allow for flexibility, rather than impose procedures or an approach on teachers. No two classes within a school are identical, even when attempts are made to make them so. When teachers and administrators understand that the guides function as a springboard for learning, they are then being used correctly.

Although flexibility is advocated, there needs to be some unity in a system's music program. By establishing what is basic in instruction, guides can provide the unity and continuity sought. They should present a "bedrock" course of study that all teachers should attempt to follow in some fashion. This portion of the music program might consume about 50 percent of the total time in an average situation, leaving the remaining 50 percent for teachers to use according to their particular situation or the needs of a particular class. This division of time provides for the desirable unity and yet allows flexibility for teacher initiative to meet special needs and interests.

A *course of study* is more specific in designating the content and sequence of a specific course. It contains not only the materials to be used but also includes suggestions for teaching procedures that will lead to the development of specific skills, musical concepts, and knowledge. Courses of study are especially helpful to new teachers, who obtain from them ideas and information as to what is expected of them in teaching the core of learning, as well as how to go about it.

The phrase *subject-matter content* refers to the topics to be taught, such as sonata allegro form, major and minor scales, shifting on a stringed instrument, or, in a graduate class, drawing conclusions from statistical data or memorizing a particular composition.

References to a *program* imply a number of courses or the type of instruction in a specific area. For example, a reference to an elementary music program concerns itself with the total musical activities and learning experiences being offered under the aegis of the music department in a particular elementary school. The same principle would apply to a description of a university's music education program.

All of the above definitions are designed to coordinate a school music program. A planned program is necessary to avoid duplication or create gaps in students' music education as they move from one school to another or one grade level to another. In large systems, where there is considerable mobility, unless there is a planned, unified sequence of content and experience, moving works against children's involvement in music and learning. It is difficult for a child who may have learned to read music under one approach to be thrust into a situation where he or she must learn a different approach to acquiring that skill.

Developing Guides

All music teachers should be interested in the course content of music classes. It is the responsibility of the supervisors and the curriculum specialists to see that the program is implemented or to provide the necessary leadership to organize opportunities for selection of content, but essentially everyone, including teachers, accepts responsibility for helping to select the musical offerings in a total curriculum. Under these conditions, the program is far more effective. Generally, district and state guides that focus on objectives are utilized in most communities where supervision is not available and therefore teachers are not provided with the necessary guidance. Under these conditions, teachers must assume responsibility for organizing class experiences and selecting the necessary music and learning activities if these guides are to be useful.

The second edition of *The School Music Program: Description and Standards* (MENC, 1986) made the list of *skills* and *understandings* more comprehensive and more specific by organizing the desired competencies or "recommended achievements" into age groups: early childhood, elementary school, middle and junior high school, high school, and beyond high school. The report also listed the student "achievements" under four specific desired outcomes for early childhood, elementary, and middle or junior high school: (1) "performing/reading"; (2) "creating"; (3) "listening/describing"; and (4) "valuing." The high school performing organizations had their list of desired "achievements" divided into three categories: (1) making music; (2) understanding music; and (3) valuing music.

Nonperforming high school organizations were expected to be able to understand music and value music.

The purpose of this publication was to provide a format for a quality school music program against which appropriate and interested individuals could compare their school music program. It not only identified the desired "achievements" for students, but also set standards for "scheduling, staffing, facilities, and materials and equipment, for determining proper levels of support" (Music Educators National Program, 1986, p. 9).

Multicultural Music Education

Americans live in a pluralistic society. For this reason alone it is incumbent upon educators to make all students aware of and sensitive to the ethnic diversity that exists not only in this society but throughout the world.

Modern transportation and media have reduced the time element and narrowed the distance in bringing nations of the world with cultures different from those in the United States closer together. Daily, one sees on television interviews, news, and stories from around the world. It is inconceivable that young people today can grow up without being exposed to other people, other countries, and other cultures.

In order to develop respect for the achievements of cultures other than their own, teachers need to integrate multicultural music into the core music curriculum. "Multicultural education clearly develops the understanding that there are many different but equally valid forms of musical and artistic expression and encourages students to develop a broad perspective based on understanding, tolerance, and respect for a variety of opinions and approaches." (Anderson & Campbell, 1989, p. 1).

Two common misconceptions regarding music that have an impact on instruction in multiethnic music are: (1) music is a universal language that is based on Western art music; and (2) the United States is a cultural melting pot. Music is *not* a universal language; it is a universal form of humanistic expression. Scales and styles vary drastically. Unless the ear has been conditioned to hear the subtle, stylistic differences or differences in scale in Asian or African music, for example, the "language" is foreign to the Western ear. To be conversant with music of other ethnic groups, one needs to be educated in those cultural manifestations.

As to the idea of the United States being a "melting pot," the suggestion implies that ethnic groups entering the United States leave their culture behind them. This may have been true during the first part of the twentieth century when immigrants were concerned about becoming assimilated in American society. However, to accept this premise today denies the existence of the beautiful, colorful music of groups other than those steeped in Western music and Western traditions. In a democracy, cultural pluralism allows diverse groups to maintain their cultural heritage or assimilate as they choose.

These are practical problems that emerge when implementing multicultural music in the curriculum:

1. The basic training of the teacher does not always include the use of multicultural music. Although the indigenous musical system of one culture may be adoptable to another, there are stylistic considerations that require additional training.

2. There exists a conditioning of the mind that when evaluating music of another culture it is mistakenly compared with a similar work of the dominant culture. For example, one should not make a comparison of a gospel song with a Protestant hymn. Although both represent a form used in the church, each one represents a different genre.

3. Selection is another problem. Every country and even specific ethnic groups contain subpopulations, each with its own music. In Africa there are more than 700 different subpopulations, and each one has its own and *different* musical scale. There is not just one type of African music any more than there is one type of American or Spanish-American music. With the time constraints as well as the curricular obligations confronting a teacher, how much time can one allot to multicultural music?

4. Probably the most difficult obstacle to overcome is dealing with students' and teachers' cultural biases and attitudes. As indicated earlier, there is a tendency to judge ethnic music in relation to one's own music, and because individuals have been trained and are more familiar with music of their own culture, they assume that theirs is a superior culture. Sociologists have identified this characteristic as *ethnocentrism* (see chapter 5 for more about this term).

To assist in solving those concerns, Joyce Jordan in writing on "Curricular Development" for multicultural experiences offers three proposals from a study by Palmer to help resolve the problems.

1. To meet the problems of great diversity of pitch phenomena of various music systems, Palmer suggests the development of an electronic instrument "capable of producing various scale structures and trainings not possible for the equal-tempered piano or other classroom instruments" (Jordan, 1992, p. 740).

2. Source books about various world music and traditions should be designed for use in elementary schools. This is the age when students

are most open-minded and have a minimum of bias (p. 740). (This is precisely what the Detroit public school system did in the 60s when there was a need to expand the knowledge and teaching of African-Americans in its schools.)

3. An extensive data bank should be established that would cross-reference information concerning materials and information to assist music teachers in teaching multicultural music (p. 740).

Additional solutions might be:

1. To solve the problem of selection and time, teachers should choose a representative sample of the various types of music. A limited number of works that might serve as models or exemplars is acceptable.

2. To present music of other cultures as authentically as possible, teachers might use recordings or invite a knowledgeable performer to perform the music of that ethnic group.

3. To overcome ethnocentrism, teachers should make every effort to instill in students an attitude of respect and acceptance toward all types of music. Although teachers cannot mandate that their students adopt accepting attitudes, they can encourage them to be informed about other cultures and their music before making judgments or expressing personal opinions about that music.

When teaching multicultural music, teachers should not lose sight of their responsibility to teach basic skills in music. The choice of material, whether it is based on ethnic music or Western music, should still focus on basic knowledge and those skills that enable the student to enjoy a lifetime of involvement with music as an art form. Focusing on essential musical skills enables students to develop those analytical skills that will assist them in understanding the development of music as an art form, especially as it is utilized throughout the world.

Interrelationships Among the Arts

The authors of this and many other books have grouped fine arts and music together when discussing certain topics, and often the arts are combined in courses, academic departments, and publications. Does this mean that to know one art is to know the others? Are the arts fundamentally unified? Is artistic talent or appreciation transferable from one art to another?

Clearly the fine arts have some things in common, or else they would not be considered together so often. They do have the same basic aesthetic reasons for being and offer the same values in human life. At some times and places they have been influenced by the same *Zeitgeist*—the same "spirit of the times"—in their attempts to fulfill general artistic goals. For example, the Classical outlook of objective detachment can be seen in the paintings of Jacques David and heard in the music of Mozart and Haydn; the Romantics' love of mystery and the unknown can be observed in Wordsworth's poetry and in Wagner's music dramas. To an extent, they can be compared on a macro level that does not delve deeply into any particular art.

Beyond their basic value and the broad outlook that has at times been influenced by cultural factors, the arts go their separate ways. To be successful in any form of art, one must learn the technique that is peculiar to that art form. It is difficult to compose music if one doesn't know notation, or at least how to manipulate the tape recorder and synthesizer. It is very hard to sculpt a fine work without knowing a great deal about different materials and techniques for making sculptures. Nor does talent in one area seem to carry over to other arts. Very few composers have tried to be painters; only Schoenberg comes to mind for such an effort, and his paintings did not earn him a place in art books. As far as the authors can determine, no recognized painter has made a major effort to be a composer, nor has any fine dancer been a performing violinist or pianist. Wagner thought of himself as the acme of German poetry, drama, and music, but today is recognized only for the music he composed. Furthermore, training in the understanding of one art does not transfer directly to other arts. If you learn what chiaroscuro is in painting, that knowledge will not tell you what a *pas de chat* is in ballet.

Sometimes teachers and writers have drawn false parallels between different arts. "Harmony is to music what perspective is to painting. It introduces the impression of musical space" (Machlis, 1977, p. 14). The problem with that statement is that music does not exist in space; it lives in time. Architecture, dance, sculpture, and painting deal with space, but not music. A student who tries to hear "space" in music is in for a frustrating and confusing time of it. An even more shaky view is presented in Robert Schumann's statement that the "cultivated musician could study Raphael's *Madonna* with the same profit as a painter a Mozart symphony . . . the musician transforms the paintings into tones" (Mueller, 1958, pp. 97–98).

The integration of music with other subjects has much to commend it, *if* done carefully and accurately. Teachers and planners of such courses must realize the limited ways in which learning in one art reinforces learning in another, and they must guard against sending the students up "blind alleys" by asking them to make false relationships among different arts. It is important that students in schools and colleges learn about the various arts. Whether such learning takes place one art at a time or in combination is not a crucial matter, providing that such learning takes place.

Essentially, all of the arts offering aesthetic and humanistic experiences are related. Therefore, school curricula should include some opportunities for a related-arts experience. This statement should be construed not as a recommendation to develop artificial similarities among the arts, but rather as a suggestion that somewhere in the curriculum there should be an opportunity to deal with the fine arts as a unit or a single course to develop an understanding of them in a larger sense.

To avoid confusion, here is a list of terms often used by music educators when discussing related-arts instruction. The terms vary from school to school.

Fine arts: A course combining art, music, dance, drama, and some of the other arts.

Related arts, or correlated arts: Very similar to the fine arts, but with an emphasis on the relationships among the arts.

Three arts: An art-music-dance course that is built around "concepts" such as line, form, rhythm, etc. The concept is then often used as a springboard for stimulating creative projects.

Humanities: The fine arts plus historical ideas and philosophical and/or political ideas. Some of these courses contain little music in them and tend to be based on the "great books" idea as first developed at the University of Chicago under Mortimer Adler in the late 1930s.

Experimental Projects in Related Arts

Two significant projects that contributed much in developing arts programs and arts materials in the late 1960s were the Interdisciplinary Model Program in the Arts for Children and Teachers (IMPACT) project, which was conducted in five school systems differing considerably in socioeconomic status and geographic location, and the Central Midwestern Regional Education Laboratory (CEMREL) project, which was an aesthetic educational program designed to assist self-contained elementary classroom teachers who were required to teach the arts with a minimum of assistance from specialists.

The IMPACT program was initiated in the following schools: the Conwell Middle School, an inner-city school in Philadelphia; Edgewood Elementary School in Eugene, Oregon, a small university city; the Eastgate and Cranbrook Elementary Schools in Columbus, Ohio, schools in a racially segregated neighborhood that was in the process of becoming integrated; the Troy, Alabama, school system, a typical rural southern school system; and the Glendale, California, schools, in a traditional suburban, middle-class community. The project proved effective in enhancing some learning and exposing students to the arts. Some improvements were also observed in reading levels, discipline, attendance, and attitudes toward school. The community as a whole became more interested and more involved in the schools, and there was an increase in parental activity.

The chief contribution made by the CEMREL project was the materials it developed for elementary classroom teachers and the impact the program had on the teachers using these materials. They developed more sensitivity to and interest in the arts, which in turn raised their level of aesthetic understanding as well as that of their students.

In developing an advocacy for related-arts programs, one needs to bear in mind that schools are primarily concerned with the education of students. The arts present an opportunity for children to enrich their lives and express themselves in sounds, shapes, and colors. The arts involve multisensory perceptions that invigorate the senses. They are not frills, but rather lasting methods of expression. Education should be just as concerned with human development as it is with skills, and the arts permit each learner to extend and expand his or her human potential.

Comprehensive Musicianship

The concept of comprehensive musicianship had its beginnings in the project first conceived by Norman Dello Joio and funded by the Ford Foundation in 1959 under the title "Contemporary Music Project," but popularly referred to as "The Young Composers Project." Young composers were selected by a panel of composers and educators to go into the schools and universities and write for music organizations in those institutions. They were assigned to areas where it was felt that the quality of music instruction, as well as the attitudes of the music teachers, would nurture and develop the creative efforts of these contemporary composers. In addition, the works of these creative artists would help the community and its satellites become sensitive to contemporary music and its several idioms.

Without going into detail regarding subsequent meetings and seminars, the actual outcome of the comprehensive musicianship concept was a consensus that courses should no longer be taught in isolation and fragmented fashion. Music students would have to learn in the course of their study of music the relationships that exist between all of the music courses studied. To do this they would need to have competency in *analyzing* music, *organizing* the sounds of music, and *performing* music. It was the basic concept of the proponents of comprehensive musicianship that students who could exhibit competencies in these three areas would then be properly equipped to deal with all forms of music, regardless of their type.

In the final analysis the comprehensive musicianship program was designed to improve the quality of instruction in school music programs.

Too often school programs that were essentially performance-oriented did little to increase the knowledge of music and the musicality of the individual student. Most of the instruction was devoted to responding to the symbols on the printed page. It was in this context that comprehensive musicianship became a significant force designed to improve all areas of music education, not just in performance organizations but in general music classes as well. It focused on the need for all students exposed to musical experiences to be able to perform, analyze, and organize sounds.

Music Education for the Handicapped

In 1975 Public Law No. 94-142 was passed by the Congress. The law provided the opportunity and right for all handicapped children to receive free, "appropriate" public education. The impact on music education was outlined in *Public Laws and the 94th Congress*, 1st Session, Vol. 89, p. 773, which states: "The use of the musical arts has long been recognized as a viable, effective teaching tool for the handicapped as well as a way of reaching youngsters who had otherwise been unteachable." The section called "Program Options" continues: "Each school system shall take steps to ensure that its handicapped children have available to them the same variety of educational programs and services available to non-handicapped children served by the school including art, music, industrial arts, [and] consumer and vocational education" (p. 774). The law makes it incumbent upon every music education program to provide music experiences for handicapped children, regardless of the nature of their handicap, and to include them in programs for the nonhandicapped students.

In the ensuing years two approaches, mainstreaming and individualized instruction, were explored to help resolve the difficulties created by this new demand for providing music instruction to handicapped children. "Mainstreaming" became a popular term. Unfortunately, it created a great deal of misunderstanding, concern, and general confusion. Too many people think that the "special child" has to be mainstreamed into *all* classes, which is not true. What is expected is that music teachers assign students to classes under the mainstreaming provision *when appropriate*. Handicapped children are expected to be given opportunities to participate in musical activities that allow them to function, particularly in the areas that are useful to their development as children. However, where this cannot be utilized, individualized instruction is an acceptable alternative.

What the law intends is that handicapped children should be given opportunities to participate in such activities as singing, listening, reading music, playing musical instruments, making large bodily movements, and generally developing behaviors that contribute to their growth and development. The law never intended that handicapped children be placed in situations where it would be impossible for them to function or in which they would prevent the other students from learning. The individualized educational program is designed to help students develop in personal situations, in which the goals are concomitant with those goals that contribute to the development of all children.

Children with minimal handicaps can be included in music classes. However, those with serious learning disabilities or emotional disturbances, and those with major physical handicaps, should be treated on an individual basis. What the law states in concept is that handicapped children are to be educated with nonhandicapped children *whenever possible or feasible*, thus opening the possibility for individualized educational programs when it is in the best interest of the students.

Discipline-Based Music Education

In the 1980s a program identified as Discipline-Based Art Education (DBAE) evolved in the visual arts with support from the Getty Center for Education in the Arts. This project met with sufficient success to warrant the Getty Foundation's expanding its support into music education and developing a comparable approach for music (Discipline-Based Music Education).

The goal of DBME is to develop students' capabilities in understanding and appreciating music. It involves not only theories and contexts of music but also includes the ability to respond as well as to compose music. The four disciplines that serve as the basis for content in this program are: (a) understanding the nature of music (aesthetics); (b) criticism, or establishing a basis for judging and valuing music; (c) contexts in which music is composed (history); and (d) processes and techniques for composing and performing music. The music utilized in the program covers every facet of musical cultures and expression—Western and non-Western, from ancient to contemporary times.

The aim of DBME is to develop mature students who are able to express their ideas through the various music media and are comfortable with the major aspects of the disciplines of music. (At this writing it is too early to determine the success of this program.) As mature adults, students should possess the ability to criticize music, be aware of the historical context of music, and possess a basic understanding of issues involving aesthetics. As its goal, DBME seeks to develop educated persons who will be capable of discriminating between simplistic or insincere expressions of musical arts and those that represent the high desirable standards of lasting musical value. It is the program's contention that when individuals become intelligent consumers who demand high standards, the end result should be higher standards of artistic production.

Music in Early Childhood Education

In today's society, with the increasing number of both parents and single parents of children between the ages of two and five being employed, it has become necessary for many children to be placed in some form of preschool situation. Unless these "schools" have personnel with some form of music training, little is done in the way of teaching music. Yet, it is universally agreed that music and musical experiences, particularly at this age, should be a regular daily activity in every preschool, day and family care center, and Head Start program. Young children in this age group respond to music in a natural, uninhibited manner, which makes musical activities extremely important to a child's development during these years.

Edwin Gordon has stated that whatever is learned in the early years of a child's life helps form the foundation for subsequent educational development. Furthermore, unless the child "has favorable early informal and formal environmental experiences with music, that level of music aptitude will never be realized in achievement" (Gordon, 1987, p. 8).

The implication in Gordon's research is that the quality of musical experiences offered at the preschool level will ultimately have an effect on the musical development of the maturing child. Thus, experiences in early childhood music can and should create a foundation upon which future learning can be built.

To implement programs that will accommodate this developmental need, the Music Educators National Conferences in its "Statement of Beliefs" has recommended the following:

45. The Music Educators National Conference believes that music should be an integral part of every preschool, kindergarten, day-care, and early intervention program. Every child should have an opportunity each day to hear, explore, and perform music.

46. The Music Educators National Conference believes that at least 12 percent of the contact time with children in every center for early childhood education should be devoted to the teaching of music.

47. The Music Educators National Conference believes that at least one staff member in every center for early childhood education should have received formal training in music, and that a music specialist qualified in early childhood education should be retained as a consultant.

48. The Music Educators National Conference believes that every center for early childhood education should have a "music corner" or similar area where children have easy access to music materials. (Music Educators National Conference, 1991, p. 3)

In its "Position Statement on Early Childhood Education," MENC has stated:

Music education for young children involves a developmentally appropriate program of singing, moving, listening, creating, playing instruments, and responding to visual and verbal representations of sound. The content of such a program should represent music of various cultures in time and place. Time should be made available during the day for activities in which music is the primary focus of attention for its own value. It may also serve as a means for teachers to facilitate the accomplishment of nonmusical goals. (Music Educators National Conference, 1992, p. 21)

Performing and Performances

For the applied musician, performing is both the end and the means. However, for school students performing should be the means, with the learning of music the ultimate goal. Unfortunately, because of the visibility and prestige that can be realized through performances, educators frequently confuse ends with means in this matter. Furthermore, if a teacher's ego becomes inordinately involved with performance and the acclaim that is received from it, this form of ego gratification can interfere with the essential satisfaction that a teacher should derive from nurturing musical growth in students.

In addition, there is some confusion regarding the term "performing." One cannot have a musical experience without a performance of music of some type. In music classes students will learn facts about and gain insight into music. However, a musical experience does not occur until the learner actually hears the music and applies the acquired knowledge and insight to his or her perceptions and reactions. In a listening portion of a class, the vehicle for a musical experience may be a performance on a record. In a large ensemble it may be the actual rehearsal of the music. In either case the end is the same: musical understanding that provides added enjoyment. Music educators should still be striving for the overall objectives of musical literacy and aesthetic development regardless of whether the class is a general music or a performing organization.

Much of the distortion of performance objectives has occurred as a result of the music contest system. When contests were first introduced into music education, they were designed as motivation for students and as a way of raising the standards of performing groups. It was never intended that they become the main goal for music performing classes. If contests are to continue, it may be more appropriate for students to take an examination in which they analyze the music performed, answer questions about general music knowledge, and do some sight-reading, as well as performing prepared literature.

In a situation in which performance becomes the end rather than the means, the emphasis shifts from learning to the gratification of the audience and performer(s). It is true that some learning occurs in all situations, but the attention is focused on pleasing an audience, not on meeting the needs of learners. The instruction is geared not to what the students will derive from the performance, but rather to what the performance will do for the organization and its director, with only side benefits for learners. This distortion of instruction has been of questionable value in music education. When it is brought up among music teachers, the misconception sometimes is "Shouldn't we have performance in music?" Of course there must be performance; one cannot have music without it! However, what educators should be concerned about in music education is the knowledge that students acquire after spending a period of time in their organizations and not just technical skill. Performance-oriented organizations can provide that knowledge if they take the time and effort to offer the proper quality of instruction.

A performing group should regard itself as a class that utilizes performance as a means of education for musical literacy and musical enjoyment. It should be committed to concern for cognitive information, such as definitions of musical idioms, as well as aesthetic and affective reactions to music. The "ideal" performing group would be involved in developing aesthetic judgment and analysis, and stimulating the creative process. It is in this manner that a school music program can develop literacy and competency extending beyond the limits of just performance or contests.

Music educators are often seduced by parental approval, but they forget that it is extremely difficult for any parent to disapprove of something that gives his or her child visibility and satisfaction. It is incumbent on the music educator to maintain the appropriate balance in the learning process. Where abuses occur, it is generally the result of distorted standards and misunderstood objectives on the part of the music educator. The success of music education in the schools of the United States is testimony to the fact that such abuses are in the minority. Most music educators are sensitive to the needs of learners and provide activities that offer an education in music.

Electronic Instruments in Curriculum Development

One of the innovative developments in recent years has been the use of electronic instruments in organizing curriculum programs and implementing instruction. A unique program demonstrating this development was created by the Yamaha Corporation and the Yamaha Music Foundation. Darrell Bailey, director of the music department at the Indiana University School of Music's Indiana-Purdue Campus in Indianapolis and a consultant for Yamaha, stated that the purpose of the courses in the Yamaha program is to develop well-rounded musicianship that includes understanding music through composition, improvisation, and performance. It is geared for adults as well as children.

There are three basic parts of the program: the Yamaha Music Education System (YMES), Keyboard Encounters, and Music in Education (MIE).

YMES is composed of two distinct courses for students eight-years-old to adult. The standard course is for hobbyist players, and the contemporary course focuses on contemporary sounds. Student instruction is delivered on an Electone keyboard, an instrument similar to an organ that utilizes "sampled" sounds and orchestral timbres activated by keyboard, pedal notes, and presets. YMES educational support materials, including aptitude and achievement tests for measuring musical skills as well as graded textbooks, augment the curriculum. However, the bulk of instruction is prepared from teachers' planning guides, which emphasize ear training, rhythm, solfège, movement, and improvisation activities.

Keyboard Encounters is a new group piano course for students ages ten to adult. It covers many musical styles, including popular, classical, jazz, and country. In addition, it provides students with a knowledge of music notation and theory. Other activities included are ear training, improvisation, and ensemble playing. Supplemental materials include textbooks and computer software, which enable the teacher to individualize instruction within the group class setting.

The Music in Education program is fundamentally a technology-assisted general music classroom. MIE is a multiyear, conceptually-based, sequential curriculum, designed in an upward spiral using one concept from one module to learn the next. Students work in cooperative "duo" group arrangements. Singing and movement are also incorporated. An assessment component in every module can be provided as hard-copy printed format to an instructor.

The Yamaha program is mentioned here as an example of recent developments that are occurring in the use of electronic instruments in curriculum development.

Summary

Philosophical and educational beliefs affect how curriculum and subject matter are approached. Four perspectives or philosophical positions describing the curriculum are: ideal, formal, instructional, and operational. They are all affected by variables such as goals and objectives, materials, content, learning activities, teaching strategies, evaluation, grouping, time, and space. Qualitative factors impinging on the curriculum are: description, decision making, rationale, priorities, attitudes, appropriateness, comprehensiveness, individualization, and barriers and facilitators (factors that obstruct and factors that make things smoother).

Curriculum guides serve such functions as: providing a source of information, aiding in-service training, helping public relations, stating the school's philosophy in music education, and establishing the basic core of a program. Guides should be developed cooperatively by teachers, with representation from the school administration and community. It is advisable to prepare a field-trial edition before assembling the final product. However, like a curriculum, guides should never be considered fixed. A course of study is more specific. It should designate the sequence of a specific course, provide helpful teaching procedures, and suggest specific subject-matter content.

The aim of a school music program is to develop music literacy and music intelligence. The materials utilized in this process should emphasize music as an art form rather than music that is ephemeral. Those who plan and work with the curriculum need to observe this tenet.

Because one cannot cover even a small portion of what could be included in a music course, curriculum planners need to make choices and establish priorities. The following guidelines are useful: Content should be educational, be valid, cover fundamental knowledge, be representative, include contemporary material, be relevant, and be learnable by the students.

Aesthetic education in music received much attention in the early 1960s and may have been a reaction to the attention given to the sciences after the Russian success with *Sputnik*. Another development that occurred in the late 1960s and 1970s was the arts-in-education movement, which was a related-arts approach. The arts-in-education movement received much support from the John D. Rockefeller III Fund.

In 1959 the Ford Foundation initiated the Contemporary Music Project, headed by Norman Dello Joio. It was soon discovered that school-teachers were not sufficiently equipped to teach contemporary idioms, so the project shifted its emphasis in 1963 to "comprehensive musicianship." The purpose of this program was to develop a college curriculum that would enable teachers to deal with all types of music. To do this future teachers needed to be able to analyze, perform, and organize sounds.

In 1975 the Congress passed Public Law No. 94-142, which stated that "each school system shall take steps to ensure that its handicapped children have available to them the same variety of educational programs and services available to non-handicapped children served by the school including art, [and] music." To accomplish the purpose of the law, schools employed two approaches, mainstreaming and individualized instruction.

In the late 1980s, based on the success achieved by its Discipline-Based Art Education program, the Getty Center for Education in the Arts expanded its programs to include Discipline-Based Music Education. The program focused on four areas: aesthetics, criticism, context of a music period, and performance.

The 1980s also saw a surge of interest and a proliferation of preschool programs. Research had established that early experiences with music increased the achievement level of a child's musical aptitude. As a result, music educators supported and initiated many of these programs.

Performance alone is insufficient in an educational setting. The ultimate goal for students in performing should be learning about music.

One of the more recent developments in curriculum programs and instruction has been the use of electronic instruments. The Yamaha program, an example of the use of electronic instruments, emphasizes music development in training its participants.

STUDY AND DISCUSSION QUESTIONS

1. What is the "operational" curriculum? An "ideal" curriculum? the "formal" curriculum? The "instructional" curriculum?

2. (a) What are the uses of a curriculum guide?

   (b) How does a "course of study" generally differ from a curriculum guide?

3. What are some reasons for a school to have a planned sequence of music instruction—a program—for a number of grade levels or classes?

4. If the music curriculum is analogous to a tree, what is the trunk of the tree? Why? What are some of the twigs? Why aren't they limbs or branches?

5. What are the three philosophical models that one may use in structuring a curriculum? How do they differ from each other in emphasis?

6. (a) What fundamental things should students learn—at least to some extent—in all music classes?

   (b) Are any of these aspects more important than others? Why or why not?

7. (a) What are the characteristics of a good curriculum guide?

   (b) How should curriculum guides be developed?

8. What were the two major projects in the late 1960s and early 1970s involving music educators in relating the other arts to music? What results were achieved by these projects?

9. What is Public Law No. 94-142? What implications and directives does it have for music education?

10. (a) What is the concept of "comprehensive musicianship"?

    (b) What practical actions did the advocates of this concept attempt to achieve?

11. Why isn't performance a sufficient end to justify maintaining school music programs?

12. How have music contests worked against the proper use of performance in music education?

13. What are the justifications for the use of music in early childhood programs?

14. What meaning do the four descriptive areas of Discipline-Based Music Education (DBME) have in terms of music terminology? How are they applied to music learning?

INDIVIDUAL OR CLASS ACTIVITIES

1. Select two curriculum guides, one elementary and the other for a secondary music activity, and examine them for the following:

    (a) Do they reflect a philosophy of music education? If so, what is it?

    (b) Is there a defined scope and sequence that leads to the acquisition of specific competencies? Discuss how this is accomplished.

    (c) Review the general format of each and how it complies with issues raised in this chapter.

2. Discuss how comprehensive musicianship may be utilized in the following: private studio, theory class, conducting class.

SUPPLEMENTARY READINGS

ANDRESS, B. (1980). *Music experiences in early childhood.* New York: Rinehart and Winston.

ANDRESS, B. (1989). *Promising practices: Prekindergarten music education.* Reston, VA: Music Educators National Conference.

BOSWELL, J. (Ed.). (1987). *The young child and music: Contemporary principles in child development and music education. Proceedings of the Music in Early Childhood Conference.* Reston, VA: Music Educators National Conference.

EISNER, E. W. (1990). *The role of discipline-based art education in America's schools.* Los Angeles: Getty Center for Education in the Arts.

FEIERABEND, J. M. (Comp.). (1990). *TIPS: Music activities in early childhood.* Reston, VA: Music Educators National Conference.

LEVINOURTZ, L. M. (1991). *Music in early childhood: A research journal*. Princeton, NJ: Sengstack Educational Foundation.

MADEJA, S. S. (Ed.). (1978). *The arts, cognition, and basic skills*. St. Louis: CEM-REL.

MCDONALD, D. T., & SIMONS, G. M. (1989). *Musical growth and development*. New York: Schirmer.

MOOMAW, S. (1984). *Discovering music in early childhood*. Newton, MA: Allyn and Bacon.

MUSIC EDUCATORS NATIONAL CONFERENCE. (1992, Winter). MENC position statement on early childhood. *Soundpost*, p. 21.

NYE, V. T. (1983). *Music for young children* (3rd ed.). Dubuque, IA: Wm. C. Brown.

ROCKEFELLER, D., JR. (Chair). (1977). *Coming to our senses: the significance of the arts for American education*. New York: McGraw-Hill.

SCHWADRON, A. A. (1965). *Comprehensive musicianship: the foundation for college education in music*. Reston, VA: Music Educators National Conference.

SCHWADRON, A. A. (1982). *Aesthetics: dimensions for music education* (2d ed.). Wakefield, NH: Longwood.

REFERENCES

ANDERSON, W. M., & CAMPBELL, P. S. (1989). *Multicultural perspectives in music education*. Reston, VA: Music Educators National Conference.

GORDON, E. E. (1987). *The nature, description, measurement, and evaluation of music aptitudes*. Chicago: G.I.A.

HOFFER, C. R. (1991). *Teaching music in the secondary schools* (4th ed.). Belmont, CA: Wadsworth.

JORDAN, JOYCE. Multicultural music education in a pluralistic society. (1992). In *Handbook of Research on Music Teaching and Learning* (pp. 735–48). New York: Schirmer Books.

KLEIN, M. F., TYE, K. A., & WRIGHT, J. E. (1979, December). A study of schooling: curriculum. *Phi Delta Kappan* (p. 472). Reprinted with permission © 1979, Phi Delta Kappa, Inc.

MACHLIS, J. (1977). *The enjoyment of music: An introduction to perceptive listening*. New York: W.W. Norton.

MALLOY, L. The case for accessibility. (1977). Pamphlet. Excerpted from *Museum News*. Washington DC: American Association of Museums.

MUELLER, J. H. (1958). *The American symphony orchestra: A social history of musical taste*. London: Calder.

MUSIC EDUCATORS NATIONAL CONFERENCE. (1986, orig. pub. 1974). *The school music program: description and standards* (2d ed.). Reston, VA: Author.

MUSIC EDUCATORS NATIONAL CONFERENCE. (1991, May). In Statement of beliefs. *Issues in Music Education* (p. 1). Reston, VA: Author.

MUSIC EDUCATORS NATIONAL CONFERENCE. MENC position statement on early childhood education. (1992, Winter). *Soundpost* (p. 21). Reston, VA: Author.

PUBLIC LAWS AND THE 94TH CONGRESS, 1ST SESSION, VOL. 89 (1977). In *United States statutes at large: Vol. 89* (p. 773). Washington, DC: U.S. Government Printing Office.

10

Assessing Musical Behaviors

THE ASSESSMENT AND evaluation of students' success in accomplishing the objectives of the music curriculum are prerequisites for any effective music program. There is a need to determine students' achievement and to gather feedback about the effectiveness of the teaching and instructional materials, as well as to identify areas in which students may need additional instruction. To be effective, teachers must assess to determine what their students have learned. Without this information, teachers do not have ways of improving their own teaching or identifying and helping students who need additional assistance.

Assessment strategies are very much intertwined with approaches to instruction; how something is taught and how it is assessed are two sides of the same coin. Teachers whose instruction is guided by sequences of behaviorally oriented objectives will employ assessment strategies that directly measure those objectives. Teachers who approach instruction with outcomes for their students stated in other ways must employ different types of assessment to determine the results of instruction.

Instructional decisions should dictate assessment strategies rather than vice versa. Teachers should not be motivated to "teach to" tests. Instead, assessment should be designed to reflect the goals of curriculum.

Assessment includes both measurement and evaluation. It is broadly used to refer to both the formal and informal determination of educational achievement. Teachers informally assess students' learning daily as they listen to students' questions and comments, and correct student performances and written assignments. The band director who recommends that a student "play that section again with 'lighter tonguing,' " illustrates the informal assessment that takes place in the music classroom. When teachers change their teaching behavior (for example, changing the organization of rehearsals, or the length and difficulty of practice assignments) based on this informal information, they should supplement this informal monitoring with measures that assess student achievement in a more systematic way. Periodic formal assessments of the objectives of the music curriculum allow teachers to reflect systematically on student progress and the effectiveness of instruction.

Evaluation includes both measuring and judging the outcomes of instruction. The word measurement implies quantifying characteristics through the assignment of numbers to a certain level of behavior; e.g., scores on a test. Evaluation includes both quantitative and qualitative descriptions of characteristics, as well as value judgments of the behavior described. Assigning a term grade to students based on their performance test scores and the quality of their preparation for lessons is an example of evaluation. Individuals as well as entire programs can be evaluated. Both measurement and evaluation as part of assessment are discussed in this chapter.

Most of the more important outcomes of music instruction are not easily measured. During the last three decades, music educators have focused considerable attention on the problems of measuring the outcomes of music instruction. Both traditional and unique approaches to assessment have been considered. The existence of several books, hundreds of articles and convention sessions, newsletters, and special interest groups of researchers who conduct studies on assessing the outcomes of music education provides ample evidence of the importance of this area to music educators.

However, music education as practiced in the schools has changed little as a result of this activity. Few music teachers consider assessment as they plan their instruction. When assessment does occur it is likely to be motivated by an administrative requirement like the assigning of grades. In such circumstances music teachers tend to turn to testing strategies with which they are most familiar, such as the typical "paper-and-pencil" test. Assessments like these are unlikely to get at the most important outcomes of music instruction. Music teachers must spend time thinking about what the most important outcomes of music instruction are, and plan their instruction and assessment strategies accordingly. Rather than focusing on the superficial and easily measured behaviors (e.g., key signatures, names of composers), music teachers must remember that performance skill, musical interpretation, attitudes, and critical thinking can all be measured. Alternative strategies that attempt to integrate music instruction and assessment in meaningful ways may provide better models for music teachers.

Some Measurement Theory

How does a teacher get an accurate assessment of a musical behavior? The question of the accuracy of measuring instruments has been and continues to be an important focus of measurement theorists. The major question revolves around the problem of knowing if the numerical value one has assigned to the behavior being sampled in a test accurately represents the level of musical knowledge or skill one is trying to assess.

Measurement theorists have attempted to explore this problem by representing the measurement situation with the following model:

$$X = T + E$$

Where X represents the raw score or the score obtained by the student on the test, T represents the true score or the actual level of the trait in the student, and E represents sources of error in the measurement process.

What types of error are likely to exist in a measurement situation? They can include transient characteristics of the student such as apprehension, fatigue, and level of motivation. They can be characteristics of the testing environment such as room temperature, noise, and the amount of padding on the desk chair seat. They can be characteristics of the test itself such as the ambiguity of the test directions or items, and the amount of time provided to complete the test. Lucky guesses or marking the wrong box on the answer sheet are also possible sources of error.

With almost an infinite number of possible sources of error, many of which cannot be controlled, the goal of accurate measurement would seem unobtainable. But measurement theorists have provided a solution. It is based on the assumption that errors that inflate the raw score are just as likely to occur as errors that make the raw score lower. If this is true, theorists suggest, several measurements are needed. The average of those measures will accurately represent the trait being measured because the *average* of the measurement errors will equal zero. The presence of the error factor still reinforces the need for assessment to be well integrated with instruction, however.

It is likely that any performing musician will be able to appreciate the following situation: After having initially learned a piece, musicians spend long hours practicing the piece. Some of these renditions are nearly perfect, while others are characterized by wrong notes, inaccurate rhythms, and less than ideal tone quality. By the time the recital or audition arrives, most musicians have developed a relatively consistent performance. The actual performance during the recital or audition is likely to be within a rather small range of quality, but can represent extremes of that range due to a variety of factors such as stage fright; that is, the performance itself can contain sources of error. A truer perspective of a performer's ability would be obtained by having the individual play the piece three times instead of once, although an increase in anxiety on the part of the performer and fatigue by the judge might be new sources of error. For this reason, music students should be given many opportunities to perform before judgment is passed on their level of development.

Reliability

The concept of reliability focuses on the consistency and stability of a test or scale. If a test of music ability produced a score of 85 for one student during one month, and a score of 35 the next month for the same student, the stability of the test and the student's performance are questionable. If a trait or behavior (for instance, the performance of a particularly difficult passage) is inconsistent, the reliability for measures of the trait tends to be lower, reflecting this inconsistency. If, for example, a performer were to record five different performances and have each one independently judged by adjudicators, fluctuations in the results could be attributed to the actual differences in the performance. They also could be attributed to inconsistency in the judges' scoring. On the other hand if a single performance was mechanically reproduced five times, adjudication differences in assessing each recording would be due solely to the judges' inconsistency. The use of the term "reliability" by measurement specialists is best illustrated by the second example, the one in which the measurement instrument, in this case "judges," is inconsistent.

When measurements are consistent over several data collections, they are said to have high reliability. Reliable scores for an individual from multiple administrations of a test tend to cluster around a central point, which is the individual's true score.

There are several different ways of estimating reliability, and each is concerned with assessing a different type of stability. Consistency over a period of time can be reported by *test-retest reliability*. To determine this type of reliability, the teacher or researcher might administer the same test twice (the second testing one week after the first) and the scores for both administrations compared. *Equivalent-form reliability* assesses whether multiple forms of the same test are interchangeable. This type of reliability can be determined by administering the different forms of a test to the same students and then comparing the results. A third type of reliability, called *internal consistency*, attempts to answer the question "Are the items on the test homogeneous? (i.e., do the items measure the same area of content?)" This type is widely reported, probably because it is the least cumbersome to determine. Although it is probably desirable to have an index for each of these three types of reliability for a test, the type of test being evaluated often dictates the type or types of reliability procedures reported.

As stated earlier, reliable scores from several tests will cluster around an individual's true score. The *standard error of measurement* (SEM), a statistic related to reliability, provides the teacher with a range within which the student's true score is likely to fall. As the reliability of a test increases, the SEM decreases; that is, for tests with high reliability the raw scores cluster more closely around the true score.

A type of reliability that plays an important role in the measurement of many musical behaviors is that of *interjudge reliability*. Interjudge reliability provides an indication of the degree of agreement among a group of judges. It is particularly important in the assessment of music performance, because it provides an index of the amount of subjectivity present in an adjudication panel. For example, if three judges are independently assessing the performance of five clarinetists, they may be asked to use a rating form to assist in rank-ordering the five performances. If their three rank-orders show substantial agreement, the form is said to have high interjudge reliability; if their orders show substantial disagreement, the form is said to have low interjudge reliability. Most investigations of the reliability of judges assessing music performances indicate that considerable agreement is present in these evaluations, although many musicians willingly relate personal experiences that seem to contradict these findings.

Validity

A good test measures the trait it claims to measure. This notion, a form of "truth in packaging," is referred to as *validity*. There are several ways to test for validity. In some cases the items on the test are compared with the content covered during the instruction, while at other times the test results are compared with the results of other tests purporting to measure the same trait. Validation strategies are generally classified into three categories: *content validity, criterion-related validity*, and *construct validity*.

Content validity is concerned with ensuring that the test covers the material taught in the class. It is determined primarily by comparing lesson plans or course outlines with the test items. In addition to ensuring that all the material covered is tested, content validity helps ensure that a test does not measure concepts not taught. Content validation should also ensure that the distribution of items on a test approximates the emphasis of the instruction. A table depicting each of the content areas covered by the instructional material and the items on the test measuring each area can help determine if a test has content validity. It is frequently the most important type of validity for achievement tests, both those used to test progress during a course and the standardized achievement tests that may be used to enable educators to compare the performance of their students with students in other communities.

Criterion-related validity compares the student scores on the test being validated with another measure of the same trait, typically other tests. It is usually mathematical in nature, with the index typically reported being a correlation coefficient between the test and the criterion. There are two subcategories of criterion-related validity that distinguish—on a temporal basis—different criteria. If the scores on the test being validated are to replace the scores of the criterion, the strategy is referred to as *concurrent criterion-related validity*. If the scores on the test being validated are to predict some future criterion, like success in college, then the strategy is referred to as *predictive criterion-related validity*.

Strategies for determining concurrent criterion-related validity can include comparing the results of a new test and a previously developed test that is generally accepted as a measure of the same trait. If the distribution of scores on both tests is approximately the same, the new test is said to be valid. Predictive criterion-related validity can be determined by administering the new test to students who already exhibit the behavior to be predicted. For example, a test designed to predict the success of high school musicians in college music theory classes could be administered to students already enrolled in such classes. The college students' performance on the test might then be compared with their grades in music theory to determine how well the test predicted such a criterion.

Criteria used in determining test validity can include a variety of measures other than additional tests: for example, grades. One criterion used often to validate music tests is teacher estimates of a trait such as music ability. Developers of music aptitude tests have frequently asked teachers (sometimes music teachers but frequently classroom teachers) to provide rankings of their students' musical ability, which are then used to establish the validity of the test. It should be noted that such estimates are likely to be less reliable and less valid, because music teachers and classroom teachers seldom have training or experience in systematically conducting such assessments.

While both content and criterion-related validity have specific practical uses, *construct validity* stresses the theoretical value of the test. Construct validity examines the extent to which a psychological construct is reflected in the results of a test. Psychological constructs are general notions not limited to a particular test result. Examples of constructs include intelligence, creativity, and music aptitude. Thus, if a score on a test of music aptitude can account for the psychological quality labeled "music aptitude," the test is said to have construct validity.

To determine construct validity, test developers typically seek out hypotheses regarding the construct in question. In the case of music aptitude, it has been suggested by some previous research that music aptitude has a low but positive relationship with intelligence. Other research suggests that members of music performing groups have a higher average of music aptitude than nonmembers. The developer of a music aptitude test who wishes to support the use of the test's scores as an indication of music aptitude might administer both the new test and a test of general intelligence to a group of students and examine the results in light of what previous research predicts. If a low positive correlation between the two measures results, the proposition that the new test is a measure of music aptitude would be supported. If the results do not parallel the predicted outcome, the test developer may conclude that the test is not a valid measure of the construct or that the previous research is erroneous.

The Relationship of Reliability and Validity

Reliability and validity are not fully independent measures of a test's value. If a test produces inconsistent results—that is, if it is not reliable—it cannot possibly be valid. Therefore, reliability is a necessary characteristic of a valid test.

Although a necessary component of validity, reliability alone is not a sufficient attribute of a valid test. Tests can be reliable without being valid. A test that examines the ability of a student to discriminate between the loudness of electronically produced sine waves presented sequentially to the right and left ear may be a very stable measure of the amount of hearing loss, but it is not likely to be a good indicator of a student's potential as a timpanist.

Types of Tests

Two factors should influence the selection of the type of assessment tool to measure a musical behavior: (1) the type of behavior being measured; and (2) the use to be made of the measurement results.

Music teachers concerned with assessing the outcomes of instruction develop *teacher-made achievement tests*. Tests that measure the present level of mastery of certain skills or understandings, usually as a result of instruction, are called *achievement tests*. Such tests are used by teachers to assess in a systematic way the progress of individuals in a class and to help determine the effectiveness of various modes of instruction. In most cases these tests are constructed by the course instructor and administered only to students enrolled in that particular class; thus they are labeled "teacher-made."

Occasionally music teachers or administrators may wish to compare the skill levels of students in their class, school, or school system with those of students across the country. *Standardized achievement tests* have been developed for this purpose. These tests are developed systematically by both content and measurement experts, who refine the tests so they are likely to be both reliable and valid. Such tests attempt to measure more universal outcomes of instruction than those developed by a particular instructor. Standardized tests provide the results of previous administrations of the test in the form of test *norms*, so that individual teachers or administrators can compare their students' performance with an appropriate reference group. When selecting a standardized achievement test, teachers and administrators should be careful to determine if the expected outcomes of instruction in their music classes are similar to the content measured on the test. Good standardized achievement tests provide a detailed description of the test's content validity.

While achievement tests focus on assessing current levels of mastery, *aptitude tests* attempt to predict future achievement by assessing innate capacities, as well as informal environmental factors. Such tests, of necessity, are standardized. Aptitude tests may be either general (attempting to measure a broad range of ability) or specific (measuring potential for a specific area such as mechanical or musical ability). While tests of general aptitude are frequently employed by educators to help provide guidance to students and teachers, the administration of specialized aptitude tests, like those measuring music aptitude, is less common. Because testing is a waste of time unless some use is to be made of the results, the absence of music aptitude testing from many school testing programs is probably appropriate. Few music educators seem to view the systematic identification of students with high musical potential through testing as an important activity. Current achievement is often the best predictor of future potential, so the tradition of identifying students with music potential through the demonstration of a high level of performing skill at a young age may continue to be the most widely employed means of identifying musically talented students.

A third type of standardized measuring instrument is the *preference inventory*. Inventories such as the *Strong Vocational Interest Blank* (1966) are used primarily by counselors to assist students, usually in high school, to identify possible vocational choices. These inventories provide students with the opportunity to examine their interests, including their interest in music, in a systematic way.

The use of standardized achievement tests for comparison purposes among schools and school districts is a widespread practice, and there are those in the government and education who promote the development of national standardized achievement tests similar to those that exist in other countries. This view seems to have had little impact on music programs. Although comparisons are made typically on reading and mathematics achievement and sometimes on science and social studies, music and the other arts are rarely if ever included in these comparisons.

There are several publications that provide detailed descriptions and reviews of standardized music tests (George, 1980; Boyle & Radocy, 1987; Boyle, 1992). Brief summaries of a few selected tests follow.

Music Aptitude Tests

Music aptitude tests comprise the largest portion of standardized music tests, but there are only a few music aptitude tests currently in print. Two of these have been developed by Edwin Gordon.

The *Musical Aptitude Profile* (MAP) was developed by Gordon and was published in 1965. It was designed to be used with students from grades 4 through 12. The test is divided into three main sections (each of which is further divided into subsections): tonal imagery (melody and harmony), rhythm imagery (tempo and meter), and musical sensitivity (phrasing, balance, and style).

The test material differs in several ways from previous tests. Rather than isolated pitches produced by oscillators, the stimuli for the MAP are musical phrases played on the violin and cello. In the first two sections, students are asked to indicate whether two phrases are the same or different. Differences in the phrases are due to the manipulation of a single dimension of music, such as tempo. The music sensitivity section requires indications of preference for a selection in pairs of phrases.

The MAP reports relatively high internal consistency reliability coefficients for its subtests. Predictive criterion-related validity for the test is reported for teachers' ratings, judges' ratings of students' instrumental performances, and musical achievement test scores.

One disadvantage of the test is the time required for administration. Each of the three sections requires approximately an hour to administer, and the manual recommends that the sections be given on three separate days within the same week. Administration of the test requires a test manual, tape, and answer sheets. The test has been the focus of numerous research studies and seems to have been generally accepted by the music education research community today as *the* measure of music aptitude.

Gordon (1979) also developed a music aptitude test for children in kindergarten through third grade, the *Primary Measures of Music Audiation* (PMMA). The two subtests require students to make same/different judgments on forty sets of "tonal stimuli" and forty pairs of "rhythm stimuli." Gordon has coined the word "audiation" for the skill required to make these judgments. It basically involves short-term music memory, which is the ability in this instance to recall the first stimuli in the pair while listening to the second in order to make the comparison.

The musical material for both the tonal and rhythm tests of the PMMA are produced with electronically synthesized tones. The tonal test contains short melodies comprised of tones of equal duration. The rhythm test examples are comprised of tones of the same frequency. The answer form employed contains pairs of similar (two smiling) and different (one smiling and one frowning) faces; the children must circle one pair of faces. Examples are provided to help the student understand the task.

Gordon reports strong (around r = .90) internal consistency reliability for the PMMA and somewhat lower (around r = .75) test-retest reliability. This lower test-retest reliability is not surprising given the age of the children. The validity of the PMMA is based on its low correlations with tests of academic achievement and intelligence and its stronger correlations with fourth grade students' MAP scores. The manual is quite complete and provides norm information for the appropriate age students. Although the test has not been as thoroughly researched as the MAP, it appears to assess effectively young children's ability to make these types of aural discriminations.

Music Achievement Tests

While considerable interest over the past six decades has been demonstrated in the measurement of music aptitude, there has been much less interest (and consequently very few tests are available) in assessing music achievement in a comprehensive way. Most of the work on developing standardized tests of music achievement has taken place since 1960.

The *Music Achievement Test* (MAT), developed by Richard Colwell in 1969, is probably the most widely used standardized test of music achievement. The test was developed to help music teachers assess a student's level of mastery of the basic objectives of the school music program.

The test is composed of four different subtests, each of which is further divided into three or four subtests. Test 1 provides information on three musical skills—pitch discrimination, interval discrimination, and meter discrimination—and does not require music-reading skill. Test 2, which also assesses three musical skills—major-minor mode discrimination, feeling for tonal center, and auditory-visual discrimination—requires some knowledge of basic music concepts but is still primarily focused on aural skills. One section of test 3, pitch recognition, requires music-reading skill, while the other two sections, tonal melody and melody recognition, do not. Test 4 is divided into four subsections: musical style, auditory-visual discrimination, chord recognition, and cadence recognition. The music examples are mostly performed on the piano, violin, viola, and cello, and the responses are in a multiple-choice format.

The reliability coefficients reported from various sources have fluctuated but are generally thought to be acceptable. The validity reported for the test has been primarily content validity, as is appropriate for achievement measures. The items on the test were based on an examination of several leading music textbook series and curriculum guides. Several conferences of music supervisors and teachers were also held during the test development to further ensure content validity. The appropriateness of the MAT for a particular school or school system ultimately depends on the correspondence of the objectives of the school and the skills measured by the test.

The test is available on records and has an interpretive manual that provides norms for geographical area, type of teacher, size of community, and grade level.

Traditional Approaches to Assessing Classroom Music Achievement

The first question a music teacher must answer when faced with the need to assess the outcomes of instruction is "What do I want to assess?" If the objectives of the instructional program have been carefully stated in behavioral terms, the development of a test to measure program outcomes relies only on the application of various assessment strategies. It is a matter of "If you don't know where you are going, you can't know when you get there."

The discussion of measurement strategies that follows is based on the assumption that objectives for the instruction material have been clearly stated, a point discussed in chapter 8.

Measuring Cognitive Outcomes of Instruction

There are two major strategies for measuring the cognitive outcomes of music instruction. *Objective tests* such as multiple-choice, matching, true-false, and short-answer (completion) tests have the advantage of *high scorer agreement*. That is, if the individual correcting the test is provided with a scoring key, no errors are likely to be made in the scoring process. In fact, multiple-choice, matching, and true-false exams are often scored by machine. Objective tests can measure large amounts of information in relatively short time periods, and the time spent correcting the tests is also short. The disadvantages of the objective test format lie in two areas: (1) good objective tests take much time to construct; and (2) they may frequently focus on objectives at lower levels of cognitive processing.

In cognitive testing the term *subjective test* is generally synonymous with the *essay test*. These tests have the advantage of taking a shorter period of time to construct, and, under some circumstances, focusing on the higher levels of the cognitive domain. The disadvantages of essay tests include the long time needed to correct them and the variability in assigning scores to the test's answers. The latter disadvantage may be sufficiently important to discourage the use of such tests for assessing most instructional outcomes.

Measuring Affective Outcomes of Instruction

Although relatively well-developed strategies are available to guide the construction of cognitive tests, assessing a student's progress toward reaching objectives in the affective domain presents more problems than solutions.

Some of the difficulties in assessing affective behavior can be illustrated by examining the model presented by Abeles (1974) below:

$$BI \approx BH = AS + En$$

where

BI = behavioral intentions, as typically might be obtained from an attitude scale response
BH = behavior, an overt action reflecting the student's values
AS = affective set, the relatively stable value for an object or event
En = environmental factors, conditions that affect the relationship between the affective set and the observed behavior

Behavioral intentions (BI) are approximately equivalent to behaviors (BH), which are due to the individual's affective set (AS) and environmental factors (En). For example, a teacher may ask a student in a music class, "Would you like to attend a symphony?" The student may say "yes" (BI) because he or she may feel that this is what the teacher wants to hear, or the response may actually indicate the intention of attending a concert (BH). While the student may sufficiently value (AS) a symphony performance, the cost of a ticket (En) may prohibit the student from attending.

This model suggests several factors for teachers to consider when attempting to assess affective behaviors.

1. Verbal measures, such as questionnaires and attitude scales, will not be as accurate an indication of attitudes as observations of behaviors.

2. Behavioral measures do not always provide a true representation of what the individual values, since they are affected by environmental factors.

3. Observations of several different behaviors may begin to neutralize the environmental effect (given that in some cases environmental factors promote certain behaviors—e.g., free concert tickets—and in other cases limit behaviors, e.g., expensive concert tickets), and eventually provide the most accurate assessment of affective set.

Although the preceding discussion suggests that a series of behavioral measurements may provide the most accurate assessment of the affective outcomes of instruction, few teachers can afford to devote so much time and effort to this task. Teachers who have attempted to assess this area have tended to rely on attitude scales and other verbal measures of affective behavior. As with the development of cognitive tests, several suggestions for the development of attitude scales are offered below.

LIKERT SCALES. Likert scales, or *summated ratings*, as they are sometimes called, are a popular form of attitude scale. They are composed of a series of statements expressing values about an object or event and a response scale on which subjects can indicate how much they agree or disagree with each statement. For example:

SA A NN D SD   Electronic music relaxes me.

SA A NN D SD   Composing electronic music is more an intellectual activity than it is a creative one.

SA A NN D SD   As more electronic music is composed, the standard for beauty in music diminishes.

The response scale employed can vary in the number of response options provided, but these generally range from three to seven. When a teacher employs a response scale with an even number of categories, the respondent is forced to indicate some degree of agreement with the statement, because the neutral response category (**NN**) is eliminated. The labels employed to identify the response categories—**SA** (strongly agree), **A** (agree), **D** (disagree), and **SD** (strongly disagree)—frequently vary. For young children they may be non-verbal; e.g., ☹ ☺ ☺

The statements to be included on such scales should be short and contain only one idea. Items expressing either a positive or negative position and covering a range of possible attitudes should be included. Statements may be generated by the instructor from writings on the topic or from the students' own statements. The latter technique, which might be facilitated by requesting students to write a short essay expressing how they feel about an object or event, has the advantage of producing statements in the respondents' own words, not the vocabulary of the scale developer.

BEHAVIORAL ASSESSMENTS. While verbal measures are easier to develop and administer, it can be argued that behavioral assessments of values probably yield more valid results. More valid results are produced when the behavioral observations are systematic rather than casual. What types of behavior might be systematically observed and employed as indicators of the effective outcomes of music instruction? Webb Campbell, Schwartz, and Sechrest (1966) provide some suggestions. The first of five behavioral-evidence categories, they suggest, consists of physical signs. These can include physical characteristics of the student, such as the violinist's "hickey," as well as physical characteristics of objects that the student has direct control over. One might consider the neatness of marching band uniforms or the care of a student's music as evidence of affective set.

The second category listed by Webb et al. is expressive movement. Evidence that falls in this category ranges from eye-pupil dilation as an indicant of fear (Darwin, 1872) to foot position of a fullback as an indication of the direction of the next play. Gilliland and Moore (1927) employed smiling as a measure in a study of students' reactions to classical and popular music selections. It is logical that conspicuous expressive behaviors would be indicants of affective set. Movement that is performed in conjunction with music, like hand clapping, might lend itself to categorization and enumeration.

Physical location is another class of behavioral evidence. An example of using physical location to examine affective set is an investigation by Campbell, Kruskal, and Wallance (1965) in which attitudes toward race were determined by recording the seating patterns of students in integrated classrooms. This type of evidence seems well suited for educational use, especially as new curricula provide the student with more opportunities to select physical location. A classroom with learning centers might well serve as a setting in which to examine students' interests in different disciplines. The proximity of a student to a stimulus such as stereo speakers, paintings, or science demonstrations can also serve to indicate interest in that stimulus. The location of a high school student in the library, music practice room, science lab, or cafeteria during a free period also provides information on the student's value system.

A fourth classification of behavioral evidence is language behavior. This type of data was employed in a study (Carlson, Cook, & Stromberg, 1936) that monitored lobby conversations during symphony concert intermissions to examine conversational differences based on gender. Procedures such as this would seem to be appropriate for the examination of attitudes. For example, the monitoring of conversations on a school bus returning from a play or concert can give some insight into appreciation of the event.

The last category Webb et al. list is that of time duration. A study by Melton (1933) examined the relationship between "degree of interest" and the value of a museum. He measured the degree of interest by observing the time spent viewing an exhibit. Greer, Dorow, and Randall (1974) employed a device that determined musical preferences by recording the amount of time students listened to different channels of a tape recording, each of which contained a different style of music. The techniques employed in both the Melton and Greer et al. studies can be readily adapted to a school setting.

Once the behaviors to be rated have been identified by the teacher, systematic procedures for collecting the observations of the behavior should be selected. The teacher needs to decide what type of observation instrument to employ, a topic that is discussed in the next section of this chapter. The teacher should also develop a scheme to sample the behavior. Some types of evidence of affective set are more difficult to sample than others. Physical signs may present no recording problem if they are relatively permanent. More temporary physical signs, such as the red lips of a trumpet player who has just finished practicing, and behaviors involving expressive movement, physical location, and language are transient in nature and should be systematically sampled to obtain representative results.

Measuring Music Performance

Of the three domains into which the outcomes of music instruction can usually be placed, the area that has the least well developed assessment techniques is the psychomotor area. This is unfortunate for music teachers because much of the focus of music instruction is on the development of psychomotor skills. However, it is not surprising, because the instructional outcomes of most of the disciplines taught in the schools lie in the cognitive and affective domains. The educational measurement community has not focused much attention on the assessment of psychomotor behaviors. A complete void does not exist, however, and most introductory measurement textbooks include a section on measuring psychomotor behaviors. A few standardized tests of music performance do exist; the most well known is the *Watkins-Farnum Performance Scale* (see Colwell, 1970).

Music educators have traditionally employed certain psychomotor measures to assess music performance. Very few music teachers have not had some exposure to an adjudication form, either as a judge or as a participant. But one problem facing the music education community is that few of those involved in the music adjudication process seem to have read the "Assessing Psychomotor Behaviors" section in an introductory measurement book.

Such a section traditionally discusses several measurement strategies, including checklists, rank-ordering, and rating scales. Checklists are composed of lists of descriptions of behaviors and a response format that allows the teacher to indicate the presence or absence of each behavior included on the list. Here is an example of one that applies to the clarinet.

YES

_____	Knows the fingering for F-sharp
_____	Can play over the "break"
_____	Plays the throat tones with good tone quality
_____	Plays the low B-flat "in tune"
_____	Can play "Lightly Row" up to tempo

Checklists require no qualitative judgments; the teacher is asked to make a simple, dichotomous, yes-no decision. Checklists seem particularly useful in assessing behaviors at the lower levels of the psychomotor domain, such as those typically found in beginning instrumental instruction. They encourage instructors to observe a student's progress systematically and to articulate, ideally with behavioral objectives, the expected outcomes of instruction. Checklists also provide a good device for providing students and parents with information regarding a student's accomplishments.

Before music students progress too far, they are likely to be compared with peers. This traditionally occurs first on an informal basis when the instructor begins to identify his or her "good" students. However, the process is soon formalized by the placement of performers in sections of ensembles, by contests and auditions, and by the assignment of grades in applied music. The checklist does not provide a qualitative index of performance, so music teachers concerned with the comparative evaluation of performers or performances must rely either on ranking procedures or rating scales.

Because music is temporal in nature, it is not possible to evaluate two performances simultaneously. Therefore, the ranking approach has limited value when more than five or six performances are to be judged. Judges simply are not able to retain a tonal image of performer number one while they are listening to performer number five. The use of tape recordings and a paired-comparison ranking approach, in which each performance is paired with each of the other performances in a group, may help solve the retention problem, but it is not practical with large numbers of performances. For example, six original performances produce fifteen possible paired comparisons.

The rating scale seems the most practical approach to music performance evaluation, and it is the format most frequently employed in contests and other situations where performance is adjudicated. Unfortunately, the forms currently in use do not reflect the current state of the art of rating scale construction.

Most music adjudication forms contain five to seven categories such as intonation, technique, and tone quality, with from one to five points to be awarded in each category. This provides a range of approximately twenty to thirty points to describe the variety of musical behaviors that a judge may be evaluating. The limited range of possible scores tends to limit the reliability and the validity of the scale.

A better procedure for constructing music performance rating scales is to model them on the Likert scale described earlier in this chapter. Such scales would include a longer list of categories to be rated, typically thirty, with a five-to-seven-option response scale. This would provide a possible score range of 120 points, and is probably a more reliable measure. Such music performance rating scales that have been developed in research projects (Abeles, 1973; Cooksey, 1977) have reported high reliability and validity coefficients. Figure 10.1 provides an example of a Likert-type music performance rating scale for a junior high school clarinetist.

The purpose of the following statements is to have you as accurately as possible evaluate the performance that you have just heard. Respond to each statement on the basis of how much you agree or disagree that the statement is descriptive of the performance. Use the following five-point scale:

HD: *highly disagree* that the statement is descriptive
D: *slightly* disagree that the statement is descriptive
NN: *neither disagree nor agree* that the statement is descriptive
A: *slightly agree* that the statement is descriptive
HA: *highly agree* that the statement is descriptive

HD D NN A HA   1. Effective musical communication.
HD D NN A HA   2. The interpretation was musical.
HD D NN A HA   3. The piece was played in character.
HD D NN A HA   4. Played with musical understanding.
HD D NN A HA   5. Played with traditional interpretation.
HD D NN A HA   6. Thin tone quality.
HD D NN A HA   7. Played with natural tone.
HD D NN A HA   8. There was a lack of tonal color.
HD D NN A HA   9. The quality of the tone was rich.
HD D NN A HA 10. Sounded shallow.
HD D NN A HA 11. Uneven rhythm.
HD D NN A HA 12. Smoothness in execution.
HD D NN A HA 13. Melodic continuation.
HD D NN A HA 14. Insecure technique.
HD D NN A HA 15. The rhythm was distorted.
HD D NN A HA 16. Played out of tune.
HD D NN A HA 17. Flat in low register.
HD D NN A HA 18. The intonation was good.
HD D NN A HA 19. Generally played flat.
HD D NN A HA 20. Tended to be flat.
HD D NN A HA 21. Played too fast.
HD D NN A HA 22. Seemed to drag.
HD D NN A HA 23. Hurried repeated notes.
HD D NN A HA 24. Played too slowly.
HD D NN A HA 25. Rushed.
HD D NN A HA 26. Squeaked.
HD D NN A HA 27. Free from tonguing noise.
HD D NN A HA 28. Attacks and releases were clean.
HD D NN A HA 29. Tonguing produced "thunkie" sound.
HD D NN A HA 30. Accents were played as indicated.

Figure 10.1 Clarinet adjudication form.

Alternative Approaches to Assessment

One of the outgrowths of the educational reform of the 1980s was a movement toward a system of national standards and assessments. This position was advocated by the America 2000 program and was endorsed by many respected education, business, and political leaders. If national standards for different subject areas are to be developed, however, a system of assessment must also be developed to determine when the standards are met. Discussions of national standards have focused much attention on what strategies might be used in such a national system of assessment. Many persons who advocate such a system assume the national tests that would be developed would be similar to other standardized national achievement tests like the Scholastic Aptitude Test (SAT), which is primarily based on a multiple-choice/objective format. There are other educators who also support the development of national standards, but who insist that alternative models of assessment must be developed that are different from existing standardized achievement tests if what students learn in schools is to be fully measured.

Advocates of alternatives to traditional standardized tests emphasize the importance of integrating assessment with learning. Thus, their recommendations imply new approaches to teaching and learning. In general, it is the perceived "artificiality" of standardized tests that has motivated the search for alternatives. Some alternative assessment strategies try to parallel "real-world" use of knowledge by asking the type of question likely to be encountered by the citizen or consumer, and it is true that many of the tasks that adults execute require time to develop, often consist of several stages, and are modified considerably before completion.

Music provides many examples of this kind of development. When experienced musicians begin to work on a new piece to perform, they often spend many hours over several days, weeks, or months to develop the level of performance that they are ready to present to others. Composers often generate copious sketches before a composition is completed, and marching band directors modify drills and arrangements as rehearsals indicate the need to do so.

Advocates of alternative modes of assessment want to move closer to modeling these learning processes with their assessment tools. One approach developed to facilitate this type of assessment use is portfolios. Portfolios are collections of a student's work. In some cases portfolios are kept while works are being developed. In a performance class, tapes of performances, rehearsals, sectionals, or practice sessions as well as written critiques of the tapes by the student, teacher, or peers, might be included in the portfolio. In a general music class, tapes of practices, class exercises, notes, and drafts of compositions, as well as finished products, might be included. In addition to examples of work at different stages of development, these portfolios should include evaluative statements, particularly those of the student. These self-critiques are viewed as an important part of the portfolio approach to assessment, because they focus the student's perception on the product being developed and help him or her reflect on the strengths and weakness of the work in its current stage of development.

The approach to the learning process that the advocates of portfolios prescribe includes three principle components: production, perception, and reflection. Production can be thought of as demonstrating levels of knowledge and skills through the activities of composing, performing and listening. Perception is the ability of students to distinguish, discriminate, or analyze critically in ways that enhance interpretation or production. By listening to their own playing, students learn to hear better, to make finer discriminations, and to see connections between events in the music. Reflection occurs when the student develops understanding through the process of self-assessment that can be demonstrated by revision and/or the reassessment of goals, methods, and the effects achieved by the product. For example, a teacher might ask students to compare a section of a rehearsal tape made one month earlier with a tape of a current rehearsal. Teachers might ask students to describe what they hear and answer questions such as "What has changed?" and "What remains the same?" It is important for students to be able to step away from the performance and think about what they are doing, why they are doing it, what they are learning, how successful they are in doing it, and how they might improve their performance.

The portfolios that have been described might be considered *process portfolios* and focus on enhancing the instructional process. Process Portfolios can also function as an evaluative tool. *Product portfolios* are used to collect student works and serve as a king of resume. These portfolios contain products that represent the different areas and techniques developed during the year. They represent the student's best work and both the student as well as the teacher are involved with the selection of items to include in the portfolio. While such product portfolios emphasize finished products, evidence of how the works evolved and were refined is also included to illustrate the student's self-assessment abilities. Product portfolios can serve as a part a student's permanent record. Some products can be culled from the portfolio each year, but a meaningful record of the student's musical development can be passed on to new instructors.

Evaluating or assigning a grade to product portfolios represent a challenge, although evaluation in music has never been as straightforward as it is in other disciplines. Students and teachers together would decide on what work best represents the student's achievement. Some portfolio advocates (e.g., Mills, 1989) recommend training *teacher assessors* to examine portfolios and prepare an analysis of student progress based on the assessor's experience with similar students. Developing procedures for evaluating portfolios continues to represent a challenge to implementing portfolio assessment in schools.

Portfolios are messy and time-consuming. They require that teachers interact with students in ways to which they are often not accustomed. Their use is contrary to the development of national standards, because they focus on individuals and do not provide easy strategies for evaluating. It is also not clear how portfolio assessment can be easily integrated in music curricula that emphasize large ensembles at the secondary-school level. The character of large ensembles in secondary schools with heavy commitments to performance schedules would have to change considerably if the portfolio approach was implemented.

Portfolio assessment does, however, have a distinct advantage for music teachers and other teachers in production-oriented subjects. It represents a more natural way of assessing progress. It is a way clearly linked to the goals and objectives of performance-oriented classes.

As stated earlier, there is a strong relationship between teaching strategies and assessment strategies. The challenge of implementing portfolio assessment procedures in music underscores this relationship. Although alternative assessment strategies demand a different approach to instruction, they may develop students' understandings and strategies and facilitate progress toward the goal of developing independent musicianship.

Program Evaluation

Evaluation should be an integral part of all levels and aspects of any music education program (Boyle, 1989, p. 22). Program evaluation often refers to the assessment of the curriculum of an educational unit such as a school or school system. The term is also used to examine the success or failure of a specific project, particularly funded projects, in which those providing the funds are interested in the success of what they have funded. Information obtained from program evaluations can inform policymakers as well as teachers about the effectiveness of an educational system or innovation.

There may be multiple reasons why program evaluations are initiated. Often they are in response to a perceived problem, such as when the children who graduate from a school system are musically illiterate. Reports like *A Nation at Risk* (National Commission on Excellence in Education, 1984) serve as catalysts for program evaluations. In general, education reform movements are accompanied by demands for objective evidence of student achievement. Sometimes school administrators undertake program evaluations for planning purposes. Accountability (discussed in chapter 8) is closely related to program evaluation because such evaluations are often the measure used to determine whether instructional systems are effective.

Evaluators have employed several different models of evaluation to assess educational programs. Traditional approaches to program evaluation have focused on the success the programs have enjoyed in achieving their stated goals and objectives. When goal-oriented evaluation models are used, programs identified as being successful are often those with clearly defined and measurable objectives, even if those objectives lack validity.

Several factors have led to the development of alternative models of evaluation. For some educational curricula and programs there are no agreed-on or easily defined criteria measures. Some evaluators emphasize that programs may yield important outcomes that were not stated as goals and not anticipated. Some evaluators (e.g., Eisner, 1979; Stake, 1983) interested in assessing the outcomes of arts education programs have tended to reject traditional approaches to program evaluation. Eisner (1979) recommends what he calls a "connoisseurship and criticism" model. In this approach to evaluation, evaluators act similarly to critics who are trained and experienced observers in the field, and provide completed and detailed descriptions of the instructional process and the results of instruction. They also place results in the context appropriate to the institution being observed. While this model may yield differing results depending on the experience and background of the evaluator, it does represent an alternative that may in some respects be more sensitive to some of the outcomes of music instruction.

Stake's (1975) "responsive approach" to program evaluation was also stimulated by the need to evaluate arts education projects. It is primarily a qualitative approach that focuses on describing what is *really* taking place in the program in contrast to what might have been intended. The tools of this approach are observing and reacting, and the data presented include narratives, testimonies of both teachers and students, and examples of products. Stake suggests that while this model does not yield quantifiable measures, it is likely to be sensitive to some outcomes of music instruction that are not easy assessed.

As stated earlier, most approaches to program evaluation have focused on the success that programs have in achieving their stated goals and objectives. Music education curricula or program innovations often state objectives in terms of student learning. For example, the state of Illinois has identified several fine-arts goals:

> As a result of schooling students will be able to: (1) understand the principal sensory, formal, technical, and expressive qualities of each of the arts; (2) identify processes and tools required to produce visual art, music, drama, and dance; (3) demonstrate the basic skills necessary to participate in the creation and/or performance of one of the arts; (4) identify significant works in the arts from major historical periods and how they reflect societies, cultures, and civilizations, past and present; (5) describe the unique characteristics of each of the arts. (Dawson, 1992, p. 1)

Traditional program evaluations in the past have relied on the assessment of what the students learn—such as information, concepts, skills, and attitudes. It is important to emphasize that program evaluation efforts should also include the assessment of the factors that concern the delivery or implementation of the music program, such as teachers, materials, equipment, and administrative schemes.

If such goal-directed program evaluations require the large-scale assessment of student achievement, objective tests are often the means employed. Several of the Illinois goals emphasize cognitive and perceptual skills for which objective test items measuring student achievement might be developed. In fact, the Illinois State Music Assessment developed many multiple-choice assessment items. Goal number 3 of the Illinois objectives focuses on student performance or production, however, which would need to be assessed by observing performances or evaluating products.

Boyle (1989) recommends that both subjective and objective information be included in evaluations. Including both, he states, leads to developing a strong information base. Teachers' informal observations and interpretations based on their experiences and training are important sources of information and strengthen the interpretation of the objective data collected.

MENC, in cooperation with the Educational Testing Service (ETS), has produced a series of program evaluation instruments designed to undertake a comprehensive assessment of instructional programs for kindergarten through grade 12. The materials include instruments to assess: (1) goals and objectives; (2) leadership; (3) staffing; (4) curriculum and scheduling; (5) instructional materials; (6) equipment; (7) facilities; and (8) outcomes (Lehman, 1992). The instruments are based on *The School Music Program. Description and Standards* (Music Educators National Conference, 1986), which describes a high-quality K–12 music curriculum. The following are examples of guidelines that Lehman (1989) provides regarding these different areas.

> Goals and objectives: Does the district have a written statement of philosophy or a rationale for its music program? Does it have a statement of goals and objectives? To what extent do these materials emphasize the various objectives and outcomes specified in *Description and Standards*?

> Leadership: Is there at least one person designated as a music administrator within the district? To what extent is the chief music administrator responsible for the music program in the district? What is the role of the chief music administrator in hiring, evaluation, and termination of music teachers and classroom teachers who teach music?

> Staffing: To what extent is music in the elementary school taught by specialists? To what extent is the ability to teach music a consideration in the hiring of elementary classroom teachers? How much planning time do music teachers have? What is the teacher/student ratio in each field of specialization (e.g., choral music) at each level?

Curriculum and Scheduling: In what grades is music required? How great an effort is made to sequential music program to every student? What is the quality of the curriculum guides? How are they used? How many minutes of music instruction do elementary students receive per week?

Instructional Materials: Is there a complete and current set of music textbooks available for each grade in the elementary and middle schools? Is there an adequate library of music for band, orchestra, choral groups, and small ensembles in every elementary and secondary school? Are there adequate materials to teach nonperformance courses in music in every secondary school?

Equipment: Is there a high-quality keyboard instrument accessible to every room in which music is taught? How adequate is the budget for the purchase of instruments and equipment? To what extent are the quantity and quality of the available instruments and equipment adequate?

Facilities: Is a room available for teaching music in every elementary school? Is a room available for teaching instrumental music? Are there separate rehearsal rooms for instrumental and choral groups in every middle school that has more than one music teacher? Are there small-ensemble rehearsal rooms (in the secondary school)? Are there adequate practice rooms? Are the music facilities acoustically isolated from one another and from the rest of the school?

Learning Outcomes: By the end of kindergarten, how many of the students can match pitches consistently? How many students at the end of the third [grade], sixth [grade], or middle school have acquired each of the skills and each type of knowledge recommended in *Description and Standards*? How many students electing band, orchestra or chorus at the secondary level have achieved the skills and acquired the knowledge recommended for those courses in *Description and Standards*? (Lehman, 1989, p. 28)

The assessment instruments that have been developed by MENC have been designed to gather both facts and opinions and are sufficiently flexible to provide for the needs of districts of different sizes and resources. The results should help districts to "identify strengths or weaknesses in its music program that might not otherwise be apparent" (Lehman, 1992, p. 290).

There are only a few examples of program evaluations of specific projects or innovations in music. Such assessments are somewhat more narrow and focused than systemwide program evaluations. Projects such as the Contemporary Music Project or IMPACT often have clearly identified objectives on which an evaluation can be based; that is, they employ goal-directed evaluation procedures, while other projects may decide to employ "goal-free" evaluation strategies. Goal-free evaluation procedures emphasize collecting information on a broad range of outcomes in order to avoid overlooking unexpected results.

Asmus (1992) describes the evaluation procedures used to assess the Southeast Institute for Education in Music, a funded project to develop discipline-based arts education concepts in music (DBAE). The institute's activities include a three-week summer institute for preparing teachers in DBAE approaches, as well as "renewal" institutes for teachers during the school year. The evaluation project assessed the effectiveness of both the components of the institute and the overall effectiveness of the project. Goal-directed and goal-free evaluation techniques were employed. Naturalistic assessment strategies, such as unobtrusive observation techniques, were used to help assess unanticipated outcomes. For instance, the evaluator would "hang-out" in the hallways between sessions during the summer institute and listen to the comments made by the participants. This information was then used to supplement the results of more formal affective measures. Objective-oriented assessment strategies (tests) were developed to measure specified goals and objectives.

The results of project evaluations provide useful information for those undertaking such curricular efforts. During the early stages of the project, formative evaluations provide insight on how the project strategies can be modified to be more effective. One characteristic of such projects is that they often exist for a specified period (highly correlated to the availability of funding!). Therefore, the summative evaluation that tries to assess the overall effectiveness of such projects is often a component of the final reports of those projects. These reports can be informative to music educators planning new projects because they provide models often of what are good strategies as well as what are less effective approaches.

The National Assessment of Music

The National Assessment of Educational Progress (NAEP) was designed to provide baseline data on the achievement of students in different subject areas, specifically "to provide helpful information about the progress of education that can be understood and accepted by laymen as well as professional educators" (National Assessment of Education Progress, 1970, p. 2). The NAEP focused on the educational achievement of three groups aged nine, thirteen, and seventeen (young adults aged from twenty-six to thirty-five were included in the first music assessment) in ten areas of instruction: reading, writing, science, mathematics, social studies, citizenship, vocational education, literature, art, and music. Music was first assessed during the 1971–1972 school year, and the results were published in 1974. The second music assessment was conducted in 1978–1979, and the results were published in 1981. The various scales and tests that were developed for the project were administered to a national sample, although each person being tested only took a portion of a test. This was deliberately planned to avoid comparisons of individuals, schools, districts, or states. Results for larger geographical regions are reported.

The assessment materials was developed by teams comprised of content scholars, professional educators, thoughtful lay citizens, and measurement experts. The initial efforts focused on structuring the area to be tested and developing statements of objectives that would reflect current instructional practices. This process eventually led to the development of groups of exercises in five major categories for the first assessment.

I. Music Performance
   A. Singing familiar songs
   B. Repeating unfamiliar material
   C. Improvising
   D. Performing from notation
   E. Performing a prepared piece
II. Notation and Terminology
   A. Vocabulary
   B. Basic notation
   C. Score-reading
III. Instrumental and Vocal Media
   A. Aural recognition
   B. Visual recognition
   C. Performance practices
IV. Music History and Literature
   A. Periods in music history
   B. Musical genres and styles
   C. Music literature
 V. Attitudes Toward Music

Because of more limited funding the second music assessment examined only three areas:

I. Value of Music
   A. Affective response to music
   B. Acquaintance with music of different periods, cultures, and genres
   C. Value of music in the life of the individual, community, and family
   D. Creation and support of aesthetic judgments about music

II. Elements and Expressive Controls of Music
  A.   Elements of music
  B.   Relationships of elements in a given composition
  C.   Music terms, expression markings, and conducting gestures
III. Music History and Culture
  A.   Features of folk, ethnic, popular, and art musics
  B.   Musical stylistic periods
  C.   Social and cultural uses of music

The First Music Assessment

The first performance testing contained fifteen performance exercises examining the five areas cited above. These performances were done individually with the test administrator. The students were generally not given pitch or tempo indications. An example of the type of experience included in subcategory A, "Singing familiar songs," is singing "America," both with and without accompaniment. The performances were recorded and judged as either acceptable or unacceptable in three areas: rhythm, pitch, and overall quality. Guidelines for scoring were provided for the judges. In the exercise that required the respondents to sing "America" with an accompaniment, over 90 percent of all age groups performed the rhythm correctly, while 70 percent of the adults to a low 48 percent of the nine-year-olds were rated acceptable on pitch. The percentage of adults performing both correctly dropped to below 50 percent with only 35 percent of the nine-year-olds' performances being acceptable.

In general, the results for the music performance exercises indicated acceptable performances for 31 percent of the nine-year-olds, 48 percent of the thirteen-year-olds, and 54 percent of the young adults.

The music notation and terminology items were in some cases presented in a multiple-choice format, while others were more analogous to short-answer items. Items in the notation section included the recognition of basic pitch and rhythmic notation from scores, and some of the exercises in the score-reading section asked students to mark the place on a musical score where the recording of an excerpt stopped. While the NAEP results for these exercises do not provide comparative scores for the nine-year-old subjects, the results report that 43 percent of the thirteen-year-olds, 47 percent of the seventeen-year-olds, and 30 percent of the adults answered correctly.

The instrumental and vocal media exercises required the students to discriminate among and label the instrument or voice performing on taped excerpts, identify pictures of instruments, and identify how certain instruments are played (e.g., by strumming). The percentages of correct responses by age group for these exercises were 84 percent for thirteen-year-olds, 89 percent for seventeen-year-olds, and 82 percent for adults. Comparative data for nine-year-olds were again not available, although the NAEP reports that these students scored acceptably on 76 percent of the items on which they were tested in this section.

Section 4 of the first music assessment examined knowledge of music history and literature. The exercises in this section tested knowledge not only of traditional Western art music, but also of popular music, folk music, music of earlier periods, and electronic music. Knowledge of music literature was tested by listening to taped performances and identifying titles (and in some cases composers) of selections from a variety of genres, such as "This Land Is Your Land," "Stars and Stripes Forever," and *Peter and the Wolf*. In this area the percentages of correct responses increased with age, with the thirteen-year-olds responding correctly to 20 percent of the items, the seventeen-year-olds to 24 percent, and the adults to 30 percent.

The final area of music on which the first national assessment was focused was that of interest in and attitude toward music. Three different subareas assessd: (1) the degree to which the respondents liked music, and what types they liked; (2) how much they liked to sing, what types of songs they preferred to sing, and whether they preferred to sing alone or with large or small groups; and (3) whether they played or would like to play an instrument, what types of music they preferred to play, and whether they preferred to play alone or with others. The reported percentages in this area represent a group's level of positive attitudes toward music. As can be seen from the results (thirteen- and seventeen-year-olds, 62 percent; adults, 56 percent) the respondents were generally willing to listen and involve themselves in musical experiences.

In 1974 the Music Educators National Conference appointed a panel to discuss the results of the first national assessment with the NAEP staff. They concluded that while the results of the assessment "made a significant contribution to their understanding of the effectiveness of music education" and provided "valuable insight into the musical competence of the 'average' citizen" (NAEP, 1974, p. 2), caution should be applied when interpreting the results, since several factors were likely to have influenced the reported outcomes, including:

1. The assessment only sampled a few specific skills of the many skills, knowledge, and attitudes that may result from music instruction, and was able to sample each skill with only a few exercises.

2. The assessment did not attempt to identify or report separately the scores of respondents with some interest or training in music.

3. Some musical knowledges and skills are likely to develop as the

result of informal exposures to music, such as media and social environment, rather than formal music instructional experiences.

The Second Music Assessment

The second music assessment placed more emphasis on assessing the affective outcomes of music instruction than the first assessment. The "value of music" was examined in a series of fifteen to twenty exercises. An example of the exercises included in this category is: "Which one of the following things would you rather do if you had one free period a day in school?

1. Play a musical instrument (14 percent)

2. Draw or paint (34 percent)

3. Write a story (9 percent)

4. Sing in a musical group (5 percent)

5. Learn a foreign language (14 percent)

6. Listen to music (11 percent)

7. None of these (10 percent)

The percentage response for the nine-year-olds in the assessment appears next to each alternative. It can be seen that only approximately 30 percent of the students selected musical alternatives.

The following item was one of the forty-five to fifty items used to examine the achievement of thirteen-year-olds in the elements-of-music category: "Listen carefully to the music. What instrument is playing the melody? (1) accordion, (2) celesta, (3) piano, (4) xylophone, (5) I don't know." Approximately 78 percent of the students correctly indicated that the melody was played by a piano (NAEP, 1981, p. 23).

The broad area of music history and culture was tested by eighteen items for the nine-year-olds and by fifty-five or sixty-one items, respectively, for the thirteen- and seventeen-year-olds. An item that was used to examine the thirteen- and seventeen-year-olds in this area was: "Listen carefully to the music. What kind of music is being performed? (1) blues song, (2) folk-rock song, (3) operatic song, (4) work song, (5) I don't know." Approximately 83 percent of the thirteen-year-olds and 95 percent of the seventeen-year-olds responded correctly to this item. The average percent of correct responses in this category was 58 percent for the nine-year-olds, 36 percent for the thirteen-year-olds, and 39 percent for the seventeen-year-olds (NAEP, 1981, p. 24)

In addition to the music achievement information collected, the second assessment collected data on the exposure of students to musical activities in school, as well as outside of school. The addition of this category seems likely to have been a result of music educators' reactions to the results of the first assessment reported previously. In this category students were asked questions that assessed such out-of-school activities as listening to music, singing just for fun, and singing in a church or community music group. Other questions examined whether the students were being taught music in their school and the type of music instruction (e.g., orchestra) they had received.

Of considerable interest for music educators is the answer to the question "Is the level of achievement in music related to music instruction in the schools?" The NAEP reported:

1. Nine-year-olds who had been taught music in the schools for two years (1977–78) performed about 6 percent better on all music exercises than those who had not been taught music during that time period.

2. Thirteen- and seventeen-year-olds who had participated in instrumental music for at least three years performed about twelve percentage points better than those with no instrumental experience, and students with three years of choral music experience scored from six to nine percentage points better than those who did not participate in choral groups. (1981, p. xiii)

The results from this section also revealed that:

- 74 percent of nine-year-olds listened to music.
- 45 percent of nine-year-olds sing just for fun.
- 28 percent of the thirteen-year-olds had never taken general music.
- 18 percent of the seventeen-year-olds had never taken general music.
- 48 percent of the thirteen-year-olds had never participated in chorus.
- 46 percent of the seventeen-year-olds had never participated in chorus.
- 50 percent of the thirteen-year-olds had never taken band.
- 52 percent of the seventeen-year-olds had never taken band.
- 90 percent of the thirteen- and seventeen-year-olds had never taken orchestra.

A Comparison of the First and Second Music Assessments

Several test items were used for both assessments to provide a means of examining any change that occurred during the seven-year interval between the two music assessments. In general, the nine-year-olds and seventeen-year-olds were slightly (approximately 3 percent) less successful in the 1978–1979 assessment than they were in the 1971–1972 assessment, while the thirteen-year-olds remained about the same. This decline was primarily due to results in the area of knowledge of elements and expressive controls of music.

The NAEP report of the second national music assessment (1981) cites the major findings of the second assessment as:

1. Students at all three ages have a high value for music.

2. Students at all three ages appear to have a somewhat superficial understanding of musical notation, terminology, and the history of music. (p. 44)

In describing the reactions of a panel of music educators to the second music assessment of students' exposure, NAEP (1981) reports:

> The members of the panel were optimistic about the future of the instrumental music program in America and hopeful about general music and greater course diversity throughout the school program in the not-too-distant future. The members of the panel expressed the belief that practically all music educators would like to see more music courses and more variety in music course offerings—particularly for the nonperforming student. (p. 45)

Evaluation of Music Teachers

Concern about the quality of the corps of teachers educating the nation's children has been an important issue in the recent education reform movement. This concern is based on the assumption that teachers' attributes are related to student learning. Some of the concern centers on ensuring that teachers have at least minimum skills and understandings. Consequently, tests that screen prospective teachers on minimal literacy and professional understandings have been adopted by many states as part of their teacher-licensing process. In some states professional entry tests have been developed for specialized teaching areas such as music. Major questions exist about the content of such tests and the relationship between the scores on the tests and effective music teaching.

There is also a need to evaluate music teachers once they occupy a teaching position. These on-the-job assessments may be helpful in improving teacher effectiveness, particularly for the beginning teacher. Ideally, music teacher evaluation can serve as an important part in developing new teachers. To be successful, such evaluation procedures must be relevant to effective teaching; that is, the characteristics assessed need to be thoughtfully developed. Educators have developed lists of teacher competencies to facilitate evaluation. Taebel (1992) points out that teacher competencies can differ in scope and specificity. He identifies several lists of "essential teacher skills" that vary in the number of competencies identified from fifteen to 511. The shorter lists define a few broad competencies (e.g., demonstration of aural music skills.), while the longer lists are more specific (e.g., demonstration of correct sight-reading of simple diatonic melodies). It is also important that the competencies cited be observable and measurable. Observing teachers perform in the classroom probably enhances the validity of teacher evaluations, but, as Taebel points out, assessing only classroom performance can be limiting. The context of such observations can greatly impact the teacher's behavior. For instance, observing a choral director in a cramped rehearsal space during a class shortened by an unexpected assembly program is not likely to be representative of that teacher's instructional skill. As a teacher moves from one situation (teaching urban junior high school general music) to another (teaching suburban elementary general music), that teacher's performance is not likely to be the same.

Problems that arise from such assessments often involve efforts to generalize across all teachers. It should not be assumed that there is one "ideal" profile for effective teachers. Furthermore, it should not be assumed that the same competencies are required for teachers in different disciplines. While general competency models may be useful for guiding beginning teachers, experienced teachers may find them limiting. The professional development of the individual teacher may be the most useful application of teacher evaluations, stressing the individual teacher's growth, rather than comparision among teachers.

Taebel (1992) recommends several policies for developing an evaluation program for music teachers. First, he suggests that a framework for evaluation be developed that includes the broad goals for music learning in the school district, as well as the major components of teaching such as subject-matter knowledge, teaching competencies, and service contributions (e.g., to the community). The purpose of the evaluations as well as the procedures should be carefully described. A variety of data-gathering tools should be developed, and experienced successful teachers should be able to select what will be most beneficial to their growth and development. All aspects of the evaluation should be developed in consultation with music teachers, music supervisors, and other administrative personnel.

Taebel's second suggestion is that training be required of those who are involved in the evaluations. The evaluators must be familiar with the procedures as well as the instruments employed, and should be able to give meaningful feedback to teachers. Third, he recommends that the school district develop plans for the professional development of music teachers. His fourth recommendation is that the evaluation system be monitored and revised when necessary. Taebel cautions that "valid outcomes of evaluation certainly are not easy to produce: the threats that may be associated with teacher evaluation must be weighed in the light of its contribution to professional development, which in turn is guided by a vision of what it means to teach music to students" (p. 324).

While most of the research on teaching evaluations has focused on classroom instruction, a few studies have examined teaching evaluations in the applied music studio (e.g., Abeles, 1975; Abeles, Goffi, & Levasseur, 1992). Abeles (1975) developed a scale for music students to use when evaluating their instructors. The scale assessed five aspects of applied teacher effectiveness: rapport, instructional systemization, instructional skill, musical knowledge, and general instructional competence. While the scale appears to be an effective measure of applied teacher effectiveness (that is, acceptable levels of reliability and validity were reported), there is the need for considerable more work in this area before music educators will begin to understand all of the components that comprise effective applied instruction.

Summary

Assessing the outcomes of instruction is an important component of the teaching-learning process. However, because of the difficulty in assessing some music behaviors, music educators have not developed ways to systematically measure some of these outcomes.

Measurement theorists suggest that a true indication of a student's level of skill or knowledge can only be obtained by eliminating error from the measurement process. One way to minimize the effect of measurement error is to take several measurements of the same trait. The average of these measurements will theoretically represent the true level of the trait.

It is important for measurement instruments to have high reliability. Test reliability is the consistency or stability of the measuring instrument. There are several different types of reliability: test-retest reliability (consistency over time), equivalent-form reliability (consistency across different forms) and internal consistency (the homogeneity of the items that constitute the test).

Validity is an equally important test characteristic. Validity assesses whether a test measures what it claims to measure. Content validity examines the content or material that a test measures; criterion-related validity compares the scores from the test being validated with some external criterion, often scores from other tests or students' grades; and construct validity compares how well the test results fit with a psychological construct. Validity is somewhat dependent on reliability; that is, if a test is not reliable it cannot possibly be valid.

Tests may be classified into several different categories. Standardized achievement tests help administrators and teachers compare the level of achievement of their students with others in different school systems. Aptitude tests attempt to predict future achievement by assessing innate capacities as well as informal environmental influences, and standardized preference inventories assist students and teachers in making vocational choices.

Music aptitude testing has been of considerable interest to music educators and music psychologists. Gordon's *Primary Measures of Music Audiation* (1979) is a recent test that is probably the most widely used measure of music aptitude.

Music achievement testing has not generated as much interest as music aptitude testing. Colwell's *Music Achievement Tests* (1969–70) is one of the more widely used music achievement tests.

Music teachers need to determine the outcomes of their instruction. Objective tests (those with high scorer agreement) have several advantages over more subjective tests. Objective tests may be composed of multiple-choice, matching, alternative-response, and/or short-answer items.

Assessing the important affective outcomes of music instruction presents several difficulties. One of the difficulties is the amount of time it takes to systematically measure affective behaviors. Another is that the instruction may not result in a change in behavior that can be readily observed. Music teachers may rely on attitude scales to help gather evidence on the affective outcomes of music instruction, but these are probably not as valid as behavioral evidence, including physical signs, expressive movement, physical location, language behavior, and duration of time spent in an activity.

Many of the outcomes of music instruction are psychomotor behaviors. This, unfortunately, is the least well developed area of measurement. It is important for music teachers to systematically rather than casually assess music performance. Music teachers can use checklists, rank-ordering, and/or rating scales to assist them in systematizing their evaluations. Of these strategies, rating scales seem to be the most advantageous in evaluating the results of applied instruction.

Alternative modes of assessment have been recently advocated by some assessment specialists and educators. The development of student portfolios is one type of alternative assessment. Collections of students' work are made up of items selected both by the teacher and the student. These portfolios can be used both to help the student reflect on their learning processes, and can be used as an evaluative tool as well.

Program evaluations are often initiated because of perceived problems. These evaluations may be of the music program of a school system or of a specific project. Many program evaluations assess how well the program is achieving its stated objectives. Other program evaluation models are "goal-free." They emphasize that programs yield important outcomes that may not have been anticipated. MENC and ETS have produced a series of program-evaluation instruments designed to undertake a comprehensive assessment of a K–12 music program.

Two national music assessments have been conducted, one during the 1971–1972 school year, the other during the 1978–1979 school year. The achievement of students from elementary through high school was assessed in areas such as music performance, music notation and terminology, instrumental and vocal media, music history and culture, and attitudes toward music. Both assessments provided important information for music teachers and administrators on the level of music understanding among the school population, and, to a lesser extent, on the effectiveness of school music instruction.

The evaluation of teachers has become increasingly important during periods of educational reform. Several states employ tests that are used to screen prospective teachers as part of the licensing process. On-the-job teacher assessments have been the focus of several studies. Typically, such assessments are based on lists of teacher competencies, and these competencies are observed and rated systematically by supervisory personnel.

STUDY AND DISCUSSION QUESTIONS

1. What are some sources of error in assessing learning? How can the effect of uncontrolled error be accounted for?

2. What is the concept of reliability? In what ways can it be estimated?

3. What is validity in testing? How does content validity differ from criterion-related validity? How does construct validity differ from other types of validity?

4. What are the characteristics of a standardized test?

5. In what ways does Gordon's *Musical Aptitude Profile* differ from his *Primary Measures of Music Audiation*?

6. What are some ways in which teachers can increase the validity of their assessments of students' attitudes?

7. What are some ways in which teachers can increase the validity of their assessments of students' musical skills, especially performance skills?

8. What are the advantages and disadvantages associated with the alternative assessment strategies described in this chapter?

9. Identify and describe at least two approaches to program evaluation. What are the advantages and disadvantages of each of the approaches?

10. (a) What was the main purpose of the National Assessment of Educational Progress?

    (b) What are categories of people did it include?

    (c) What areas of music were examined?

11. What are the primary reasons to establish teacher evaluation programs? Describe the components of a model teacher evaluation program.

INDIVIDUAL OR CLASS ACTIVITIES

1. Provide the students with a short (ten- to fifteen-item) rating scale to measure the solo performance of an instrument. Distribute the form to the students in the class and ask them to use it to evaluate a recording of a solo performance of the instrument. Summarize the ratings for each of the items and discuss items that show considerable agreement among the raters (students), as well as those items on which the raters disagreed.

2. Divide the class into several groups of three or four students. Ask each group to develop a strategy for collecting behavioral responses that show middle-school students' affective reactions to a school performance of a visiting professional ensemble.

SUPPLEMENTARY READINGS

BOYLE, J. D. (1992). Evaluation of music ability. In R. Colwell (Ed.), *Handbook of research on music teaching and learning* (pp. 247–65). New York: Schirmer Books.

CUTIETTA, R. A. (1992). The measurement of attitudes and preferences in music education. In R. Colwell (Ed.), *Handbook of research on music teaching and learning* (pp. 295–309). New York: Schirmer Books.

LEHMAN, P. R. (1992). Curriculum and program evaluation. In R. Colwell (Ed.), *Handbook of research on music teaching and learning* (pp. 281–94) New York: Schirmer Books.

TAEBEL, D. K. (1992). The evaluation of music teachers and teaching. In R. Colwell (Ed.), *Handbook of research on music teaching and learning* (pp. 310–30). New York: Schirmer Books.

REFERENCES

ABELES, H. F. (1973). Development and validation of a clarinet performance adjudication scale. *Journal of Research in Music Education, 21*(3), 246–55.

ABELES, H. F. (1974, April). *Value judgments and construction of rating instruments to measure affective behavior.* Paper presented at the National Council on Measurement in Education Convention, Chicago.

ABELES, H. F. (1975). Student perceptions of characteristics of effective applied music instructors. *Journal of Research in Music Education, 23*(2), 147–54.

ABELES, H. F., GOFFI, J., & LEVASSEUR, S. (1992). The components of effective applied instruction. *The Quarterly Journal of Music Teaching and Learning, 3*(2), 17–23.

ASMUS, E. P. (1992, Spring). Evaluating the Southeast Institute for Education in Music. *Special Research Interest Group in Measurement and Evaluation Newsletter* (13), 5–11.

BOYLE, J. D. (1989). Perspective on evaluation. *Music Educators Journal, 76*(4), 22–25.

BOYLE, J. D. (1992). Evaluation of music ability. In R. Colwell (Ed.), *Handbook of research on music teaching and learning* (pp. 247–65). New York: Schirmer Books.

BOYLE, J. D., & RADOCY, R. E. (1987). *Measurement and evaluation of musical experiences.* New York: Schirmer Books.

CAMPBELL, D. T., KRUSKAL, W. H., & WALLANCE, W. P. (1965). Seating aggregation as an index of attitude. *Sociometry, 29.*

CARLSON, J., COOK, S. W., & STROMBERG, E. L. (1936). Sex differences in conversation. *Journal of Applied Psychology, 20*(2), 727–35.

COLWELL, R. (1969). *Music achievement tests.* Chicago: Follett Educational Corp.

COLWELL, R. (1970). *The evaluation of music teaching and learning.* Englewood Cliffs, NJ: Prentice-Hall.

COOKSEY, J. M. (1977). A facet-factorial approach to rating high school choral music performance. *Journal of Research in Music Education 25*(2), 100–114.

DARWIN, C. (1872). *The expression of the emotions in man and animals.* London: Murray.

DAWSON, J. A. (1992, Spring). Development of the state music assessment in Illinois. *Special Research Interest Group in Measurement and Evaluation Newsletter* (13), 1–4.

EISNER, E. W. (1979). *The educational imagination.* New York: Macmillan.

GEORGE, W. E. (1980). Measurement and evaluation of musical behavior. In D. Hodges (Ed.), *Handbook of music psychology* (pp. 291–392). Lawrence, KS: National Association of Music Therapy.

GILLILAND, A. R., & MOORE, H. T. (1927). The immediate and long-time effects of classical and popular phonograph selections. In M. Schoen (Ed.), *The effects of music* (pp. 211–22). New York: Harcourt, Brace.

GORDON, E. (1965). *The musical aptitude profile.* Boston: Houghton Mifflin.

GORDON, E. (1979). *Primary measures of music audiation.* Chicago: G.I.A.

GREER, R. D., DOROW, L. G., & RANDALL, A. (1974). Music listening preferences of elementary school children. *Journal of Research in Music Education, 22*(4), 284–91.

LEHMAN, P. R. (1989). Assessing your program's effectiveness. *Music Educators Journal, 76*(4), 26–29.

LEHMAN, P. R. (1992). Curriculum and program evaluation. In R. Colwell (Ed.), *Handbook of research on music teaching and learning* (281–94). New York: Schirmer Books.

MELTON, A. W. (1933). Some behavior characteristics of museum vistors. *Psychological Bulletin, 30*, 720–721.

MILLS, R. P. (1989, December). Portfolios capture rich array of student performance. *The School Administrator*, pp. 8–11.

MUSIC EDUCATORS NATIONAL CONFERENCE (1986). *The school music program: Description and standards* (2d ed.). Reston, VA: Music Educators National Conference.

NATIONAL ASSESSMENT OF EDUCATIONAL PROGRESS (1970). *Music objectives*. Ann Arbor, MI: Author.

NATIONAL ASSESSMENT OF EDUCATIONAL PROGRESS (1974). *A perspective on the first music assessment* (Report No. 3-MU-02). Washington, DC: U.S. Government Printing Office.

NATIONAL ASSESSMENT OF EDUCATIONAL PROGRESS (1981). *Music 1971–79: Results from the second national music assessment* (Report No. 10-MU-01). Denver, CO: Educational Commission of the States.

NATIONAL COMMISSION ON EXCELLENCE IN EDUCATION (1984). *A nation at risk: The full account*. Westford, MA: Murray Printing Co.

STAKE, R. E. (1975). *Evaluating the arts in education: A responsive approach*. Columbus, OH: Charles E. Merrill.

STAKE, R. E. (1983). Program evaluation, particularly responsive evaluation. In G. F. Madaus, M. S. Scriven & D. L. Stufflebeam (Eds.), *Evaluation models* (pp. 279–86). Boston: Kluwer-Nijhoff.

STRONG, E. K. (1966). *Strong vocational interest blank for men and women*. New York: Consulting Psychologists Press.

TAEBEL, D. K. (1992). The evaluation of music teachers and teaching. In R. Colwell (Ed.), *Handbook of research on music teaching and learning* (pp. 310–30). New York: Schirmer Books.

WEBB, E. J., CAMPBELL, D. T., SCHWARTZ, R. D., & Sechrest, L. (1966). *Unobtrusive measures: Nonreactive research in the social sciences*. Chicago: Rand McNally.

CHAPTER 11

Research and Music Education

RESEARCH IN MUSIC EDUCATION or any other field represents the search for new knowledge. In a genuine sense, it is a seeking for reality and truth. As was pointed out in chapter 2, John Dewey and other pragmatists made scientific inquiry their chief means for determining what was true, and proposed the five steps outlined on page 46. Dewey's outline for scientific inquiry provides the structure that serves as a basis for what is often termed the *scientific method*.

Research is a key to progress in music education. Without it, the profession would be caught in a quagmire of conflicting opinions based on the personal experiences of thousands of music teachers who would probably continue to do things in the future in much the same way as they have been done in the past. Music education cannot afford such stagnation. New music will be composed, new means and equipment for teaching will be developed, and students will come to music classes with new interests and backgrounds. Continued progress in the profession is not only desirable, it is mandatory.

Science and Personal Experience

Why aren't personal impressions of what is truth good enough? After all, humankind has existed for thousands of years on the basis of people's personal perceptions without subjecting these views to scientific validation. And it is true that human beings can get along without research. The problem is that personal experience and opinion are unsystematic and subjective. There is an old tale about three blind men who happen on an elephant. Each grabs a different part of the animal and gains a different impression of it. The man holding the tusk says that an elephant must be hard and smooth; the man who grabbed the tail thinks the elephant is like a rope; the man who wrapped his arms around one of the elephant's legs thinks the animal must be like a large tree.

Each of the men in the tale tried to generalize from his own limited data. Human observation is inaccurate, however, people miss many things and incorrectly observe others. People also tend to see and hear what they want to see and hear; they practice what is termed "selective observation." The phenomenon is represented by an old saying having its words transposed to become "Believing is seeing." While watching a basketball game, the spectators are quick to note any pushing and shoving on the part of the visiting team and to overlook similar actions on the part of their home team. Furthermore, to keep from changing the beliefs they hold, people often make faulty deductions about an event that will allow them to retain their opinions. People's reasoning is often not logical. In other cases, people let their egos affect their objectivity. Once a person adopts a position publicly, it is a bit embarrassing to change it. Too often people have formed opinions that they do not wish to be altered by facts.

It is not being suggested here that research and scientific inquiry are a foolproof solution to the limitations and weaknesses of individual perception and objectivity. Scientists are human, and they also make mistakes. What research can do is significantly reduce the likelihood of the errors cited in the preceding paragraph. It reduces inaccurate observation by the simple fact that it is a *conscious* activity. If asked what your professor wore to class on the first day, the chances are that you would probably not remember. However, if you went to the first class knowing that you were going to record in your notebook what the professor wore, you would probably be quite accurate in gathering that piece of information. Research guards against overgeneralization by drawing on a number of instances. It encourages replication and/or collection of data from a large sample of subjects. Selective observation is avoided by establishing *before* the study begins what observations will be made, before egos and predispositions become too involved. Although research involves logic, it does not stop there. It also includes the process of objective study and often consists of studying phenomena under controlled conditions. Research may have its limitations, as a portion of this chapter points out, but to paraphrase Winston Churchill's comment about democracy, "Research may not be a very good way to arrive at the truth, but it is the best way that humankind has been able to develop."[*]

Because the information provided by research is subjected to more tests than personal impressions and opinions, it provides a better basis on which to make decisions. Many of us have faced the decision about whether or not to trade in a car. While we have our impressions about the condition and value of the old car, most of us want more facts before arriving at a decision about the new car. We want to know how much it would cost to get the rust spots fixed, the brakes relined, and the rip in the driver's seat repaired, as well as other pertinent facts. Such information cannot tell us what the decision should be, a point that will be discussed more fully later in this chapter. However, if we are to be clear on our priorities regarding a car (is it only for transportation or do we also want to impress people with it?), the information uncovered by our practical research efforts will aid in making a better decision than if we merely guessed at the various costs.

Values of Research

A hammer is a very useful tool—for certain purposes. It is fine for cracking walnuts or pounding nails; but if you try to fix a watch with it, you can do a great deal of damage. It is a bit like that with research. Used properly, research can be of much value to music educators, but it can be misunderstood or applied incorrectly. Therefore, being aware of what research can and cannot do is not only useful but mandatory for growth in the profession.

Differences Between the Physical and Social Sciences

People generally have great confidence in, and understand to some degree, the scientific method as applied to physical phenomena. And the results of the physical and biological sciences are impressive. The application of the scientific method to the social sciences—the study of human behavior—is a somewhat different matter. Although both physical and social sciences utilize the same general principles, there are some important differences between them.

To begin with, most of the topics studied in the social sciences are generalized notions or mental constructs that actually exist only in the human mind, and are not physical phenomena like sulfur and chlorophyll.

---

[*]The actual statement, made in the House of Commons on November 11, 1947, is: "Indeed, it has been said that democracy is the worst form of Government except all those other forms that have been tried from time to time" (*Oxford Dictionary of Quotations*, 1979, p. 150).

Musicianship, musical talent, creativity, attitudes, leadership, and many other potential research areas are mental constructs that people form from observing human behavior. None of these concepts can be held in the hand, photographed, or weighed on a scale, and therefore are somewhat subject to interpretation by each individual. Probably each one of us has a slightly different idea in our mind when we use a term like "musicianship." For this reason, when the topic is vague and poorly defined, a research study in the social sciences has a serious problem even before the data are gathered.

This is not to say that research on music aptitude and other mental constructs cannot be conducted. Rather, it means that constructs cannot be measured directly. Instead, researchers must study *indicators* of music aptitude or whatever construct is being studied. Think of the various subtests that are included in music-aptitude tests. The subjects are asked to do such things as discriminate between two pitch levels, select the better harmony or meter of two examples, and determine if the tempo of an example speeds up or slows down. Each subtest represents one indicator of what the maker of that test considered to be a part of the construct of music aptitude. The combination of a number of indicators, then, offers some information about a person's music aptitude as indicated by a particular test.

The precise definition of a concept in terms of indicators is no easy task. It is an important one, however, for anyone who tries to understand what the results of a research study indicate. Each research study must be considered in terms of the indicators chosen by the researcher to define the concepts being studied. Many disputes in education have arisen because people have chosen to define the same mental construct with somewhat different indicators. For example, does the ability to discriminate between the loudness levels of two tones indicate an aptitude for music or just good hearing? Does the ability to select what the test maker considers to be the better phrasing of two examples represent music aptitude or cultural conditioning? Although the results of research in music aptitude have produced few generalizations that everyone agrees with, a better understanding of musical ability exists today than would have been possible without such research.

Frequently people are disappointed that the social sciences cannot produce information of the same exactness and consistency as the physical sciences. The physical and biological sciences enjoy the advantage of being able to deal with more constant elements—temperature, chemical properties, molecular structure, and so on. An African violet plant reacts the same way whether or not people are watching it, while human beings usually react differently if they realize that someone is observing them. African violets can be given any amount or type of fertilizer or light, can be dismembered and examined, and so on. A researcher cannot do that with human beings! The conditions in which research in the social sciences is carried out can never be as tightly controlled as research in the "hard" sciences.

The physical sciences have another advantage. Most of us admit that we know little about physics or biochemistry, but few of us are lacking in ideas about how people should or do act. We are not as ready and willing to accept the findings of social scientists as we are those of physical scientists. Usually we are somewhat involved in the social science topic, be it learning, economics, or stereotyped thinking, and we have some practical knowledge about it. Therefore, we are not as objective in considering it.

One of the aims of science is to develop generalizations in the form of theories or laws describing the relationship between objects or events. Theories can be tested or validated by research. Theories are also successful in predicting events most (but not all) of the time. This is true of theories in the physical and biological sciences, as well as theories in the social sciences. For example, most of us can readily accept the tentativeness of the relationship between height and weight. In general, the taller an individual is, the heavier he or she is, but sometimes tall, thin people do weigh less than short, plump people. This notion of the "exception to the rule" also applies to theories of physics, but because the components of theories that the physical scientist is dealing with are more stable than the components of social science theories, theories in the "hard" sciences tend to produce better predictions.

In the social sciences, therefore, researchers must report results largely in terms of *tendencies* or *probabilities*. Furthermore, the results apply to groups or classes of persons, not individuals. For example, in the Abeles and Porter study (1978) of preferences for musical instruments according to gender, it was found that girls tended to choose flute while boys selected trombone. Those results do not mean that Heather Smith will choose flute instead of trombone; they merely indicate that the chances are greater that Heather and other girls will choose flute over trombone. The tentativeness of the conclusions of the social scientist, however, causes some people to question the value of such research.

Usually the physical sciences deal with quantities—so many grams of this, so many centimeters of that, and the like. Some of the time the social sciences also work with quantities; the U.S. census is an obvious example of this because it reports quantities of people in different locations. However, research in social sciences frequently involves *qualities*—which is better and which is not as good, which is more musical, and so on. Sometimes numerical values are assigned to qualities by evaluators, as when a pianist's interpretation of a Beethoven sonata is awarded so many points. The transformation from a quality to a quantity is not, however, straightforward. Suppose that one pianist is awarded ten points and another five. Is the high-scoring pianist twice as good an interpreter as the pianist with the lower score? Are two pianists who each score five equal in ability? Clearly that isn't so, which indicates the presence of errors in the assigning of numerical values to qualitative phenomena. The basic problem here is the ethereal nature of mental constructs, a topic discussed earlier. Transforming qualitative evaluations into quantities is often a necessary process in social science research. However, one should realize that the result of this transformation does involve a certain amount of error.

Proof or Confirmation?

One of the more confusing and perplexing matters in research concerns the idea of proof. The search for conclusive, "once and for all" proof makes scientists uneasy, for several reasons. Science always leaves open the possibility that an event, no matter how unlikely, could happen; it never assumes that all possible knowledge about a phenomenon has been uncovered. Countless times in the past, new discoveries have rendered old facts obsolete. Therefore, researchers report results as "confirming" or "accepting" a conditional idea (referred to as a *hypothesis* in research terminology) instead of "proving" an established fact.

Another reason for hesitation in claiming proof is the fact that the results of any study apply only to the particular conditions studied. Suppose that a researcher wished to learn about the musical preferences of teenagers. A survey conducted in 1965 might give one set of data and a survey in 1995 might produce another result. Yet both sets of information might be accurate for the time in which they were conducted and for the age of the group surveyed.

The hesitation in using the word "proved" can also be attributed to the fact that human behavior is far too complex for absolute statements to be made about it. Human beings have a way of upsetting any hard and fast predictions about what they will do. If anyone tells you that he or she is sure of which way you will vote in an election, you just might be perverse enough to vote the opposite way. Compared to human beings, the elements that chemists and biologists deal with seem simple.

Researchers are careful about claiming proof in yet another way. When they analyze the results of a study involving comparisons of two or more variables, they require that the burden of proof be in terms of establishing a difference.* This procedure might be compared to a basic tenet in the American system of justice that a defendant is presumed innocent until found guilty in a court of law. It is up to the prosecution to establish "beyond a reasonable doubt" that the defendant did commit the crime. What if guilt is not established? Does that confirm that the defendant is innocent? No; it merely means that it has not been established that he or she is guilty.

---

*In research parlance, a statement assuming no significant difference is a *null hypothesis*.

There is an important point here in understanding research. Suppose that two methods of teaching children to sing are tested, and when the results are analyzed, there is found to be no statistically significant difference between them. Has the study established that one method is as effective as the other? Not really. It merely indicates that *in this particular experiment* no significant difference was found between the two methods. Were the experiment to be replicated with one variable changed (maybe conducted over a longer period of time or with second-grade students or in conjunction with the use of hand signs) the results *might* be quite different—or they might not be different.

Can researchers ever come to the point of asserting that there is no significant difference between the two methods of teaching songs? Yes, but only after a number of trials of the methods have been conducted under somewhat different conditions and with results indicating no significant difference. Never should a general result be claimed on the basis of one or two studies.

Causation

Research studies can report accurately on what happened in a particular situation. Coming up with a reason or reasons *why* something happened is a far more difficult undertaking. This is true for several reasons. Any condition or fact rarely has a single cause; usually several factors influence a phenomenon. Things are rarely as simple as they seem. Musical preferences, for example, are affected not only by the year in which a preference study is conducted, but also by the subjects' age, musical background, intelligence, ethnic group, family background, self-image, and on and on. As biologist Garret Hardin has said, the first law of ecology is: "You can't do *one* thing" (Babbie, 1979, p. 428). Whatever action is taken always affects something else, because in life (and apparently in ecology), phenomena are very much intertwined with each other, and each affects something else.

If a student clarinetist plays a particular passage badly and is moved down a chair by the director, it may be accurately (although superficially) stated that he or she has been demoted for musical reasons. However, the matter of causation is usually deeper than the immediate cause. In this case there are probably other factors that have contributed to the demotion. Perhaps there is a personality conflict between the director and the clarinetist, who may have been resentful when previous efforts were made to improve his or her performance; or maybe the director is merely exhibiting egocentricity or an obsessive need to dominate a situation. If it is a matter of personality, what factors have contributed to the director's aggressive behavior or the clarinetist's uncooperative attitude? Perhaps it was the recent loss of a loved one, or a case of peptic ulcers, or a drive for perfection brought on years ago by an excessively domineering parent, or overanxiety created by fear of a poor rating in a music contest.

The chain of causation is continuous and complex, with no clear beginning or end, as Herbert Spencer pointed out well over a century ago (1860, p. 62) in telling about finding a fallen bird in a field and wondering why it could no longer fly. Each explanation brought him to a more general proposition until, as he concludes, "Of necessity, therefore, explanation must eventually bring us down to the inexplicable. The deepest truth which we can get at must be unaccountable." If nothing else, the complex chain of interrelated causes and explanations should make anyone, especially researchers, cautious in making claims about knowing the cause for something.

Not only is the matter of cause an intricate one, it is also easy to be mistaken about it. Each spring in the northern half of the United States the grass turns green and the birds come flocking back. Does the greening of the grass cause the birds to return, or possibly does the return of the birds cause the grass to become green? The two events are related in that they happen at about the same time; therefore, according to common sense, one must cause the other. However, neither the birds nor the green grass influences the other; a third factor—warm weather—is the immediate cause of both events. Therefore, what is related may or may not be causally related, although superficially it may appear that way.

Data and Values

As mentioned earlier in this chapter, research results can provide information, but they cannot make decisions; only people can do that. Often decisions are made on the basis of values as much as they are on facts. For example, a research study might show that one method of teaching clarinet tends to improve the ability to finger notes but also encourages poor methods of tone production and consequently a less-than-desirable tone quality. Whether one should use that method would depend on one's values regarding the relative importance of tone quality v. finger technique, and research data cannot decide that question. However, research findings can provide information about the extent to which finger technique is improved and tone quality reduced. Knowing that, one could make a more intelligent decision, which is certainly preferable to deciding on the basis of intuition or personal bias.

Acceptance of Research by Music Educators

Unfortunately, many music teachers find research difficult to understand, and they harbor doubts about its value. Seldom are these doubts openly expressed, because music educators, at least those who teach at the college level, feel that they ought to be interested in research. For them, opposing research would be a bit like disapproving of good weather; it just isn't done. Instead, many music teachers secretly question the usefulness of it all, and whether it makes any difference in what they should do when they stand before their classes.

Part of the trouble with research may stem from an inherent contradiction between the "artistic" aspect of music and the more "scientific" process involving an objective analysis of teaching. Reading an analysis of systematically collected data may seem rather sterile and cold to people who are fond of the emotional qualities of a fine musical work. Reconciling the intellectual and emotional sides of the human personality is never easy, but to music teachers, who are so involved with feelings and personal expression, the reconciliation is probably particularly difficult.

The dichotomy between art and science is not the only reason why many music teachers ignore research; in fact, it may not even be an important one. As is true of most areas of life, there is no simple, single reason. Here are several circumstances that appear to contribute to the situation, in spite of the efforts of a number of music educators who have been active in such research organizations as the Music Education Research Council of MENC.

1. Often, or so it seems, the results of research studies end up confirming what most people already know or think they know; little that is new and startling is revealed. There appears to be a human tendency, however, to think one already knew what he or she later finds out is fact. So common is this human foible that social psychologists have given it a name: the "I-knew-it-all-along" phenomenon (Myers, 1990, pp. 20–22). For example, data from the U.S. Bureau of the Census confirm the general opinion that women live longer than men, so to the lay public that fact seems hardly worth studying. Researchers, however, value the knowledge that common belief and perception in this matter is supported by reliable data.

There is a more important reason, however, for conducting research on what may appear to be something that everyone "knows." Every so often research uncovers information that is contrary to what nearly everyone thinks is so. For example, at one time it was believed that the best way to teach reading was to have students learn the letters of the alphabet, then words, then phrases, and then sentences (Swaby, 1984, p. 29). This method, called the "ABC method," seems logical. However, people do not always operate logically, or what appears to be logically. Research studies uncovered the fact that people actually read by fixing their eyes on groups of words, not letters or individual words. The faster readers have fewer fixations per line than the slower readers. Hence, what had been accepted as the truth about reading was abandoned, and better methods for teaching reading are the result.

2. In the past many studies were (and some being conducted today still are) irrelevant and insignificant in terms of being useful to the field of music education. Such studies cannot be generalized to other situations. Even the philosopher-psychologist William James complained about instances in which researchers "would go off by themselves and use apparatus and consult sources in such a way as to grind out in the requisite number of months some little peppercorn of new truth worthy of being added to the store of extant information on the subject" (James, 1958, p. 38). Clearly, what is irrelevant to one person may be of much interest to another person, so the matter of the usefulness of a study is partly a matter of opinion. Music teachers, however, find studies that can be applied to teaching situations to be more relevant and useful to music education, and many studies have been conducted in the field that do not directly fulfill that condition.

3. Many teachers do not realize that one or two studies on a topic rarely provide an adequate amount of research information, no matter how competently they may have been conducted. This fact is especially true of complex topics, and most matters involved with teaching are complex. Studies are frequently replicated in the physical sciences, and only after several studies have produced consistent results are findings generally accepted.

4. The number of areas in music education in which a sufficient amount of research has been conducted to form conclusions is quite small. Music education is not a large field like reading or biological science, and the funds available from the U.S. Department of Education, the National Endowment for the Arts, and other sources for research are very limited. As a result, there simply is not a great deal of research data on which music educators can build, even if they wished to do so. The limited amount of research studies available discourages the basing of educational practices on objective data, which in turn discourages research, thus creating a cyclical situation that is detrimental to progress in the profession.

5. Sometimes the writing used in research reports seems to be foggy and abstruse. While this criticism of research writing is somewhat true, some use of precise, specialized terminology and statistical techniques is unavoidable if accuracy is desired. Some readers falsely assume that what they do not understand is just so much "mumbo-jumbo" and reject it out of hand. Other readers try to wade through the sometimes needlessly complex prose and statistical analysis, only to find it quite unrewarding.

6. Many researchers see their role as being that of producers of knowledge; the application of the information they uncover is left to others. Teachers sometimes read research studies hoping to find suggestions for applying the data to classroom situations. Usually they are disappointed in finding nothing about application, because most research reports are written for other researchers. The research community has recognized this

problem and has made attempts to address it by publishing practitioner-oriented articles in state music journals and *UPDATE.*

Often the setting of the research project affects the ease with which the results can be applied to the music classroom. If the project is carried out in a laboratory, it can be tightly controlled, which will probably lead to results in which the researcher has considerable confidence. But the results of the experiment cannot be generalized easily to the "real world." When studies are conducted in the field (that is, actually in the music classroom), much less control is possible. Therefore, the researcher has less confidence that the results of the experiment are valid, but such experiments are more easily generalized to the music teaching-learning situation.

7. It is not uncommon in research in the behavioral sciences for the results of one study to contradict the results of another study. This can occur for several different reasons, some of which were mentioned earlier in this chapter and are inherent in applying the scientific method to the social sciences. One reason for apparently contradictory results is that the researchers may not have the same mental constructs in mind, even though they employ the same words for the constructs. A second reason is the conditional nature of research data. What is true under one set of conditions may not be true under another; sometimes a small change in a study can dramatically affect the results obtained.

Of course, not all studies are conducted competently. Researchers are human; occasionally they make mistakes. In music education a great deal of the available research consists of doctoral dissertations. These dissertations are usually a person's first sizable piece of research and writing. Normally such studies are done with little or no financial support, and the doctoral candidates are under pressure to complete their work within a specified number of years. Therefore, the topics doctoral candidates can hope to study are limited to those they can do on their own and complete in a reasonable amount of time.

8. Teachers sometimes find research reports frustrating because the studies end up raising more questions than they answered. Actually, this is to be expected. Research studies do provide new information, but that new information usually raises additional questions. Let's return to the hypothetical study in which the results clearly indicate that a certain method of teaching clarinet results in better finger technique but a poorer tone quality. What seems to contribute to this result? Could better finger technique be achieved without hurting tone quality? Is the loss in tone quality only temporary? Do most students react to the method in about the same way, or are certain types of students not affected? And one could go on and on with similar questions. Although at first glance the presence of new questions may seem undesirable, that is not so. The new questions are based on better information than was previously available, and more pertinent than they would have been without the research data. In short,

the researcher (and music education) are better off, even if more questions have been raised.

Locating Research Reports

It is not the purpose of this chapter to delve deeply into matters related to carrying out research studies. There are number of books devoted exclusively to that matter, and this book centers on the foundations of music education, of which research is only one aspect. However, an awareness of and interest in research is important for any music educator. For most music teachers the form that such an interest takes is the reading of reports about research, with the subsequent application of the results to classroom activities.

Locating reports of research in music education may be approached in several ways. Ideally music educators will, as a part of their routine professional activity, read research journals in the field. The most widely read refereed journal (i.e., the articles are reviewed by other researchers before they are accepted for publication) in the field is the *Journal of Research in Music Education*. Other journals, such as the *Bulletin of the Council for Research in Music Education* and the *Quarterly Journal of Music Teaching and Learning* publish research-based articles as well as position or policy papers. There are also more specialized research journals to which music professionals in specific areas may wish to subscribe. These include the *Journal of Band Research*, the *Bulletin of Historical Research in Music Education, Journal of Research in Singing,* and *Dialogue in Instrumental Music Education*. In addition, a few states (e.g., Ohio) publish their own music education research journals. Other published sources of reports of research are state music education magazines or newsletters, many of which contain columns that summarize research studies of interest.

UPDATE: The Applications of Research in Music Education is a journal that was begun in 1982 and published by MENC since 1990. It is an important source of research information for practitioners because its goal is to disseminate research findings through articles written in nontechnical terms. Many of the articles published in *UPDATE* are syntheses of research. Each synthesis summarizes an area of music education (e.g., choral rehearsals or mainstreaming in music education) in which several studies have been conducted and some practical applications may be developed.

In 1992 MENC and Schirmer Books joined forces to publish the *Handbook of Research on Music Teaching and Learning*, which was edited by Richard Colwell. The handbook is comprised of fifty-five chapters, each by a different author or group of authors. Many of the chapters include comprehensive reviews of research in the focus area of the chapter. The handbook is divided into eight sections: "Conceptual Framework,"

"Research Modes and Techniques," "Evaluation," "Perception and Cognition," "Teaching and Learning Strategies," "The Teaching of Specific Musical Skills and Knowledge in Different Instructional Settings" (e.g., teaching singing or teaching middle-school general music), "Schools/Curriculum," and "Social and Institutional Settings." In the preface, Colwell states: "Use of the handbook will allow individuals in teaching and research to avoid pitfalls already encountered by our colleagues and to capitalize on strengths that have been attained by many successful teachers but not disseminated to the profession (p. xi)." Clearly this volume is a valuable resource for the researcher as well as the practitioner in music education.

Another source readily available to all music education professionals is the presentations of research reports at professional meetings. Many state meetings and all national MENC meetings have sessions devoted to reporting research results. While some of the sessions may be oriented mainly toward communicating with other researchers, other sessions are devoted to applying research results. This is particularly true of sessions at state music education meetings. Music educators should seek out opportunities to discuss projects that interest them with the researchers who conducted them.

Occasionally the professional music educator needs to locate research information on a specific topic. This can most readily be obtained by systematically searching several available bibliographical sources. If the subject is not too narrow, one might start with the card catalog of a good library. Often the reference lists of books with general chapters on the topic are a good starting place for leads to other, more specific primary sources. In addition to books, the general reference section of the library contains bibliographical materials with indexes to help locate topics. Bibliographical sources that may be of particular value for music education researchers include *Music Index, Current Index to Journals in Education*, and *Music Psychology Index*. Other useful bibliographical sources include the Educational Retrieval Information Center (ERIC) and Répertoire International de la Musique (RILM). *Dissertation Abstracts International* is also an important source for the music education researcher because much of the research conducted in the field consists of doctoral dissertations. Many reference sources contain abstracts in addition to information to assist the reader in locating documents (e.g., *Dissertation Abstracts International*). Abstracts are brief summaries of documents that assist the researcher in determining whether a document is truly relevant to their area of interest. Many journals also include abstracts at the beginning of articles to help readers quickly decide which reports are worth reading in depth.

More recently many researchers have found it efficient to use computer search and retrieval systems. There are several such systems available.

They are usually located at university libraries, and usually there is some search fee charged, but the time saved by using such systems is usually well worth the cost involved. In choosing a computer search system, it is important for the music educator to know precisely what sources are available in the system. One that does not include articles from the *Journal of Research in Music Education* will miss important information on many topics in the field. It would also be important for the system to include dissertations, for the reasons stated earlier.

Analysis of Research Results

Securing a report on research is just the first step. To read it with understanding is the primary objective. Many dissertations and reports follow a similar pattern. First, the background and need for the study is described; such information places the study in the field. Second, a brief summary of related research follows. Third, the research procedures followed in the study are described: the length of the study, types of tests and subjects used, experimental procedures (if any), and so on. Finally, the researcher-writer presents the results and offers his or her interpretation of them, and often makes suggestions for further research. The sequence of sections in a research report may vary for historical, philosophical, and ethnographic studies.

Once readers have decided that the study is of interest, usually by examining the first section of the report, they may then be curious to find out "what happened." This information is reported in the results and discussion sections. In the last several decades it has become quite common for the results section to include statistics. This has been necessitated by the use of certain research methods (to be described later in this chapter) and by the need for precision in reporting results. Statistics are a powerful tool for the researcher, and they can be rather easily interpreted by research consumers who keep in mind a few general points about statistics.

There are two general categories of research techniques: *descriptive* statistics and *inferential* statistics. The primary objective of statistics belonging to the descriptive family is to describe the data obtained in the study. There are usually three ways in which data are described. First, if there is a group of scores, researchers frequently want to be able to report one number that succinctly describes the group's relative position on a scale. This can be achieved by reporting the arithmetic average, or *mean*, of the scores in the group. Another aspect of this group of scores that researchers may wish to describe is the spread, or distribution, of the scores. One way this can be summarized is by reporting the distance between the lowest and highest scores, or the *range*. Finally, if there are two sets of data, researchers may wish to describe the extent to which they are related.

Describing the relationship between different characteristics of things or people is a common practice. Some examples include the relationship between rate of speed and miles per gallon in automobiles, or between height and weight in an individual. When such relationships need to be described precisely, researchers employ a statistic called the *correlation coefficient*. Bar graphs and line graphs also belong to the descriptive statistical family.

The other family of statistics is inferential statistics. The major function of this type of statistical data is to indicate when researchers can have sufficient confidence in their results to say that they are likely to occur again if their procedures were to be repeated. This ability to *generalize* is an indispensable tool for social science researchers. It allows them to work with a *sample*, or small group, and then make statements regarding a much larger *population* with similar characteristics (e.g., fourth-grade students in rural schools).

Researchers, of course, can never be certain that what occurs in one sample will occur in another, so they usually talk in terms of what will *probably* occur in other groups. Because of their desire to be precise, researchers usually indicate exactly how confident they are that a result they obtained is likely to occur again. If they are not very confident that the result they obtained is replicable, they say that it probably occurred by chance.

The researchers' way of identifying to other researchers whether or not they think the results they obtained were due to chance or a function of the procedure employed in the study is to use the term *statistical significance*. When researchers say the results are statistically significant, they are telling the reader that the results will probably generalize to other samples. Researchers are quite precise in their description of how much confidence they have in the generalizability of their results. They report a level of significance of confidence, traditionally .05, which indicates to the reader precisely how much chance there is that they may have been incorrect in the conclusions they drew. The .05 level indicates that there are five chances out of 100 that the results obtained could have been due to chance rather than the procedures of the study. The use of the .05 level of confidence is a convention that has generally been adopted by researchers in the social sciences as the appropriate risk level for making decisions regarding results. However, there is nothing magic about that number.

Often the notion of statistical significance is confused with the vernacular use of the term *importance*. They are *not* the same. "Statistical significance" simply refers to how much confidence can be placed in the results. The practitioner, of course, also needs to know how "important" a result is. This may be referred to as *practical significance*. For example, an experiment comparing methods of teaching ear training involving large number of students may produce a statistically significant result, but the mean of the group may be only a point or two apart. This difference is so small that it is of little value in deciding which method of ear training is more effective. In other words, one can have confidence in the results of a study, but the difference in scores between the groups may be so modest that they are meaningless.

It should be emphasized that the interpretation of the results of a study begins rather than ends with the decision regarding statistical significance. The practitioner's knowledge of the "real world" is critical in deciding whether the results of a study are of sufficient importance.

Research Methods

The steps of scientific approach described earlier in chapter 2 provide a general outline for designing systematic investigations, but are too general for conducting actual studies. Therefore, more specific sets of procedures have been developed to help find data related to certain types of problems. Although different writers have different systems for categorizing these methods and different labels to identify them, five broad categories seem to be generally agreed on: experimental research, historical research, descriptive research, ethnographic research, and philosophical research. It is helpful for readers of research to become acquainted with the general strategies and limitations of each method so that they are better able to understand reports of research employing these different methods.

Descriptive Research

When music educators seek to answer "What is?" questions, they read and/or conduct studies employing *descriptive research* methods. Such studies may seek to describe the existing state of an individual, group, or phenomenon. They describe trends and relationships, and also compare or contrast differences and similarities among phenomena in an effort to discover possible reasons for any differences that are observed. Descriptive research, however, cannot establish cause-effect relationships.

All of us at one time or another have participated in descriptive research studies. The most common subtype, *survey research*, seeks to provide information regarding the current status of phenomena. Survey research frequently employs questionnaires and/or interview strategies for collecting data. Public opinion polls such as those frequently reported in the media are a common example of this approach. Surveys not only seek to describe the characteristics of a particular group or phenomenon but often provide information allowing comparisons (e.g., Republicans vs. Democrats; instrumental music teachers vs. choral music teachers).

While surveys tend to be somewhat superficial descriptions, *case studies* are intensive investigations focusing on an individual or social unit. They often employ a variety of data collection techniques over a period of time in an effort to describe the unique features of the individual or group under investigation. Classic studies such as the *Middletown, U.S.A.* study, which focuses on Muncie, Indiana, and the famous *Two Faces of Eve* illustrate this approach. Reports of case studies are not common in music education. They are more often seen in music therapy journals, where clinical descriptions of individual clients are a well-established research approach.

Correlation studies seek to describe the relationship between two or more characteristics or phenomena. Such studies typically first gather information on the characteristics being compared through the administration of tests or surveys. The relationship of the results of these tests or surveys is then described quantitatively employing a correlation coefficient. The correlation of coefficient is an index ranging from -1.00 to $+1.00$, which provides information on the direction and strength of a relationship. Correlation coefficients around $+1.00$ or -1.00 (e.g., .92, $-.85$) indicate strong relationships. A positive coefficient indicates that the items increase or decrease together, such as the tightness of a violin string and the frequency that the string produces (as tension increases, pitch goes up). Negative coefficients indicate that the items being compared move in opposite directions, such as the length of a violin string and the pitch the string produces (as length increases, pitch goes down).

Correlation studies are frequently used to examine how the characteristics of individuals may be related. A typical study might report a correlation coefficient between scores on a music aptitude test and scores on an intelligence test in an effort to discover if these two traits are related. Other typical correlation studies may compare questionnaire responses to such items as the number of marching band contests participated in and the size of band parent support organizations.

It must again be emphasized that correlation studies do not establish cause and effect. One may find that two characteristics are highly correlated, for instance, height and weight. This does not suggest that weighing a lot *causes* one to be tall, or vice versa. Rather, it is likely that other factors, such as eating habits or genetic inheritance, influence both factors.

Another type of descriptive study is the *developmental study*. In this type of investigation the primary focus is on examining changes that occur as a function of time. Longitudinal studies in music education, for example, might examine any changes that occur in music ability as children mature. However, such studies are not very common in music education, because they require longer periods of time to complete than most other research strategies. This is unfortunate, because many important questions in the field require a developmental approach.

Ethnographic Research

During the decade of the 1980s there was a rapid increase in the number of research studies in education published using ethnographic research methods. This emphasis is also reflected in research in music education, where a small but increasing number of studies employing ethnographic strategies have appeared. Some researchers consider ethnographic research as a subcategory of descriptive research because it shares many of the same characteristics. The strategies employed in such studies are often identified by different labels including ethnography, qualitative research, naturalistic research, case studies, and field research. They all have similar characteristics. Researchers employing these methods seek to describe phenomena in the settings in which they exist naturally. This is in contrast to experimental researchers who purposefully manipulate the experimental circumstance to observe the consequences of the manipulation. Bresler and Stake (1992, p. 79) list seven characteristics of qualitative research:

1. *It is holistic.* It considers the contexts of the study.

2. *It is empirical.* There is an emphasis on unobtrusive observation.

3. *It is descriptive.* The descriptions are more often qualitative than quantitative.

4. *It is interpretive.* Researchers attempt to assign meaning to their observations.

5. *It is empathic.* It attempts to understand the motives of the players in the research setting.

6. *Some researchers emphasize working from the bottom up.* Ethnographic researchers do not generally use hypotheses to direct their work, but instead may develop hypotheses as a consequence of their research.

7. *Observations and immediate interpretations are validated.* Researchers seek multiple sources of information to assist in confirming or challenging their interpretations.

An early and classic series of studies in music education sponsored by the Pillsbury Foundation employed ethnographic methods (Moorhead & Pond, 1941, 1942, 1944, 1951). The research focused on the musical creativity of three-to six-year old children. The children were in a particularly creative environment and were encouraged to explore. The primary method of the study was detailed observation. The research reports included detailed descriptions of the creative activities of the children, and the final report consisted of cases studies including biographical information and family background.

There are strengths and weakness to the strategy of each research method. The strengths of ethnographic studies are the rich understandings of the environment in which the phenomenon occurs—the real context of music education with all its messiness (e.g., the classroom or rehearsal room, with its infinite number of uncontrolled variables). The ethnographer is not satisfied with the constraints of other empiricists or what is seen as the imposed sterility of the experimental research setting. However, ethnographers need to be concerned about the subjectivity of their observations, the difficulty of organizing voluminous and idiosyncratic data, and the ability to generalize the results of their studies to relate to other settings. The uniqueness of the research environment that is the strength of the ethnographic method is therefore at the same time also limiting.

Historical Research

While historical studies focus on the question "What was?" it is important to remember that these studies are initiated primarily to help understand the present. They are similar to studies employing descriptive research methods in that the primary activity involved is the collection of data. However, the type of evidence collected by the historical researcher differs considerably from that employed in descriptive studies. While music educators employing descriptive research techniques frequently have the "luxury" of asking subjects specific questions designed to elicit responses directly related to the research concerns under investigation, historical researchers must rely on evidence that was not necessarily specifically designed to meet those concerns. Thus, the type and validity of source materials becomes a major issue for the historical researcher.

Historical researchers classify sources of evidence into two categories: *primary sources* and *secondary sources*. Primary sources are original records, eyewitness descriptions, photographs, tape recordings, and similar sources that provide for a minimum amount of interpretation that may influence the evidence. Secondary sources provide evidence that is at least one step removed from the actual event. Examples of secondary sources include newspaper stories, textbooks, and other sources that allow for the distortion of events by the interpretation of the author. It may be best to think of historical research sources as being on a continuum, with one end of the continuum representing primary sources characterized by no possibility of distortion through interpretation and the other end of the continuum representing the most secondary sources, characterized by being several steps removed from the event and subject to considerable interpretation.

It should be obvious that the music educator employing historical research strategies should first seek out primary sources of evidence. When primary sources are not available, secondary sources must be employed.

The skilled historian is never completely confident of the evidence provided by such sources and always attempts to establish their validity.

The veracity of historical evidence has two dimensions labeled by historians as *external criticism* and *internal criticism*. Is the diary genuine? Was the score actually written by a certain composer? These are questions of external criticism that are concerned with the genuineness or validity of the data employed by the historical researcher. Internal criticism focuses on the truthfulness of the information reported in a document that has already been established as valid. Do the descriptions of the events contained in the diary actually depict the events? Was the recording equipment of such poor quality that the performance is distorted? Internal criticism seeks to establish the true meaning of the content of a data source.

The value of historical research to the music educator is strongly related to the question of relevance. As Heller and Wilson (1982) state: "Methods and materials, techniques and literature, skills and concepts are the accumulated wisdom of many past labors. It is not necessary for teachers to reinvent the wheel at each moment of the instructional process. Trends in music education recur" (p. 16).

Experimental Research

"What happened under carefully controlled conditions?" is the question answered by experimental research studies. Experimental research strategies differ from other research methods in that they allow the researcher to identify *cause-effect* relationships to a limited extent. These strategies, therefore, allow researchers to draw conclusions regarding the prediction of behavior (i.e., if this procedure is followed, the students will be more likely to do this). No other research strategy provides researchers with this capability.

Experimental research follows the scientific method, employing the problem identification-hypothesis-observation-conclusion sequence that was mentioned in chapter 2. Experimental investigators endeavor to control the observational setting and attempt to eliminate all explanations for the observed "effect" other than the one under investigation. In descriptive research, on the other hand, events are reported as they occur without researcher intervention.

A *variable* can be thought of as a characteristic or procedure that is changeable; that is, it can take on different characteristics or quantities (e.g., instrumental performer: clarinetist, pianist, flutist, etc.). In experimental studies the procedure or method being examined is labeled the *independent* (or *treatment* or *experimental*) variable, and its effect is measured on the *dependent* (or *criterion*) variable. An independent variable is one that has been selected for examination by the experimenter. It is changed or manipulated by the researcher, and the effect of this manipulation is observed on one or more dependent variables. The key words in this definition of "independent variable" are "selected" and "manipulated." The manipulation of the independent variable typically involves presentation of different levels or types (e.g., programmed instruction, lectures, textbooks) to different groups of students in a controlled situation. Changes in the students' behavior that result from the exposure are measured by the students' performances on the dependent variable (e.g., a music fundamentals test or the playing of a specified exercise). The dependent variable evolves directly from the hypothesis, and it often produces quantitative data that can be analyzed statistically. It is selected by the researcher to assess the effects of the experimental treatment of the independent variable, which then allows a researcher to make a judgment regarding a hypothesis.

The *research hypothesis* is a tentative statement describing what effect in the dependent variable is likely to occur by manipulating the independent variable. It may attempt to explain previously observed phenomena. For example, a researcher may observe that some students perform well on an entrance audition while others perform poorly. To confirm these observations, the researcher might hypothesize that those who have had solo performance experience prior to the audition are less anxious and therefore perform better. In this case the researcher is attempting to account for the differences among performers by hypothesizing that previous solo experience may affect performance during an audition. The hypothesis ("Students with previous solo experience will generally receive higher audition scores than other students") is based upon the researcher's experience of sitting on many entrance audition juries and observing the characteristics of students who do well. This hypothesis may also be based on observations or on research that others have done.

A hypothesis stating that a cause-effect relationship exists between good audition performances and the gender of the performer would probably not explain a large proportion of the observed differences among those who audition; there is little evidence that gender affects the ability to play at auditions. Researchers endeavor to select hypotheses that account for large portions of the observed differences. The ability to select plausible hypotheses is probably related to the familiarity of researchers with the field being investigated, so experienced music educators are likely to make the best music education researchers—a statement that is itself a hypothesis.

The manipulation of the independent variable takes place in a controlled situation. This allows researchers to isolate the independent variable so that they have confidence that any effects observed in the dependent variable were the result of changes in the independent variable. Chemists control their experiments by carefully measuring the amounts of the substances used and keeping them at a consistent temperature. Educational researchers employ some of the same strategies to add control to their studies, such as using the same textbook for each class in the study, teaching comparison classes at the same time of day, and making sure all the saxophonists play "Exercise No. 16" at $\downarrow = 72$.

The major difficulty in establishing control of the experimental setting for educational researchers is the main material they work with—people. While chemists can take two teaspoons of NaCl from the same bottle, put three grams each into two different beakers, and be relatively confident the materials they are working with are homogeneous, the music education researcher cannot place the students in the left half of an orchestra in one group, and the students in the right half in another group, and expect any kind of equivalence. The students in each half will differ in a variety of ways. They will play different instruments, be of different genders, sizes, and shapes, and have different intellectual and musical abilities. All of these differences could serve as alternative explanations to the independent variable for any effects observed in the dependent variable.

Because people possess so many characteristics that can serve as alternative explanations for an effect in an experiment, educational researchers have determined that, when possible, the *random assignment* of people to groups is the best strategy to employ. This procedure allows only *chance* differences to occur between the groups, rather than systematic differences in the subjects that might affect the results. These chance differences can then be evaluated with inferential statistical techniques that are based on chance.

Thus, much care must be taken in designing experiments in music education. The use of comparable groups of subjects whose members have been randomly assigned, the control of other situational factors, and the use of inferential statistics are all important characteristics of well-designed experiments. The number and sophistication of experimental research studies in music education have increased in recent decades. In many experimental studies the statistical manipulations seem overwhelming to music educators. However, by keeping in mind the general principles of experimental research described in this chapter, many of these studies can be understood.

The Philosophical Method

There is considerable disagreement on whether the terms "philosophical" and "research" (as in "philosophical research") can correctly be linked together. In general, philosophy and science are viewed as involving different activities and having different goals. Scientists are primarily concerned with describing phenomena. Science tries to answer the questions "What?" "What is?" "What was?" "What will be under certain conditions?" Philosophy, on the other hand, is concerned with interpreting phenomena:

"philosophy seeks to identify and evaluate the lenses through which we construct experience" (Stubley, 1992, p. 44). "Essentially the music educator comes to philosophy . . . to seek critical and logical grounds for developing consistencies between contemplation *and* action, between what is *and* what could (or should) be" (Schwadron, 1973, p. 42). Actually philosophy and science seem to play complementary roles, with science providing the foundation of knowledge around which philosophy can develop value judgments.

Regardless of whether one chooses to label this philosophical activity as research, it is valuable to the profession because it provides both practitioners and researchers with a sense of direction and purpose. This method provides a systematic way of working with ideas by theorizing, speculating, and evaluating.

The "system" that scholars employing the philosophical method use can be viewed as being somewhat similar to the scientific method. The methods of philosophy are logical induction and logical deduction, and the tools the philosopher employs are rigorous analysis and synthesis. Frequently philosophers begin with isolated phenomena. They then may attempt to identify patterns or relationships from which general principles inherent in these patterns are derived. These general principles may then be stated in the form of hypotheses. These hypotheses can then be tested logically for consistency and validity. It should be remembered that logic is a mental process, so while other methods discussed in this section strive for objectivity by observing phenomena, the philosophical approach is based on the process of logical thinking. This does not suggest that one strategy is more likely to arrive at the "truth" than another, but it does clearly distinguish between the approaches.

There are several examples of studies employing the philosophical method in the professional literature of music education research. These include studies focusing on aesthetics as a rationale for music education, curriculum studies that are applications of theoretical or philosophical positions, and studies that explore the rationale for certain professional goals. Philosophical research therefore has the potential for complementing, as well as providing new directions for, music education research.

Reading Research Reports

Professional music educators need to keep abreast of new knowledge in the field. One source of such information is the articles published in music education research journals. When reading research articles it is helpful to have a systematic procedure for organizing the information they present. The following outline provides questions organized into categories that can assist readers in understanding research reports.

I. What research method was employed? Which of the following questions did it attempt to answer?
  A. What was? (historical)
  B. What is? (descriptive)
  C. What will be under certain conditions? (experimental)
  D. What should be? (philosophical)
II. Why was the study undertaken?
  A. What was the problem being investigated?
  B. How did it relate to previous research?
III. What were the major factors or variables considered in the study? How are they defined?
IV. What was the major research question or hypothesis? Were there subquestions?
V. What were the sample and sources?
  A. If it was an experimental or descriptive study, who was included in the sample?
    1. Was the sample randomly selected?
    2. Was it representative?
    3. To whom can the results of the study be generalized?
  B. If it was a historical study, what types of sources were employed?
VI. What procedure was followed by the researcher?
  A. Was it logically derived from the hypothesis?
  B. If it was an experimental study, how was the experimental setting controlled?
  C. If it was a historical study, how was the validity of the sources and the truthfulness of their content established?
VII. How were the data analyzed?
VIII. What were the results?
  A. Which presentation of results was most informative?
  B. Did the author succinctly state what happened?
  C. Can the results be generalized to other situations?
IX. What are the implications for teaching music?
  A. Did the study answer the research question posed?
  B. Did the results agree with prior research in the area?
  C. Can the results be applied? How?

The following article appeared in the *Journal of Research in Music Education* (Winter, 1988).

ROSEANNE K. ROSENTHAL, MARY WILSON,
MADELINE EVANS, LARRY GREENWALT,
VANDERCOOK COLLEGE OF MUSIC, CHICAGO

Effects of Different Practice Conditions on Advanced Instrumentalists' Performance Accuracy[*]

Listening, singing, and silent analysis are common practice techniques that musicians use to help themselves and others master music literature. For example, listening to a model of music to be learned (as well as observing techniques to be learned) plays a critical role in the Suzuki approach to music education (Suzuki, 1969) as well as in more traditional teaching, during which the teacher, perhaps less formally, sings or plays a part to be learned. Puopolo (1971) and Zurcher (1975) found that modeling can be effectively used to facilitate children's practice at home, and Rosenthal (1984) found that modeling aids college students' mastery of a musical selection. Other researchers have suggested that children may learn to prefer an inappropriate rendition of a song if it is what they have been hearing (Baker, 1980). Even creativity in melodic improvisation may be influenced by modeling (Partchey, 1973).

Authorities in music have also frequently emphasized singing as an effective learning technique (Choksy, 1974; De Young, 1977; Kress, 1960; Whybrew, 1956). Elliott (1972) demonstrated that students who used daily vocalization as part of their practice sessions were superior to those not using vocalization in their ability to discriminate pitch, relate musical sounds to musical notation, and convert musical notation to musical sounds. Froseth (1971) found that students who received individualized instruction that included singing obtained a higher degree of musical achievement than did those who received a traditional, nonsinging group approach.

Some researchers have also suggested that silent analysis of a work to be learned enables the musician to "hear" the music with his or her "inner ear." In fact, in Rubin-Rabson's (1941) study, in which skillful pianists acted as subjects, silent reading produced (according to her subjects) nearly as vivid "inner" tonal hearing as did actual keyboard performance. Researchers have also demonstrated the value of silent analysis in learning to play the trombone (Wapnick, Gilsig, & Hummel, 1982).

Thus, evidence from various sources suggests that modeling, singing, and silent analysis are all effective practice techniques. This study is a report of a comparison of the relative effectiveness of these techniques in helping advanced instrumentalists master a musical selection quickly. The specific research questions addressed were: (a) Are modeling, singing, and silent analysis effective practice techniques when compared with free practice or simply sight-reading? (b) Do modeling, singing, and silent analysis differ in their effectiveness as aids to practice?

METHOD

We examined the relative effectiveness of five experimental practice conditions on musical performance:

- *Group 1, modeling*—subjects used their practice time to listen to a recording of the composition, with the written music available.
- *Group 2, singing*—subjects used their practice time to sing the composition.
- *Group 3, silent analysis*—subjects spent time silently studying the music.
- *Group 4, free practice*—subjects practiced the selection using their instruments, playing continuously.
- *Group 5, control*—subjects practiced an unrelated musical composition and then performed the experimental composition.

We included the control group to enable us to compare the effectiveness of the practice techniques with the effectiveness of sight-reading.

We selected "Etude No. 96" from a collection for various brass instruments by P. Bona (1969) for mastery by the subjects because it fulfilled the criteria of being relatively obscure and complex enough to be challenging for graduate students in music education. We transposed the étude for each band instrument to maintain the original tonality and rewrote some notes an octave higher or lower to make the composition playable on particular instruments. We added tempo, phrasing, and dynamic markings to increase the complexity of the work. A professional violinist performed a model of the musical selection to avoid bias toward any of the band instruments in the study, and the model was recorded using an NAD Stereo Amplifier #3020, a Yamaha K-200 Cassette Recorder, and Maxell High-bias CrO_2 cassette recording tape.

Subjects for this study were 60 graduate and upper-level undergraduate students majoring on either a woodwind or brass instrument and attending VanderCook College of Music, Chicago, during the summer of 1985. We randomly assigned each student to one of the five treatments.

We conducted the experiment in a small room equipped with microphone, amplifier, headphones, cassette recorder, Casio keyboard, and a metronome. When subjects arrived, we thanked them for participating in the study and asked them to be seated. We assured them that their participation in the study was absolutely confidential and gave them instructions according to the groups in which we had placed them.

Group 1—Modeling

Please look at the music on your stand. You will be asked to listen to a recording of a violin performing this selection. Please set your instrument aside and listen to the tape. I will be back to stop the tape. You will be asked to play the selection to the best of your ability. Do you have any questions?

Group 2—Singing

Please look at the music on your stand. To learn this selection we ask that you sing it using your full voice on any syllable. You are welcome to use the electronic keyboard to aid in finding pitches. Please practice singing this selection for 3 minutes.

I will be back when this time is up. Then we will ask you to play this selection to the best of your ability. Do you have any questions?

Group 3—Silent Analysis

Please study the music on your stand silently for 3 minutes. When the time is up, I will return to this room, and you will be asked to perform this selection to the best of your ability. Do you have any questions?

Group 4—Free Practice

Please look at the music on your stand. Take 3 minutes to practice it. Please continue to play during this time. When the time is up, I will return to this room, and you will be asked to perform this selection to the best of your ability. Do you have any questions?

Group 5—Control

Please look at the music on your stand. Practice this music for the next 3 minutes. When the time is up, I will return to this room, and an exercise will be given to you. Please perform it to the best of your ability. Do you have any questions? [Subjects received a copy of the Watkins-Farnum Test of Musical Performance (Watkins & Farnum, 1954) written for their instrument.]

The experimenter answered any questions and left the room for 3 minutes. Upon returning, the experimenter asked the subject to play through the étude one time to warm up his or her instrument. Then, the experimenter turned on the audiotape, announced an identification number, and played six beats on the metronome. The experimenter then left the room, returning at the end of the subject's performance.

We analyzed each musical excerpt with respect to correct notes, rhythms, articulation, phrasing or dynamics, and tempo. We evaluated notes, rhythms, and articulations on a beat-by-beat basis; these items had a maximum possible score of 39. There were 10 phrasing or dynamic markings. We determined tempo accuracy in terms of seconds of deviation from the model's performance.

A trained musician listened to all tapes with respect to either notes, rhythms, articulation and phrasing, or dynamics. Performances were randomly mixed so that it was impossible to know to which group a performance belonged. An independent observer listened to 20% of the tapes with respect to each variable to establish reliability. We obtained the degree of agreement between evaluators using the formula of agreements divided by agreements plus disagreements and found this degree to be acceptable. Agreement quotients for each variable are given in Table 1. A single observer timed each performance using a stopwatch to determine tempo accuracy.

RESULTS

We analyzed the subjects' scores using the Kruskal-Wallis non-parametric analysis of variance (Siegel, 1956) to determine whether there were significant differences among the practice techniques. We ran separate tests for notes, rhythm, articulation, phrasing or dynamics, and tempo. We chose the Kruskal-Wallis analysis because of the ordinal nature of the data and to compensate for occasional outlying scores.

We found significant differences ($p < .05$) among the practice techniques in subjects' performance of phrasing or dynamics and tempo. Probability of less than .10 was observed among subjects' performance of correct rhythms. We found nonsignificant difference among practice techniques in subjects' performances of correct notes

TABLE 1
Agreement Quotients between Evaluators

VARIABLE	AGREEMENT QUOTIENT
Notes	.96
Rhythm	.91
Articulation	.93
Phrasing or dynamics	.84

TABLE 2

Probability of Differences Occurring among
Groups on Each Dependent Measure Using the
Kruskal Wallis Analysis of Variance

VARIABLE	PROBABILITY
Notes	$p < .40$ (N.S.[a])
Rhythm	$p < .10$
Phrasing or dynamics	$p < .001$
Articulation	$p < .25$ (N.S.[a])
Tempo	$p < .02$

[a] N.S. = not significant.

TABLE 3

Dunn's Multiple Comparison among the Means of the Ranks on Each
Dependent Measure

	GROUPS				
VARIABLE	MODEL	SINGING	SILENT ANALYSIS	PRACTICE	CONTROL
Notes (N.S.[a])	35.83	30.75	28.70	33.88	23.33
Rhythm	34.17	21.33	41.29	30.46	24.04
Phrasing or dynamics	39.75	20.75	27.75	43.75	20.50
Articulation (N.S.[a])	36.08	28.25	28.08	34.58	25.50
Tempo (lowest score reflects most accuracy)	23.08	44.25	25.00	25.92	34.25

Note: Underlined means are significantly different at $\alpha = .05$.
[a] N.S. = not significant.

and articulation (see Table 2). We used Dunn's multiple comparison procedure to compare the means of the ranks among practice techniques (Madsen & Moore, 1978). We set a critical difference of 12.48 or more between a set of ranks as the basis of significance (see Table 3).

Subjects' performance of correct notes did not significantly differ among the practice groups, although subjects in the model group obtained the highest scores. Rhythmic accuracy was best among subjects in the silent analysis group, whose results differed significantly from scores in the singing and control groups. Accuracy of phrasing was most pronounced in the practice and modeling groups: These subjects performed significantly better than did subjects in the singing and control groups. Although we observed no significant differences among groups on articulation, subjects in the model group attained the highest scores and subjects in the control group obtained the lowest scores. Tempo accuracy of subjects in the modeling, practice, and silent analysis groups was significantly better than that of subjects in the singing group.

Thus, as shown in the data in Table 3, subjects in the control and singing groups generally produced the least accurate scores. Scores of subjects in the silent analysis groups were low on all variables except tempo. Subjects in the modeling and practice groups had the most accurate scores.

DISCUSSION

The most important outcome of this study is that listening to a model alone (without opportunity for practice) seems to be about as effective as practicing with the instrument in hand. Silent analysis did not seem to provide any immediate benefits over sight-reading except in subjects' performance of rhythms. Performance of rhythms was most accurate in the silent analysis group.

The results of this study with respect to the effectiveness of modeling confirm the results of previous research (Rosenthal, 1984; Zurcher, 1975). This study's results may also lend credence to the use of teaching methods that make considerable use of modeling either formally, as in the Suzuki approach, or less formally, as in the case of teachers who advocate listening to music to be learned or who sing or play parts for their students in private lessons or ensemble rehearsals.

Singing alone, without any opportunity for practice, offered no immediate benefits over sight-reading. We observed informally that subjects in the singing group seemed uncomfortable with the task; it is possible that these subjects simply did not have enough vocal background to deal with the fairly difficult composition and became absorbed with the task of finding pitches rather than working out rhythmic and technical problems. Although previous research indicates that singing is an important aspect of musical training, the results of this study suggest that singing alone is not a practical means of attaining immediate mastery (at least of the selection studied in this experiment). Singing may be more helpful for improving overall musicianship.

Silent analysis had a relatively positive outcome on subjects' rhythmic mastery. Although the statistical probability of the difference occurring by chance was less than .10, the scores obtained suggest that silent analysis may have been effective in facilitating rhythmic mastery but was clearly ineffective in improving the other variables. Perhaps these results occurred because the exercise we selected for this study was rhythmically complex and the opportunity for silent analysis enabled the subjects to work out the analytical aspects of the rhythms. Had they received more practice time, the subjects in this group, as well as those in the other practice groups, might eventually have focused their attention on the other elements of the music.

Additional research is needed to examine such concerns as subjects' previous sight-reading experiences and the long-and short-term effects of practice conditions on mastery of musical selections with different musical demands. It would also be particularly useful to examine the effects of various practice techniques on the short- and long-term musical achievement of young children.

The results of this study may have some practical implications for students and teachers. Providing a model of the music to be learned seems to be effective in helping students master musical compositions and thus seems to be a technique that music teachers can use to good advantage during a rehearsal or lesson. The finding of positive outcomes in this study after only a 3-minute practice treatment lends support to modeling's efficiency. The results of this study also suggest that silent analysis may be helpful in facilitating rhythmic accuracy, although it may not necessarily improve accuracy in the other elements of a composition. On the other hand, singing may not be particularly effective as a practice aid, at least not when the selection is rhythmically and melodically complicated as was the composition that we selected for this study.

REFERENCES

BAKER, D. (1980). The effect of appropriate and inappropriate in-class song performance models on performance preference of third- and fourth-grade students. *Journal of Research in Music Education, 28*, 3–17.

BONA, P. (1969). *Rhythmical articulation*. New York: Carl Fischer.

CHOKSY, L. (1974). *The Kodaly method*. Englewood Cliffs, NJ: Prentice-Hall.

DE YOUNG, D. (1977). Singing as an aid to brass performance. *The Instrumentalist, 31*(11), 49–50.

ELLIOTT, C. A. (1972). The effectiveness of singing in the beginning band class. *Journal of Band Research, 9*, 38–39.

FROSETH, J. (1971). Individualizing instruction in the beginning instrumental music class. *Journal of Band Research, 8*, 11–18.

KRESS, V. (1960). The voice in brass playing. *The Instrumentalist, 14*(7), 49–50.

MADSEN, C.K., & MOORE, R. S. (1978). *Experimental research in music.* Raleigh, NC: Contemporary Publishing.

PARTCHEY, K. C. (1973). The effects of feedback, models, and repetition on the ability to improvise melodies. *Bulletin of the Council of Research in Music Education, 4,* 9–11.

PUOPOLO, V. (1971). The development and experimental application of self-instructional practice materials for beginning instrumentalists. *Journal of Research in Music Education, 19,* 342–349.

ROSENTHAL, R. K. (1984). Relative effects of guided model, model only, guide only, and practice only treatments on the accuracy of advanced instrumentalists' musical performance. *Journal of Research in Music Education, 32,* 265–273.

ROSS, S. L. (1985). The effectiveness of mental practice in improving the performance of college trombonists. *Journal of Research in Music Education, 33,* 221–231.

RUBIN-RABSON, G. (1941). Studies in the psychology of memorizing piano music: V. A comparison of pre-study periods of varied length. *Journal of Educational Psychology, 32,* 101–112.

SIEGEL, S. (1956). *Nonparametric statistics for the behavioral sciences.* New York: McGraw-Hill.

SUZUKI, S. (1969). *Nurtured by love: A new approach to education.* New York: Exposition Press.

WAPNICK, J., GILSIG, M., & HUMMEL, T. (1982, February). *Relative effects of psychomotoric practice, mental rehearsal, and guided mental rehearsal on performances of undergraduate brass and piano music majors.* Paper presented at the National Convention of the Music Educators National Conference, San Antonio.

WATKINS, J. G., & FARNUM, S. E. (1954). *The Watkins-Farnum Performance Scale, Form A: A standardized achievement test for all band instruments.* Milwaukee, WI: Hal Leonard.

WHYBREW, W. (1956). Singing approach to the brasses. *The Instrumentalist 11*(2), 22–25.

ZURCHER, W. (1975). The effect of model-supportive practice on beginning brass instrumentalists. In C. K. Madsen, R. D. Greer, & C. H. Madsen, Jr. (Eds.), *Research in music behavior* (pp. 131–138). New York: Teachers College Press.

Analysis of the Study

The success of applied music instruction depends to a great extend on the effectiveness of the practicing the student does between lessons. The study by Rosenthal, Wilson, Evans, and Greenwalt presented above examines five approaches to practice with the goal of increasing the effectiveness of practice.

METHOD. Because of the active nature of the data-gathering in the Rosenthal et al. study, it is clear that the study is neither philosophical nor historical. To judge whether the study is descriptive or experimental, answer the question: "Does the study attempt simply to ask 'What is?' or does it ask 'What will be under certain conditions?' " It should be clear in this case because the researchers employ five different practice conditions with their students (particularly because some of these conditions are not normally a part of applied instruction) that the study best fits into the experimental research model. As you have read previously, experimental research is obtrusive; it manipulates the research environment in order to observe the effects of the manipulation. Again, the use of five different experimental practice conditions reinforces the initial judgment that this is an experimental study.

PROBLEM. In the beginning of their report, Rosenthal et al. describe how there is evidence that different approaches to structuring music practice are effective. While there are several studies that report individually on these practice techniques, there are none that provide a comparison of these techniques. It is that lack of information, that need for the specific knowledge to assist in decision making, that is the motivator of this study. This motivating problem is clearly a logical extension of previous research. The previous work does not provide a direct answer to the question "Which technique is best?" because the characteristics of the subjects and the operational definitions of the variables differed in each of the studies.

VARIABLES. The independent variable in this study is "practice technique." There are five types or levels of this variable: modeling, singing, silent analysis, free practice, and control, all of which are carefully defined both by their initial description and by the reporting of the instructions given to the subjects in the different groups. The dependent variable is multidimensional. The performances were judged on the correct notes, rhythms, articulation, phrasing or dynamics, and tempo. The evaluations were made by judges and the reliability of their judgments is reported in table 1.

HYPOTHESES OR RESEARCH QUESTIONS. Two specific research questions are stated: "Are modeling, singing, and silent analysis effective as practice techniques when compared with free practice or simply sightreading?" and "Do modeling, singing, and silent analysis differ in their effectiveness as aids to practice?"

SAMPLE.   Rosenthal et al. chose a sample that might be characterized as a "sample of convenience." It was not randomly selected from a larger population of graduate and upper-level undergraduate wind-instrument students. To the extent that wind-instrument students at the particular college of music differ from wind-instrument students at other schools or colleges of music, or from applied music students in general, the study has limited generalizability *on the variables being examined*. The italicized phrase in the preceding sentence is important because, while it is known these different populations differ in some ways (for instance, in preferences for college basketball teams), they may not differ on variables important to this investigation. Therefore, researchers in such circumstances tentatively may logically generalize to other populations. Other researchers, of course, may wish to challenge this by identifying variables that might limit the generalizability of the results. An interesting discussion might center on the appropriateness of generalizing the results of this study to other areas of applied music such as string, piano, or voice instruction.

PROCEDURE.   The procedure is relatively straightforward. Once the students were randomly assigned to a practice condition (e.g., modeling), they arrived at a small room, were shown an étude and given a set of instructions that differed for each of the practicing techniques. Then, they were given three minutes in which to "practice" employing the strategy described in the directions. After the three minutes the researcher returned, asked the student to warm up by playing through the étude one time, and then recorded the second playing of the étude. The recordings were then evaluated by a trained musician according to specified criteria.

STATISTICAL ANALYSIS.   The authors first checked for the reliability of the judges' evaluations employing a strategy identified as "Agreement Quotients," which they described. The major research questions are analyzed using the *Kruskal-Wallis nonparametric analysis of variance* and then *Dunn's multiple comparison procedure*. It is really not necessary to know the intricacies of calculating these statistics to understand the article. However, the question of whether the statistical procedure is appropriate is important. For the statistically unsophisticated examiner of research, the appropriateness of the statistical treatment must be left to the screening committee for the professional meeting or publication in which the research appears. In other words, if the report appears in a refereed journal or at a professional meeting for which the papers have been selected, then to some extent the profession has approved the research competence demonstrated in the report. That approval should include an evaluation of the statistical procedures.

RESULTS.   The authors state that they found significant differences among the practice techniques regarding the students' performance of phrasing or dynamics and tempo. This fact means the results are generaliz-able. They further analyzed the results and found that the students in the "modeling" and "free-practice" groups had the most accurate scores. The results are best observed in tables 2 and 3. An examination of these tables and the brief statements describing them should provide a basic under-standing of "what happened."

IMPLICATIONS.   The discussion section is the place to look for implica-tions. The authors emphasize that listening to a model alone was as effective as practicing with an instrument. The effectiveness of modeling is confirmed by the results of previous research. The problem that initi-ated the study focused on a comparison of these five different approach-es to practicing. The results appear to contain implications for applied music instruction, particularly if further studies continue to support these findings.

The authors of this book strongly believe that it is the obligation of all professional music educators to increase their competence by seeking new knowledge through research. This chapter provides a base on which music educators can build a greater understanding of research.

Summary

Research is the best way humankind has yet been able to devise for acquir-ing truth. Although not foolproof, research is superior to other forms of human inquiry. It is, therefore, necessary for progress in music education.

Although the scientific method functions in the same basic way for both the physical and social sciences, there are some important differences. Social scientists deal with mental constructs, human beings and their com-plex nature, and tendencies and probabilities rather than constant physical properties.

Science is cautious about claiming proof. New knowledge may yet be discovered that will render old truths obsolete, and the results of a research study may be true for only that one particular set of circum-stances. In order to be especially careful about claiming a result, researchers require that the data resulting from a study establish a statisti-cally significant difference between groups.

Determining more than the immediate cause-effect relationship of a phenomenon is difficult and prone to error. Usually events or conditions have more than one cause, and trying to delve deeper into the chain of causation soon leads to a point at which no answer is possible.

Although research is vital to the progress of the music education profes-sion, many music educators have not been particularly interested in it, for a variety of reasons. Some of these reasons stem from a lack of under-standing about what research can do; some are due to the limited amount of research data available in music education; and some are due to the manner in which research results are reported.

Reports of research studies are available in a number of journals and are presented at professional meetings. To be able to read a research article intelligently, one needs to understand certain basic statistical concepts such as the difference between descriptive and inferential statistics. Also necessary is an understanding of the five approaches to research:

1. Descriptive: studies that seek to describe an existing situation.
2. Ethnographic: studies that seek to describe phenomena in natural settings employing unobtrusive and often qualitative research strategies.
3. Historical: the examination and analysis of past events and situations.
4. Experimental: studies conducted under conditions that are controlled and manipulated by the researcher.
5. Philosophical: the objective analysis and synthesis of information with regard to goals and methods.

When reading a research report, one should attempt to answer the following questions:

- What research method was employed?
- Why was the study undertaken?
- What major factors were considered in the study?
- What was the major research question?
- What constituted the sample of subjects or sources of information?
- What procedures were used?
- How were the data analyzed?
- What were the results?
- What are the implications of the results for teaching music?

STUDY AND DISCUSSION QUESTIONS

1. (a) What are the limitations of personal impressions as a way of determining what is true?

   (b) How does research attempt to overcome these limitations?

2. Although both the physical and social sciences apply research procedures to gathering information, the social sciences have a number of

problems and limitations that are not present in the physical sciences. What are those limitations?

3. Why do researchers tend to avoid the idea of definitive proof?

4. Why is it difficult for research studies to pin down the cause for some situation or event?

5. What factors have made many music educators cool toward research and its benefits?

6. Suppose that you wish to examine the available research data on helping children in the primary grades who have a problem singing on pitch. Where would you look for reports of research on the topic?

7. Suppose that you locate reports of a number of studies on helping singers to sing better.

   (a) What would the descriptive statistical data tell you?

   (b) What would the inferential statistical data tell you?

   (c) What characteristics would tell you if a research study is descriptive, ethnographic, historical, experimental, or philosophical?

   (d) Which type of research studies would be of the most value to you as a teacher of music in the primary grades?

8. Suppose that you find one report of research that looks especially interesting. What questions should you try to answer as you read the report?

INDIVIDUAL OR CLASS ACTIVITIES

Several or all of the class members can select articles from the *Journal of Research in Music Education*. The title and abstract can be read to determine the topic of the study and the type of research utilized. If time permits, the article can be read, and the rest of the questions suggested for analyzing a study listed on page 364 can be answered.

SUPPLEMENTARY READINGS

ABELES, H. F. (1992). A guide to interpreting research in music education. In R. Colwell (Ed.), *Handbook of research on teaching and learning* (pp. 227–44). New York: Schirmer Books.

BRESLER, L., & STAKE, R. E. (1992). Qualitative research methodology in music education. In R. Colwell (Ed.), *Handbook of research on music teaching and learning* (pp. 75–90). New York: Schirmer Books.

BUSCH, J. C., & SHERBON, J. W. (1992). Experimental research methodology. In R. Colwell (Ed.), *Handbook of research on music teaching and learning* (pp. 124–40). New York: Schirmer Books

CASEY, D. E. (1992). Descriptive research: Techniques and procedures. In R. Colwell (Ed.), *Handbook of research on music teaching and learning* (pp. 115–23). New York: Schirmer Books.

HELLER, G. N., & WILSON, B. D. (1992). Historical Research. In R. Colwell (Ed.), *Handbook of research on music teaching and learning* (pp. 102–14). New York: Schirmer Books.

RAINBOW, E. L., & FROEHLICH, H. C. (1987). *Research in music education*. New York: Schirmer Books.

STUBLEY, E. V. (1992). Philosophy as a method of inquiry. *The Quarterly Journal of Music Teaching and Learning, 3*(1), 44–55.

REFERENCES

ABELES, H. F., & PORTER, S. Y. (1978). The sex-stereotyping of music instruments. *Journal of Research in Music Education, 26*(1), 65–75.

BABBIE, E. (1979). *The practice of social research* (2d ed.). Belmont, CA: Wadsworth.

BRESLER, L., & STAKE, R. E. (1992). Qualitative research methodology in music education. In R. Colwell (Ed.), *Handbook of research on music teaching and learning* (pp. 75–90). New York: Schirmer Books.

COLWELL, R. (1992). *Handbook of research on music teaching and learning*. New York: Schirmer Books.

HELLER, G. N., & WILSON, B. D. (1992, Winter). Historical research in music education: a prolegomenon. *Council for Research in Music Education Bulletin, 69*, 1–20.

JAMES, W. (1958). *Talks with teachers*. New York: W. W. Norton.

MOORHEAD, G., & POND D. (1941, 1942, 1944, 1951). *Music of young children: Vols. 1–4*. Vancouver, WA: Pillsbury Foundation.

MYERS, D. G. (1990). *Social psychology* (3rd ed.). New York: McGraw-Hill.

OXFORD DICTIONARY OF QUOTATIONS (1979). London: Oxford University Press.

SCHWADRON. A. A. (1973, Fall). Philosophy in music education: state of the research. *Council for Research in Music Education Bulletin 34*, pp. 41–53.

SPENCER, H. (1860). *First principles*. New York: A. L. Burt.

STUBLEY, E. V. (1992). Philosophy as a method of inquiry. *The Quarterly Journal of Music Teaching and Learning, 3*(1), 44–55.

SWABY, B. E. R. (1984). *Teaching and learning reading*. Boston: Little, Brown.

12

Teacher Education and Future Directions

INHERENT IN ANY PROFESSION is the need to continue growing and be revitalized. Because of this basic need, it is appropriate that a text on the foundations of music education examine the most active arena that not only prepares members for the profession but also is the chief means for the inservice training of its members already in the field, namely the university or college.

Music Education as a Profession

In order to understand better the training of a professional, one needs to know what distinguishes a profession from being just a routine job that merely requires a skill. First, there must be an accumulated body of knowledge that requires lengthy, continuous study, usually culminating in a college degree. This knowledge is not static, but is in a constant state of flux as research and technical advancements open and expand new horizons for learning. Second, there must be established standards that permit members to enter the profession. Third, if the profession requires education, there need to be objectives that are constantly assessed and evaluated in terms of knowledge, growth, and their impact on learning. Fourth, members of a profession have a genuine commitment to their discipline; it is not just a nine-to-five job. Fifth, professionals have responsibility for making judgments and decisions. For example, a doctor prescribes medication; a nurse can only administer medicine. Teachers make decisions regarding what students must study; teachers' aides may follow up with a review or explanation of the material, but they should not determine class content.

As in medicine, one cannot isolate one's specialty from the total professional responsibility. Just as eye, ear, and nose specialists have to understand the impact of their specialty on the whole body, instrumental music teachers need to be aware of the musical needs of choral directors and general music teachers, and vice versa. In fact, music training, just as in medical training, which begins with the basic exposure to the totality of the human body, focuses initially on acquiring the basic skills of the art of music.

As you read these lines, teaching is changing. In years past people thought of teaching as a personal relationship between a teacher and his or her class, although virtually no one claimed that the teacher was the exclusive means of instruction. In contrast to the early days of blackboards and books, today's teachers and students have an impressive array of technological resources to aid them.

It is also characteristic of a profession that there exists a national organization that represents the discipline as a whole, one that encompasses all of the segments or subspecialties within the profession. A responsibility of this organization—which in the case of music education is MENC—is to raise pertinent issues and examine them as they pertain to the professional concerns of its members. It was just such a concern that caused MENC to create commissions to examine the nature and direction of teacher education in music as it currently existed and to propose needed changes.

Most concerns in teacher training have not changed. They revolve around three basic responsibilities: (1) curricular decisions as to what students should learn to achieve professional competency, (2) classroom procedures that implement these decisions, and (3) evaluaton of student achievement. Successful teaching requires integrating all three concerns into a coherent, meaningful unit of instruction, and the use of technological media does not alter this basic paradigm.

First priority among faculty members is the course content. Those who might become enamored or preoccupied with technical development should not lose sight of the fact that the content is more important than the medium. Basically, most college teachers are subject-matter specialists, and by using newer technologies they may expand their contribution of reference books, texts, and syllabi through films, slides, videotapes, and computer programs. However, in the final analysis all of this preparation is designed to turn out a professional music educator with the competencies that will enable him or her to provide optimum learning experiences for music students.

Teacher Education in Music: Final Report

In 1968 the MENC president, Wiley L. Housewright, along with Frances Andrews, then president-elect, appointed a commission to examine teacher education programs in music and to recommend changes that would lead to the improvement of these programs. *Teacher Education in Music: Final Report* (Klotman et al., 1972), which incorporated the work of the commission during the four years between 1968 and 1972, not only developed a set of recommendations designed to strengthen the training of individuals preparing to be music educators, but also identified qualities and competencies necessary for such teachers. Frances Andrews, in accepting the *Final Report*, stated:

> It [the report] recognizes the need for a well-prepared musician-educator who will function in various instructional modes and roles; it makes clear the fact that the music educator must be prepared to deal with youth from widely disparate socioeconomic backgrounds, maximizing their interests and talents while still striving for excellence. The Commission report, in its attitude toward teacher preparation, clearly implies that all pupils have a right to music and suggests ways to prepare future teachers who will be equipped to employ various avenues, approaches, and viable alternatives in their teaching styles. . . . Best of all the report is structured in terms of needed competency, and includes provision for evaluation. (Klotman et al., 1972)

To establish a means by which music education departments in colleges and universities could evaluate their offerings, the commission published "Recommended Standards and Evaluative Criteria" (Klotman et al., 1972).

Each criterion in the *Final Report* identified a specific competency and provided pertinent questions for determining what existing conditions were available to assist in promoting skills and competencies and how well these conditions fulfilled this need (see figure 12.1). The three major areas of music teacher training are: (1) general education, (2) music, and (3) professional education. In addition, the *Final Report* reviewed personal qualities, musical competencies, and professional qualities involved in selecting and training future music teachers for the schools.

In 1974, the National Association of Schools of Music endorsed the basic tenets of the *Final Report* by using much of it in establishing its own criteria for assessing schools and departments of music engaged in the training of music teachers.

Figure 12.1. Task Group 1: Qualities and Competencies for Music Educators. Copyright © 1972 by Music Educators National Conference. Used by permission.

A new type of teacher education in music is needed in order to provide "music educators who are competent, flexible, creative, curious, and prepared to survive and flourish in a world of change" (the terminal objective established by the Commission in its first report December 1968). The accompanying list of qualities needed by music educators for today's schools may not, at first glance, appear significantly different

Figure 12.1 (*continued*)

from those that colleges say they are striving to produce with present curricula. It would be most unfortunate if this list should be so interpreted, for many, if not most, of today's graduates are finding major areas of their preparation neither sufficient nor relevant to the problems they face in their first jobs. Clearly, a different kind of preparation is needed—one that derives from and supports the following basic assumptions.

BASIC ASSUMPTIONS

The development of music teacher competencies should result from the total program of the teacher training institution. The demonstration of competence, rather than the passing of a course, should be the deciding factor in certification. This means that proficiency tests, practical applications of historical, theoretical, and stylistic techniques, and advanced standing procedures should be employed; that screening procedures for admission to the program should be enforced; and that an adequate means of final assessment should be developed and implemented.

Musical skill and understanding must be acquired more through aural than through visual perception. For example, the emphasis on improvisation demands this approach.

Music educators need to demonstrate at least a minimum knowledge of and competence to teach in all musics, and cannot be restricted in their training to the styles represented by a few hundred years of Western art music. The enormous task of becoming competent to function within the whole spectrum of music dictates the need for a new set of tools. Music educators need something more than performance skills. They must develop a comprehensive musicianship that, coupled with an open-mindedness toward the use of any sounds combined in a musical context, will enable them to address themselves to any music they encounter.

Throughout their preparation, they must never lose sight of the fact that a major goal as music educators is to bring the joy of music to others and to lead all students from a musical experience in the classroom to the broad world of musical art.

PERSONAL QUALITIES

Music educators must:

Inspire others.

Continue to learn in their own and in other fields.

Relate to other disciplines and arts.

Identify and evaluate new ideas.

Use their imaginations.

Understand the role of the teacher.

MUSICAL COMPETENCIES

Producing Sounds (Performance)

All music educators must be able to:

Perform with musical understanding and technical proficiency.

Play accompaniments.

Sing.

Conduct.

Supervise and evaluate the performance of others.

Organizing Sounds (Composition)

All music educators must be able to:

Organize sounds for personal expression.

Demonstrate an understanding of the elements of music through original composition and improvisation in a variety of styles.

Demonstrate the ability to identify and explain compositional choices of satisfactory and less-than-satisfactory nature.

Notate and arrange sounds for performance in school situations.

Describing Sounds (Analysis)

All music educators must be able to:

Identify and explain compositional devices as they are employed in all musics.

Describe the affective results of compositional devices.

Describe the means by which the sounds used in music are created.

Figure 12.1 (*continued*)

PROFESSIONAL QUALITIES

The ability to communicate with students is essential for teachers. Therefore, music educators must be able to:

Express their philosophy of music and education.

Demonstrate a familiarity with contemporary educational thought.

Apply a broad knowledge of musical repertory to the learning problems of music students.

Demonstrate, by example, the concept of the comprehensive musician dedicated to teaching.

Graduate Music Teacher Education Report

In 1976, the president of MENC, Robert Klotman, along with President-elect James Mason, appointed a commission to make a study of recommended directions for graduate music teacher education. This commission was first chaired by Robert Bays and later by Charles Ball. After four years of study, it submitted its report to MENC. Its recommendations appeared in the *Music Educators Journal* of October 1980, and the complete document, *Graduate Music Teacher Education Report*, was published in 1982 (see Ball et al., 1982). It was this commission's general recommendation that graduate programs needed to be imaginative and flexible while maintaining and improving standards that affect quality.

The commission felt that graduate study at both the masters and the doctoral levels should function to provide for

1. The improvement of knowledge and competence in the craft of music teaching and musical performance.
2. The development of insight into the nature and acquisition of musical knowledge.
3. The development of a rational basis for professional commitment and continued growth.
4. The development of research competence.
5. The development of both added depth and breadth in knowledge of the field of music (not limited to Western art music) and other liberal studies. (Ball et al., 1982, p. 4)

In describing what graduates of masters programs in music education should possess, the commission listed the following:

1. A basic understanding of the historical, philosophical, and sociological foundations of music education.

2. A basic understanding of psychological principles and learning theories as applied to music education.

3. A functional acquaintance with research in music education, with emphasis on the guided, critical interpretation of research reports and the practical application of valid research findings.

4. A basic knowledge of current teaching methods and techniques, including an understanding of their philosophical, psychological, sociological, and aesthetic implications.

5. A functional level of performance skill.

6. A functional knowledge of music theory.

7. A basic knowledge of music literature, including jazz, popular, ethnic, and non-Western music.

8. An acquaintance with instructional materials that address multicultural needs.

9. A knowledge of techniques for motivation and relating to students of diverse cultures.

10. A basic understanding of the impact of technology on music and education.

11. A functional knowledge of basic techniques of evaluation. (Ball et al., 1982, p. 5)

It is interesting to note that recommendations 1–4 and 11 are closely related to the purpose of this book.

The commission's recommendations were aimed to develop students at the masters level who could *analyze, synthesize,* and *generalize* at a more advanced level than undergraduates.

In general, the commission felt that doctoral programs should allow students to comprehend in greater depth the theoretical basis of music education. In addition, each doctoral student is expected to gain comprehensive knowledge and understanding of "all aspects of one major area of music education, for example, research design, administration and supervising, history and philosophy, psychology, methodology" (Ball et al., 1982, p. 6).

A graduate faculty, according to the commission, should be made up of individuals who are experts and scholars in the history and philosophy of music education, in research techniques, in learning theories and the psychology of music, and in advanced methodology. In addition, in recent years a need has arisen to include faculty with specialized knowledge in special education, computer-assisted instruction, continuing education, and music in adult education, as well as in recreational music. More recently there has been substantial study in both historical and scientific research. The need for graduate music students who are capable both musically and in research methodology is becoming more urgent as advanced study in music education continues to increase.

The Task Force on Music Teacher Education for the Nineties formed in the fall of 1984 by MENC expanded the concern in teacher training to include recruitment, selection, and retention. It identified the personal, intellectual, musical, and instructional traits for potential teachers. Traditionally, retention of music education majors depended primarily on passing course work. However, the 1984 commission supported the concept that "retention should be dependent on students demonstrating their growth, knowledge and understanding through formal calculations prior to admittance to student teaching" (Task Force on Music Teacher Education, 1987, p. 25).

The Competency-Based Teacher Education Movement

The frequent references to "competencies" in the preceding material should provide a clue to indicate that in the mid-1960s a movement developed that would affect the nature of teacher training: namely, competency-based or performance-based education. The shift in emphasis in this development was from the completion of courses to the acquisition of the specific skills and knowledge needed to do the job. It was a direct outgrowth of the accountability movement mentioned in chapter 8, which focused on the ability of the educational system to provide students who could *demonstrate* behaviors acquired from the school training program rather than having merely taken a class that might or might not have developed such ability.

Competency-based teacher education (CBTE) was not new or revolutionary. Professionals in many areas have always been asked to demonstrate competence. Furthermore, it was not an emphasis only upon the ends of a program. Means were also important. For example, what prospective teachers do on the podium may be the end objective, but in competency-based education it was just as important to know how to prepare a score. CBTE attempted to document what was necessary to make a competent music educator so that teachers could agree on goals and on the means to evaluate their success in meeting them. Students in CBTE systems indicated that they liked knowing specifically what they were supposed to be doing and learning.

Since the accountability movement, which prompted this examination of teacher-training programs, was based in behaviorism, it seemed reasonable that the solution advocated by many regarding the inadequacy of current programs in the educational system would be based in behavioral theory. Competency-based teacher education might therefore be viewed as accountability applied to the education of teachers (see chapter 8).

A significant characteristic of CBTE is the strong relationship between the real world of the music classroom and the teacher-training program. This relationship appears in several aspects of the program. The identification of the competencies that serve as the exit criteria for training programs are based on the needs of the classroom. Therefore, the first task of CBTE developers is to identify factors critical to successful teaching. In some cases this task has been undertaken by professional groups, such as the MENC Teacher Education Commission's *Final Report*. Faculty of institutions implementing CBTE programs and state certifying bodies have also contributed to the task of identifying competencies. The actual training programs, particularly in the later stages, tend to be field-oriented; that is, the demonstration of the required competencies is done in actual music classrooms.

Although CBTE is an outgrowth of the accountability movement, its emphasis was not only on what is measurable but also on the necessary competencies to achieve the measurable. One cannot measure the beauty of an orchestra's performance, but one can expect an individual violin player to demonstrate certain competencies in order to be a member of that orchestra. Despite some misconceptions regarding the so-called "impersonal nature" of CBTE, it did not underestimate the complexity of individuals and of systems.

In summary, to be effective, CBTE programs should contain the following six basic elements:

1. Demonstrable, precise objectives for the entire program as it relates to the students' ultimate goal.

2. Predetermined competencies identified and acknowledged by both student and teacher that are based on the actual requirements of the particular class in which the student is enrolled.

3. Step-by-step mastery of specific competencies through a series of identified levels. These competencies are applied and exhibited in a variety of situations, either live or simulated, both on and off campus.

4. Responsibility for the acquisition of competencies resulting with the individual student.

5. Progression from one phase of the program to the next dependent on meeting the appropriate competency.

6. Constant evaluation and opportunities for modification when and where changes in the professional requirements indicate the need for such adjustment.

The CBTE movement seemed most energetic in the early 1970s, when considerable federal funding was available for colleges and universities to experiment with such programs and for professional organizations to disseminate ideas. The MENC reflected this situation by producing documents such as the *Final Report* promoting CBTE ideas. The National Association of Schools of Music included in its *Proceedings of the 49th Annual Meeting*, published in March 1974, an article by Gretchen Hieronymus, "Competency-Based Programs in Teacher Education" (p. 78). An overview can be found in "An Analysis of the Origins of Competency-Based Teacher Education," a doctoral dissertation by Gordon R. Meek that was reviewed by Michael Mark in the Fall 1981 *Bulletin of the Council for Research in Music Education* (p. 69).

During this period many state teacher certifying agencies also developed requirements for certification in music reflecting the CBTE movement. An examination of music education professional publications and conference programs also reveals an interest in and concern for the implications of CBTE for music education. (The National Association of Schools of Music publications likewise reflect this concern in their recommendations.) By the early 1980s, however, this energy that was so evident earlier seemed to have dissipated. In the penny-pinching atmosphere of the 1980s many college programs were more concerned with maintenance than innovation. In addition, the bureaucratic interest from state certifying bodies had subsided, and the pressure for college programs to conform had diminished.

Although the systemized programs of CBTE may not increase in number in the future, some components of the program will continue to have an impact on teacher-training programs. The emphasis on demonstrating the mastery of competencies, field-based preservice experiences, and individualization continues to have strong support in the educational community. Many of these concepts appear in the 1987 report of the Task Force on Music Teacher Education for the Nineties.

The Holmes Group

In 1983 the Holmes Group, a consortium of education deans and chief academic officers from the major research universities in each of the fifty states, came together because they felt that their own institutions were not doing the appropriate job in teacher education. It was their contention that if American students' performances were to improve, there needed to be dramatic improvement in teacher education.

After two years of study the group identified the following goals for improving teacher education:

1. To make the education of teachers intellectually more solid.

2. To recognize differences in teachers' knowledge, skill, and commitment, in their education, certification, and work.

3. To create standards of entry to the profession—examinations and educational requirements—that are professionally relevant and intellectually defensible.

4. To connect our own institutions to schools.

5. To make schools better places for teachers to work and learn. (The Holmes Group, 1986, p. 4)

In identifying these goals, the Holmes Group felt that teacher education as practiced then (1983–85) was not only intellectually weak, but it also encouraged many people who were inadequately prepared to enter teaching. This practice contributed further to the erosion of the prestige of the profession, which at that time was already held in low esteem. Another concern identified by this distinguished panel was that good teachers who were knowledgeable and skillful were afforded little opportunity to advance within the profession and received inadequate remuneration. Furthermore, the group stated that students were able to utilize some of the most amazing achievements of modern technology and science in learning while their teachers were still working with the same job descriptions and technology of the mid-1800s.

Beginning with teacher licensing, the group suggested the following three-tier system:

1. No professional certificate should be available to a teacher who has only an undergraduate degree (The Holmes Group, 1986, p. 10). These individuals would receive a temporary certificate and be called *instructors*. They would be required to take an intensive professional development course before being permitted to practice. [This is the incipient stage of a recommended five-year teacher training program.] In addition, instructors would be required to pass a general test that included reading and writing ability, and a test of the rudiments of pedagogy.

2. The first full professional certificate should be for the *professional teacher* who has completed a master's degree in teaching. It would include continued study in the candidate's major or minor field, work with children who were at risk, and a full year of supervised teaching as well as taking the same examinations as those given to *instructors* in subjects they teach.

3. The highest license in teaching would be the *career professional* certificate. To receive this certificate a teacher would need to: (1) complete with satisfaction all of the requirements for the *professional teacher* license; (2) to have extensive experience as a professional teacher, with outstanding performance; and (3) to complete "further specialized study, ordinarily for the doctorate either in an academic subject or in some other specialty" (The Holmes Group, 1986, p. 13).

It was the position of the Holmes Group that one could not improve the quality of education without improving the quality of teachers and their training. Therefore, the universities must accept responsibility for change within their institutions to achieve the desired improvement in teaching. To accomplish this objective, the Homes Group set as its five major goals the following:

> To Make the Education of Teachers Intellectually Sound . . .
>
> To Recognize Differences in Knowledge, Skill, and Commitment, Among Teachers . . .
>
> To Create Relevant and Defensible Standards of Entry to the Profession of Teaching . . .
>
> To Connect Schools of Education with Schools . . .
>
> To Make Schools Better Places for Practicing Teachers to Work, and Learn. (The Holmes Group, 1986, pp. 62–67)

In its commitment statement the group recognized that if it wanted to create a profession that represented the larger society, schools of education needed to recruit and encourage more minority representatives. To achieve this objective of having a better representation of minorities in teaching positions, institutions need to endorse loan-forgiveness programs for minority students entering teaching; develop programs that increase retention of minority students; and assure that "evaluations of professional competence minimize the influence of handicapping conditions, poverty, race, and ethnicity on entry to the profession" (The Holmes Group, 1986, p. 66).

The Carnegie Task Force on Teaching as a Profession

In January of 1985 the trustees of the Carnegie Corporation of New York assembled the Carnegie Forum on Education and the Economy. The first recommendation that came out of this assembly was that a Task Force on Teaching as a Profession be established. In the spring of 1986 the task force submitted its report, *A Nation Prepared: Teachers for the Twenty-first Century*, at the first annual meeting of the forum.

The report pointed out that with the declining economy of the late 80s and early 90s, Americans needed to turn to education for a solution to their economic and social crises. Too many American children were unaware of our nation's past economic accomplishments and were unprepared for the future. Furthermore, these young people were not just leaving school but abandoning their role and responsibility for creating a productive society.

In advocating an educational renaissance to solve this condition, the report pointed out that to achieve a better standard of education, the quality of teaching and teachers needed to improve. First, educational standards needed to be raised to a far more demanding level than had been attempted ever before. Second, there needed to be a profession of well-prepared teachers who were equal to the task of raising these standards.

To construct such a professional force, the Task Force on Teaching as a Profession recommended the following sweeping changes in education policy:

- Create a National Board for Professional Teaching Standards, organized with a regional and state membership structure, to establish high standards for what teachers need to know and be able to do, and to certify teachers who meet that standard.

- Restructure schools to provide a professional environment for teaching, freeing them to decide how best to meet state and local goals for children while holding them accountable for student progress.

- Restructure the teaching force, and introduce a new category of Lead teachers with the proven ability to provide active leadership in the redesign of the schools and in helping their colleagues to uphold high standards of learning and teaching.

- Require a bachelor's degree in the arts and sciences as a prerequisite for the professional study of teaching. [This implies that a four-year undergraduate course is insufficient training for teachers, and that those entering the profession would require at least five years of training.]

- Develop a new professional curriculum in graduate schools of education leading to a Master in Teaching degree, based on systematic knowledge of teaching and including internships and residencies in the schools.

- Mobilize the nation's resources to prepare minority youngsters for teaching careers.

- Relate incentives for teachers to schoolwide student performance, and provide schools with the technology, services, and staff essential to teacher productivity.

- Make teacher's salaries and career opportunities competitive with those in other professions. (Carnegie Forum Task Force on Teaching as a Profession, 1986, p. 3)

Accomplishing the needed reform recommended by the task force will be expensive, but the report insisted that it was affordable. If the investment in this proposed education reform is not made, it contends, the nation will suffer as it becomes increasingly noncompetitive in the world markets.

What are the ramifications of the reports cited above as they affect music education? As yet there is an insufficient number of new, quality teachers who meet the professional criteria established by these groups. String positions are closed in our nation's schools not only because of the economy in some situations but also because qualified string teachers are not available. To complicate the situation, the Holmes Group, although not specifically identifying music, points out that in today's society women have a wide range of professional choices. Many are abandoning teaching for more prestigious and better-paying situations. Teaching and more specifically music education need to take the necessary measures to improve the professional environment. Society needs to offer appropriate incentives that will attract the best minded and most talented to teaching music. Only then will education achieve the renaissance aimed at in the Carnegie report.

Music Teacher Education: Partnership and Process

In calling for a new model in the training of potential music educators, the Teacher Education Commission, organized in 1984, recommended that partnerships and bonds be established among the nation's elementary and secondary music teachers, college music teachers, and music educators. The focus of this effort would be on the *process* that occurs in developing an excellent music educator rather than just on subject matter. Furthermore, in the minds of the commission, the *process* should begin prior to admission to a college training program and should be extended throughout one's career. The commission also called for a closer examination of the standards on which potential teachers are evaluated, and it created a high priority for membership in the partnership to find and attract potential music teachers equipped to teach in the twenty-first century.

In its section on "Teacher Certification Program: The Process of Developing Music Educators," the report suggests that faculty participants in their areas of expertise should focus on making the content of their courses meaningful in such a way that students understand how the course applies to their needs. As prospective students comprehend how the content is applicable, they should then be able to transfer this insight to diverse and new situations. Under these conditions students will then begin "to integrate the elements of education so as to make intelligent judgements for its future use" (Olson, et al., 1987, p. 30).

To achieve the above objective, the report identifies goals for student growth under the following categories: personal, intellectual, musical, and instructional. Its recommendations for program implementation are divided into the following categories: integrative learning experiences, laboratory experiences, early field experiences, teaching practice, and student teaching.

The *content* of the coursework elected by the future teacher should be designed to continue the development of the student's depth and breadth in music, liberal studies, and education. As foundation courses, these studies must provide content and stimulation that will accompany the student through a lifetime of growth. The experiences and understanding that the commission deemed necessary for the development of competent, effective teachers are organized around personal, intellectual, musical, and instructional needs.

In its deliberations, the commission established guidelines for a professional development program that would promote a process that would enable teachers to extend their personal growth and development beyond certification. In fact, this process is designed to assist them throughout their careers.

The last section of the 1984 commission's report dealt with "Music Teacher Educators: Partners in Music Teacher Education." It is the premise of this segment of the report that the burden for change "and the exciting potential for the future rests in the imaginative approaches to graduate-level preparation of those involved in school music teacher preparation, whether as college faculty or school music personnel" (Olson et al., 1987, p. 47).

The list of attributes that identify the profile of a desirable music teacher educator is included in the section with the personal, intellectual, musical, and instructional qualifications. Professional music educators seeking graduate degrees will have the potential to become partners in preparing prospective teachers in schools and institutions of higher education. Standards for selecting graduate students are a concern of the report and it suggests that these standards be based on the same skills and dispositions that are necessary for leadership responsibilities in preparing future music teachers. The qualifications listed fall under personal, intellectual, musical, and instructional categories. Counseling of graduate students by the select partners in music and music education at the college level is crucial—the report recommends specific courses offered by cooperating school music educators, music education professors, and music professors.

The report recognized that if changes in teacher education were to occur, the impetus needed to come from professors in music education. Their responsibilities are as follows:

- identify potential music education students and assist with the recruitment process
- design the curriculum in music education
- set and administer the standards for acceptance into the certification program in music education
- monitor student progress in general education, music, and professional education courses
- teach and supervise the music education methods course, observation programs, early field experiences and teaching practica
- identify cooperating school sites for placement of student teachers
- supervise the growth of student teachers in conjunction with cooperating school music educators
- prepare written evaluations and recommendations for certification and employing agencies

- assist in forming professional development programs for advisees and former students (Olson et al., 1987, p. 51)[*]

Comprehensive Musicianship and Teacher Training

It is not the purpose of this book to include all of the MENC *Final Report*. It is, however, important not only to call attention to this significant document but also to discuss its philosophical viewpoint.

In addition to the accountability movement of the 1960s, another development affecting teacher training in music was initiated through the Contemporary Music Project (CMP) (see pp. 290–291). The introduction to the "Musical Competence" section of the *Final Report* states the following:

> The development of musical competencies is essential in the music teacher education program. Comprehensive musicianship based on skills, knowledge, and understanding enables the music educator to instruct others confidently and effectively. The music competencies considered necessary for music educators are reflected in the standards below.
>
> Related competencies are grouped under appropriate headings: Producing Sounds, Organizing Sounds, Describing Sounds, and Knowledge of History, Repertoire, and Performance Practices. (p. 27)

For those already familiar with the CMP it is evident that this section was organized according to and based on the principles established by the project: namely, competence in organizing, analyzing, and performing music. The basic idea is that students who can exhibit competencies by responding to behavioral objectives in these three areas will be equipped to deal with all types of music.

Although the Contemporary Music Project and competency-based teacher education (accountability) seem to belong to an earlier era historically, the concerns regarding improved education and improved teacher education remain current. CMP advocated better, in-depth training of music as a discipline, a concern of the Holmes Group as well, while the phrase "accountable for student progress" appears in the statement for sweeping change released by the Carnegie Task Force on Teaching as a Profession (1986, p. 3).

---

[*]From *Music Teacher Education: Partnership and Process*, published by Music Educators National Conference, Reston, VA. Copyright ©1987. Reprinted with permission from MENC.

Teaching as an Art

Teaching is no longer isolated as just an academic profession. To many it is a performance discipline as well. Leon Lessinger and Don Gillis make an analogy between teaching and performing in their book *Teaching as a Performing Art* (1976). Teaching is seen as being closely related to performing. There are, however, some differences. For example, for a teacher performance is merely a means to the end, which is students' learning. For the artist/performer, performing is both the end and the means, even though he or she is teaching indirectly by conveying musical standards and tastes. In a sense, the teacher's objective is always a group or individual involvement in music, with the ultimate end being a student's performance as it relates to demonstrating musical competencies and ideas. The performer's ultimate end is the quality or achievement of his or her personal performance whether in a group or as a soloist.

Teachers and performers have many common areas. The performing artist reacts to audiences' applause, while the teacher's satisfaction is a reflection of students' learning. Both are dedicated individuals; the performer to the art of music, and the teacher to learning and preserving that art. Teachers and artists are both involved in "rehearsal"; in the case of one it is preparing lessons, and in the case of the other it is individual practice. Teachers need to keep abreast of current professional developments, while artists need to constantly expand and develop their repertoire. Both teachers and artists need to develop efficiency on their instrument, whether it be their own personality or classroom manner in the case of teachers or technical proficiency in the case of performers. Able performers can improvise in that they can organize sounds as they hear them and perform them in a creative fashion when called upon to do so, while teachers' ability to improvise is inherent in the concept of flexibility in teaching. As issues come up in the classroom, teachers need to be able to adjust and respond to the developments as they occur. As true professionals, performing artists and teachers have common goals in that their presentations need to reflect honesty, integrity, and dedication toward achieving the goals of their chosen profession.

But even beyond teaching being a performing art, it is also a creative art. The nature of teaching is that it is based on the information, interpretation, and experiences derived from the past. With a knowledge of previous accomplishments one may understand the present and then make appropriate decisions regarding future directions. Unfortunately, sometimes teachers become preoccupied with the past and have little interest in developing new directions for a future society. It is easy to do this, because one need not use imagination, research, analysis, and interpretation. All one needs to do is merely be satisfied with existing facts, music, and interpretations of developments of the past. Truly artistic teachers go beyond that and attempt to instill in students an attitude of looking forward to circumstances that they may not be able to anticipate in today's classrooms. It is these creative teachers who will lay a foundation for the generations yet to come.

"America 2000"

In 1989 President George Bush met with the nation's governors in Charlottesville, Virginia, to initiate a decade-long campaign to raise educational standards and performance at all levels of instruction. This summit meeting was identified by the title "America 2000," and it established six goals for the year 2000 as its national educational agenda. They were:

1. All children in America will start school ready to learn.
2. The high school graduation rate will increase to at least 90 percent.
3. American students will leave grades four, eight, and twelve having demonstrated competency in challenging subject matter including English, mathematics, science, history, and geography; and every school in America will ensure that all students learn to use their minds well, so they may be prepared for responsible citizenship, further learning, and productive employment in our modern economy.
4. U.S. students will be first in the world in science and mathematics achievements.
5. Every adult American will be literate and will possess the knowledge and skills necessary to compete in a global economy and exercise the rights and responsibilities of citizenship.
6. Every school in America will be free of drugs and violence and will offer a disciplined environment conducive to learning. (*America 2000*, 1992, inside cover)

To implement the initiative for achieving these goals, each state organized its own communitywide meetings and steering committees to develop strategies for meeting this challenge.

In its statement of what competencies children in grades 4, 8, and 12 should demonstrate satisfactorily, the *America 2000* report identified only English, mathematics, science, history, and geography. The arts were omitted from their concerns and the arts community made this ommission an issue (see Eisner, 1992, p. 591). In May of 1992 a national conference was convened in Annapolis, Maryland, by the U.S. Department of Education and the National Endowment for the Arts to launch the process of developing a research agenda for the next decade in arts education. This purpose of the coalition is to advance the "America 2000" Arts Partnership in support of the national effort to develop world-class standards that describe the knowledge, skills, and understandings that all students should acquire in the arts.

The idea of a system of world-class standards and assessments is provocative. There is concern that a system of uniform standards linked to examinations that have high-risk emphasis will be even more damaging to disadvantaged students who are already victimized by discrimination and inequities that exist in schools. Other critics fear that this system may erode local control of their schools. If this occurs, the implications are that it will detract from local financial resources and financial responsibility as well as interfere with local control of school reform when necessary.

Just how successful this initiative toward "America 2000" will be remains to be assessed. Progress of the program will be carefully observed and analyzed during the next decade.

Summary

Teaching is a constantly changing field of work. The traditional blackboards and books have been supplemented by an impressive array of technological resources. However, in spite of all these developments, three basic concerns have remained constant: (1) curricular decisions, (2) classroom procedures, and (3) evaluating student achievement.

In the mid-1960s a movement called "competency-based" or "performance-based" education had an effect on the nature of teacher training. It was a direct outgrowth of the accountability movement that focused on the learner, who was expected to demonstrate specific behaviors as a result of the training.

One of the significant documents that emerged from this movement was the *Final Report*. To assist the profession in keeping abreast of changes occurring in the field, in 1968 a commission had been appointed to recommend the necessary changes that would lead to improving the training of the prospective music teacher. It was this commission that produced the *Final Report* in 1972. Much of the philosophical content of this report was based on the work of the Comprehensive Musicianship Project, which was functioning during this same period.

The Contemporary Music Project, or "Young Composers Project," was organized and funded by the Ford Foundation in 1959. Later, when its focus changed to comprehensive musicianship around 1963, MENC provided additional funding.

When the Young Composers Project was instituted in 1959, it was discovered that members of the music education profession were not properly trained to deal with the music created by the young composers assigned to various schools. To assist in correcting this deficiency, the project changed its focus and moved toward comprehensive musicianship in the training of prospective teachers.

A commission to study graduate training for music educators was appointed in 1976. Its *Graduate Music Teacher Education Report* was published in 1982 and contained a variety of recommendations, including a call for more in-depth understandings and research.

In 1983 the Holmes Group, a consortium of education deans and chief academic officers from major research universities in each of the fifty states met to improve teacher education in the members' own institutions. Its report, which was published in 1986, recommended specific licensing procedures and focused on the need to strengthen the academic training of teachers in their specific disciplines.

The Carnegie Forum on Education and the Economy met in 1985. In the spring of 1986 in its report to the first annual meeting of the forum, the Task Force on Teaching as a Profession focused on the critical need to achieve a better standard of education. To accomplish this objective, the report emphasized that the quality of teaching and teachers who would be well prepared for the tasks of raising standards needed to be increased.

The Music Educators National Conference, in response to these calls for improved teacher education in music, introduced its program in the publication *Music Teacher Education: Partnership and Process*. The program established a profile of a desirable music teacher education. Those music teachers fitting this profile would then have the potential to become partners in preparing prospective music teachers in schools and institutions of higher education.

As teaching music has become more and more complex, it is no longer considered just an academic profession. It is now considered a performing art as well by modern thinkers and writers.

In 1989 President George Bush met with the nation's governors in Charlottesville, Virginia, to initiate a decade-long campaign to raise educational standards and performance at all levels of instruction. The meeting established a program of national goals for the year 2000 under the title "America 2000." Arts educators were disturbed that the arts were omitted from the conference's agenda. As a result, a coalition consisting of the U.S. Department of Education and the National Endowment of the Arts was formed. They met in Annapolis, Maryland, in May of 1992 and developed a research agenda for the next decade that would be a part of the "America 2000" program.

STUDY AND DISCUSSION QUESTIONS

1. (a) What are the characteristics of a profession?

   (b) Is music education a profession or a skilled trade? Explain your position.

2. (a) What are the main personal qualities advocated by the Teacher Education Commission of MENC in its *Final Report*?

   (b) What professional and musical competencies are advocated in the *Final Report*?

   (c) Are there some competencies that you believe should be added to the list completed by the Teacher Education Commission? Are there any that should be deleted or altered?

3. What is the function of graduate study as described by the Graduate Music Education Commission?

4. Characterize the ideal graduate faculty as described by the Graduate Music Education Commission.

5. How does competency-based teacher education differ from traditional teacher education programs?

6. What is the condition of competency-based teacher education programs today?

7. What were the main characteristics of the Comprehensive Musicianship Project?

8. In what way are performers and teachers similar in their work? In what ways do they differ?

9. What are some of the unique recommendations made by the Task Force on Music Education for the Nineties?

10. What is your reaction to the recommendations made in the Holmes Group report?

INDIVIDUAL OR CLASS ACTIVITIES

1. Select an undergraduate program, perhaps your own, and using the "Task Group V: Recommended Standards and Evaluative Criteria for the Education of Music Teachers" from the *Teacher Education in Music: Final Report* assess how well it meets the criteria established by the undergraduate commission.

2. Follow the above procedure and apply it to the report *Music Teacher Education: Partnership and Process*.

SUPPLEMENTARY READINGS

ABELES, H. F. (1975). Student perceptions of characteristics of effective applied music instructors. *Journal of Research Education* 23(2), 147–54.

AQUINO, J. T. (1978). *Artists as teachers*. Bloomington, IN: Phi Delta Kappa, Fastback 113.

AXELROD, J. (1973). *The university teacher as artist*. San Francisco: Jossey-Bass.

CARNEGIE TASK FORCE ON TEACHING AS A PROFESSION. (1986). *A nation prepared: Teachers for the twenty-first century*. Hyattsville, MD: Carnegie Forum on Education and the Economy.

GOODLAND, J. (1983). *A place called school: Prospects for the future*. New York: McGraw-Hill.

HIPP, W. J. (1982). Practices in the evaluation of music facility in higher education. (Dissertation, University of Texas at Austin, 1979.) *Council for Research in Music Education Bulletin 72*, 52–58.

LESSINGER, L., & GILLIS, D. (1976). *Teaching as a performing art*. Dallas: Crescendo Publications.

MILTON, O., & ASSOCIATES. (1978). *On college teaching*. San Francisco: Jossey-Bass.

WERNER, R. J. (1971). Graduate education of the musician-teacher. In *College Music Symposium: Vol. II* (pp. 103–7). Boulder, CO: College Music Society.

REFERENCES

AMERICA 2000. (1992). Washington, DC: U.S. Department Education.

BALL, C. (Chair), et al. (1982). *Graduate music teacher education report*. Reston, VA: Music Educators National Conference.

CARNEGIE TASK FORCE ON TEACHING AS A PROFESSION. (1986). *A nation prepared: Teachers for the twenty-first century*. Hyattsville, MD: Carnegie Forum on Education and the Economy.

EISNER, W. (1992, April). The misunderstood role of the arts in human development. *Phi Delta Kappa*, p. 591.

HIERONYMUS, G. (1974). Competency-based programs in teacher education. In *Proceedings of the 49th Annual Meeting* (No. 62, pp. 78–84). Washington, DC: National Association of Schools of Music.

THE HOLMES GROUP. (1986). *Tomorrow's teachers: a report of the Holmes Group*. East Lansing: Michigan State University.

LESSINGER, L., & GILLIS, D. (1976). *Teaching as a performing art*. Dallas: Crescendo.

KLOTMAN, R. H. (chair), et al. (1972). *Teacher education in music: Final report*. Washington, DC: Music Educators National Conference.

MEEK, G. R. (1981). An analysis of the origins of competency-based teacher education. (Dissertation, University of Toledo, 1979.) *Council for Research in Music Education Bulletin 68*, 69–72.

OLSON, G. B. (chair), et al. (1987). *Music Teacher Education: Partnership and Process*. Reston, VA: Music Educators National Conference.

Index